REGARDLESS OF FRONTIERS

Regardless of Frontiers

*Global Freedom of Expression in
a Troubled World*

Edited by

Lee C. Bollinger
and
Agnès Callamard

COLUMBIA UNIVERSITY PRESS New York

Columbia University Press
Publishers Since 1893
New York   Chichester, West Sussex
cup.columbia.edu
Copyright © 2021 Columbia University Press
All rights reserved

Library of Congress Cataloging-in-Publication Data

Names: Bollinger, Lee C., 1946– editor. | Callamard, Agnès, editor.
Title: Regardless of frontiers : global freedom of expression in a
troubled world / edited by Lee C. Bollinger, Agnès Callamard.
Description: New York : Columbia University Press, [2021] |
Includes bibliographical references and index.
Identifiers: LCCN 2020026141 (print) | LCCN 2020026142 (ebook) |
ISBN 9780231196987 (hardback) | ISBN 9780231196994
(trade paperback) | ISBN 9780231551922 (ebook)
Subjects: LCSH: Freedom of expression. | Freedom of speech. |
Sovereignty. | European Court of Human Rights.
Classification: LCC K3253 .R44 2021 (print) | LCC K3253 (ebook) |
DDC 341.4/833—dc23
LC record available at https://lccn.loc.gov/2020026141
LC ebook record available at https://lccn.loc.gov/2020026142

Columbia University Press books are printed on permanent and durable acid-free paper.
Printed in the United States of America

Cover design: Julia Kushnirsky

We dedicate this book to all those women and men around the world who are standing up in courtrooms and newsrooms, in the academy and in international organizations, in exercise of their freedom of expression and information and in defense of ours.

Contents

Preface

The Idea of Global Norms of Freedom of Speech and Press

LEE C. BOLLINGER

From my vantage point, this volume of essays originated more than a decade ago, when I began to realize that the reality of what we, for good or bad, call "globalization" was fundamentally changing the problems of freedom of speech and press. The increasing interconnectedness of the world was having a profound impact on individual nations while creating issues and challenges that required collective action at a global level. The near-universal embrace of some version of capitalism and open markets, the easing of barriers to the movements of people, and the emergence of the first ever truly global communications system (led, of course, by the Internet, but preceded and supported by satellite broadcasting and other forms of communication) together augmented trends toward integration of the world that, in turn, would reshape how we communicate and need to communicate in order to cope with a new level of shared life.[1] Climate change, economic bubbles, recessions—and, yes, pandemics—would offer undeniable proof that global discussion of global issues was more and more the order of the day.[2]

But it was also increasingly apparent that this new world required a different level of political structure or framework. The international institutions established in the wake of World War II needed to be refreshed or replaced.[3] Life in whatever form it takes—economic, social, political, cultural—was racing ahead of our capacities to govern it. Such changes were emphatically not self-effectuating. For them to happen, we needed a public square—a place where all this and more could be debated and understood and decided. Some of this would happen, of course, within existing nations, though each system would be affected by the whole, and some would happen across nations in the broader public sphere. This, in turn, would necessitate expansive rules and norms about communication and media, and that's what the principles of freedom of speech and press are all about.

For me, the problem was that my primary academic expertise, my scholarly knowledge, essentially ended at the borders of the United States. I was, and am, an expert on the First Amendment to the U.S. Constitution. My education occurred in the 1960s and 1970s, resulting in becoming a law professor in 1973, which corresponded with that particular period of American history—indeed, a seminal period—when the modern First Amendment was born and a new generation of scholars was created. This moment of enormous social and political ferment, following the Supreme Court's 1954 decision in *Brown v. Board of Education* and centered around the civil rights movement and dissent over America's involvement in the Vietnam War, laid bare the gap between the realities of American life and our ideals. It was also a period when virtually every major controversy and argument was refracted through the lens of the Constitution and brought to a receptive court. The constitutional jurisprudence of this era was so rich and important, spanning such a wide swath of American life, that the scholarly community responded, appropriately, by subdividing what had until then been regarded as one field of expertise—constitutional law—into dozens of distinct scholarly pursuits. Some law professors became experts on the Fourteenth Amendment, some on the Fourth Amendment, and some, like me, on the First Amendment. By the 1970s, the ranks of every law school faculty were dominated by constitutional law scholars. The First Amendment rights of freedom of speech and press became a "field" unto itself, and every law school had its First Amendment experts, with courses and textbooks, academic conferences, and journals to support this work.

A different world of expertise, however, centered on freedom of speech and press in other nations (often focusing on comparative law) and at the international level (typically grounded in international human rights law).[4] The work of scholars in these fields, who came from different intellectual traditions and who expressed their thinking through separate journals, textbooks, and conferences, would occasionally overlap with the world inhabited by First Amendment scholars in the United States, but serious cross-pollination was rare. The

First Amendment had, of course, been part of the U.S. Constitution since the adoption of the Bill of Rights in 1789.[5] But, for various reasons, the Supreme Court did not interpret those simple words "Congress shall make no law . . . abridging the freedom of speech, or of the press" until just after World War I, in 1919.[6] Those early cases and the decisions in the decades that followed, leading up to that extraordinary period of the 1960s, were in effect trial runs in which different ways of thinking about freedom of speech and press were tested.[7]

Even though all of this jurisprudence evolved from a felt need to design principles and doctrines for the political system within the United States, in retrospect one can see that, certainly since this seminal period in the 1960s, the world was watching, and that it absorbed many of the ideas that emerged from the United States' quest. And there were signal moments on the international stage that gave birth to the equivalent of the U.S. First Amendment. The most significant came in 1948 with the adoption of the Universal Declaration of Human Rights (UDHR).[8] Article 19 of the declaration addressed freedom of expression in stirring language: "Everyone has the right to freedom of opinion and expression; this right includes freedom to hold opinions without interference and to seek, receive and impart information and ideas through any media and regardless of frontiers."[9]

The UDHR was followed with the 1967 International Covenant on Civil and Political Rights, which, among other things, codified Article 19.[10] For freedom of speech and press in the international arena, these are the critical foundational texts. Yet, as a symbol of the separation of the academic fields of First Amendment law and international law, it is worth noting that casebooks on American constitutional law typically will make no reference to these treaties. In contrast, as contributors to this volume of essays demonstrate (see part 2), beginning in the 1960s, divisions that had existed in international jurisdictions were being bridged by the establishment of courts and regional institutions, particularly in Africa, that encouraged regional political and legal integration and, eventually, enabled international legal integration.

This progression in the United States was largely foreseeable. During an extended period after World War II, the United States held the status of an international superpower experiencing both the Cold War threat presented by the Soviet Union and a profound internal societal reorganization. Locked in an ideological battle against totalitarian regimes, the nation assumed the responsibility of setting an example for the world and subscribed to the belief that getting it right would convey symbolic authority internationally.[11] The collapse of the Soviet Union and the rise of capitalism, with policies favorable to expanding free trade and the accompanying ubiquity of foreign investment, magnified a process under way for decades and created a new degree of interdependence demanding an overlay of global oversight. This transition built upon the accumulation of global norms that took root after the end of dictatorships in the Americas, the dismantling of apartheid, and the erosion of the Soviet bloc, and can be traced back even further, to the proliferation of international treaties and regional institutions in the 1960s and 1970s.[12]

The pace of change in the 1990s was radically accelerated by the phenomenal development of the global communications system.[13] And by the beginning of the twenty-first century, we were in a new world, where each nation would have to figure out how its citizenry would or would not participate in the global marketplace of ideas and how it would interact with citizens from other nations who did so, as well. These were very real and very practical questions, different from the foremost concerns of the prior era, when we were focused on the degree to which respective nations embraced "universal human rights" and how best to leverage the developing human rights system and the ethos it embodied to impede the belligerence of totalitarian governments and lessen the possibility of another world war, which were the well-founded objectives of the Universal Declaration of Human Rights and its progeny.[14]

Here are some examples of this highly complex new reality.

Every nation must decide to what extent its own public forum will be permeable to the peoples and governments around the world. Will its own citizens be protected domestically when they engage in free speech work around the world? In the United States, there is one set of doctrines for citizens who provide advice and assistance to radical domestic political organizations and another (less protective) set of doctrines for citizens who do this for foreign political groups.[15] Will the domestic public forum be open to foreign citizens and governments wishing to communicate with its citizens? In the United States, there have been enormous concerns about foreign interests (governments) trying to disrupt and manipulate domestic deliberations.[16] Yet, clearly, we all have a significant interest in hearing from peoples beyond our borders about issues we all face. Will a nation's public forum be open to foreigners seeking to better understand and report on that nation? In the United States, the foreign press must receive special visas from the government before operating as journalists.[17] Recent controversies surrounding the denial of visas to members of the Chinese media are illustrative of this issue.[18]

Here is another set of problems in the new world of an instantaneous and pervasive global communications system. One's own citizens may be "censored" by foreign governments for exercising their free speech rights within their own national borders. We see civil (for instance, libel) and criminal actions brought in foreign jurisdictions against American citizens for exercising their rights of expression in the United States.[19] The most heinous example of this, of course, is the murder by Saudi Arabia of Jamal Khashoggi, in part for viewpoints he expressed as a columnist for the *Washington Post*.[20] I have written about the ways in which international and U.S. law might be deployed to punish this extreme form of "censorship."[21]

And yet another set of problems: In this new world, with its urgent problems to be discussed and resolved, we now have a much stronger interest in how citizens in other countries are treated by their own governments. Since what they know and decide are crucial to things we all care about, in the most practical sense, we have a stake in how their governments treat discussion within that state. As I have said many times, in the modern world, censorship anywhere is censorship everywhere.[22]

As I laid out in the Tanner Lectures at Clare Hall, University of Cambridge, in 2018,[23] in a profound sense what we are encountering now on the global level is a continuation of a process that began to unfold in the last century, starting with the movement within societies from the local to the national levels. I see this as having happened in the United States during that seminal period of the 1960s, to which I referred earlier. By the mid-twentieth century, America was well into the development of a national economy, with a strengthened and expanded federal government, facing issues national in scope, new technology of communication that emphasized national conversations (namely, broadcasting, with first radio and then television), and a rising sensibility that whatever happens anywhere is consequential for those elsewhere (leading examples being de jure segregation in the South, actions involving the environment, and local economic policies).

With regard to the First Amendment, this shift from local to national standards was represented by the Supreme Court's decision in *New York Times Co. v. Sullivan* in 1964.[24] Protections for an individual's reputation through the civil law of defamation had long been regarded as a matter for individual states and local jurisdictions to handle.[25] As a result, libel laws across the country varied significantly. But, in a case involving an attempt by the state of Alabama to impose its speech-restricting defamation law against the *New York Times* for publishing a (concededly factually incorrect) advertisement by a civil rights group seeking to raise funds to continue protesting racial discrimination by the Alabama state police, the court in *Sullivan* intervened and established national constitutional standards necessary for "uninhibited, robust, and wide-open" national debate.[26] (Many of those standards have been embraced by courts and intergovernmental watchdogs around the world, as Hawley Johnson and Peter Noorlander examine extensively in their contributions to this collection.)

Just as the course of history with respect to freedom of speech and press has been to move to national principles as issues have become more national in scope, so too must that happen on a global scale as the issues have become global in scope. The problem is, of course, that while this could happen in the United States through the institution of the Supreme Court, there is no comparable institution at the international level that could take the norms of the UDHR, for example, and make them into a global jurisprudence of free speech and press—although, as the contributions in this volume demonstrate, a number of others have played this role.

Nevertheless, the project we have embarked upon is no less clear: to evolve global norms about these rights and to determine which global freedom of expression norms are essential for this interconnected world. That is the fundamental issue for the essays in this book. My reference point for this inquiry is also the development of the common law in the twentieth century, particularly in fields like contract law. Great treatise writers such as Arthur Corbin and Samuel Williston scoured the decisions in states across the country and brought them together in major reference books.[27] By aggregating these cases and highlighting them over the decades, a consciousness and reality of a national body of law were created. It was, in one sense, basic assembling. But, in a much more profound sense, the process became meaningful in its own right and over time fulfilled what it assumed—namely, that there was a coherent whole emerging from discrete parts. The idea behind this volume is to help create that similar whole.

The search for global norms on freedom of expression and information is crucial in its own right. It is also, however, a matter of enormous importance to the state of the world generally. As global communication expands, many governments are responding to the sense of loss of control not only by increasing censorship but also by turning to techniques of authoritarianism, such as inciting extreme forms of nationalism, engaging in the politics of populism, and exhibiting animosity toward and demonization of marginalized groups, especially foreigners.[28] General norms of freedom of expression, therefore, are inherently important, but they also are critical to avoiding further descent into the new forms of authoritarianism and to finding effective solutions to shared global problems.

Let me take a moment to speak about the direction I believe we should take in the years ahead. As I have indicated, unfortunately but realistically there is no way to establish enforceable global principles and rules about freedom of speech and press under the current international institutional framework, nor does it seem likely that this state of affairs will change anytime soon. The absence of any institution within the UN framework that possesses the power to enforce the texts of international law on freedom of expression in disputes between states and their citizens is a hard fact of life—well known, of course, and, at least in the free speech community, widely lamented.

This does not mean, however, that there is a complete absence of international bodies with institutional authority in these matters. They exist at the regional level. The emergence since World War II of regional human rights courts in Africa,[29] Latin America,[30] and Europe[31] has been one of the signal areas of advancement in the development of enforceable legal doctrines concerning freedom of expression. Everything must be done to support this trend in the world. Important essays in this volume address this development.

Still, the bulk of what happens, and will continue to happen, in the realm of free speech and press on a day-to-day basis occurs at the level of individual nations and, increasingly, at the level of the private corporate actors powering the Internet. Any strategy to advance these rights must accommodate that reality. There are several points that follow from this.

First, for a variety of reasons, freedom of speech and the press seem to be best articulated and preserved by the judicial branch of government, provided it is independent of the political process and characterized by respect for the rule of law. This seems to me to be based in experience, not necessarily in any preordained theoretical truth. To be sure, other government institutions are important to the development of free speech rights, sometimes even more important, but it is the judiciary that seems again and again to be the primary source of respect for those rights. My personal sense is that this is due to a natural alignment between the way of thinking that characterizes the legal mind and the values inherent in the principle of freedom of expression (that is, receptivity to the give-and-take of argument and an attitude of skepticism). Whatever the underlying reason, if this is true, then we must do all we can to support independent judiciaries.

Second, we should not be thinking about freedom of speech and press as rooted only in the idea of democracy and Madisonian self-government. In the United States, linking the First Amendment and freedom of expression to democratic self-government has become the conventional theoretical basis for analyzing cases ever since the court's decision in *New York Times Co. v. Sullivan*. With the influence of the writings of Alexander Meiklejohn, the relationship between the "search for truth" and the First Amendment, which emerged at the very beginning of First Amendment jurisprudence in the first half of the twentieth century, has taken a secondary position.[32] But, in my view, that has been a mistake, and it certainly does not work well, given the variety of systems of government around the world.

For the "search for truth" rationale to gain greater currency, it must be linked more persuasively to all the ways in which we benefit from it. In particular, the system of research universities, both in the United States and around the world, is entirely devoted to advancing knowledge and truth, and over the past century, in particular, has brought more benefits to humanity in every facet of life than any other institution. At its best, journalism and its institutions are similarly dedicated to finding and conveying to the broader public the truth of current events. Tying freedom of speech and press to this entire enterprise is more likely to be palatable and compelling in most nations, especially in those that do not begin with the premise that Western-style democracy is the way to organize their societies. It is a fact that economic progress, at least beyond the level of a mercantile, basic manufacturing economy, is dependent upon an underlying creativity in the society, one linked to a commitment to expanding knowledge.[33] This is a commonly shared interest across most of the world and, therefore, a solid basis on which to argue for strong protections for speech and press.

Third, we need to decide (informally, of course) the scope of protections for freedom of expression that should be considered foundational, or vital, and in what areas reasonable but different approaches might be taken. I am thinking here specifically about what to do with extremist speech, which is often but not always about so-called hate speech. This is a very complicated subject, about which I have written and spoken extensively over the course of my career.[34] While the U.S. Supreme Court has squarely come down on the side of extraordinary protections for this kind of speech,[35] and while I believe there is a very good rationale for this approach, I do not think it is a necessary condition of a strong commitment to free speech and press. This is one area where reasonable people and nations may come to different conclusions, and we should be prepared to have those debates and discussions without assuming that the entire edifice of rights is at stake.

Fourth, as we engage in this sometimes laborious process of going case by case, court by court, and nation by nation in trying to build up norms around freedom of expression, it is critically important that we realize that this is necessarily a project that will take decades rather than years. As one surveys the world at this moment, it is easy to become discouraged, as nation after nation drifts further and further into an authoritarian, autocratic mind-set and system. Free speech and press seem under assault from every direction, more so than at any time since the collapse of the Soviet Union.

I will conclude, just as I began, on a personal note. As president of one of the world's great research universities, the operative question for me over the past decade has been how Columbia University should respond to all of this. We took a number of related actions. To help faculty and students find ways to engage in teaching and research around the world, we established what are now nine Columbia Global Centers.[36] These are currently operating in Amman, Beijing, Istanbul, Mumbai, Nairobi, Paris, Rio de Janeiro, Santiago, and Tunis, and they have become essential aids for our community to expand our physical and intellectual presence beyond the boundaries of New York City. These are not branch campuses, with separate faculty and students, but rather are facilities led by distinguished and highly knowledgeable individuals who can help guide our faculty and students to do their teaching and research more effectively in this far more integrated and interdependent world. The Global Centers reflect our sense that we are too ignorant of the vast changes that are occurring across the planet and that we, as scholars and teachers, need to be out there, physically as well as imaginatively, in order to grasp and critique what is happening. It is intellectual modesty, not the arrogance of superior expertise, that drives this initiative.

We also have embarked on a major effort to add to the basic mission of the modern university the purpose of having a direct impact on the world by bringing research into action through partnerships with outside entities. I have called this the "fourth purpose" of the university. Traditionally, universities have been thought of as being about expanding and conveying knowledge, while also being a good neighbor and engaging in public service. The fourth purpose adds a mission of action, or impact. Although this is not by any means unheard of within universities (for instance, medical research is often connected to delivery of health care; commercialization of academic research has become a widely accepted function of universities; and individual faculty often act on their own initiative to bring their research insights into the world of action), no university has been deliberate and comprehensive about making this a key element of what it is about.

To realize this new mission, we have created several new entities within the university. Related to Columbia Global Freedom of Expression, about which I will speak in a moment, is the Knight First Amendment Institute, which we launched with a $50 million endowment and the mission of advancing research, teaching, public education, and—more to the point—litigation on freedom of speech and press.[37] The institute is the result of a collaboration between the John S. and James L. Knight Foundation and Columbia to lodge within a secure and independent institution (namely, a university) an organization engaged in helping to foster as meaningful a place for the First Amendment in this century as it occupied in the last century.

The new media concerns at the helm of today's digital world, though possessing abundant wealth, have so far not embraced to the same degree the journalistic ethos of their traditional media predecessors, nor have they exhibited a willingness to shoulder the costly and sustained legal advocacy needed to repel government abuse of power. Our intention in establishing the Knight First Amendment Institute is that it will be there to fill the gap, and in its first years of existence it is admirably accomplishing this purpose.[38] Nongovernmental organizations and public-minded law firms have for decades provided invaluable support in setting and safeguarding norms for the protection of freedom of expression, frequently advancing novel or progressive interpretations of the law that have had a global reach. Lodged in a great university and, therefore, distinctive, the Knight Institute is now among their ranks.

Consistent with this intellectual framework and these related ideas and initiatives, I decided in 2014 to establish the Columbia Global Freedom of Expression project.[39] As the founding director, I hired Agnès Callamard, then the head of the nongovernmental organization Article 19. Agnès has been spectacular in this role. She knows what needs to be done and is clear-sighted about the forces in the world that have to be reckoned with, courageous in person, scrupulous in character, imaginative in how to move the world forward, and generous to a fault in supporting others and never making herself the center of attention, even when she deserves it. It has been a joy and a privilege to work with Agnès on this far-reaching and long-term goal of advancing the development of global norms of freedom of speech and press.

The most important of the many activities and initiatives taken on by Columbia Global Freedom of Expression—though it is in many ways the least likely to be heralded—is the simple idea of creating a database of decisions related to freedom of expression around the globe. Amazingly, before we developed this, there was no place one could go to get a comprehensive sense of the judicial (and legislative) decisions regarding freedom of speech and press, referencing international principles. To date, more than 1,300 decisions have been analyzed, and there are thirty thousand visitors each month, demonstrating the need for and interest in such a tool.[40]

Ultimately, my hope and objective is to encourage an integrated approach and understanding of freedom of expression and press freedom, one that borrows from, and builds bridges across, multiple jurisdictions and disciplines. To protect freedom of expression globally and to establish the norms needed for creating and then safeguarding a robust global public square, we must see a willingness on the part of scholars, intellectual leaders, and policy makers around the world to reach across national, regional, and international—and intellectual—borders. Scholars of the First Amendment must become central participants in this effort, committed to interacting with international human rights lawyers, and vice versa.

This, then, provides the background and framework for this particular book. We hope that assembling many of the greatest experts in the fields related to global norms of freedom of expression will yield yet another milestone in the advancement of free speech and press in the world. I am deeply grateful and indebted to Agnès and to the authors who have worked so diligently and creatively to make the idea of this book, and this large project, a reality.

NOTES

1. See Artur Borcuch, Magdalena Piłat-Borcuch, and Urszula Świerczyńska-Kaczor, "The Influence of the Internet on Globalization Process," *Journal of Economics and Business Research* 18, no. 1 (2012): 118–129.

2. See Karen Pashby, "The Global, Citizenship, and Education as Discursive Fields: Towards Disrupting the Reproduction of Colonial Systems of Power," in *Globalization and Global Citizenship: Interdisciplinary Approaches*, ed. Irene Langran and Tammy Birk (London: Routledge, 2016), 69, 71 (describing a "world [that] seems more global than ever before," in which "global issues take on a particular urgency and schooling is required to attend to the global").

3. See Bruce W. Jentleson, "The Liberal Order Isn't Coming Back: What Next?," *Democracy: A Journal of Ideas* (Spring 2018), https://democracyjournal.org/magazine /48/the-liberal-order-isnt-coming-back-what-next (describing international institutions as "underperforming" and suggesting that "their failings are the result of the constraints and inefficiencies imposed on them by the states that constitute and control them"). See also Tine Hanrieder, "The Reform Reformation: International Organizations and the Challenge of Change," *Foreign Affairs*, April 8, 2016, https://www .foreignaffairs.com/articles/2016-04-08/reform-reformation.

4. See, for example, Sarah H. Cleveland, "Hate Speech at Home and Abroad," in *The Free Speech Century*, ed. Lee C. Bollinger and Geoffrey R. Stone (Oxford: Oxford University Press, 2018), 210–231; and Albie Sachs, "Reflections on the Firstness of the First Amendment in the United States," in *The Free Speech Century*, ed. Lee C. Bollinger and Geoffrey R. Stone (Oxford: Oxford University Press, 2018), 179–192.

5. Daniel Baracskay, "Bill of Rights," *The First Amendment Encyclopedia*, February 2018, https://www.mtsu.edu/first-amendment/article/1448/bill-of-rights.

6. Schenck v. United States, 249 U.S. 47 (1919); Abrams v. United States, 250 U.S. 616 (1919); Debs v. United States, 249 U.S. 211 (1919).

7. See Brandenburg v. Ohio, 395 U.S. 444 (1969); Tinker v. Des Moines, 393 U.S. 503 (1969); United States v. O'Brien, 391 U.S. 367 (1968).

8. "Universal Declaration of Human Rights: History of the Document," United Nations, https://www.un.org/en/sections/universal-declaration/history-document /index.html.

9. G.A. Res. 217 (III) A, Universal Declaration of Human Rights, art. 19 (Dec. 10, 1948).

10. International Covenant on Civil and Political Rights, art. 19, Dec. 19, 1966, 999 U.N.T.S. 171.

11. George C. Herring, *From Colony to Superpower: US Foreign Relations Since 1776* (Oxford: Oxford University Press, 2008), 2–4.

12. See UN Department of Economic and Social Affairs, *World Economic and Social Survey 2017: Reflecting on Seventy Years of Development Policy Analysis* 24 (2017), https://www.un.org/development/desa/dpad/wp-content/uploads/sites/45 /publication/WESS_2017-FullReport.pdf (discussing the rise of capitalism following the end of World War II and the impact on international institutions).

13. See Ivo H. Daalder and James M. Lindsay, "The Globalization of Politics: American Foreign Policy for a New Century," Brookings, January 1, 2003, https://www .brookings.edu/articles/the-globalization-of-politics-american-foreign-policy-for -a-new-century/.

14. See "Universal Declaration of Human Rights," Amnesty International, https:// www.amnesty.org/en/what-we-do/universal-declaration-of-human-rights.

15. Holder v. Humanitarian Law Project, 561 U.S. 1 (2010) (holding that the United States' prohibition on providing material support to terrorist organizations barred a nonprofit from providing conflict resolution training to designated foreign groups, and that the statute did not violate the nonprofit's First Amendment rights).

16. Gabriela Schulte, "Poll: Voter Fraud, Foreign Interference Top Election Security Concerns," *The Hill*, February 21, 2020, https://thehill.com/hilltv/what-americas -thinking/484061-poll-voter-fraud-foreign-interference-top-election-security.

17. "Visas for Members of the Foreign Media, Press, and Radio," US Department of State, Bureau of Consular Affairs, https://travel.state.gov/content/travel/en/us-visas /employment/visas-members-foreign-media-press-radio.html (accessed April 8, 2020).

18. See Lily Kuo, "US–China Media Row Deepens as Beijing Hints at Revenge over Curbs on State Media," *Guardian*, March 5, 2020, https://www.theguardian.com /us-news/2020/mar/05/us-china-media-row-deepens-as-beijing-hints-at-revenge -over-curbs-on-state-media.

19. See, generally, Kathleen A. O'Connell, "Libel Suits Against American Media in Foreign Courts," *Dickinson Journal of International Law* 9, no. 1 (1991): 147–175.

20. See Ben Hubbard, "One Year On, Shadow of Khashoggi's Killing Stalks Saudi Prince," *New York Times*, October 2, 2019, https://www.nytimes.com/2019/10/02 /world/middleeast/khashoggi-killing-mbs-anniversary.html.

21. Lee C. Bollinger, "How the US Could Prosecute Jamal Khashoggi's Killers," *Washington Post*, March 31, 2019, https://www.washingtonpost.com/opinions/how-the -us-could-prosecute-jamal-khashoggis-killers/2019/03/31/1f8a7f4c-5180–11e9–88a1 -ed346foec94f_story.html.

22. See, generally, Lee C. Bollinger, " 'The Free Speech Century': A Retrospective and a Guide," 2018 Clare Hall Tanner Lectures, Clare Hall, University of Cambridge, November 5, 2018, https://tannerlectures.utah.edu/Bollinger%20Lecture.pdf.

23. See Georgette Jasen, "University Awards First-Ever Global Freedom of Expression Prizes," *Columbia News*, March 24, 2015, https://news.columbia.edu/news/university -awards-first-ever-global-freedom-expression-prizes.

24. New York Times Co. v. Sullivan, 376 U.S. 254 (1964).

25. See Rick Schmitt, "Window to the Past: New York Times Co. v. Sullivan," DC Bar, October 2014.

26. New York Times Co., 376 U.S. at 270.

27. Arthur L. Corbin, *Corbin on Contracts* (St. Paul, MN: West Publishing, 1993); Samuel Williston, *A Treatise on the Law of Contracts* (Mount Kisco, NY: Baker, Voorhis, 1936).

28. See Z. Umut Türem, "Rising Authoritarianism(s) and the Globalization of Law: An Initial Exploration," *Indiana Journal of Global Legal Studies* 26, no. 1 (2019): 1–30 (describing the implications of the rise of authoritarianism in the late 2010s).

29. "African Human Rights System," International Justice Resource Center, https:// ijrcenter.org/regional/african.

30. "Inter-American Human Rights System," International Justice Resource Center, https://ijrcenter.org/regional/inter-american-system.

31. "European Human Rights Bodies," International Justice Resource Center, https:// ijrcenter.org/regional/europe.

32. See, generally, Alexander Meiklejohn, *Political Freedom: The Constitutional Powers of the People* (New York: Harper, 1960); and Meiklejohn, *Free Speech and Its Relation to Self-Government* (New York: Harper, 1948).

33. Phillip LeBel, "The Role of Creative Innovation in Economic Growth: Some International Comparisons," *Journal of Asian Economics* 19, no. 4 (2008): 334–347.

34. See, for instance, Lee C. Bollinger, *The Tolerant Society* (Oxford: Oxford University Press, 1986).

35. See Brandenburg v. Ohio, 395 U.S. 444 (1969); National Socialist Party of America v. Village of Skokie, 432 U.S. 43 (1977).

36. Columbia Global Centers, Columbia University, https://globalcenters.columbia.edu.

37. "Knight Foundation, Columbia University Launch First Amendment Institute, $60 Million Project to Promote Free Expression in the Digital Age," press release, *Columbia News*, February 1, 2017, https://news.columbia.edu/news/knight-foundation-columbia-university-launch-first-amendment-institute-60-million-project.

38. Knight First Amendment Institute v. Donald J. Trump, 928 F.3d 226 (2d Cir. 2019) (holding that Donald Trump's blocking of Twitter users constituted unconstitutional viewpoint discrimination).

39. Columbia University, Global Freedom of Expression, "About," https://globalfreedomofexpression.columbia.edu/about.

40. Columbia University, Global Freedom of Expression, "Case Law," https://globalfreedomofexpression.columbia.edu/cases.

REGARDLESS OF FRONTIERS

Introduction

Regardless of Frontiers?
Global Freedom of Expression
Norms for a Troubled World

AGNÈS CALLAMARD

It may seem paradoxical to embark on a publication focused on global norms for freedom of expression at a time when the post–World War II global human rights system and the information regime it helped establish are, at the very least, being questioned, if not thoroughly undermined. The unraveling of the so-called global project and its associated multilateralism have been the object of much analysis, centering on the rise of populist politics and leadership, the emergence of a multipolar international system, the rise of neoliberalism, and widening inequality,[1] to name but a few topics.

Within the community defending freedoms of expression and the media, equally forceful warnings emerge, including from media outlets, journalists, Internet companies, and freedom of expression activists. Freedom of the media is under assault, they warn;[2] online content is censored and overly regulated,[3] including by monopolistic private companies;[4] the dissemination of false news is undermining democratic institutions, discrediting quality information and facts.[5]

Although their emphases vary, often the main conclusions or findings of these analyses are similar: liberal and democratic values are in jeopardy, as is the rules-based international system, both being subject to multiple attacks that, once taboo, are now, quite to the contrary, both claimed and carried out with pride.

(Potential) readers thus would be excused for giving the volume but a cursory look before setting it aside as merely the final gasps of (analog) idealists of a global project in its death throes.

To be clear, the challenges *are* substantial. But assaults on global norms, values, and systems cannot be understood without an adequate and accurate reading of what is being rejected, railed against, or demonized. We won't respond effectively to the onslaught if we do not also take stock of what these global norms, values, and systems have and have not achieved. It is thus both timely and particularly relevant to analyze the last seventy years' achievements, specifically in terms of adopting, spreading, and strengthening international standards on freedom of expression, and ultimately establishing global norms.

That is the focus of this volume, not a naive or idealistic reading of the world but a realistic one, revealing how far the world has come with regard to the global norms that have protected and continue to protect the free flow of information in an increasingly interconnected global community. This book does not assume that those norms are implemented everywhere or that they have been challenged only recently. But it suggests that those norms, along with the actors and "forces" that have helped sow and grow them, constitute a necessary starting point from which to better understand the current push back against their global penetration. Finally, to the extent that the world may be standing on the brink of renouncing the core values and commitments of the post–World War II regime, this book serves as a reminder of just what is at stake, at least as far as freedom of expression is concerned.[6]

OBJECTIVES AND THEORETICAL FRAMEWORK

The objectives of this book are to explore whether legal norms on freedom of expression have emerged that have sufficient consensus and collective commitment to now qualify them as truly "global," and to look at how it was that those norms came about. Ultimately, and more ambitiously, the collection seeks to lay the groundwork for the development of a coherent international legal doctrine on the various freedom of expression global norms that we examine here, from access to government-held information to media diversity and political expression.

The volume emerges from two distinct theoretical sources: constructivism and comparative law. These are described in broad strokes here. However, it is not our purpose to offer a theoretical contribution to either. Rather, the volume's contributions are largely empirical, being loosely or firmly grounded in constructivist and comparative jurisprudence predispositions for the purpose of mapping out the global information system, including its norms and actors, that has developed in the past seventy years.

This is a huge subject. The collection could not examine every freedom of expression standard or principle nor comprehensively identify which of them has been reborn as a global norm. Nor, realistically, could we review here all the actors that have worked to globalize the freedom of expression normative framework over seventy years. However, we do offer a unique exploration of the emergence and global circulation of freedom of expression norms, and more global perspectives[7] into freedom of expression than does much of the literature.

Global Norms and Comparative Law

Under constructivist theories of international relations, to which the volume's initial approach is indebted, ideas and norms are considered to play a determining role in shaping international relations and individual states' interests. The definition of norms on which it has largely relied is that of the standard of appropriate behavior for actors with a given identity.[8] Norms are deemed to be the expression of collective and convergent expectations[9] and are inherently consensual.[10]

In their seminal work on norms development, Martha Finnemore and Kathryn Sikkink argue that norms go through a life cycle composed of three phases, which they call norm emergence; norm cascade, defined by broad norm acceptance; and norm internalization, when norms achieve a "'taken-for-granted' quality that makes conformance with the norm almost automatic."[11] *Norm emergence* is heavily dependent upon "entrepreneurs." Often members of civil society, entrepreneurs are those who are convinced that something must be changed. They are responsible for the formulation, negotiation, and advocacy of a particular norm, using existing organizations and norms as a platform from which to proselytize, and framing their issue so as to reach a broader audience. *Norm cascade* occurs when norms reach a "tipping point" or critical mass of state endorsements. According to Finnemore and Sikkink, up to the tipping point, "little normative change occurs without significant domestic movements supporting such change." Afterwards, "more countries begin to adopt new norms more rapidly, even without domestic pressure."[12] The normative cascade may require diplomatic praise or censure by states and also may entail advocacy by, and technical assistance from, norm entrepreneurs. The cascade is followed by *norm internalization*, when a global norm meets and shapes domestic legislation, policies, and/or politics. Finnemore and Sikkink warn us, though, that completion of the life cycle is not inevitable and that a number of norms may never reach the tipping point.

The first two sections of the book focus largely on the first two stages of the norms cycle, attesting to the emergence and (relative) cascade of a range of free speech global norms. With few exceptions, the volume has also prioritized largely legal, as opposed to moral or social, norms. This is partly due to the contributors' field of expertise—the law—and partly due to the methodological difficulties inherent in the exploration of practices based on social mores. It is also a product perhaps of the human rights project's overemphasis on the state's legal obligations and practices.

The normative cycle model has not been without its critics. Of particular importance to this volume are the suggestions that constructivist theories on global norms do not sufficiently take into account the importance of conflicts and contests over norms, the messiness of the real political world of norm adoption, and the various types of adaptation and translation of norms. Amitav Acharya, for instance, introduced the concept of "norm localization" to describe processes of framing and grafting by local actors to create greater congruence with local practices, giving a norm its legitimacy, while Antje Wiener highlights the instability of norms, citing their evolution through interpretation and dialogues.[13] Both analyses find resonance in the volume.

Until the early years of the twenty-first century, fundamental conflicts over liberal norms were not even considered. Not surprisingly however, the century's second decade has seen a multiplication of research into normative battles.[14] Alan Bloomfield suggests that counternorms are led by norm "antipreneurs," who resist new norms or advocate for the normative status quo: "Emerging norms may (therefore) struggle to establish themselves even after status quo norms fail catastrophically. The mere fact they are unproven provides 'naysaying' antipreneurs opportunities to pick holes in the new norms, and/or tag the norm entrepreneurs as idealistic, naive dreamers (at best; or dangerous radicals at worst)."[15] Rebecca Sanders advances the notion of "norm proxy war" to describe how norms challengers frustrated by the pace of institutionalization of human rights patronize surrogates in countries where international norms are weak, "in the hope that victories abroad will reverberate internationally and at home."[16] The normative conflicts and actors described in the third section of the volume highlight some of these dimensions, and others related, in part, to the specificities of freedom of expression.

A second theoretical source for the volume is derived from comparative law, which seeks to interpret domestic laws in comparison with others and, by so doing, to bring closer to each other various national legal approaches. In theory, the field of comparative law should contribute to convergence and harmonization across domestic laws, while also constructing international law.[17] In reality, two factors militated against such a role. First, academic comparative law or comparative jurisprudence studies privileged the study of differences across legal systems and rarely did it seek to identify what may bind various legal systems or jurisprudences together, such as similar legal standards, reasoning, and precedents, across countries or regional and historical-political blocs, such as the Commonwealth. Second, as noted by a group of experts brought together by Columbia Global Freedom of Expression, comparative media law tends to compare the same countries (within the common law system, usually the United States, United Kingdom, Australia, Canada, South Africa, Singapore, and sometimes India), leaving out many others, particularly but not exclusively from the Global South.[18] Comparisons among common and civil law freedom of expression regimes are very rare. European and Latin American comparative jurisprudence studies tend to include a focus on regional standards and on the jurisprudence of the regional courts, but far more rarely does it compare regional courts jurisprudences. Further, legal studies of freedom of expression are largely monojurisdictional, and so is the teaching of freedom of expression or media law.

The volume borrows from the methodology of comparative law but seeks to address some of its aforementioned limitations. In particular, we have sought to balance out the overemphasis on legal or jurisprudential differences. We have looked for, and identified, commonalities across legal systems, suggesting, highlighting, or indeed constructing legal coherence where there may have thought to be only legal disorder or confusion.

A Treaty-Initiated and Treaty-Based Process

The volume tells a remarkable story, but it is neither a linear nor a predictable story.

The story begins in 1948, when the Universal Declaration of Human Rights (UDHR) was promulgated, defining freedom of expression as the right "to seek, receive, and impart information and ideas through any media and regardless of frontiers."

The International Covenant on Civil and Political Rights (ICCPR), adopted in the late 1960s, and regional human rights instruments[19] elaborated on the initial broad aspiration by fleshing out states' responsibilities and largely (if narrowly) restricting the exercise of the right:

1. Everyone shall have the right to hold opinions without interference.
2. Everyone shall have the right to freedom of expression; this right shall include freedom to seek, receive and impart information and ideas of all kinds, regardless of frontiers, either orally, in writing or in print, in the form of art, or through any other media of his choice.
3. The exercise of the rights provided for in paragraph 2 of this article carries with it special duties and responsibilities. It may therefore be subject to certain restrictions, but these shall only be such as are provided by law and are necessary:
   (a) For respect of the rights or reputations of others;
   (b) For the protection of national security or of public order (ordre public), or of public health or morals.

The text of Article 19 of the ICCPR borrowed heavily from Article 10 of the European Convention for the Protection of Human Rights and Fundamental Freedoms,[20] adopted some ten years earlier, and in turn served as a model for Article 13 of the American Convention on Human Rights.[21] The African Charter on Human and Peoples' Rights,[22] the last of the regional conventions to be adopted to date, has a different wording, but the language of the ICCPR has largely served as the model for subsequent legal and judicial developments. The text of Article 19 also served as a "source of inspiration" for many comparable provisions in other treaties, such as the Convention on the Rights of the Child, and for national constitutions around the world.[23]

Treaties in general, and human rights treaties in particular, are the pillars of a rule-based international system, even though there are no (or only limited) means for their enforcement or punitive mechanisms if breached. Nonetheless, historically, these rules have been fundamental to interstate relations; they are the centerpiece of the post–World War II international regime, seeking to regulate as well the relationship between citizens and their governments, between the governed and their governors. The adoption of the ICCPR and its subsequent ratification by 164 states, along with the adoption of regional conventions, underscores a degree of international consensus over, and national commitments to, associated human rights protection that should not be undervalued. Its significance may become more painfully clear as its provisions are challenged.

This collection suggests that, while vague and imperfect, freedom of expression treaty provisions did establish a foundation on which to build and nurture strong and global norms of freedom of expression protection.[24] It also highlights the importance of the processes and actors that have addressed the vagueness of these provisions (largely inherent to declamatory texts) and have given them meaning, depth, and scope. Indeed, the legal journeys traveled by Article 19 are all the more interesting in that, unlike a number of other provisions in the ICCPR, the right to freedom of expression or information has not been the object of additional conventions, despite some efforts in the early 1950s,[25] or subsequent conventions on more specific areas of communication.[26] Instead, and necessarily so, Article 19 was clarified and took meaning through interpretation,[27] a right conferred to state parties and to the Human Rights Committee, the body established by the ICCPR to monitor its implementation.

Importantly, the present volume shows that Article 19 interpretations have involved interactions and dialogue between civil, judicial, and legislative actors around the world—domestic, regional, and international. Just as importantly, the seventy years of journeys have crisscrossed countries, regions, and international events, borrowing heavily along the way from "soft" law, including from declarations, principles, and guidelines. These journeys challenge the traditional normative hierarchy, drawing instead on intersecting soft norms, principles, rules, and regulations of international, regional, and state laws.[28]

A Global Village of Constitutions, Principles, and Precedents

"The emergence of a global village of precedents" was how the late Kevin Boyle[29] described the state of global jurisprudence on freedom of expression some twenty years ago. This visually elegant depiction is most appropriate, describing the roles played by courts in developing and cascading global norms. This is not to suggest, as highlighted below, that there are coherent international doctrines on all free speech issues. But the scale of judicial integration across some regions of the world (such as Europe, Central and South America, and Africa) and a few countries elsewhere (Canada, India, and South Korea, for instance) is nothing short of impressive.

Regional Institutions

The cascade of freedom of expression norms in many parts of the world was made possible by a range of political and legal shifts that accompanied the first seventy years of the post–World War II system, such as growing acceptance of supranational jurisdictions' oversight and constraints on national power and control. The process was made possible by the existence of regional membership bodies and regional courts overseeing the implementation of regional conventions.

Regional courts in Europe, Latin America, and more recently in Africa, have played a central role in the emergence and cascading of norms. There is no evidence of norm entrepreneurship per se on the part of courts and judges, that is, of judges proselytizing over specific norms or decisions. But they have given greater scope, meaning, and value to what may initially have been loose principles, while establishing as well the bases for regional legal integration.

The European Union, the Council of Europe, and the European courts have allowed for the "Europeanization" of domestic laws and precedents on freedom of expression.[30] Such a transformative process also characterized the circulation of free speech principles in Latin America, leading to what scholars have referred to as the "inter-Americanization" of national legal orders. The European Court of Human Rights and the Inter-American commission and court have played a central function in legally integrating freedom of expression norms, very much coherently within their jurisdictions.[31] In Africa, the regional legal integration process has begun, as evidenced by the laws and decisions on criminal defamation, for instance, but is not yet quite expanded and solidified.

Under the inter-American system, the doctrine of conventionality control, requiring national judges to apply the convention as interpreted by the Inter-American Court of Human Rights,[32] has facilitated the emergence of a coherent and integrated body of law across the country signatories to the American convention, as has the doctrine on "integral reparations" for human rights violations, which include guarantees of nonrepetition. It is under this doctrine that the court was able to request that Chile amend its constitution to strike out film censorship,[33] and to adopt laws and regulations to guarantee access to information.[34] The inter-American system has yet to delve into and deliver decisions on online freedom of expression, on hate speech, or on incitement, to name but a few topics—or, indeed, on privacy. Given the approach it has taken to date on freedom of expression questions, given its solid and impressive jurisprudential and theoretical work on a range of human rights questions, there is no doubt that greater contributions from the court and the commission are yet to come.

Far less ambitiously, the "margin of appreciation" doctrine of the European Court nevertheless has assisted in the general acceptance of supranational judicial authority by carving out specific judicial spaces dominated by the principle of subsidiarity.[35] However, this has not been without risk, and it has failed to establish much-needed judicial pathways for the difficult task of balancing the exercise of competing rights, such as those related to "hate speech," blasphemy, and incitement.[36]

Exchanges Across Regional Blocs

Constructivist research into the emergence and cascade of global norms has highlighted the crucial role played by national tribunals and national jurisprudence. What makes a norm "global" is, in part, the extent to which courts are making reference to it, citing it, justifying it, or giving it substantive, legal, and political meaning and resonance. Sikkink, for her part, highlights the existence of a "global judicial system," whereby courts cite and reference decisions and concepts, contributing (along with other actors) to a "justice cascade." This volume gives much credence to this theory.

The remarkable journeys of free speech norms also emphasize the extent of the exchange between and within regional blocs. Ideas and precedents on freedom of expression have traveled extensively over the past seven decades. There is limited evidence of formal dialogue among courts[37] but many indications that parties to cases, including national and international law firms and nongovernmental organizations (NGOs), have played key roles in identifying and "exporting" key principles and decisions cross-jurisdictionally.[38]

Cross-regional integration does not necessarily mean that interpretations travel unchanged from one regional court to another. Seizing upon a precedent from another regional jurisdiction, courts have often filled "interpretive gaps," adding locally specific contours and meaning without undermining the existence of a norm. Further, each regional court plays a distinct role in the protection of freedom of expression and in the emergence of global norms. For instance, the Inter-American Court has been instrumental in interpreting the right to freedom of expression to include access to government-held information.[39]

In the process of globalizing themselves, freedom of expression norms may thus be infused with local dimensions or interpretations. There is little evidence of "passive" transplant of norms from one region or country to another. Rather, courts or other actors involved, such as NGOs and lawyers, adapt the norm to the circumstances. There is an ownership process, which may be an essential rite of passage for norms cascading and internalization. This is clearly the rule when it comes to the way in which judicial decisions are cited, referenced, or exported. The examples provided in this collection demonstrate that the principles the court's decisions embody (from the protection of offensive ideas under *Handyside* to the high level of protection of political expression under *Sullivan* and including the right to be forgotten under *Google Spain*, for instance) may be adopted, while the doctrine or standards (such as strict scrutiny for defamation of public officials) may not.[40]

For example, the right to be forgotten, as it was initially conceived by the European Court of Justice in *Google Spain SL v. Agencia Española de Protección de Datos*,[41] has been the object of different interpretations by courts around the world. This does not, however, invalidate the notion that there is an emerging or cascading norm at the moment, regarding the specific application of the right to privacy in an online context. Similarly, decisions, laws, or policies related to the protection of sources may approach the application of the right in different fashions. Some courts may limit it to journalists working for traditional media outlets, thus excluding freelancers or those working in an online context. Such an approach may weaken the extent of the norm application, but it cannot be said to invalidate its existence.[42]

Besides regional judicial entities, political membership may also play a role in creating this global village of precedents. The chapters in the first section of this volume show precedents traveling across country members of the Commonwealth, for instance, with some members (such as the United Kingdom, South Africa, India, and Australia) playing a central role in establishing and reshaping principles and standards. Judicial integration and the production of global norms have also taken place nationally. Regional courts cite national jurisprudence, while domestic courts cite other courts' decisions, thus further contributing to the process of norms cascade, norms internalization, and judicial integration, characterized by coherent reasoning and approach across principles.

The Importance of Soft Law and Nonstate Actors

The remarkable journeys undertaken by freedom of expression global norms demonstrate that law does not need to be "hard" and that norms do not need to be legally detailed to have powerful influence on states and other actors. State behaviors with regard to freedom of expression have been influenced, if not shaped, by soft norms developed by intergovernmental bodies, nongovernmental organizations, and other nonstate actors. They, too, have given shape, scope, meaning, and depth to the original treaties' provisions, conferring to their necessary legal interpretation flexibility and the capacity to adapt to a rapidly changing environment.

Soft freedom of expression law comes in many shapes and forms; the past seventy years have seen an explosion of comments, guidelines, declarations, and opinions that have sought to interpret legally binding but imprecise legal rules and address conflicts of interpretations, gaps in implementation, or emerging freedom of expression issues.[43] These efforts have not always succeeded, as this volume's case study on hate speech or defamation of religion demonstrates, but their importance to global norms formation is undeniable. The volume shows how much these "soft norms" have tended to build on and solidify one another, and how the technique of soft norms development has largely mirrored that found in the formal legal field.[44]

Such rigorous approaches may explain why a number of such soft norms cited here have morphed over time into law or, at the very least, have produced legal effects, particularly by and through the courts, but also through state legislatures or executives in the context of their policy making. The majority of the chapters in the volume highlight the importance of the Human Rights Committee, and in particular its General Comment no. 34, which serves as a benchmark for regional institutions and other actors. Also often cited are the so-called joint declarations by independent experts representing regional and political intergovernmental organizations, singling these out as a particularly effective exercise in the process of norms emergence or cascading.

The seventy years' journeys are also a celebration of the work of nongovernmental organizations, and individuals within NGOs, in developing (emerging) a norm and advocating for it. Within the freedom of expression and press freedom activist communities, a number of individuals and organizations have been directly involved in interpreting practices, laws, and jurisprudence and identifying convergence, with the view to building a common body of principles. It is said that "Legal revolutions'—[as they call] revolutions set in motion by law—do not end with the passing of the law, but begin with it."[45] This is certainly true for the freedom of expression revolution that was unleashed by the adoption of the UDHR, of the ICCPR, and its regional counterparts. In no way was this a historical "given" or a logically inevitable outcome.

Indeed, more than half of the seventy years were dominated by polarization under the Cold War and "the deep incompatibilities between the communist and liberal approaches to the functions of the press."[46] At least a third of those seventy years were dominated by the struggle against apartheid and other denials of rights on the basis of race, ethnicity, gender, or religion, and by the deep-seated ambivalence of Western countries toward decolonization, self-determination, and civil rights. Several decades of these seventy years were overshadowed by dictatorship in Latin America and elsewhere. It is only against the backdrop of these historical realities that one can truly assess the significance of the global journeys of freedom of expression norms and more truly understand the role of the people drafting, driving, and protecting them.

Broader transformation of societies brought about by peace, the end of the Cold War, economic growth, and new technology may have played a role in the emergence and cascading of the norms highlighted in this volume. But seizing upon opportunities, capturing the meaning of a political moment, and translating these into a normative advancement—that work was done with and by individuals and their organizations, mostly, but not only, within civil society. As Sikkink well captures in her analysis of the cascade of international criminal law and the fight against impunity: "At the beginning of any norm cascade, specific people work hard to propose new ideas and policies, and they share their ideas with others, who carry them to new settings. The early adopters of new human rights norms don't contract the ideas through the air like a virus, but always through struggle, innovations, and often just plain luck." Later she adds, "Change cannot be understood without seeing how new ideas emerge and spread. These new ideas often challenge the older ideas that constitute the international system."[47]

The role of agency against otherwise unforgiving structures is noted in the vast majority of the contributions here, offering compelling examples of the work of transnational norm entrepreneurs in the field of freedom of expression, from those drafting cutting-edge principles to those lobbying over years for the adoption of a declaration, including many engaging in strategic litigation. They also have played a central role in the emergence of global standards applied to the digital world and era, adopted in turn by intergovernmental bodies, which have recognized that people depend upon online media "to access and exchange information, publish content, interact, communicate, and associate with each other,"[48] and to "engage in debate and participate in democratic processes."[49]

The Human Rights Council and regional intergovernmental organizations also have moved toward insisting on the important role of new information and communications technologies in enabling and facilitating the enjoyment of the rights to freedom of assembly and of association[50] and the rights of the media in covering protests.[51] Digital technologies and "online spaces" have been highlighted as crucial vectors for mobilizing, organizing, and holding protests,[52] and for bringing external attention to protests. The normative implications of these developments have been at the heart of more recent standard-setting initiatives. Crucially, these have called for the expansion of the protection afforded to journalists. In this respect, human rights bodies have increasingly recognized that journalism should be seen as "a function shared by a wide range of actors, including professional full-time reporters and analysts, as well as bloggers and others who engage in forms of self-publication in print, on the Internet or else-where,"[53] or indeed those who are documenting protests. These conclusions have been supported by the decisions of regional human rights bodies. These latest normative developments, however, are increasingly at odds with those espoused by governments eager to impose principles of national sovereignty over the Internet, and corporations eager to maximize data-driven profit.

THE NORMATIVE CONFLICTS OF THE TWENTY-FIRST CENTURY

Constructivists have tended to see norms contestation, conflicts, or competi-tion as occurring when the norm emerges and when it is in the process of dif-fusion (cascade). Norms competitors may share the same basic normative understandings but propose alternative approaches. Antipreneurs, on the other hand, resist any attempt to change the normative status quo and to advance new norms.

The normative world of the 2010s has been far messier, being at the conflu-ence of several forms of normative conflicts and contests.

First, some normative contestations or conflicts, such as that over hate speech and incitement, still have not found closure, or even strong convergence, despite years having elapsed since it was first exposed. This failure reveals ten-sions, insufficiently addressed, in the *idea* of freedom of expression, tensions between autonomy and dignity, on the one hand, and the exercise of free speech on the other.[54]

Second, the advent of the Internet and concerns over national security have further exacerbated original tensions that had not previously found closure, while also creating new ones. The difficulties inherent in the cascading and internalization of global norms related to freedom of expression were com-pounded at the beginning of the twentieth century by the September 11, 2001, terror attack and its domino-like impacts on many aspects of international and domestic relations. Nongovernmental actors advocating for the protection of freedom of expression found themselves increasingly at odds with the general public and with governments that, in the name of national security, were push-ing for greater constraints on free speech.

Thus, the first decade of the twenty-first century witnessed an explosion of counterterrorism resolutions, laws, and policies grounded in or espousing secu-ritization and implicitly rejecting norms related to civic and personal freedoms. When played out in the globalized communication environment of the Inter-net, the measures to counter incitement to "terrorism," "radicalization," and "extremism" have included further laws or policies that sought to regulate not only freedom of online expression but also the practices of the private actors powering the Internet. States have demanded "backdoor keys" and an end to encryption, have justified greater surveillance, and have weakened what were well-entrenched norms (or so they seemed). The result has been the multiplication of normative battlefields.

Third, while the speed, growth, and transborder nature of online speech could have incentivized governments to agree on common norms, thus far, the opposite has happened. The Internet has brought about additional normative storms,[55] whose resolutions are further complicated because of new *sources* of norms—namely the large, mostly American, Internet service providers powering the online world[56]—and because of new *forms* or *language* of norms: namely, algorithms, codes, artificial intelligence, and machine learning, which have also taken on a global normative character.

The advent of the digital world has brought new instruments of codification, including codification of speech and behaviors, which have challenged the idea of what constitutes a legal and normative system. Lawrence Lessig well captured the legal idiosyncrasies of cyberspace when he coined the now famous principle that "code is law," by which he meant that the (obscure, nontransparent) instructions embedded in the software and hardware that makes cyberspace also regulates it.[57]

Code has not been the only attempt to offset and compete with governments' laws and constitutions. Terms of service agreements enacted by social media and other private companies also serve a function similar to that of the law, but they are not quite like the law—or at least not quite as a law ought to be—in being transparent, easy to access and understand, fair and just in their application. As Chinmayi Arun shows in her contribution, none of these characteristics apply to terms of service, which, from both a procedural and substantive standpoint, undermine the very notion of legality as well as international standards and global norms.

These codes and terms of service immensely complicate the (traditional) normative system, as far as freedom of expression is concerned—and in other ways, too. Even in a context where states are progressively reasserting their control over the technology and its regulation,[58] code and terms of service continue to enact quasi-legal functions, which are both intertwined with state laws and yet also autonomous. Cyberspace, in fact, offers a practical instance of multiple legal and normative orders, with nonstate actors competing with states as both the source and the adjudicator of regulation. As theoreticians of global legal pluralism have shown, the existence of multiple legal orders does not need to be a source of concern per se, to the extent that the interaction between these orders produces dialogues and results in the strengthening or emergence of common global norms.[59]

Indeed, the global norms studied in this volume are themselves the products of interaction and dialogues among different legal systems and actors. But an evident difficulty one confronts in applying this model to cyberspace is that of language. Codes and algorithms embody values and seek to be the "law." These are expressed in a language, a mathematical mode of transmission, that very much complicates "traditional" normative dialogue, or indeed normative conflicts. Normative dialogue gets lost in translation, literally *and* metaphorically. A second difficulty is that the online space is not *only* a space of and for expression. It is the economic, political, social, cultural space of the twenty-first century, and increasingly the space where wars are waged and national security and interests are advanced or protected. It is a space of powers contestation, confrontation, and dominance.

The fourth dimension of twenty-first-century normative conflicts is linked to the (re)construction of the international political system toward a bipolar or, more likely, a multipolar system, with subregional systems adding further complexity and instability. China and Russia are usually singled out as leaders of the counternorms onslaught. China is a complicated, multidimensional but ultimately pragmatic player.[60] It is advocating for cyber sovereignty as the leading normative framework for global cyber governance, but the country has also adopted, and adapted to, a version of the values of "multistakeholderism," so long as doing so does not interfere with its understanding of "political stability." The sheer extent of its e-market (the largest in the world) allows China to attract foreign companies willing to set aside their own values to comply with China's invasive free speech norms. The China case study in this volume (chapter 13) points to a side of normative development and conflicts that is rarely studied; it may be far more commercial, mercantilist, and transactional than the literature thus far has suggested. Normative quid pro quos are the untold stories of the seventy years' normative journeys.

The normative conflicts of this decade are not necessarily directed at emerging or cascading norms. More often than not, they are targeted at undermining norms that had already reached their tipping point and, indeed, had already been "internalized"—or so we thought. Nowhere is this more significant than in the United States, for instance, where as of this writing the press is regularly criticized by the country's president, Donald Trump, and freedom of the press and other constitutional First Amendment values are being attacked or deliberately undermined. Normative conflicts thus are not driven only by authoritarian regimes and their leaders; they may be initiated, too, from within liberal democracies or may find great resonance and many allies within those democracies. This may include not only "emerging" countervalues but also undermining and stigmatizing actors who have painstakingly constructed global norms for the protection of freedom of expression over the past seventy years. The current conflicts, driven as they are by political leaders, the "street," and the online world, may feel closer to a normative counterrevolution than to the norms contestations of the second half of the twentieth century, with normative changes brought about and imposed through fear, the removal of the levers of control,[61] and institutionalized violence.

Such a finding has to be contrasted with the main conclusions of this volume. Freedom of expression norms related to political expression, defamation, access to information, protection of sources, or media diversity are in place. There are inconsistencies or weaknesses, and some aspects of these norms have stronger protection than others. But many have consolidated into legal norms and thus far have withstood a range of normative attacks. Actors responsible for their initial emergence or growth, particularly courts, legal scholars, international civil servants, or civil society activists, are showing little indication of faltering. The free speech norms described in this volume have emerged, developed, and transformed over a seventy-year period through careful effort and work across sectors, nations, and regions. To "debunk" them, counternorm entrepreneurs and their supporters would have to go through similar and lengthy processes.

THE MANUFACTURING OF GLOBAL NORMS
AND INTERNATIONAL LAW

Violations of a global norm do not invalidate its existence or call its legitimacy into question. However, repeated violations across the world—when justified, for example, on the basis of national security or in defense of "traditional family values"—can call into question the strength of the norm and may impede its progress toward the tipping point required for it to truly cascade into broad-based application.

Incidents of violations of norms and, critically, the value-based justifications behind these must be examined closely, including in terms of their nature and extent as well as in the impact of the resistance that they provoke, domestically and internationally. Determining and understanding the degree to which norms (and counternorms) emerge and spread requires careful analysis, including assessment both of convergences in norms and the significance and consequence of comparable divergence. Means of diffusion of norms (and counternorms), internationally and across national borders, may take a variety of forms and may lead to local internalization in a variety of ways. A norm may be steadfastly rejected in its entirety or only in some elements of it. What is important, and useful too, is to evaluate whether modifications to, and rejections of, a norm, on their own or when taken together, amount to an invalidation of the norm in question or suggest perhaps even the emergence of new norm altogether.

The field of international public law has long sought to manage these "vagaries" inherent in a global codification project by resorting to a range of rules that seek to condition interpretation and assessment of legal norms/ standards, such as those related to the sources of law. Article 38(1) of the Statute of the International Court of Justice, widely recognized as the most authoritative and complete statement about the sources of international law,[62] identifies primary sources as being international conventions, international custom, the general principles of law recognized by civilized nations (the peremptory norms, or *jus cogens*), or a fourth, "subsidiary" means for the determination of rules of law, namely judicial decisions and the teachings of the most highly qualified publicists of the various nations. The International Law Commission, for its part, notes three subsidiary means for determining the existence and content of customary international legal norms, in declining order of evidentiary weight: the decisions of international courts and tribunals, including regional human rights courts; the decisions of national courts; and the "teachings of the most highly qualified publicists of the various nations."[63]

The field of freedom of expression, the media, and information, on line or not, has not been the object of specific international conventions,[64] although some related matters have been the subject of international legal development under the auspices of the International Telecommunication Union. To date, there has been no known attempt to suggest that some freedom of expression norms amount to international customary law, let alone peremptory norms. Despite the globalization of content and medium, the legal framework for freedom of expression and information is largely framed as matters between a country's government and a country's residents or citizens. An ever-increasing number of legal matters involving social media companies and online content spread over two or more countries raise complex questions related to who has jurisdiction, standing, control over content, or control over data, to name but a few issues.[65]

However, such matters are still largely addressed through national laws and policies or the law and policy of the European Union, with courts around the world somehow "competing" with one another. International customary law doctrine for cyberspace has not yet developed (with the possible exception of armed conflicts scenarios). More broadly, it is truly remarkable how little progress has been realized in terms of developing new notions of sources of law, international legal personality, and subjecthood of international law in response to the challenges of the online world.[66]

In such a vacuum, national and regional jurisprudence, soft norms development by expert bodies, along with expert writings on the existence and content of global norms constitute crucial avenues for the international protection of freedom of expression. They may also, over time, allow for the development of international (customary) law for freedom of expression both on and off line. As this volume highlights, each of the subsidiary means and sources of law identified by the International Court of Justice and the International Law Commission with regard to international customary law figures large in the field of freedom of expression, influencing their emergence, allowing for their cascading and their internalization,[67] while narrating as well the very facts of their existence and their content. The assessment of subsidiary sources by judges and scholars in turn becomes part and parcel of the emergence, cascading, and internalization of global norms.

The task of extracting a coherent and intelligible narrative of such global norms from a swelling number of opinions, documents, and experiences, being produced by an ever-growing number of actors, sometimes working in contradiction to each other, may seem daunting—even impossible. Yet, as Lee C. Bollinger wisely suggests, "In this process, experience and time are the great validators and the givers of higher meaning. Through a largely indecipherable process, various fragments of statements in judicial opinions and other writings, and the factual narratives around which those statements were made, are plucked from the ever-increasing mass of material; these take on the status of higher text, of near biblical significance, to which nearly everyone regularly refers in trying to provide a coherent and intelligible account of the field."[68]

In the late nineteenth and early twentieth centuries, legal scholars in the United States engaged in the drafting of what became known as "legal treatises," tying together vast masses of cases, across the various states of the Union, and giving them a real (or imaginary) coherence.[69] This effort was born out of "despair" at the sheer number of cases and "the impenetrable vagaries" of common law, made worse by the increasing number of states federated into the

United States.[70] The legal treatise had both a deductive and doctrinal component. Scholars created an "interpretive framework" by "categorizing authorities, interpreting authoritative texts within the categories, demonstrating what the law requires, and highlighting gaps."[71]

It is our hope that this volume will help to lay the methodological groundwork for a comparable project: the development of coherent global doctrines on freedom of expression, from the many and diverse sources and experiences that are now, following World War II, part of the global information and human rights ecosystem. In a decade dominated by normative counterrevolution, decision makers and freedom of expression experts and lawyers would benefit more than ever from authoritative works on a range of free speech principles, which interpret the various sources around the world and offer the makings of a coherent, reliable, relevant, and robust international interpretive framework.

NOTES

The author is indebted to Malwina E. Lys-Dobradin for her invaluable research and contribution to this volume.

1. See, for instance, Joseph Stiglitz, *Globalization and Its Discontents Revisited: Anti-Globalization in the Era of Trump* (New York: Norton, 2017); Bernard Harcourt, *The Counterrevolution: How Our Government Went to War Against Our Own Citizens* (New York: Basic Books, 2018); Adam Tooze, *How a Decade of Global Financial Crisis Changed the World* (London: Penguin Random House, 2018).

2. See, for instance, Article 19, *The Expression Agenda Report 2017/2018: The State of Freedom of Expression Around the World* (London: Article 19), 2018.

3. Freedom House, *Freedom on the Net: The Rise of Digital Authoritarianism* (Washington, DC: Freedom House, 2018).

4. Martin Moore and Damian Tambini, eds., *Digital Dominance, The Power of Google, Amazon, Facebook, and Apple* (Oxford: Oxford University Press, 2018).

5. Brian McNair, *Fake News: Falsehood, Fabrication, and Fantasy in Journalism* (London: Routledge, 2017); Edward S. Herman and Noam Chomsky, *Manufacturing Consent: The Political Economy of the Mass Media* (Montreal: Pantheon Books, 1988).

6. To borrow from the conclusion of Oona A. Hathaway and Scott J. Shapiro, *The Internationalists: How a Radical Plan to Outlaw War Remade the World* (New York: Simon and Schuster, 2017).

7. See Frederick Schauer, "Freedom of Expression and Three Conceptions of the Global," introductory chapter in this volume.

8. Peter Katzenstein, ed., *The Culture of National Security: Norms and Identity in World Politics* (New York: Columbia University Press, 1996), 5.

9. Stephen Krasner, "Structural Causes and Regime Consequences: Regimes as Intervening Variables," in *International Regimes*, ed. Stephen Krasner (Ithaca, NY: Cornell University Press, 1983); Ronald L. Jepperson, Alexander Wendt, and Peter J. Katzenstein, "Norms, Identity, and Culture in National Security," in *Culture of National Security: Norms and Identity in World Politics*, ed. Peter Katzenstein (New York: Columbia University Press, 1996), 33–75; Rodger A. Payne, "Persuasion, Frames, and Norm Construction," *European Journal of International Relations* 7, no. 1 (2001): 37–61

10. Jepperson, Wendt, and Katzenstein, "Norms, Identity, and Culture"; Martha Finnemore and Kathryn Sikkink, "International Norm Dynamics and Political Change," *International Organization* 52, no. 4 (1998).

11. Finnemore and Sikkink, "International Norm Dynamics," 895, 904.

12. Finnemore and Sikkink, "International Norm Dynamics," 902.

13. Amitav Acharya, "How Ideas Spread: Whose Norms Matter? Norm Localization and Institutional Change in Asian Regionalism," *International Organization* 58, no. 2 (2004): 239–275; Antje Wiener, "Contested Compliance: Interventions on the Normative Structure of World Politics," *European Journal of International Relations* 10, no. 2 (2004): 189–234.

14. See, for instance, Holger Niemann and Henrik Schillinger, "Contestation 'All the Way Down'? The Grammar of Contestation in Norm Research," *Review of International Studies* 43, no. 1 (2017): 29–49; and Jonas Wolff and Lisbeth Zimmermann, "Between Banyans and Battle Scenes: Liberal Norms, Contestation, and the Limits of Critique," *Review of International Studies* 42, no. 3 (July 2016): 513–534.

15. Alan Bloomfield, "Norm Antipreneurs and Theorising Resistance to Normative Change," *Review of International Studies* 42, no. 2 (2016): 310–333, at 314.

16. Rebecca Sanders, "Norm Proxy War and Resistance Through Outsourcing: The Dynamics of Transnational Human Rights Contestation," *Human Rights Review* 17, no. 2 (2016).

17. See, for instance L. C. Green, "Comparative Law as a Source of International Law," *Tulane Law Review* 42, no. 1 (1967): 52–65.

18. According to contributor Catalina Botero, the problem is particularly acute from a South–South standpoint, for which there is almost no existing comparative work.

19. The first elaboration of Article 19 of the Universal Declaration of Human Rights had been European, whose European integration project had included in the early 1950s the elaboration of a European Convention on Human Rights, whose aspects of Article 10 may have served as a model for the International Covenant on Civil and Political Rights.

20. Adopted November 4, 1950; entered into force September 3, 1953.

21. Adopted at San José, Costa Rica, November 22, 1969; entered into force July 18, 1978.

22. Adopted at Nairobi, Kenya, June 26, 1981; entered into force October 12, 1986.

23. See Tarlach McGonagle and Emmanuel Vargas Penagos, "The Norm Entrepreneurship of the United Nations," chapter 6 in this volume.

24. See Lee C. Bollinger, *Uninhibited, Robust, and Wide-Open: A Free Press for a New Century* (New York: Oxford University Press, 2010), 141.

25. See McGonagle and Penagos, "Norm Entrepreneurship."

26. For instance, in 2012, the World Conference on International Telecommunications 2012 sought to create a global regime for monitoring Internet communications. The proposal and its development process were heavily criticized by a number of member states, including the European Union and the United States, and by a range of nonstate actors, including nongovernmental organizations and the industry. The treaty was eventually signed by 89 of the 152 countries (above the 50 percent margin). But it is safe to say that the treaty has thus far failed to deliver anything other than the paper it has been drafted upon. The conference well illustrates the difficulties with treaty-based governance of freedom of expression, either on line or off line, and the necessity to resort to a more flexible and multistakeholder approach to rules and regulation as far as the Internet is concerned.

27. See Toby Mendel, "Global Norms on Media Regulation: The Devil Is in the Detail," chapter 1 in this volume.

28. To borrow from Mariela Morales Antoniazzi and Pablo Saavedra Alessandri, "Inter-Americanization: Its Legal Bases and Political Impact," in *Transformative Constitutionalism in Latin America: The Emergence of a New Ius Commune*, ed. Armin von Bogdandy, Eduardo Ferrer Mac-Gregor, Mariela Morales Antoniazzi, and Flavia Piovesan (Oxford University Press, 2017), 255–276, at 255.

29. Founding director of Article 19, Professor Kevin Boyle, went on to establish the University College Galway human rights center and to cofound the Human Rights Law Centre at the University of Essex. He advanced many human rights claims at the European Court for Human Rights and was an expert on both freedom of expression and antidiscrimination law.

30. Antoniazzi and Alessandri, "Inter-Americanization," 255–276.

31. Antoniazzi and Alessandri, "Inter-Americanization," note 35.

32. Case of Almonacid-Arellano et al. v. Chile: "The Judiciary must exercise a sort of 'conventionality control' between the domestic legal provisions which are applied to specific cases and the American Convention on Human Rights. To perform this task, the Judiciary has to take into account not only the treaty, but also the interpretation thereof made by the Inter-American Court, which is the ultimate

interpreter of the American Convention." http://www.corteidh.or.cr/docs/casos /articulos/seriec_154_ing.pdf.

33. Inter-American Court of Human Rights, *The Last Temptation of the Christ* (Olmedo Bustos and Others) v. Chile (February 5, 2001), Series C, No. 73, Merits, Reparations and Costs.

34. Inter-American Court of Human Rights, Claude Reyes et al. v. Chile. See also Sandra Coliver, "The Right to Access Information Held by Public Authorities: Emergence as a Global Norm," chapter 2 in this volume; and Sofía Jaramillo-Otoya, "*Claude Reyes et al. v. Chile*: A Global Trailblazer," chapter 17 in this volume.

35. F. Tulkens and L. Donnay, "L'usage de la marge d'appréciation par la Cour européenne des droits de l'homme: Paravent juridique superflu ou mécanisme indispensable par nature," *Revue de Science criminelle et de droit pénal comparé* 1 (2006); L. Burgorgue-Larsen, "Les standards: Normes imposées ou consenties?," in *Existe-t-il une exception française en matière de droits fondamentaux?*, ed. Marthe Fatin-Rouge Stéfanini and Guy Scoffoni (Aix-en-Provence: Presses Universitaires d'Aix Marseille, Cahiers de l'Institut Louis Favoreu, 2013), 15–30.

36. See Agnès Callamard and Sejal Parmar, "Norms in Conflict: The Restraints on the Emergence of a Global Free Speech Norm," chapter 11 in this volume.

37. But examples of such dialogues seem to be increasing, including at the level of judges and among clerks. The United Nations Educational, Scientific and Cultural Organization, Open Society, and other intergovernmental organizations have been instrumental in creating the space and avenues for cross-jurisdictional fertilization.

38. See Richard Winfield, *Exporting the Matrix: The Campaign to Reform Media Laws Abroad* (Durham, NC: Carolina Academic Press, 2012).

39. See Coliver, "Right to Access Information"; Catalina Botero-Marino, "Role of the Inter-American Human Rights System"; and Jaramillo-Otoya, *Claude Reyes et al. v. Chile* (chapters 2, 8, and 17 of this volume).

40. See section 4 of this volume.

41. See Bach Avezdjanov, "Fast, Far, and Deep: The Journey of the Right to Be Forgotten," chapter 19 in this volume.

42. See Richard Danbury, "Is There a Global Norm for the Protection of Journalists' Sources?," chapter 5 in this volume.

43. Andrew T. Guzman and Timothy L. Meyer, "International Soft Law," *Berkeley Law Scholarship Repository* 1, no. 1 (2010).

44. See, in particular, Mendel, "Global Norms."

45. Oliver Diggelmann, "The Internationalists as Grand Narrative: Key Elements and Dilemmata," *Global Constitutionalism* 7, no. 3 (2018): 297–314.

46. John P. Humphrey, *Human Rights and the United Nations: A Great Adventure* (Dobbs Ferry, NY: Transnational Publishers, 1984), 36.

47. Kathryn Sikkink, *The Justice Cascade: How Human Rights Prosecutions Are Changing World Politics* (New York: Norton, 2012), 23, 237.

48. Committee of Ministers, "Declaration on the Protection of Freedom of Expression and Freedom of Assembly and Association with Regard to Privately Operated Internet Platforms and Online Service Providers," adopted on December 7, 2011, para. 2.

49. Committee of Ministers, "Recommendation CM/Rec(2012)3 on the Protection of Human Rights with Regard to Search Engines," adopted on April 4, 2012, para. 1.

50. Resolution 28/16, adopted on September 27, 2012, A/HRC/RES/21/16; Resolution 25/36, adopted on March 24, 2014, A/HRC/25/L.20; OEA/SER.L/V/II CIDH/RELE/INF.22/19 September 2019; Committee of Ministers, "Declaration on the Protection of Freedom of Expression," para. 6. The UN Human Rights Committee is currently drafting General Comment no. 37 on Article 21 of the International Covenant on Civil and Political Rights, which guarantees the right of peaceful assembly.

51. Resolution 25/36, adopted on March 24, 2014, A/HRC/25/L.20; Report of the Special Rapporteur on the Promotion and Protection of the Right to Freedom of Peaceful Assembly and of Association, May 21, 2012, A/HRC/20/27, para. 48.

52. Personal communication, Barbora Bukovska, senior legal director, Article 19. I am also indebted to one of the reviewers of the volume for highlighting normative developments with regard to freedom of association and protests.

53. General Comment no. 34, para. 44.

54. See Callamard and Parmer, "Norms in Conflict."

55. See Chinmayi Arun, "Making Choices: Social Media Platforms and Freedom of Expression Norms," chapter 12 in this volume.

56. Jeff Rosen, "Who Decides? Civility v. Hate Speech on the Internet," in *Insights on Law and Society*, American Bar Association, Winter 2013, http://www.americanbar.org/publications/insights_on_law_andsociety/13/winter_2013/who_decides_civilityvhatespeechontheinternet.html.

57. Lawrence Lessig, *Code Version 2.0* (New York: Basic Books, 2006).

58. Agnès Callamard, "Are Courts Re-inventing Internet Regulation?," *International Review of Law, Computers and Technology* 31, no. 3 (2017): 323–339; Callamard, "The Control of 'Invasive' Ideas in a Digital Age," *Social Research* 84, no. 1 (2017): 119–145.

59. Paul Schiff Berman, in particular, sees global legal pluralism as a normative project aimed at striking a middle ground between strict territorialism and open-ended universalism. Berman, "From International Law to Law and Globalization,"

Colombia Journal of Transnational Law 43 (2005); and "Global Legal Pluralism," *Southern California Law Review* 80 (2007).

60. See Séverine Arsène, "China, Information Technology, and Global Freedom of Expression: A Story of Sovereignty and Global Capitalism," chapter 13 in this volume.

61. M. Teitgen, Rapporteur for the Committee on Legal and Administrative Questions for the Council of Europe, delivered a speech on September 7, 1949, in which he said, "Democracies do not become Nazi countries in one day. Evil progresses cunningly, with a minority operating, as it were, to remove the levers of control. One by one freedoms are suppressed in one sphere after another. Public opinion and the entire national conscience are asphyxiated. And then, when everything is in order, the Fuhrer is installed and the evolution continues even to the oven of the crematorium . . . A conscience must exist somewhere which will sound the alarm to the minds of a nation menaced by this progressive corruption. An international Court and a system of supervision and guarantees could be the conscience of which we all have need."

62. Malcolm N. Shaw, *International Law*, 6th ed. (Cambridge University Press, 2008).

63. International Law Commission, Draft Conclusions 13 and 14, and commentary to Draft Conclusion 13, para. 4.

64. See McGonagle and Vargas Penagos, "Norm Entrepreneurship of the United Nations."

65. Callamard, "Are Courts Re-inventing Internet Regulation?"

66. See the excellent analysis and proposal in Daniel Bethlehem, "The End of Geography," *European Journal of International Law* 25, no. 1 (2014).

67. International Court of Justice statute, October 24, 1945, Article 38(1)(b), Draft Conclusion 14, para. 5.

68. Lee C. Bollinger, *The Tolerant Society* (Oxford: Oxford University Press, 1986), 6.

69. To paraphrase Lawrence M. Friedman, *American Law in the 20th Century* (New Haven, CT: Yale University Press, 2004), 487.

70. Richard A. Danner, "Oh, the Treatise!," *Michigan Law Review* 111, no. 6 (2013).

71. Danner, "Oh, the Treatise!," 833–834.

Freedom of Expression and
Three Concepts of the Global

FREDERICK SCHAUER

As the contributions in this volume show, freedom of expression is, importantly, a global and not merely a national phenomenon, and a global and not merely a national set of problems and issues. But just what is it for some phenomenon, whether it be freedom of expression or anything else, to be "global"? As an introductory matter, therefore, it may be useful to clarify the very idea of the global, using freedom of expression as an example, but in ways that might be helpful in the consideration of other topics as well. More particularly, it appears that both the descriptive and the normative dimensions of the idea of the global can be divided into three quite distinct forms of inquiry, all of which are represented in this volume. My aim in this introduction is to distinguish these three different conceptions of the global, to show how each is applicable to important questions about freedom of expression, and to offer a framing that it is hoped will be of assistance in understanding and evaluating the contributions that follow in this volume.

GLOBALIZATION AS COMPARISON

For freedom of expression, more than for many other topics, and for freedom of expression in the United States even more particularly, both the academic and the policy literatures tend to be highly provincial. Scholars, advocates, and practitioners all describe the law in their own jurisdiction, sometimes applaud the law in their own jurisdiction, and often criticize the law in their own jurisdiction. But even when they criticize the law in their own jurisdiction, critics are prone to use as a standard against which the system's norms are measured either some never-realized ideal or various ideas from politics, philosophy, sociology, or any of a number of other disciplines. The phenomenon is especially extreme with respect to freedom of expression in the United States, where a vast body of case law and a rich literature going back at least a century has been focused almost exclusively on American law, American history, and the American free speech tradition, with remarkably little attention to issues of freedom of expression as they arise in other jurisdictions.

In recent years, however, the study of freedom of expression, even in the United States, has become far more explicitly comparative across jurisdictions.[1] In precisely this sense, the study of, and advocacy about, freedom of expression has thus become far more global. Scholars in one country will, far more often than in the past, describe the freedom of expression regimes—legal, political, and cultural—that exist in other nations. Sometimes, advocates for a change in freedom of expression laws, institutions, and cultural practices in their own country will (again, more often than in the past) use another country as a model for what they argue that their own country ought to do. Less commonly, but still worthy of note, scholars and advocates in one country will argue that the laws and practices in other countries ought to be changed in light of global trends or in view of the advantages that the advocates perceive in their own country's laws and practices.[2]

One sense of the global, therefore, is comparative, with those in one nation consciously seeking to learn about, to use, and sometimes to attempt to influence the law and the practices elsewhere. Again, the phenomenon is hardly restricted to freedom of expression, but freedom of expression appears to be not only an example but also an especially prevalent one. Comparison itself, therefore, can take any of several different forms, with commensurately different goals. One of these forms and goals, perhaps the most traditional, is simply descriptive. If one is a freedom of expression scholar, practitioner, or advocate in France, for example, one might be—and, it seems, ought to be—at least interested in knowing about freedom of expression laws and practices in Germany, in Argentina, in

Australia, and in South Africa, simply as a way of increasing one's knowledge base of the topic with which one is professionally interested and involved.

In the academic study of comparative law and comparative politics, however, comparison merely as description has a bit of a bad odor these days, largely because many social scientists see their enterprise as one principally focused on the search for the causes and consequences of various social phenomena rather than as simply reporting or describing the phenomena.[3] And even without getting into the question (or dispute) about whether this understanding of the social science enterprise is or is not too narrow, we can still understand the virtues of viewing cross-national comparisons as a way of examining and exposing deeper causal forces.

The United States, for example, has stronger protections for racist speech, for defamation of public figures and public officials, and for the communication of unlawfully obtained information than do other countries, even other common law jurisdictions.[4] But why is this so? Is it because of an especially strong libertarian strain in American political culture, coupled with an equally strong distrust of government? Is it because of the subsequent consequences, themselves partially a product of the path-dependence of law and the strong role of precedent within it, of judicial and political decisions made in the context of protests central to the civil rights movement and against the unpopular Vietnam War?[5] Is it because the absence of a tradition of government broadcasting has produced in the broadcasting industry a strong free expression advocacy faction that is largely absent in countries without the same history of private broadcasting? Is it because the excessive censorship and repression of the 1919 Red Scare and the late 1940s and early 1950s McCarthy era have spawned a strong counter-reaction?

These are only hypotheses, and there could be others,[6] but similar questions can be asked about other comparisons. Is the strong protection of human dignity in the German Basic Law one cause of Germany's approach to freedom of expression and the appropriate limitations on it, and is the protection of human dignity, even against freedom of expression claims, itself a product of reactions against the Nazi era? Is a communitarian—as opposed to individualistic—approach to freedom of expression in Singapore and Hong Kong, among other places, a consequence of the existence of an Asian value system that is dramatically different from the so-called Western values that inform European and North American freedom of expression doctrines?[7] And is South Africa's special sensitivity to racist speech an only-to-be-expected reaction to South Africa's history of apartheid, a history that may be more extreme in its racism than even the racism that exists in much of the rest of the world?

All of these examples are, to repeat, merely questions and not answers. They are hypotheses and not conclusions. But these questions and hypotheses suggest that even if the goal is purely academic, in the best sense of that term, freedom of expression can, and increasingly does, provide a platform for a range of interesting and important questions of comparative law and comparative politics. In addition, however, cross-national—global—comparisons may often inform advocacy. Around the world, advocates for greater press immunity from libel judgments rely on American law,[8] and the 1964 case of *New York Times Co. v. Sullivan* (376 U.S. 254) in particular,[9] to inform their work and help persuade courts to change domestic law, and American advocates do much the same thing with respect to press immunity from mandated disclosure of confidential sources, an area in which the United States, at least as a matter of constitutional law, is less protective than many other nations.

The globalization of freedom of expression discourse, in this sense of comparison, tracks larger legal and political developments. Although the debate in the United States about the use of foreign law by American courts (as authority, or for guidance) has been especially acrimonious and salient,[10] there is increasing worldwide attention to legal and constitutional uses, borrowing, transplants, and related phenomena.[11] The American approach to freedom of expression, which remains largely provincial, stands as an exception to this trend. Indeed, even those American scholars, practitioners, and activists who are in general sympathetic to American use of non-American law for guidance and perhaps authority remain largely resistant to such use with respect to freedom of expression. But if globalization is understood to mean the cross-border exchange of information and ideas, and cross-border influence from one system to another, freedom of expression stands out as a primary example of this form of globalization, with the United States increasingly an outlier to the worldwide willingness to learn from other systems, to use the law of other systems, and to modify a domestic system in view of the lessons to be gained from other approaches.[12]

GLOBALIZATION AND THE DEVELOPMENT
OF INTERNATIONAL NORMS

In the cross-national and comparative sense of the global discussed in the previous section, the norms about freedom of expression—or anything else, for that matter—remain largely domestic. Increasingly, nations learn from others, and domestic advocates, scholars, and norm entrepreneurs draw on (or self-consciously avoid)[13] models and examples from other nations to support their activities, but the object still ultimately remains a freedom of expression regime that is located within the legal system, the political and economic structures, and the cultural institutions of a particular country.

By contrast, there are also freedom of expression norms that are genuinely and pervasively supranational. Article 19 of the Universal Declaration of Human Rights,[14] Article 10 of the European Convention on Human Rights, and quite a few other sources of international human rights law, or of international law generally, contain guarantees of freedom of expression of varying strength and scope. In addition, there are, as several of the contributions in this volume describe and analyze, increasingly pervasive and influential international human rights norms, norms that may have even greater effect on national practices than formal international positive law.[15]

The details of these various laws, treaties, documents, and norms are less important here than the very fact of their existence. And what their existence establishes is the idea of an international law of freedom of expression, or international norms of freedom of expression—laws or norms that thus have a global impact in a quite different way. The most obvious difference is that the laws or norms emanate internationally and are not situated within a particular jurisdiction. But a less obvious but even more important difference stems from the important principle that such norms establish a minimum standard but still allow considerable nation-to-nation variance within the boundaries of that standard. In the law of the European Convention on Human Rights, for example, the idea of the "margin of appreciation"[16] acknowledges that different nations have different traditions, different values, different legal and political systems, and different priorities, and as a result, the decisions of the adjudicating and enforcement bodies allow for national variation as long as a nation's practices do not fall below a minimum standard.[17] So too, even if often less explicitly so, with a broad collection of other international laws, conventions, treaties, and norms dealing with freedom of expression.

Many Americans, or at least many Americans with typical American enthusiasm for freedom of the press, consider *New York Times Co. v. Sullivan* to be a landmark of press freedom, especially the freedom of the press to criticize, even harshly and sometimes mistakenly, those who wield political power. But few of even those most committed to the *Sullivan* approach believe that this is the approach that every country should follow.[18] And so too, I suspect, with French views about the importance of privacy, or the Scandinavian perspective on a mandated right of reply.[19] Indeed, the fact that the Grand Chamber of the European Court of Human Rights has held that punishment for denying the

Armenian genocide violates Article 10 of the European Convention on Human Rights[20] while allowing signatory nations to criminalize Holocaust denial suggests not only that freedom of expression norms are variable and culturally contingent but also that there still remains the idea that there is floor below which nations should not go. And insofar as that floor is the subject of international norms, laws, conventions, and treaties, the cross-national floor itself has a global dimension that is quite different from the globalization by which nations adapt their own domestic laws to the domestic laws of other countries.

THE SPECIAL PROBLEM OF GLOBAL EXPRESSION

There exists an interesting and revealing debate, if we can really call it that, about how to label the right about which we are speaking. Historically, the terms "freedom of speech" and "freedom of the press" have the longest lineage, but more recently those terms have come into disfavor, in part because the right encompasses far more than just "speech" or even "press" in their literal senses. Most liberal democracies, after all, consider flag waving (and sometimes flag burning), armband wearing, picket sign carrying, parades, demonstrations, art, and music to be within the ambit of the right, although none of these is "speech" in the literal and ordinary sense.

As a result, "freedom of expression" has become a somewhat more popular term, although it too is beset with problems, albeit of a different kind. If the problem with "freedom of speech" is that it is too narrow, the problem with "freedom of expression" is that it is too broad. The clothes we wear, the style of our hair, the hobbies or sports in which we choose to indulge, the professions or occupations we elect to pursue, and even where we love and with whom we live are all forms of expression, or forms of self-expression, but the right under discussion here and elsewhere is widely understood to be something narrower than the right to engage in all activities that might in some way be considered to be self-expressive.[21] Thus, perhaps the best among some number of imperfect terms is "freedom of communication," and, indeed, that term and its non-English equivalents are increasingly prevalent in international circles.

If what we are discussing is freedom of communication, however, then we need to face the fact that communication itself is, increasingly, a global phenomenon. I have been discussing here largely domestic communication, first in the context of domestic protections against domestic communication-restrictive laws and practices and then with respect to international protections, whether formal or informal, again against domestic communication-restrictive laws and practices. But neither of those perspectives on freedom of communication in a global context addresses the way in which communication itself is ever more frequently global.

The Internet is, of course, the most obvious example of a global medium of communication, but even more traditional forms of communication increasingly have global origins, global audiences, and global content, with the *International New York Times*, the *Economist*, the *Financial Times*, CNN, Sky News, and the Fox Broadcasting Company being only the most obvious examples. And insofar as communication itself is global in just this way, then the threats to its freedoms take on a different dimension. To what extent do restrictive libel laws in just one jurisdiction, for example, make genuine international publication substantially more difficult? May a broadcaster or an Internet service provider distribute worldwide without a license from each recipient nation? Do nations have the ability to block content coming to their country? To other countries? To all countries? And so on.

In some sense, each of the problems just mentioned is small. That is, each of these represents a specific problem, albeit possibly with major consequences, that might be amenable to a specific solution. But the large problem created by the idea of an international communications network is the poor fit between the transnational or supranational phenomenon of communication that knows no borders and the fact that the world's governing structures have, from the time that government first emerged, been largely national and thus bordered institutions. As a matter of truly ideal theory, genuinely international communications would be governed by an equally genuinely international governance structure and set of international governance institutions.

Such a solution to the problem of global communication is unlikely to emerge in the lifetimes of anyone who is reading this book. That said, however, the contributions that follow may provide the resources to begin to think about many of these issues. And, at the very least, recognizing that the problems of global communications and global freedom of expression come in three quite distinct varieties may provide a useful starting point for confronting the issues.

NOTES

1. An early forerunner of this trend is Pnina Lahav, ed., *Press Law in Modern Democracies* (New York: Longman, 1985). More recent English-language comparative contributions include Ivan Hare and James Weinstein, eds., *Extreme Speech and Democracy* (Oxford: Oxford University Press, 2009); Ludovic Hennebel and

Thomas Hochmann, eds., *Genocide Denials and the Law* (New York: Oxford University Press, 2011); Michael Herz and Peter Molnar, eds., *The Content and Context of Hate Speech: Rethinking Regulation and Responses* (New York: Cambridge University Press, 2012); David Kretzmer and Francine Kershman Hazan, eds., *Freedom of Speech and Incitement Against Democracy* (The Hague: Kluwer, 2000); Ian Loveland, *Political Libels: A Comparative Study* (Oxford: Hart Publishing, 2000); Ian Loveland, ed., *Importing the First Amendment: Freedom of Speech and Expression in Britain, Europe and the USA* (Oxford: Hart Publishing, 1998); W. J. Waluchow, ed., *Free Expression: Essays in Law and Philosophy* (Oxford: Clarendon Press, 1994).

2. See, for example, Richard N. Winfield, ed., *Exporting the Matrix: The Campaign to Reform Media Laws Abroad* (Durham, NC: Carolina Academic Press, 2012).

3. See Gary King, Robert Keohane, and Sidney Verba, *Designing Social Inquiry: Scientific Inference in Qualitative Research* (Princeton, NJ: Princeton University Press, 1994).

4. See Frederick Schauer, "The Exceptional First Amendment," in *American Exceptionalism and Human Rights*, ed. Michael Ignatieff (Princeton, NJ: Princeton University Press, 2005), 29–56.

5. Indeed, much that makes the American approach to freedom of expression unique, whether for better or for worse, derives from a series of Supreme Court decisions in only a twelve-year period, starting with *New York Times v. Sullivan*, 376 U.S. 254 (1964), which transformed defamation law in the context of the civil rights movement, and perhaps ending with *Virginia State Board of Pharmacy v. Virginia Citizens Consumer Council*, 425 U.S. 748 (1976). In between came, inter alia, *Brandenburg v. Ohio*, 395 U.S. 444 (1969), protecting the advocacy of racial violence by a leader of the Ku Klux Klan; *Cohen v. California*, 403 U.S. 15 (1971), protecting the public use of epithets that would offend unwilling viewers in public spaces; and *New York Times Co. v. United States* (the Pentagon Papers Case), 403 U.S. 713 (1971), protecting against injunction the publication of stolen documents whose publication might harm national security. In important respects, these cases constitute the building blocks of American exceptionalism with respect to freedom of expression, an exceptionalism that continues to this day.

6. Including simply the possibility that the sheer volume of free expression litigation and advocacy in the United States has produced doctrinal developments not seen in nations with less experience dealing with the issues. See Frederick Schauer, "Freedom of Expression Adjudication in Europe and America: A Case Study in Comparative Constitutional Architecture," in *European and U.S. Constitutionalism*, ed. Georg Nolte (Cambridge: Council of Europe and Cambridge University Press, 2005), 47–64.

7. On the debate between so-called Asian and Western values, a debate that was especially prominent in the 1990s, see, for example, Alfred M. Boll, "The Asian Values Debate and Its Relevance to International Humanitarian Law," *International Review of the Red Cross*, Paper No. 841 (March 31, 2001); and John Ingleson, "The Asian Values Debate: Accommodating Dissenting Voices," *Social Semiotics* 8 (1998): 227–237.

8. See Loveland, *Importing the First Amendment*; and Winfield, *Exporting the Matrix*.

9. See especially Kyu Ho Youm, "The 'Actual Malice' of *New York Times Co. v. Sullivan*: A Free Speech Touchstone in a Global Century," *Communications Law and Policy* 19 (2014): 185–210.

10. See, among many examples, Vicki C. Jackson, *Constitutional Engagement in a Transnational Era* (New York: Oxford University Press, 2010); Jeremy Waldron, *Partly Laws Common to All Mankind: Foreign Law in American Courts* (New Haven, CT: Yale University Press, 2012); Nelson Lund and John O. McGinnis, "*Lawrence v. Texas* and Judicial Hubris," *Michigan Law Review* 102 (2004): 1555; Ernest A. Young, "Foreign Law and the Denominator Problem," *Harvard Law Review* 119 (2005): 148.

11. See Elaine Mak, *Judicial Decision-Making in a Globalised World: A Comparative Analysis of the Changing Practices of Western Highest Courts* (Oxford: Hart Publishing, 2013); and Tania Groppi and Marie Claire Ponthoreau, eds., *The Use of Foreign Precedents by Constitutional Judges* (Oxford: Hart Publishing, 2013).

12. An interesting hypothesis is that the American comparative reluctance to draw on non-American legal and constitutional sources is one of the causes of decreasing American cross-border legal and constitutional influence. See David Law and Mila Versteeg, "The Declining Influence of the United States Constitution," *New York University Law Review* 87 (2012): 762.

13. Although nations frequently draw on the experience of other nations for guidance, they often do so for reasons unrelated to the substance of the matter at hand. In the early 1990s, for example, Estonia made a conscious effort to harmonize its law with that of Germany, and it did so largely in an effort to increase the likelihood of acceptance into the European Union. Similarly, the United States–Vietnam Bilateral Trade Agreement imposes on Vietnam requirements for modification of its judicial procedures, modifications that Vietnam often accepts not because it thinks those modifications intrinsically desirable but because of the economic advantages of trade with the United States. Once we recognize the frequency of such substance-independent decisions about cross-border legal borrowings, we can understand why similar factors might produce resistance as well as acceptance, such as the increased reluctance of Canadian courts to use American precedents and the increased reluctance of Irish courts to use British ones. On

all of this, see Frederick Schauer, "The Politics and Incentives of Legal Transplantation," in *Governance in a Globalizing World*, ed. Joseph S. Nye Jr. and John D. Donahue (Washington, DC: Brookings Institution Press, 2000), 253–270.

14. As well as Article 18 on freedom of thought and Article 20 on freedom of assembly.

15. See Kathryn Sikkink, *Evidence for Hope: Making Human Rights Work in the 21st Century* (Princeton, NJ: Princeton University Press, 2017).

16. See Steven Greer, *The Margin of Appreciation: Interpretation and Discretion under the European Convention on Human Rights* (Strasbourg: Council of Europe Publishing, 2000).

17. Here, I refer to those international or supranational bodies that adjudicate international and supranational law, but it is important not to forget that these various international legal sources may also have an authoritative effect on domestic law. In the context of freedom of expression, for example, Article 10 of the European Convention on Human Rights has a significant impact on the domestic law of signatory nations. With respect to the United Kingdom, see Andrew Clapham, "The European Convention on Human Rights in the British Courts: Problems Associated with the Incorporation of International Human Rights," in *Promoting Human Rights Through Bills of Rights*, ed. Philip Alston (Oxford: Oxford University Press, 1999), 95–157, at 108–110.

18. For an example of the widespread international view that *Sullivan* goes too far in the protection of the press at the expense of legitimate interests in reputation, see New South Wales Law Reform Commission, *Report 75: Defamation* (Sydney: New South Wales Law Reform Commission, 1995).

19. A valuable comparative description and analysis of right of reply laws worldwide is Kyu Ho Youm, "The Right of Reply and Freedom of the Press: An International and Comparative Perspective," *George Washington Law Review* 76 (2008): 1017–1064.

20. *Perincek v. Switzerland* (2015).

21. See Frederick Schauer, *Free Speech: A Philosophical Enquiry* (Cambridge: Cambridge University Press, 1982), 47–59.

A Global Threshold | **PART I**

Global Norms on Media Regulation | **ONE**

The Devil Is in the Detail

TOBY MENDEL

In November 2005, I had the honor of giving a keynote presentation at the Sixth National and Second International Congress of Information Law, hosted in Mexico City by the Universidad Nacional Autónoma de México. As part of my presentation, I opined that access to information held by public authorities had matured into a human right, part of the wider right to freedom of expression. I based my claim on a collection of soft law statements by various international actors and the growing number of countries that had adopted right to information laws (and constitutional guarantees of this right), as well as a principled extrapolation from the language of international guarantees of freedom of expression.

A well-known expert, commenting on my presentation, challenged my claim, saying that legal opinion on this issue was not sufficiently established and that, in any case, I was a leading author of many of the soft law statements I had quoted.[1] Less than a year later, the Inter-American Court of Human Rights adopted its leading decision on the matter, *Claude Reyes et al. v. Chile,*[2] which held clearly and unequivocally that the right to freedom of expression did encompass the right to access information. The European Court of Human

Rights followed suit a few years later,[3] and today few would disagree that access to public information is a human right.[4]

Was I an early innovator for this norm, a norm entrepreneur, someone who was able to foresee the way in which relevant international standards and practices would trend, or was I an irresponsible civil society activist making an essentially unfounded human rights claim? This chapter explores the issue of what constitutes a global norm and, in particular, a human rights norm. Within that wide field, the chapter focuses on media regulation, specifically broadcast regulation, providing a case study of one norm that has been asserted by human rights activists, namely that a key goal of broadcast regulation should be to support diversity through promoting a three-tier system of broadcasting.

WHAT IS A GLOBAL NORM?

International Law

Formally, the international legal system contains a well-established definition of what constitutes international law, found at Article 38(1) of the Statute of the International Court of Justice. This recognizes four sources of international law, namely treaties, customary international law, general principles of law, and "the teachings of the most highly qualified publicists of the various nations," as a subsidiary source.

The definition covers both general and particular rules of international law, and hence cannot be equated with the idea of a global norm. However, customary international law and general principles of law inherently refer to general rules, and it would be easy enough at least to propose reasonable standards for how widely ratified a general convention would need to be before it could be considered to establish global norms.

It seems clear that general legal rules are global norms—even if global norms go beyond the scope of general legal rules—so an assessment of legal rules can shed important light on the nature of global norms.

Interpretation

The presence of the fourth source of international law, in subarticle 38(1)(d), reminds us that any system of law depends on authoritative interpretation of what are, of necessity, less than perfectly clear rules. This is true of even the most developed legal system, because the complexity of human life will always transcend the level of detail provided by the legal system. In other words, no system of rules, even governing a clearly defined area, could comprehensively and without the benefit of human interpretation resolve every dispute that might arise among humans (or states) in that area.

This is all the more true of general international law, given what a terribly cumbersome process it is to create it. The process of adopting treaties of general application, for example, is enormously challenging and lengthy. This has resulted in what might be described as the underdevelopment of the normative framework of rules in international law, at least as assessed by reference to the need for such rules. Systems of interpretation can play an invaluable, albeit only partial, role in addressing gaps in the normative framework.

The idea that interpretation needs to fill gaps is not a theoretical one. The main treaty guarantee of the right to freedom of expression is found in two sentences in subarticles 19(2) and (3) of the International Covenant on Civil and Political Rights (ICCPR). This is a far-reaching and in many ways prescient statement of this right, and yet it is more than clear that extensive interpretation is required to understand its full meaning. None of the issues addressed in this section of this book—political expression, defamation, protection of sources, access to information, and media regulation—can be understood properly without adding enormously (including through interpretation) to the words of subarticles 19(2) and (3).

Yet the existence of actors with the authority to provide binding interpretations is precisely where international law, and international human rights law in particular, is weakest compared to national law. At the national level, complex hierarchies of courts are constitutionally empowered, in almost every state, to provide binding interpretations of the law. Although there are dedicated human rights courts in the three more developed regional systems for the protection of human rights—namely in Africa, the Americas, and Europe—no equivalent exists at the global level.

Even where international courts or entities with more limited powers to resolve human rights disputes, such as the UN Human Rights Committee, do exist, however, there are important limits to the role they can play in interpreting human rights. First, there are strict limits on approaching international human rights bodies in individual cases, namely that one has to exhaust local remedies first.

Second, there are important structural biases in the subject matter of these cases because they are essentially limited to matters where those involved have a very strong personal vested interest. As Toby Mendel notes, "Thus, while there are numerous defamation cases [before international human rights courts], there is relatively little jurisprudence on issues like the responsibility of the State to ensure diversity in the media or to respect the independence of public broadcasters."[5]

Third, international and regional human rights courts tend to be quite cautious in their rulings, in part because they are conscious of the limits of their power. In particular, they normally limit their decisions to what is required to decide the case at hand and refrain from making wider statements of principle. Given the other constraints, this limits their role in developing interpretive positions.

Although, formally, interpretation relates to both treaties and customary international law, there are important differences between these two types of international law. First, the power of most of the more authoritative actors to interpret human rights—including all of the regional human rights courts and the UN Human Rights Committee—is formally limited to interpretation of the treaties that created them.

Second, interpretation of a treaty is a very different process than interpretation of a customary norm. The former consists of determining what the language that has been agreed upon by the parties to the treaty actually means. There are established rules and systems for doing this, which not only appropriately constrain the discretion of the interpreter but also allow for progressive development of the rules over time. It is completely different with customary rules, where the process normally involves an assessment of whether a rule exists in the first place. This, in turn, requires an assessment of whether enough states have acted in accordance with a practice out of a sense of legal obligation. Interpretation might then be required to assess the scope or implications of the rule.

Third, and closely related, when interpreting a treaty, a decision-maker must choose the meaning, from among the competing meanings that are being asserted, which makes best sense and best resolves the issue at hand. The situation for customary law is simply not analogous to this, since the decision focuses on whether a rule exists in the first place.

As a result, treaties are far better suited to the progressive development of international law, through interpretation, than is customary international law. Put differently, while some level of innovation and progressive development is inherent in treaty interpretation, the bar in this regard is very high for customary international law.

Global Norms

Martha Finnemore and Kathryn Sikkink defined the core idea of a global norm in 1998 as a "standard of appropriate behavior for actors with a given identity."[6] This is helpful inasmuch as it provides some definitional specificity—a certain type of behavior that applies to a defined set of actors—but it is still undoubtedly too vague for current purposes inasmuch as it fails to identify what "appropriate" might mean and whether, and to what degree, acceptance by or binding power over the actors to whom it relates would be required for it to qualify as a "standard."

International human rights law rules are also global norms (including in the way Finnemore and Sikkink define that idea). But, as the story at the beginning of this paper suggests, for a human rights activist—that is, for someone who is committed to change—strictly limiting the idea of a global norm to international law rules is unduly confining. The challenges described here in terms of both creating and interpreting international law suggest that a more practical definition of a global norm is needed, one that captures standards that, even if they have not fully crystalized into international law rules, still provide normative guidance as to how states or other actors should behave.

I would like to suggest a utilitarian definition of a global norm, at least for purposes of human rights. Specifically, I would define a global human rights norm as "a standard that, whatever the underlying reasons, has sufficient authority to be able to influence the behavior of state actors, and as relevant, others, reasonably consistently over time."

There are problems with this definition, inasmuch as it is vague in terms of how much influence would be required, and what would suffice to qualify as "reasonably consistently over time." Some degree of spread, or a tipping point in terms of the number of countries adopting the norm, would be required. There also may need to be a degree of spread in terms of countries in different regions of the world, because a practice that was restricted to just one region could not claim to be global. At the same time, it would be unduly rigid to require countries in all regions to adopt a human rights norm before it could be considered global.[7]

Another tension inherent in this definition is between standards and practice, both of which it incorporates, because there is not infrequently a gap between what is accepted as an authoritative standard and what state actors actually do in practice. Even widely accepted human rights are sometimes denied or repudiated in practice. The extent of this can ebb and flow depending on wider geopolitical factors. Furthermore, even widely accepted standards may suffer from general breaches. One reason for this is that, unlike national law, the international system lacks effective institutions and procedures for enforcing even its clearest human rights rules. This alone cannot defeat the emergence of a global norm or the notion would have no power. However, where lack of respect for a norm in practice was sufficiently widespread, its quality as a global norm would be vitiated, which is why the idea of practice was incorporated into the definition.

Another consideration is the extent to which a state adapts or reframes the norm when adopting it locally (that is, nationally). As I will explore, many global norms leave states a lot of leeway in terms of implementation. International human rights law recognizes this as potentially being legitimate, as, for example, in the notion of states' "margin of appreciation" when giving national effect to rules.[8]

Some combination of acceptance of a norm and respecting it in practice is needed before it can deliver the qualities posited here for a global norm. Perhaps there is some sliding scale, so that a norm that is very widely accepted would need less conforming practice to qualify. However, the opposite cannot be true, because a "mere" practice (something states do, but without any sense that they are bound to do it) cannot qualify as a "standard."

An interesting issue arising from this definition is what gives norms sufficient authority to influence behavior. This is addressed in the next section.

HOW GLOBAL NORMS ATTRACT THE REQUISITE "AUTHORITY"

The formal sources of international law, as described in Article 38(1) of the Statute of the International Court of Justice, are very state oriented. Conventions are adopted by states, customary international law requires states to accept a general practice as law, and general principles also have to be recognized by (civilized) states. Only in subarticle (d) are other actors brought in, as a subsidiary source, and even then, only judges and "the most highly qualified publicists" are considered to qualify.

In somewhat stark contrast to this, there are many ways in which global norms, as I have defined this idea, can attract authority, albeit sometimes by feeding into the Article 38(1) sources. Some observations about how this may come about are relevant here.

First, as Finnemore and Sikkink point out, national norms can mature into global ones.[9] However, at least in the area of human rights, the actors that drive or lead this process are more likely to be development actors, such as civil society organizations and sometimes intergovernmental organizations, than states.

In relation to human rights, it is common for development actors to transfer from one country to another approaches deemed to be "successful" (whether in terms of promoting respect for human rights or justice values or simply as a practical way of delivering other development objectives). Practices can spread, sometimes widely, in this way. At some point a practice may start to become widespread—such as, for example, the growth in the rate of adoption of right to information legislation, starting around 1997—and thus become a potential candidate for recognition as a global norm.

However, as noted, a shared practice, even one that is widespread and recognized to be highly effective, cannot by itself constitute a global norm, because such a practice is not a "standard" but just a commonly employed approach. To become a standard, some normative element—"accepted as law," in the words of Article 38(1) of the Statute of the International Court of Justice—must attach to the practice. Put differently, while one can market a good practice only on the basis of what it delivers, it is possible to advocate in favor of a global norm on the basis that it *should* be respected.

Promoting the normative aspect, whether or not this is based on an established practice, can happen in a variety of ways. In some cases, normative value can attach simply because states widely agree that the arrangement is an efficient and fair way to manage international affairs. This could be said to be the case, for example, with the recognition by states of the exclusive economic maritime zone of two hundred nautical miles.

Different considerations normally propel recognition of human rights, given that these essentially constrain the power of the state to act and hence are unlikely to have the same sorts of state-negotiated drivers that underlie many other branches of international law.

Looking at this specifically from the perspective of freedom of expression, and based on my own involvement in "normative development" activities, it is impossible not to recognize the power of extrapolating from or interpreting basic guarantees based on principled analysis and, ultimately, the power of (good) ideas.

International law provides a brief, if sophisticated, statement of the right to freedom of expression. The guarantee says almost nothing about what it means in relation to specific freedom of expression issues, such as protection of reputation or regulation of the media.[10] To understand how to strike an appropriate balance between freedom of expression and protection of reputation, or what might be appropriate in terms of media regulation, one is therefore required to extrapolate from the core guarantee.

There is no shortage of normative statements being made by academics, journalists, nongovernmental organization (NGO) activists, media owners, or simply interested individuals. Sometimes, certain statements contradict those made by others. For example, media owners often take a strong position against the imposition of regulatory regimes on the media, while civil society actors may support such regulation as a way of improving the quality of media reporting.

The question then arises as to what gives certain statements the authority that is required to create a global norm, while other statements fail to attract that status (or power). Ultimately, the adoption of a position by an international human rights court is among the strongest ways to impart authority to it. However, as noted, there are important limits to this at the international level, which generates a need for (alternative) authoritative normative development (in addition to the courts), which strong existing institutional and civil society structures for human rights are ideally placed to provide.

An important official voice here is the UN Human Rights Committee, a soft law body operating under the ICCPR. In addition to its decisions ("Views") on individual cases,[11] the committee produces periodic concluding observations on states' periodic reports, which collectively serve as a sort of common law set of standards regarding different rights.[12]

More influential, however, are the committee's explicitly standard-setting general comments, which it produces about once every two or three years.[13] The most recent statement on freedom of expression is the 2011 General Comment no. 34,[14] which covers a wide range of freedom of expression issues, including many that do not naturally find their way to courts (such as diversity in the media and the independence of public service broadcasters). However, the large number of issues embraced by freedom of expression means that only a paragraph or two is devoted to each one, even in this lengthy general comment. As a result, the contribution of general comments to global norms is only quite general in nature.

Another very important source of soft law in relation to freedom of expression is the joint declarations that the special international mandates on freedom of expression[15] have adopted on an annual basis since 1999.[16] Each joint declaration focuses on a different freedom of expression theme; the last few, in reverse chronological order, have focused on freedom of expression and elections, challenges to freedom of expression in the coming decade, media independence, and "fake news." This allows for far more precise and detailed treatment of an issue than is possible with general comments. Based on the collective status of the four mandate holders, these statements carry a lot of authoritative weight.[17]

It would be a mistake, however, to attribute either the development of these sorts of statements themselves or their subsequent impact only to the official actors that adopt them. On the development side, academics, civil society actors, professional bodies, and sometimes even media outlets feed into the process. For example, several rounds of both formal and informal consultations with a range of actors significantly shaped General Comment no. 34.

Behind joint declarations and general comments is an enormous body of work contributing to the ideas in these statements. This includes academic writings, reports by NGOs, statements by intergovernmental organizations or state-level leaders, media reporting, conference declarations, and so on. In some cases, this background material helps define the standards in the statements, so that the latter can be described as elaborating on previously developed ideas. In other cases, the statements reframe or recast the background material in a more developmental way. In yet other cases, the statements work by analogy, applying previously established standards to new areas, such as the Internet, or to new contexts, such as during elections. Regardless of how it is used, background material provides a base from which authoritative statements develop and distill ideas.

In terms of impact, again, it is the promotion of these statements by a range of actors—academics, NGOs, professional bodies, lawyers, and others—that move them up the "value chain" in terms of normative influence, whether this is by getting courts, either national or international, to refer to them in judgments or by getting states to follow their prescriptions. Without this promotional work, the behavioral impact of these statements would be far reduced.

Getting states to follow these normative statements is often a complex political (advocacy) process. However, the ability of these statements to influence at least independent courts depends not only on their formal status, in the sense of who adopted them, but also on what may broadly be called the power of the ideas they contain.

These statements essentially represent an extrapolation from or interpretation of the core international guarantees of freedom of expression, and this can be done more or less "powerfully." A number of factors may contribute to their power. An important one is the coherence of the vision underlying the specific normative statements, whether this vision is based on a conception of freedom of expression or on wider human rights or, indeed, even on social values. In many cases, they involve a balancing or calibration between rights, such as freedom of expression and privacy, or other social interests, such as freedom of expression and national security. In the area of media regulation, they may even involve a balancing between different freedom of expression interests, such as those of owners and of media consumers. An unsophisticated or ultimately unworkable attempt to balance or calibrate competing interests will be far less likely to gain wide acceptance than a more sophisticated one.

Another factor is the extent to which statements reflect a global understanding. Simply seeking to project a national practice globally will almost never work. There needs to be wider acceptance and some cross-regional adoption.

The clarity and force of the statements—ultimately their persuasive power—is another factor. This is complex, because some ideas represent inherently more obvious claims for inclusion within the scope of freedom of expression. The idea that bodies that regulate the media need to be independent of government falls into this "more obvious" category. On the other hand, decriminalizing defamation is far more complex. Beyond this, there are different ways of presenting normative claims, even where they are substantively similar, some of which have greater persuasive power.

The extent to which statements progressively develop international law is a delicate balancing act. Going too far in this respect can undermine the authoritative weight of the statements (that is, if they are seen as overstepping or being too radical), whereas being too timid not only can result in a lost opportunity (if an idea's time has come) but also may trench on the coherence of the underlying vision.[18] Linking to wider developmental goals and benefits can be important as well, especially in terms of bolstering support for a larger progressive development leap.

These factors all impact on the standard-setting power of statements and hence on their contribution to the development of global norms. In my experience of working on these sorts of statements, I have found it imperative to try to be as strategic and high-powered as possible in relation to these factors, taking into account the particular value in relation to which one is trying to develop a global norm.

Any normative statement will almost inevitably have to compete with countervailing claims, because there will always be those who wish to project different ideas. In the end, a number of additional factors will affect the emergence of a global freedom of expression norm, including resistance by states and other political considerations. However, where it is a question of assessing what the meaning of the words in a treaty mean, including Article 19 of the ICCPR, the most powerful vision, based on the factors outlined above, should ideally win out.

CASE STUDY: A THREE-TIER BROADCASTING SYSTEM

These days, commentators often refer to the idea that systems for broadcast regulation should provide for equitable recognition of three different types of broadcasters: public service, commercial, and community. Thus, paragraph 39 of the UN Human Rights Committee's 2011 General Comment no. 34 states, "Licensing regimes for broadcasting via media with limited capacity, such as audiovisual terrestrial and satellite services, should provide for an equitable allocation of access and frequencies between public, commercial and community broadcasters." Whether this qualifies as a global norm, and, if so, where it came from, is a complex question.

The normative essence of this standard is rooted in two attributes of freedom of expression. The first, derived directly from the language of Article 19 of the ICCPR, is that the right applies not only to the speaker but also to the recipient of a communication, based on the protection in Article 19(2) of the rights to "*seek, receive* and impart information and ideas" [emphasis added]. The second is that the right is not only negative in nature—barring the state from interfering with expressive activities—but also has a positive aspect—requiring the state to take steps to foster the free flow of information and ideas in society. This has been widely recognized, including in an oft-repeated quotation by the European Court of Human Rights: "The Court recalls the key importance of freedom of expression as one of the preconditions for a functioning democracy. Genuine, effective exercise of this freedom does not depend merely on the State's duty not to interfere, but may require positive measures of protection, even in the sphere of relations between individuals."[19]

States' positive obligation to promote diversity in the media—so that individuals can receive a plurality of information and ideas—follows from the combination of these two ideas. These ideas also underpin other obligations—including to protect the right to information—but many of the positive obligations that have been recognized are essentially about promoting media diversity, whether generally or within a specific media outlet.

The idea of diversity has received a lot of attention in authoritative soft law statements. Some of the earliest regulatory measures that promoted diversity were rules prohibiting media monopolies. To some extent, these ran in parallel to general antimonopoly rules, which were designed to protect fair market competition rather than diversity per se. But many states put in place far more stringent antimonopoly rules specifically for the media based on the overriding need to promote media diversity.[20]

One of the earliest, more general statements on diversity, albeit limited in scope to the print media, is the Declaration of Windhoek, adopted under the auspices of the United Nations Educational, Scientific and Cultural Organization (UNESCO) on May 3, 1991, which states, "Consistent with Article 19 of the Universal Declaration of Human Rights, the establishment, maintenance and fostering of an independent, pluralistic and free press is essential to the development and maintenance of democracy in a nation, and for economic development."[21]

There also have been some general statements on this by international courts. For example, the Inter-American Court of Human Rights has recognized that realization of the right to seek and receive information and ideas is possible only in the context of a diverse media, stating, in 1985, "It is the mass media that make the exercise of freedom of expression a reality. This means that the conditions of its use must conform to the requirements of this freedom, with the result that there must be, inter alia, a plurality of means of communication, the barring of all monopolies thereof, in whatever form, and guarantees for the protection of the freedom and independence of journalists."[22]

The European Court of Human Rights has often repeated the phrase "[Imparting] information and ideas of general interest . . . cannot be successfully accomplished unless it is grounded in the principle of pluralism."[23] In a 2012 case decided by a Grand Chamber,[24] *Centro Europa 7 S.R.L. and Di Stefano v. Italy*, the European Court of Human Rights set out in some detail the key principles governing diversity:

> The Court considers it appropriate at the outset to recapitulate the general principles established in its case-law concerning pluralism in the audiovisual media. As it has often noted, there can be no democracy without pluralism. . . . In this connection, the Court observes that to ensure true pluralism in the audiovisual sector in a democratic society, it is not sufficient to provide for the existence of several channels or the theoretical possibility for potential operators to access the audiovisual market. It is necessary in addition to allow effective access to the market so as to guarantee diversity of overall programme content, reflecting as far as possible the variety of opinions encountered in the society at which the programmes are aimed.[25]

The UN Human Rights Committee has also noted, "States parties should take particular care to encourage an independent and diverse media."[26] It is, therefore, probably fair to conclude that the idea that states are under a general positive obligation to ensure media diversity has attained the status of a global norm. To fully establish this, evidence would need to be presented that this idea had influenced state behavior over time, something for which there is at least anecdotal support.

It also seems reasonable to conclude, at least in a traditional broadcasting environment, that the state should use the licensing process to promote diversity on the airwaves—again, something that has attracted widespread support, even if sometimes it is not well reflected in practice. Most democracies, for example, have, over time, developed at least a dual broadcasting system whereby public broadcasters exist alongside commercial broadcasters.[27] The European Court of Human Rights has held in a number of cases that a public broadcasting monopoly is a breach of the right to freedom of expression.[28]

On the other hand, a few countries, such as the United States and some countries in Latin America, do not have any—or have only very weak—public broadcasters, as that term is used here, namely to denote public ownership.[29] However, a global norm does not require universal state practice, and there are other examples of the United States diverging from even clearly established freedom of expression rules.[30] Furthermore, licensing in the United States has been used to foster a very robust and diverse commercial broadcasting sector, which may arguably reduce the need for public service broadcasting.[31]

The next step, to call for community broadcasting to be recognized, is less well established as a matter of both practice and normative development. In terms of practice, although some countries formally recognized community broadcasting quite a long time ago, such recognition is less widespread than with public and commercial broadcasting and, in many countries, far more recent.[32] Similarly, normative statements about this, whether cast as a need to recognize community broadcasting or as a need to recognize a three-tier broadcasting system, are of more recent vintage.

The World Association of Community Radio Broadcasters, the representative organization for this sector, has been calling for this for some time. One of the earlier independent statements about this is found in the African Charter on Broadcasting 2001, adopted at a UNESCO-sponsored conference held ten years after the original Windhoek conference. The very first substantive clause of the charter states, "The legal framework for broadcasting should include a clear statement of the principles underpinning broadcast regulation, including promoting respect for freedom of expression, diversity, and the free flow of information and ideas, as well as a three-tier system for broadcasting: public service, commercial and community."[33]

The need to recognize the three tiers of broadcasting has been reiterated in the declarations adopted at a number of the annual conferences that UNESCO holds to celebrate World Press Freedom Day each year on May 3.[34] The Council of Europe's 2009 Declaration of the Committee of Ministers also "recognises community media as a distinct media sector."[35]

A number of authoritative statements go beyond merely indicating a need for recognition and call on states to allocate frequencies equitably among the three types of broadcasters. An early statement of this is found in a set of principles on broadcast regulation published by Article 19.[36] In 2003, the African Commission on Human and People's Rights adopted a Declaration of Principles on Freedom of Expression in Africa, principle 5(2) of which calls on states to ensure that the regulatory system for broadcasting recognizes the principle of "equitable allocation of frequencies between private broadcasting uses, both commercial and community."[37] Statements along these lines are also found in the 2009 Council of Europe Declaration (clause 2), the UN Human Rights Committee's General Comment no. 34 (paragraph 39), and the 2007 joint declaration of the special international mandates on freedom of expression, which states, "Different types of broadcasters—commercial, public service and community—should be able to operate on, and have equitable access to, all available distribution platforms. Specific measures to promote diversity may include reservation of adequate frequencies for different types of broadcasters, must-carry rules, a requirement that both distribution and reception technologies are complementary and/or interoperable, including across national frontiers, and non-discriminatory access to support services, such as electronic programme guides."[38]

Despite this, it remains debatable whether the need to recognize a three-tier system of broadcasting has emerged as a global norm. So far, no international human rights court has specifically decided this. However, using the definition of a global norm proposed here, focusing on the ability to influence the behavior of state actors, it probably does meet this standard. A growing number of states in all regions of the world are formally recognizing community broadcasting, and the pace of recognition has certainly increased in recent years.[39]

GENERAL NORMS VERSUS SPECIFIC PRACTICES

If we assume, for argument's sake, that a three-tier system of broadcasting is a global norm, there remains the important question of how this should be implemented. Even if it is a norm, that does not provide much guidance in terms of what, specifically, is required to implement it. UNESCO, in collaboration with the Centre for Law and Democracy, recently launched a Community Media

Sustainability Policy Series, setting out detailed standards for regulating community media and including seven policy papers and a policy checklist.[40] Creating a three-tier system of broadcasting is complex, and there are numerous potential ways of going about it, which may deliver more or less respect for the norm in practice.

States clearly have some leeway in terms of how they create a three-tier broadcasting system, but there are equally clearly limits to that. A system that formally provided for community broadcasters but then made it impossible for them to operate in practice—for example, because they were simply not being awarded licenses or because they had no viable sources of funding—would be a charade and so clearly would fail to deliver the norm.

But the reality is more subtle, and it may be challenging in relation to many global norms, at least those covering more complex issues, to decide whether the behavior of any particular state is compliant with the norm. Legal reflection of a global norm, even if that legal regime is not properly implemented, would serve as verification of the norm. But what if the legal framework significantly reframes or locally adapts the norm?

In relation to community broadcasting, for example, in Brazil, a constitutional rule (Article 223[3]) allocates the authority to issue broadcasting licenses exclusively to the national congress. The result, for various reasons—including that many members of congress have some involvement in the commercial broadcasting sector—has been a huge backlog in the approval of community licenses in the country.[41]

Clause 8 of *Policy Guidelines for Setting Up Community Radio Stations in India*, adopted by the Ministry of Information and Broadcasting, imposes strict limits on the ability of community radios to raise funds. Contributions from foreign donors must be cleared in accordance with the Foreign Contribution Regulation Act. A very low maximum of five minutes per hour of commercial advertising is allowed. Program sponsorship is strictly limited to government bodies and to public interest programming. There is a system for registering to be eligible to receive government advertising, which has strict conditions and rates. Because it is almost impossible to survive without government advertising, in practice the government exercises significant indirect control over the community broadcasting sector.[42]

In Ethiopia, there are strict rules governing the establishment of community broadcasters, including that there be an annual general assembly for members of the community, which should then elect a seven-member board and a full-time general manager. Through its power to ratify these procedures, local government exercises significant control over this sector.[43]

These three examples are far from worst-case scenarios, but they still represent clear examples of legal and policy environments that undermine community broadcasting and that fail in important ways to conform to UNESCO's policy prescriptions. There are many other countries where community broadcasters are struggling in the face of less hostile but also less than robustly supportive environments. At what point along the spectrum, ranging from a fantastically supportive environment to one in which it is impossible to survive, is a state failing to respect the relevant global norm?

The practice of many countries in terms of recognition of community broadcasting is the result of negotiations between various interested stakeholders—including the government, aspirant community broadcast operators, commercial media actors, NGOs, and others—rather than of a strict application of established standards. In such a context, the more detailed standards, such as those adopted by UNESCO, can be an important bargaining chip. It would be difficult to argue that all thirty-eight of UNESCO's recommendations are part of the global norm relating to media diversity, or even the norm relating to a three-tier broadcasting system. On the other hand, many of them, at least, can be expected to "influence the behavior of states," some "reasonably consistently over time."

CONCLUSION

This chapter defines a global norm as a standard that has sufficient authority to be able to influence the behavior of states reasonably consistently over time. This has both a normative and a practical element (that is, it must be a standard, but it must also be reasonably widely observed in practice). Although a number of limitations and tensions are inherent within this definition—including the possibility of a major gap between recognition of a norm and respecting it in practice—it still provides useful definitional power.

Stringent practical limits are inherent within the international legal system for human rights, in terms both of establishing primary rules and of providing authoritative interpretations of those rules. Despite this, strong global norms that go beyond the relatively sparse formal legal framework are needed. As a result, at least in practice, we often look to other actors as sources of authoritative statements that constitute or can develop into global norms.

There are a number of ways in which normative statements can attract the requisite authority to develop into global norms. It is important, for this purpose, that there is a body of state practice that aligns with or delivers the norm, but that alone is not enough because in itself it lacks standard-setting value. A range of both official and other actors regularly contribute to the development of normative statements about freedom of expression values. However, only some garner sufficient authoritative weight to be able to affect state behavior reasonably consistently. Various factors contribute to this, including the status of the body making the statement. An important ingredient is what might be described as the "inherent power" of the ideas in a statement, in terms of reflecting a wide and coherent vision of human rights, their persuasive power, and whether they strike the right balance when progressively developing international law.

We can see all of these factors at play in the development of normative values around the idea of a three-tier system of broadcasting, involving public service, commercial, and community broadcasters. It may be debated whether this has developed into a global norm, but it certainly seems to meet at least the basic conditions of the definition put forward in this chapter.

The challenge here, as with many other global norms, is that its normative clarity or detail is insufficient to dictate even the main features of the practical systems that are inevitably needed to deliver or implement it. States have numerous options for doing this, which may be more or less effective in terms of delivering the underlying values that inspired the global norm. Assessing whether an option is sufficiently effective to qualify as meeting the norm is a very challenging task. In the end, as important as it is to have high-level global norms, the real devil is in the detail.

NOTES

1. This was partially true, in the sense that I had played a supporting and drafting role for many of the statements, but they had all been formally adopted by official actors.
2. September 19, 2006, series C, no. 151.
3. *Társaság A Szabadságjogokért v. Hungary*, April 14, 2009, application no. 37374/05.
4. See Sandra Coliver, "The Right of Access to Information Held by Public Authorities: Emergence as a Global Norm," chapter 2 of this volume.
5. Toby Mendel, "The UN Special Rapporteur on Freedom of Opinion and Expression: Progressive Development of International Standards Relating to Freedom of Expression," in *The United Nations and Freedom of Expression and Information: Critical Perspectives*, ed. Tarlach McGonagle and Yvonne Donders (Cambridge: Cambridge University Press, 2015), 235–268, at 248.

6. Martha Finnemore and Kathryn Sikkink, "International Norm Dynamics and Political Change," *International Organization* 52, no. 4 (1998): 891.

7. Among other things, some regions include few countries that are robust democracies, so requiring every region to participate would pose a considerable barrier to the development of global human rights norms.

8. See, for example, European Court of Human Rights, *Handyside v. the United Kingdom*, December 7, 1976, application no. 5493/72, para. 48.

9. Finnemore and Sikkink, "International Norm Dynamics," 893–894.

10. The protection of reputation at least gets a one-word nod in the part of the guarantee focusing on restrictions, in subarticle 19(3), but media regulation is not mentioned even once.

11. A searchable database of these decisions is available from the Office of the United Nations High Commissioner for Human Rights, http://juris.ohchr.org.

12. These are available at "UN Treaty Body Database," Office of the United Nations High Commissioner for Human Rights, http://tbinternet.ohchr.org/_layouts/treatybodyexternal/TBSearch.aspx?Lang=en&TreatyID=8&DocTypeID=5. Accessed July 1, 2020.

13. These are available at "UN Treaty Body Database," http://tbinternet.ohchr.org/_layouts/treatybodyexternal/TBSearch.aspx?Lang=en&TreatyID=8&DocTypeID=11. Accessed July 1, 2020.

14. September 12, 2011, U.N. Doc. CCPR/C/GC/34. Available in various formats and languages at "UN Treaty Body Database," http://tbinternet.ohchr.org/_layouts/treatybodyexternal/Download.aspx?symbolno=CCPR%2fC%2fGC%2f34&Lang=en. Accessed July 1, 2020.

15. Currently, these include the United Nations Special Rapporteur on Freedom of Opinion and Expression, the Organization for Security and Co-operation in Europe Representative on Freedom of the Media, the Organization of American States Special Rapporteur on Freedom of Expression, and the African Commission on Human and Peoples' Rights Special Rapporteur on Freedom of Expression and Access to Information.

16. The recent joint declarations are available at "Standard-Setting," Centre for Law and Democracy, https://www.law-democracy.org/live/legal-work/standard-setting. Originally conceived of by Article 19, these are now developed jointly with the Centre for Law and Democracy.

17. For a detailed description of the development and influence of the joint declarations, see Mendel, "UN Special Rapporteur," 251–265.

18. The European Court of Human Rights arguably did this in the piecemeal and not very coherent way it recognized the right to information. See Toby Mendel, "Global Recognition of the Right to Information as a Human Right," in *Comparative RTI*

Laws in the SAARC Nations, ed. Jeet Singh Mann (New Delhi: Centre for Transparency and Accountability in Governance, 2017), 1–26, at 15–21.

19. European Court of Human Rights, *Özgür Gündem v. Turkey*, March 16, 2000, application no. 23144/93, para. 43.

20. See Toby Mendel and Eve Salomon, *The Regulatory Environment for Broadcasting: An International Best Practice Survey for Brazilian Stakeholders* (Brasilia: UNESCO, 2011), 59–64. http://unesdoc.unesco.org/images/0019/001916/191622e .pdf.

21. The declaration was endorsed by the United Nations Educational, Scientific and Cultural Organization (UNESCO) General Conference at its twenty-sixth session, in 1991.

22. Inter-American Court of Human Rights, *Compulsory Membership in an Association Prescribed by Law for the Practice of Journalism*, November 13, 1985, series A, no. 5, para. 34.

23. See, for example, European Court of Human Rights, *Informationsverein Lentia and Others v. Austria*, November 24, 1993, application nos. 13914/88, 15041/89, 15717/89, 15779/89, and 17207/90, para. 38.

24. These cases are decided by a larger panel of judges and, as a result, have more weight.

25. European Court of Human Rights, *Centro Europa 7 S.R.L. and Di Stefano v. Italy*, June 7, 2012, application no. 38433/09, paras. 129–130.

26. Human Rights Committee, General Comment no. 34, para. 14.

27. The reference here to "public" rather than to "public service" broadcasters is intentional. Not all publicly owned broadcasters qualify as public service broadcasters. The characteristics of public service broadcasters are discussed in Toby Mendel, *Public Service Broadcasting: A Comparative Legal Survey*, 2nd ed. (Paris: UNESCO 2011), 6–8.

28. Starting with *Informationsverein Lentia and Others v. Austria*.

29. The United States' Public Broadcasting Service and the stations that are associated with it, despite the similarity in the name, is a privately run nongovernmental organization.

30. In some cases, this even applies to rules that are explicitly spelled out in human rights treaties, such as in relation to incitement to hatred, which is constitutionally protected in the United States but is required to be prohibited under Article 20(2) of the International Covenant on Civil and Political Rights.

31. Although it is also arguable that the absence of public service broadcasting in the media ecology of the United States has negatively affected diversity.

32. See Toby Mendel, *Tuning into Development: International Comparative Survey of Community Broadcasting Regulation* (Paris: UNESCO, 2013), 29–39.

33. Adopted May 5, 2001. See *African Charter on Broadcasting,* https://en.unesco.org /sites/default/files/african_charter.pdf.

34. See, for example, the 2008 Maputo Declaration, https://en.unesco.org/sites/default /files/maputo_declaration.pdf; and the 2012 Carthage Declaration, http://www .unesco.org/new/fileadmin/MULTIMEDIA/HQ/CI/CI/pdf/WPFD/carthage _declaration_2012_en.pdf.

35. Council of Europe, Committee of Ministers, *Declaration of the Committee of Ministers on the Role of Community Media in Promoting Social Cohesion and Intercultural Dialogue* (February 11, 2009), preamble. https://go.coe.int/DOmlX.

36. Toby Mendel, *Access to the Airwaves: Principles on Freedom of Expression and Broadcast Regulation* (London: Article 19, March 2002), principle 9.3. http://www .article19.org/data/files/pdfs/standards/accessairwaves.pdf.

37. Adopted at its thirty-second session, October 17–23, 2002. See also the African Charter on Broadcasting, principle 1(4).

38. Joint Declaration on Promoting Diversity in the Broadcast Media, December 12, 2007. https://www.osce.org/fom/66176.

39. Mendel, *Tuning into Development,* 29–39.

40. See UNESCO, Community Media Sustainability Policy Series, http://en.unesco .org/community-media-sustainability/policy-series.

41. Mendel, *Tuning into Development,* 61.

42. Ministry of Information and Broadcasting, *Policy Guidelines for Setting up Community Radio Stations in India,* 2006. https://mib.gov.in/sites/default/files/c1_0 .pdf.

43. Mendel, *Tuning into Development,* 44.

The Right of Access
to Information Held by
Public Authorities

TWO

Emergence as a Global Norm

SANDRA COLIVER

Of all of the rights that are facets of the right to freedom of expression, the right of access to information held by public authorities has arguably enjoyed the most precipitous growth in recognition over the past two decades, at both the national and international levels. Moreover, not only have international courts and other authoritative norm definers recognized the right as a fundamental human right, but also there is considerable agreement among national laws and international instruments about the scope and contents of the right.

This chapter examines the extent to which the right of access to information held by public authorities has become a global norm as well as a rule of international law. The chapter begins with an examination of the meaning of rules of customary international law and the way in which global norms differ from them. It then reviews the historical development of the right of access to information held by public authorities at the international, regional, and national levels; examines the extent to which the right to information (RTI) can be said to have achieved the status of a rule of customary international law and a global norm; and discusses the content of the norm in different regions.

GLOBAL NORMS AND NORMS OF CUSTOMARY INTERNATIONAL LAW

Definition of a Global Norm

This chapter focuses on the first two stages of the norm life cycle developed by Martha Finnemore and Kathryn Sikkink,[1] namely, norm emergence and cascade, and on norms concerning the behavior of states; it does not address the third stage of norm internalization, when the behavior of nonstate actors (officials, civil servants, public watchdogs, and citizens) becomes as significant as the behavior of state actors.

Definition of Customary International Law

Two types of international law are relevant to the right of access to public information (and other human rights): treaty law and customary international law (CIL). A treaty provision is binding only on the states that have adhered to the treaty. In contrast, a CIL rule is binding on all states, including those that came into being after the norm's crystallization. A state may be exempted only if it persistently objected to the rule during its formation and only if the rule is not considered *jus cogens*, or peremptory, meaning that a majority of states consider the rule to be so vital that it must be binding on all.[2]

CIL is based on the general practice of states, followed out of a sense of legal obligation.[3] According to the International Law Commission, evidence that may prove that a general practice is "accepted as law" includes "public statements made on behalf of states; official publications;... decisions of national courts; treaty provisions; and conduct in connection with resolutions adopted by an international organization or at an intergovernmental conference."[4]

Breaches of a rule do not necessarily prevent a general practice from being established. This is particularly so when the state concerned denies the violation and/or seeks to justify its conduct by invoking an exception to the rule.[5] Thus, for instance, the prohibition of torture was widely accepted to have ripened into CIL by the 1980s,[6] even though Amnesty International documented that more than sixty states (about 40 percent) systematically engaged in torture and another thirty committed acts of torture.

Similarities and Differences Between a Global Norm and a Customary International Law Rule

There is considerable overlap between a global norm of state practice as defined by Finnemore and Sikkink and a rule of CIL. Most importantly, both require a general practice of states. How many states need to engage in the practice is to be assessed, taking account of the context. In order to transform a treaty provision into a CIL rule, "widespread and representative" acceptance of the treaty may suffice, and "widespread" does not require adherence by even a majority of states.[7] As with norm emergence,[8] an important factor in the ripening of a CIL rule is "the extent to which those States that are particularly involved in the relevant activity have participated."[9] Regarding the right of access to information, all states arguably are equally concerned, because all hold information that is critical for those who live in, or are otherwise subject to, their jurisdictions. On the other hand, states with large populations may carry more weight in developing the RTI norm by virtue of their holding greater amounts of information that is of interest to more people, and critical states could also include those that are viewed—globally or regionally—as leaders in governance reform trends.

The main difference between a CIL rule and a global norm is that a CIL rule imposes a legal obligation, and is followed out of a sense of legal obligation, whereas a global norm, at least one that is prescriptive, has a quality of "oughtness" that influences behavior as a result of primarily social and sometimes moral and political influences. In practice, however, the development of global norms of state behavior are often closely linked to the development of international law. Finnemore and Sikkink state that, in most cases, for an emergent norm to reach a tipping point, it "must become institutionalized in specific sets of international rules and organizations," including international law.[10]

A second difference is that a rule of CIL is deemed global when the sense of legal obligation arises from a decision or instrument of a United Nations or other universal body, so long as there is conforming practice in all major regions. For a *norm* to be considered global, Finnemore and Sikkink suggest, not only should it be embraced by at least one-third of all states but also there should be momentum toward increased adoption, and while acceptance of the norm may not be advancing at the same rate in all regions, there should be evidence that the norm likely will take hold in all regions and become dominant over any counternorms.

THE EMERGENCE OF THE RIGHT OF ACCESS TO INFORMATION AS CUSTOMARY INTERNATIONAL LAW AND A GLOBAL NORM

This part begins with a section on the emergence of RTI at the national level through the end of the twentieth century, and then examines RTI's development at the international and regional levels. A consistent theme is the role of civil society organizations (CSOs) and experts (often called special rapporteurs) appointed by intergovernmental organizations (IGOs) as norm entrepreneurs, both in generating support for the norm and in providing expertise in norm elaboration to IGOs and makers of domestic law and policy.[11]

It is important to note that *domestic* social, cultural, and political dynamics played a more important role in many, if not most, countries in the norm's emergence and cascade than did the UN and regional human rights and political bodies, and other IGOs, including the World Bank and NATO, contributed as well. These other influences have been examined in depth elsewhere and are beyond the scope of this chapter.[12]

Suffice it to note that the right initially was urged in a few countries primarily by legislators who sought to assert power over the executive and administrative agencies and by individuals seeking information relevant to protecting their rights. By the 1970s, the right also increasingly came to be pressed by public demand for good governance, democratic oversight of public institutions, protection against authoritarianism, and the right to participate in public affairs. Only at the dawn of the twenty-first century was the right recognized by the United Nations and regional IGOs as a component of the human right to freedom of expression. That emergence of the CIL norm, which coalesced during the period 2006 to 2011—at least a decade or two later than other core elements of the right to freedom of expression—fed back into the adoption of more, and more robust, national and subnational laws reflecting increasing convergence of the content of the norm across all regions.

The Right of Access to Information in National Law Through the End of the Twentieth Century

The first right to information law, Sweden's Freedom of Printing Act, was passed in 1766 by a parliament whose political parties found common interest in gaining access to government files.[13] Colombia adopted a law granting access to government records in 1888, and Finland, historically part of Sweden, passed a relevant law in 1951.[14] The United States became the next country to pass a right to information law, in 1966, motivated by legislators seeking to reinforce their capacity to control and supervise the executive branch.[15] However, it was not until 1974, prompted by the Watergate scandal, that the U.S. Freedom of Information Act got real teeth, including a presumption of access, narrow exemptions, and court review of decisions to withhold information.[16]

By 1989, thirteen countries had RTI laws (figure 2.1)—some of them just a few provisions in administrative procedure codes—granting a right to information held by public authorities.

A wave of new laws was prompted by the collapse of totalitarian regimes in Central and Eastern Europe, and transitions from authoritarian to (progressively more) democratic governments in Latin America, accompanied by high public demand to disclose their secrets, as well as by secrecy scandals in longstanding democracies, demand for democratic oversight, and/or an interest in the use of foreign development and investment funds. Most campaigns were advanced by civil society organizations, which sought allies among opposition legislators, news publishers, and citizens aggrieved by poor public service delivery. Beginning in the early 1990s, international CSOs, including Article 19 and the Open Society Justice Initiative, and, over time, regional and new national CSOs, played an increasingly important role; they facilitated exchanges among national CSOs about benefits of RTI, strategies for adoption and implementation, and lessons learned; provided technical support to UN and regional IGO expert bodies to draft reports and elaborate the norm's content; and advocated with the political bodies of the UN and regional IGOs to recognize the norm and to monitor compliance.[17]

Development of the Right at the International Level

The right to freedom of expression, set forth in the Universal Declaration of Human Rights of 1948 and codified in the International Covenant on Civil and Political Rights (ICCPR) and the main regional human rights treaties—the African Charter on Human and Peoples' Rights, the American Convention on Human Rights (ACHR), and the European Convention on Human Rights (ECHR)—was for decades interpreted to provide only a right to seek, receive, and impart information and ideas free from government interference.[18] The right to access information held by public authorities started to receive recognition by the UN as a human right only in the late 1990s. Shortly thereafter, it was recognized by regional bodies in the Americas and Africa, but was recognized in Europe only in 2009. The lateness of this normative recognition likely is due to the fact that civil society actors did not begin to press for recognition of the right as a component of the human right to freedom of expression until the early 1990s, motivated in large part by demands for information from civil society groups in countries previously part of, or in the sphere of influence of, the Soviet Union. The following sections examine the development of this right by the UN

OPEN SOCIETY
JUSTICE INITIATIVE

**Countries that Guarantee a Right of Access to Information (RTI)
in National/Federal Laws or Decrees + Dates of Adoption & Significant Amendments:
126 (out of 193) UN Member States + 2 non-UN Members,
as of June 2020[1]**

African Union w/o North Africa (22/48)[2]
Angola 2002, 2006
Benin 2015
Burkina Faso 2015
Cote d'Ivoire 2013
*Ethiopia 2008
Ghana 2019
Kenya, 2016
Liberia 2010
Malawi 2017
Mozambique 2015
^Niger 2011
*Nigeria 2011
Rwanda 2013
Seychelles 2018
Sierra Leone 2013
*South Africa 2000
*Sudan 2015
*Sudan, South 2013
*Tanzania 2016
Togo 2016
Uganda 2005
Zimbabwe 2002, '07, '20

North Africa (2/7)[3]
Morocco 2018
Tunisia 2011, 2016

Org. of American States-English speaking (10/13)[4]
Antigua & Barbuda 2004
Bahamas 2017
Belize 1994, 2000
*Canada 1983, 2001, 2016
Guyana 2011
Jamaica 2002
St. Kitts & Nevis 2018
St. Vinc. & Grenadines 2003
Trinidad&Tobago 1999,2011
*USA 1966,'74,'96,2007,'16

OAS non-English (16/22)[5]
*Argentina 2003, 2016
^*Bolivia 2004, 2005
*Brazil 2011
Chile 2008
Colombia 1888, 1985, 2014
Dominican Republic 2004
Ecuador 2004
El Salvador 2011

Guatemala 2008
Honduras 2006
*Mexico 2002, 2006, 2016
Nicaragua 2007
Panama 2002, 2013
Paraguay 2014
Peru 2002, 2017
Uruguay 2008

Asia, South (7/8)[6]
Afghanistan 2014
Bangladesh 2008, 2009
*India 2005
Maldives, 2014
*Nepal 2007
^*Pakistan 2002, 2017
Sri Lanka 2016

Asia, Central (4/5)[7]
Kazakhstan 2015
Kyrgyzstan 2006,2016
Tajikistan 2002
Uzbekistan 1997

Asia, East/ Southeast (10/17)[8]
^China 2007
*Indonesia 2008
Japan 1999, 2003
Korea, South 1996,2004,'13
Mongolia, 2011
^*Philippines 2016
±Taiwan 2005
Thailand 1997
Timor-Leste 2016
Vietnam 2016

EU (27/27)
*Austria 1987, 2005
*Belgium 1994, 2000
Bulgaria 2000
Croatia 2003, 2013
Cyprus 2017
Czech Republic 1999, 2006
Denmark 1985, 2000
Estonia 2000, 2009
Finland 1951, 1999, 2009
*France 1978, 2005
*Germany 2005
Greece 1986, 1999
Hungary 1992, 2003
Ireland 1997, 2003, 2005
*Italy 1990, 1997, 2016

Latvia 1998
Lithuania 2000, 2005
Luxembourg 2018
Malta 2009, 2012
*Netherlands 1978, 2005
Poland 2001
*Portugal 1993, 1999
Romania 2001, 2007
Slovakia 2000, 2008
Slovenia 2003, 2005, 2017
*Spain 2013
Sweden 1766, 1976

Council of Europe Non-EU (19/20)[9]
Albania 1999, 2014
Armenia 2003
Azerbaijan 2005
*Bosnia Herzegovina 2000
Georgia 1998, 2001
Iceland 1996, 2003, 2012
Liechtenstein 1999
Macedonia 2006, 2008
Moldova 2000, 2003
Monaco 2011, 2013
Montenegro 2005, 2017
Norway 1970, 2006
*Russia 2009, 2011
†San Marino 2011, 2016
Serbia 2003, 2007
*Switzerland 2004
Turkey 2003
*Ukraine 1992, '02,'11, '15
*United Kingdom 2000

Europe, Non-CoE (1/2)[10]
±Kosovo 2003

Middle East (5/14) [11]
Iran, 2011
Israel 1998, 2009
Jordan 2007
Lebanon 2017
Yemen 2012

Pacific (5/14)[12]
*Australia 1982, '04, '09
Fiji 2018
New Zealand 1982, 2003
*Palau 2014
Vanuatu 2013, 2016

Territories[13]

± - Country not formally recognized by the UN   ^- Actionable RTI regulation/decree rather than a law
† - Not rated by RTI-Rating.org   *- Federal system, several states also have laws

Figure 2.1 RTI laws around the world.
Source: Open Society Justice Initiative

Countries without RTI Laws or Decrees:
67 UN Member States

Notes

1. These numbers are consistent with, and partly based on, the two main expert lists of RTI laws, compiled by Article 19 and by the Global RTI Rating (RTI-Rating.org), which rates 128 countries, including the 2 non-UN member states here listed, plus the Cook Islands (here considered a territory and not counted as an independent state), and has yet to rate one country: San Marino. See also Article 19, "Open Development: Access to Information and the Sustainable Development Goals," (July 2017), Appendix (118 UN member states with RTI laws or regulations).

2. African Union countries (not including 7 countries of North Africa that are listed separately): 26 w/o RTI laws – Botswana, Burundi, Cameroon, Cabo Verde, Central African Rep., Chad, Comoros, Congo (Brazzaville), Democratic Rep. of Congo, Djibouti, Equatorial Guinea, Eritrea, eSwatini (previously Swaziland), Gabon, Gambia, Guinea-Bissau, Guinea Conakry, Lesotho, Madagascar, Mali, Mauritius, Namibia, Sao Tome & Principe, Senegal, Somalia, Zambia.

3. North Africa: 5 countries w/o an RTI law - Algeria, Egypt, Libya, Mauritania, Saharawi Republic (Western Sahara) [not a UN member state].

4. OAS English-speaking: 3 countries w/o an RTI law - Barbados, Grenada, and St. Lucia.

5. OAS non-English-speaking: 6 countries w/o an RTI law - Costa Rica, Cuba, Dominica, Haiti, Suriname, Venezuela.

6. Asia, South (countries of South Asian Association for Regional Cooperation): 1 country w/o an RTI law – Bhutan.

7. Asia, Central: one country w/o an RTI law - Turkmenistan.

8. Asia, East/ Southeast: 7 countries w/o an RTI law - Brunei, Cambodia, Korea (North), Laos, Malaysia, Myanmar, Singapore.

9. Council of Europe, non-EU: one country w/o an RTI law - Andorra.

10. Europe, non-Council of Europe: one country w/o an RTI law – Belarus.

11. Middle East: 9 countries w/o an RTI law - Bahrain, Iraq, Kuwait, Oman, Palestine [not a UN member state], Qatar, Saudi Arabia, Syria and United Arab Emirates.

12. Pacific: 9 countries w/o an RTI law - Kiribati, Marshall Islands, Micronesia, Nauru, Papua New Guinea, Samoa, Solomon Islands, Tonga, Tuvalu.

13. There are at least 61 territories or dependencies, governed by 8 countries: Australia (6), Denmark (2), Netherlands (2), France (16), New Zealand (3), Norway (3), United Kingdom (15), and the United States (14). See https://www.infoplease.com/world/countries/territories-colonies-and-dependencies. A few have RTI laws, including Bermuda 2010, Cayman Islands 2007, Cook Islands 2007, and Guernsey 2013.

For more information, see www.right2info.org and http://www.rti-rating.org/country-data.

Figure 2.1 *(continued)*

and in the three regions with active human rights institutions and treaties—the Americas, Europe, and Africa.

United Nations

In 1993, the UN Human Rights Commission, then comprising representatives of fifty-three member states, by consensus created the post of UN Special Rapporteur on Freedom of Opinion and Expression. In his 1998 annual report, the special rapporteur stated that "the right to seek, receive and impart information imposes a positive obligation on states to ensure access to information" and that "the right to access to information held by the government must be the rule rather than the exception."[19] In subsequent reports, welcomed by the commission,[20] the rapporteur noted the fundamental relationship between the right of access to government-held information and democracy, public participation, and realization of the right to development.[21] In 2004, the rapporteur, along with special experts of the Organization of American States (OAS) and the Organization for Security and Co-operation in Europe (OSCE), and facilitated by the CSO Article 19, issued a joint declaration affirming the access right as a fundamental human right based on the principle of maximum disclosure, subject only to narrowly drawn exceptions set forth in law[22] which they, together with the special rapporteur of the African Commission on Human and Peoples' Rights, affirmed in 2006 and 2010.

In 2011, the UN Human Rights Committee adopted a general comment affirming that the right to freedom of expression guarantees to everyone the right of access to information held by public bodies, and it elaborated that right at some length.[23] General comments are considered authoritative interpretations of treaty provisions and, accordingly, play an important role in establishing both the existence and the contents of CIL rules.

The right to information has also been widely recognized in international agreements, in part because of its importance in enabling public participation and protecting other rights. These agreements include international and regional treaties and other instruments on corruption, development, the environment, and food and agriculture, and the 2015 UN Sustainable Development Goals.[24]

Americas

The OAS Inter-American Commission on Human Rights appointed a Special Rapporteur on Freedom of Expression in 1997 and began to address the right of access to state-held information in 2000, at about the same time as did the UN Human Rights Commission. As Catalina Botero-Marino describes in chapter 8 of the present volume, the right developed rapidly and achieved the status of a fundamental, regional norm as a result of the efforts of a combination of actors: civil society, including the Oaxaca Group, several groups that advocated for adoption of normative OAS statements, and Chilean groups that brought the *Claude Reyes* case to the Inter-American Commission; the Office of the Special Rapporteur, which in its 2003 report developed the arguments to support recognition of the right as a component of the right to freedom of expression; the Inter-American Court of Human Rights—in particular the Mexican judge Sergio García Ramírez, who sat as president—which, in 2006, issued its groundbreaking judgment in the *Claude Reyes* case, becoming the first international court to recognize RTI as an essential element of freedom of expression; the governments of Mexico and Peru, which pressed for crucial OAS resolutions; and the OAS General Assembly itself, which issued several normative statements.

The *Claude Reyes* judgment confirmed the right as a regional law rule (both treaty and customary) for the Americas. The tipping point for emergence of the regional norm arguably occurred a few years earlier, in 2004, by which time fourteen, or 40 percent, of the OAS's thirty-five member states had adopted laws. Five more countries adopted laws at the time of the *Claude Reyes* judgment or in the three years following, and five more enacted laws within a few years of the OAS General Assembly's welcoming, in 2010, of the Model Inter-American Law on Access to Public Information. As of September 2019, twenty-six of the thirty-five member states of the OAS had laws on access to information. The main ones that did not are Costa Rica, Cuba, Haiti, and Venezuela.[25] However, Costa Rica's Supreme Court, citing the *Claude Reyes* judgment, ruled in 2014 that the right of access to information is a fundamental human right,[26] and neither Haiti nor Cuba has challenged the right at the UN or at the OAS (in Cuba's case, because it has been excluded from the OAS by member states since 1962). Only Venezuela—which has objected to the right before OAS bodies and whose Supreme Court has systematically rebuffed efforts to implement it—could be considered a persistent objector.[27]

Europe

In Europe, the right to obtain information from public authorities was recognized earlier than in other systems, but as a corollary of democratic governance. Only recently, by virtue of judgments of the European Court of Human Rights in 2009 and 2016, has it been clearly recognized as a component of the human right to freedom of expression, although as an instrumental rather than an intrinsic component.

In 1981, the Committee of Ministers of the Council of Europe (comparable in function to the General Assemblies of the UN and OAS) called on member states to ensure that everyone within their jurisdictions "shall have the right to obtain, on request, information held by the public authorities other than legislative bodies and judicial authorities."[28] In 2002, the Committee of Ministers adopted a second recommendation, strengthening the 1981 recommendation: member states ought to guarantee the right of access to "everyone," not just to persons within the state's jurisdiction, and should examine "to what extent the principles of this recommendation could be applied to information held by legislative bodies and judicial authorities."[29] The recommendation set forth the legitimate scope of restrictions, procedural matters, costs, the right to independent review of denials, promotional measures, and proactive publication.

In 2008, the Committee of Ministers adopted the Convention on Access to Official Documents (called the Tromsø Convention), the first, and to date only, multilateral convention affirming and articulating an enforceable, general right to information.[30] However, the convention has not entered into force because it has been ratified by only nine out of a necessary ten countries. Moreover, the convention has been roundly criticized, including by the Parliamentary Assembly of the Council of Europe, because it fails "to enshrine modern standards for access to information," such as by requiring that laws apply only to the administrative functions of legislative and judicial bodies.[31]

In April 2009, a seven-judge chamber of the European Court of Human Rights expressly declared, in *Társaság a Szabadságjogokért v. Hungary* (known as the *TASZ* case, brought by the Hungarian Civil Liberties Union), that the human right to freedom of expression gives rise to a right to information held by public authorities when the requester needs the information to contribute to public debate and the public authority, in essence, has monopoly control of the information.[32] In 2016, in the case of *Magyar Helsinki*, the Grand Chamber (comprising seventeen judges) authoritatively affirmed the 2009 judgment. It concluded, following an extensive examination of the *travaux preparatoires* of the ECHR, its own case law, other relevant developments within and outside the Council of Europe, case law of other human rights bodies, and legislation of member states, that "there [now] exists a broad consensus in Europe (and beyond) on the need to recognize an individual right of access to state-held information in order to assist the public in forming an opinion on matters of general interest."[33] The court, stressing the "instrumental nature" of access to information for the proper functioning of a democratic society, ruled that a right to state-held information arises when the requester is a "public watchdog" that requests information of public interest in order to contribute to public debate and the information is "ready and available" to the public authorities (paras. 156–170). The term "public watchdog" includes the press and civil society organizations, as well as academic researchers and authors on matters of public concern, and may include "bloggers and popular users of the social media" (para. 168). The European Court's view of the right of access to information is thus more circumscribed than that of the UN and OAS bodies, which view the right as both an intrinsic element of the right to freedom of expression, belonging to everyone, and an instrumental right.

The European Union has recognized a right of citizens and residents of EU countries to information held by community institutions since 2001; in that year, the European Parliament adopted Regulation (EC) no. 1049/2001, which provides a right of public access to documents of the European Parliament, Commission, and Council. The Charter of Fundamental Rights of the EU, which became binding on EU member states with adoption of the Treaty of Lisbon in 2009, guarantees both a right to "everyone" to "receive or communicate information or ideas without interference from public authorities" (Article 11) and a right to EU citizens and residents to access EU documents (Article 42).

As of September 2019, of the forty-seven member states of the Council of Europe (with a combined population of some 820 million), all but one state (Andorra, with a population of less than 100,000) have RTI laws. The tipping point, when the norm emerged and started to cascade, occurred around 1997. By that date, sixteen (one-third) of the member states had RTI laws. However, the right arguably ripened into European regional law only twenty years later, with the 2016 issuance of the *Magyar Helsinki* judgment. The United Kingdom has been the main persistent objector to recognition of RTI as a component of the human right to freedom of expression.[34] The countries of northern Europe— Sweden, Norway, and Finland—are among the strongest promoters of the regional customary law rule.

Africa

South Africa's 1996 constitution, aiming to "lay the foundations for a democratic and open society in which government is based on the will of the people," includes a strong protection of the right to access information held by the state as well as "any information that is held by another person and that is required for the exercise or protection of any rights." In 2000, South Africa became the first country in Africa to enact an RTI law, which remains one of the strongest in the world. In 2002, the African Commission on Human and Peoples' Rights adopted the Declaration of Principles on Freedom of Expression in Africa to supplement the right to freedom of expression set forth in the African Charter, a treaty that entered into force in 1986 and has been ratified by all fifty-five member states of the African Union, save Morocco. Article 1 of the declaration affirms the right to freedom of expression in language similar to that of the ICCPR and the ACHR; namely, it includes the right to "seek, receive and impart information and ideas." Moreover, the right is declared to be "a fundamental and inalienable human right and an indispensable component of democracy." Principle 4 of the declaration sets forth the elements of, and states' obligations to fulfill, the right of access to information held by public bodies.[35]

In December 2004, the African Commission, urged by civil society, created the mandate of Special Rapporteur on Freedom of Expression, and in November 2007, it expanded the mandate and title to include "Access to Information." When Pansy Tlakula became rapporteur, in late 2005, only four countries had RTI laws, and of those, only South Africa's law was being actively implemented. By the time Tlakula's mandate ended, in November 2017, twenty-one countries—nearly 40 percent of the African Union's member states—had RTI laws on the books, and bills were pending in a half dozen additional countries. The rate of adoption, as well as the content of the laws (as will be discussed), were clearly influenced by the Model Law on Access to Information for Africa, adopted in 2013 by the African Commission, after a three-year process involving widespread consultations with governments, civil society, and independent experts, led by Rapporteur Tlakula.[36]

The Right of Access to Information: *When* Did It Emerge into a Global Norm?

Taking into consideration the definitions and information in the preceding sections, it may be concluded that the right of access to information ripened into a CIL right by 2011, if not earlier. By that date, eighty-eight countries, in all parts of the world, had enacted RTI laws. The sense of legal obligation was supplied by the 2011 UN Human Rights Committee General Comment no. 34, which states expressly and authoritatively that Article 19 of the ICCPR guarantees the right as a fundamental component of the right to freedom of expression. That conclusion was reinforced by the Inter-American Court's 2006 judgment in *Claude Reyes*, the African Commission's 2002 Declaration of Principles on Freedom of Expression, and (to a limited extent) the European Court's 2009 judgment in the *TASZ* case. Several experts have endorsed the conclusion that the right was guaranteed by international treaty law by 2011 or earlier.[37]

By 2011, the norm had clearly reached a tipping point and was cascading in Latin America and Europe, though not so clearly in other regions. By the end of 2019, the numbers were sufficiently compelling to make a strong case for the existence of a global norm: nearly two-thirds of all UN member states had an RTI law, including virtually all countries in the Council of Europe and South Asia; more than two-thirds in the Americas (Latin and English speaking); nearly two-thirds in Central, East, and Southeast Asia (including the population giants of China, Indonesia, and Japan); 45 percent of countries in sub-Saharan Africa; 40 percent in the Pacific; and one-third of the countries in the Middle East and North Africa. Nearly 90 percent of the world's 7.5 billion people now live in countries that provide an enforceable right, at least in law, to obtain information from their governments.[38]

The regions that have been the slowest to embrace the right to information are the Middle East and North Africa, but even there, all subregions but the Arabian peninsula seem open to the norm. Of the thirteen countries without RTI laws in these two regions, only four (Oman, Qatar, Saudi Arabia, and the United Arab Emirates) are *not* parties to the ICCPR, and the nine that are parties did not object to the development of the right, suggesting at least tacit acceptance of the CIL rule. Moreover, there have been sustained citizen campaigns for laws in Palestine and Egypt, and Article 68 of Egypt's 2014 constitution unambiguously grants the right to all citizens.

RIGHT OF ACCESS TO INFORMATION: CONTENTS OF THE NORM

A more complex question than whether the right of access to information is a global norm or only one embraced by most regions is the question of the norm's content. The following sections examine the content of both the CIL right as set forth in the most authoritative statements of international and regional law as well as the content of the global norm as evidenced by national laws. Much of the information about national laws is drawn from the Global Right to Information Rating, which, by June 2020, had analyzed 128 RTI laws, using more than sixty indicators.[39]

Areas of Norm Convergence

Authoritative statements of international and regional law concerning the content of the right to information all agree that there is a presumption in favor of disclosure, subject only to exceptions that are set forth in law and that advance a legitimate interest, and that any withholding of information should be neces-sary and proportionate to the legitimate aim;[40] that procedures for requesting information should be easy, prompt, practical, and affordable; that public authorities should state reasons for any refusal to provide information; and that requesters should have the opportunity to appeal denials to an independent court or administrative body.[41] More than two-thirds of national laws comply with these essential requirements.[42] Implementation of the right lags behind the normative commitments, but as has been noted, breaches of a rule do not pre-vent the ripening of a norm of practice or CIL.[43]

Areas of Norm Divergence

Despite convergence concerning the core elements of the CIL rule and global norm, there are a few notable areas of divergence among the regions concerning the customary law rules, and these divergences appear to roughly correlate with differences among the norms of practice as reflected in national law.

Differences Among International and Regional Customary Law

The main difference among the international and regional law norms concerns the intrinsic versus the instrumental nature of the right. The UN, OAS, and African Union bodies all view RTI as both an intrinsic component of the human right to freedom of expression as well as an instrumental element of freedom of expression, democratic participation, and other rights.[44] In contrast, the institu-tions of the Council of Europe and the EU emphasize the value of the right as instrumental to the proper functioning of a democratic society, good gover-nance, and freedom of expression about matters of general public interest.

A second, related difference concerns who may exercise the right. State-ments of relevant UN, OAS, and AU bodies assert that, as a component of the human right to freedom of expression, the right to information belongs to "everyone" (citizens, residents, and nonresidents alike) and "information should be provided without the need to prove direct interest or personal involvement in order to obtain it, except in cases in which a legitimate restriction is applied."[45] In contrast, the European Court of Human Rights has ruled that the right accrues only to public watchdogs (although this is expansively construed) who seek information of public interest in order to contribute to public debate,[46] and the EU Charter of Fundamental Rights guarantees a right to access EU docu-ments only to citizens and residents of the union.

A third difference concerns the bodies to which RTI applies. The UN general comment issued in 2011, and the model laws issued by the OAS in 2010 and the African Commission in 2013, call for RTI laws to be applied to information held by all public authorities (executive, judicial, and legislative), reflecting the recognition that human rights impose obligations, at a minimum, on all state bodies. Both model laws also call for application of RTI to private bodies that perform public functions and/or receive public funds, with regard to those funds, and the Model Law for Africa goes one step further by calling for RTI laws also to apply to private bodies to the extent that information they hold "may assist in the exercise or protection of any right."[47]

In contrast, the Tromsø Convention, adopted by the Committee of Ministers of the Council of Europe in 2009, calls for the right to be applied to judicial and legislative bodies only when it concerns their administrative functions, and to private bodies that exercise administrative authority (but not to those that perform public functions or receive public funds). Although that convention has been ratified by only nine of the Council of Europe's forty-seven member states, it reflects the view of RTI shared by most of the twenty or so "old" democracies of Western Europe, about 60 percent of which do not apply their laws to their legislatures or judiciaries at all, or apply them only to administrative information held by those bodies.[48]

The right of access to information under European customary law is thus more circumscribed than the right as set forth by the UN, American, and African systems, all of which recognize that the right belongs to everyone and not merely to public watchdogs or citizens, is an intrinsic and not merely an instrumental component of the right to freedom of expression, and applies to all information held by all public authorities.

Regional Trends as Reflected in National Laws

These differences among the customary law rules of the UN and regional systems reflect, and have impacted, regional norms of practice, as evidenced by national legal frameworks, through a dialectical process. Through the 1990s, virtually all of the national laws treated RTI as an administrative right or as a component of the state's duty of accountability and good governance. As the international and regional human rights law principles began to emerge and consolidate in the first decade of the twenty-first century, they contributed not only to the cascade of norm diffusion but also to development of the content of the norm, as noted in the previous section on norm convergence, and to recognition in national legal frameworks—whether set forth in the constitution or elaborated by the courts—of the right as a fundamental human or citizen's right.[49]

The fact that European bodies have conceived of the right in more circumscribed terms than have the UN, American, and African bodies correlates with the lower percentage of countries in Europe, especially in Western Europe, that treat the right as fundamental, and with the fact that European laws, on average, are weaker than laws in the two other regions, as measured by the Right to Information Rating. Outside of Europe, the Americas, and Africa, laws tend to be even weaker than in Western Europe, except in South Asia, where India's leadership may be credited with having inspired relatively strong laws.

In the Americas, where the intrinsic, fundamental nature of the right has been emphasized by the Inter-American Court and the OAS General Assembly, most national legal frameworks treat the right as a fundamental human right of everyone, which has both intrinsic as well as instrumental value and which applies to all public bodies and to private bodies that receive substantial public funds or perform public functions. The right is also treated as a fundamental right, though only of citizens, in South Asia, where India's robust Right to Information Act of 2005 (which grants RTI only to citizens), coupled with jurisprudence of India's Supreme Court recognizing a right of access to information as a corollary of freedom of expression and participation rights,[50] has had substantial impact. The strongest laws in the world, according to the Global Right to Information Rating, are found in these regions—Latin America and South Asia—and also in the countries of the former Yugoslavia, perhaps owing to the influence of the international community there following the 1992–1995 war.

In Western Europe, the strongest laws are those of Norway, Sweden, and Finland, the product of long-standing societal and legal traditions embracing the fundamental importance of the right. These countries, along with Belgium, are the only "old democracies" of Western Europe whose legal frameworks protect RTI as a fundamental right. The other 80 percent treat RTI as a component of good governance; only the right to access information of personal interest is treated as fundamental.[51] The laws of many of these countries are among the weakest in the world, according to the Global Right to Information Rating. In contrast, in more than two-thirds of the countries of Central and Eastern Europe, including Russia, RTI received protection as a fundamental right by constitution in the flush of democratic transitions following the fall of the Berlin Wall, and the laws of most of these countries rank in the middle or higher ranges of the Right to Information Rating.

Other countries that have middling laws are most of the Anglophone Western democracies—Australia, Canada, New Zealand, the United Kingdom, and the United States—and several other countries that were influenced by the U.S. Freedom of Information Act, including most of the English-speaking Caribbean, Japan, South Korea, and Thailand.[52]

The impact of international and regional law norms has been less pronounced in Africa. Only 45 percent of the countries of sub-Saharan Africa, and one-third in North Africa, have RTI laws. Of the twenty-two laws in sub-Saharan Africa, seven are ranked in the middle and six are in the lowest third, according to the Global Right to Information Rating. This low rate of incorporating regional legal norms into domestic law can be explained in part by the fact that the RTI law norms developed later in Africa than in the Americas and Europe. Additional significant factors are the lower levels of democratic development in many of the countries, the negative influence of the Francophone tradition (France has one of the weakest RTI laws in Europe), and the fact that, in several countries, undemocratic ruling parties adopted laws as window dressing in order to burnish their democratic credentials. Nonetheless, the thirteen laws passed in or since 2013, when the Model Law for Africa was issued, suggest increasing domestication of the regional law norms. More than two-thirds of these laws apply RTI to all public bodies and to private bodies that perform public functions or receive public funds, and six of the countries (all English speaking)[53] have incorporated the distinctive African norm that RTI should also apply to private bodies that hold information that is needed for the exercise or protection of a right. There also is a trend toward rejecting one of the key requirements of the international and regional legal norms: six countries grant the right only to citizens. The norm cascade (involving adoption of more and stronger laws) generated by Special Rapporteur Tlakula during the twelve years of her mandate appears likely to continue, though at a slower rate than during her tenure. Some of the next countries expected to adopt laws include three whose constitutions recognize RTI as a fundamental right—the Democratic Republic of the Congo, Madagascar, and Senegal.

The regions with the weakest, and lowest concentration of, RTI laws—the Middle East and Asia (excluding South Asia)—have neither regional human rights instruments that elaborate RTI nor individual countries to serve as norm leaders. A counternorm appears to be emerging in these regions, as in Africa and pressed by China, to limit the right only to citizens or to citizens plus non-citizens from countries that grant reciprocal RTI rights.[54] The fact that 60 percent of countries in the Pacific region do not have RTI laws may be explained by their small populations and low demand for RTI in most of those countries.

CONCLUSION

Although cultures of secrecy undeniably persist, the growing adoption of national RTI laws and international and regional normative standards is chipping away at those cultures and replacing them with the presumption that good governance requires transparency and that disclosure is the rule, subject only to narrowly drawn exceptions necessary to protect legitimate interests. Countries adopt RTI laws for a range of reasons, most related to domestic political demands and to cultural, historical, and developmental considerations. Nonetheless, the influence of global and regional norms and of norm entrepreneurs and leaders is unmistakable. Progress in strengthening the right to information in all parts of the world correlates with civil society activism and with the emergence of customary international and regional norms, set forth by the UN and by regional IGOs, that protect the right in clear, detailed, and largely consistent terms. A greater percentage of states have adopted laws, and more robust laws, in regions that have detailed regional instruments setting forth RTI law norms (namely, the Americas, Europe, and Africa), or that have norm leaders (South Asia, led by India), than in regions without them. Other regions have weaker laws, on average, and an apparent emerging counternorm limiting RTI to citizens and to citizens of countries that grant reciprocal RTI rights.

As noted, the right to information emerged as a customary international law norm by 2011, if not earlier. It had by that time reached the tipping point of a norm of state practice in the Americas and Europe, and within the past few years has arguably become a global norm, given that it has been embraced by nearly two-thirds of all states, representing 90 percent of the world's population, and that it is taking hold in all regions, with only minor regional variations. From 2001 to 2018, countries adopted laws at the rate of five per year, on average, and the new laws tend to be stronger and to apply to more bodies than those passed before 2001. Moreover, countries passed considerably more amendments to strengthen RTI laws than to weaken them.[55] Although that norm cascade has slowed, it has not stopped.

Questions that warrant further research include the extent to which regional legal norms will contribute not only to national laws but also to norm internalization by political, social, and bureaucratic actors, and the extent to which the absence of regional legal norms in the Middle East and Asia will lead to the emergence in those regions of norms contrary to those generated by the UN and regional bodies.

NOTES

I gratefully acknowledge the comments on earlier drafts from several colleagues, in particular, Daniel Berliner, Agnès Callamard, Toby Mendel, and Kathryn Sikkink.

1. Martha Finnemore and Kathryn Sikkink, "International Norm Dynamics and Political Change," *International Organization* 52, no. 4 (1998): 891, 895, 902, 904. See also the introduction to this volume.

2. Roozbeh B. Baker, "Customary International Law in the 21st Century: Old Challenges and New Debates," *European Journal of International Law* 21, no. 1 (2010): 177.

3. International Court of Justice statute, October 24, 1945, Article 38(1)(b).

4. Report of the International Law Commission, UN Doc. A/71/10 (2016), Draft Conclusion 10(2).

5. International Court of Justice, Nicaragua v. United States, judgment of June 27, 1986, para. 186.

6. American Law Institute, *Restatement (Third) of Foreign Relations Law of the United States*, vol. 2 (1987), sections 102, 702c.

7. International Court of Justice, North Sea Continental Shelf (1969), ICJ Report 3, 41–43.

8. See introduction to this volume.

9. International Law Commission Draft Conclusion 8, commentary, para. 4.

10. Finnemore and Sikkink, "International Norm Dynamics," 891, 900.

11. Regarding the role of civil society in influencing the development of right to information (RTI) norms, see, for instance, Daniel Berliner, "The Political Origins of Transparency," *Journal of Politics* 76, no. 2 (2014): 479–491; and Andrew Puddephatt, "Exploring the Role of Civil Society in the Formulation and Adoption of Access to Information Laws," *Access to Information Working Paper Series* (World Bank Institute 2009).

12. See, for instance, John M. Ackerman and Irma E. Sandoval-Ballesteros, "The Global Explosion of Freedom of Information Laws," *Administrative Law Review* 58, no. 1 (2006): 85–130; Gregory Michener, "Assessing Freedom of Information in Latin America a Decade Later: Illuminating a Transparency Causal Mechanism," *Latin American Politics and Society* 57, no. 3 (2015): 77–79; Stephen Lamble, "United States FOI Laws Are a Poor Model for Statutes in Other Nations," *Freedom of Information Review* 106 (2003): 50–56; Sheila Coronel, ed., *The Right to Know: Access to Information in Southeast Asia* (Quezon City: Philippine Center for Investigative Journalism, 2001); and Thomas Blanton, "The World's Right to Know," *Foreign Policy* 131 (July–August 2002).

13. David Goldberg, "From Sweden to the Global Stage: FOI as European Human Right?," *Journal of International Media and Entertainment Law* 7, no. 1 (2017): 7 (quoting Hans Gunnar Axberg).

14. Toby Mendel, *Freedom of Information: A Comparative Legal Survey*, 2nd ed. (Paris: UNESCO, 2008), 22; David Goldberg, *Advocating for the Right to Information—the Swedish "Oddity"?*, Campaign for Freedom of Information in Scotland, December 2002, 8. http://www.humanrightsinitiative.org/old/programs/ai/rti/articles /foi_advocacy_swedish_oddity.pdf.

15. Ackerman and Sandoval-Ballesteros, "Global Explosion," 116, 118. See also David E. Pozen, "Transparency's Ideological Drift," *Yale Law Journal* 128 (2018); and Blanton, "World's Right to Know," 52.

16. Blanton, "World's Right to Know," 52.

17. Regarding Article 19's influence, see Daniel Berliner, "Transnational Advocacy and Domestic Law: International NGOs and the Design of Freedom of Information Laws," *Review of International Organizations* 11, no. 1 (2016):121–144.

18. Toby Mendel, *The Right to Information in Latin America* (Paris: UNESCO, 2006), 9–10. See also European Court of Human Rights Grand Chamber, Magyar Helsinki Bizottság v. Hungary, judgment of November 8, 2016, para. 134; and Goldberg, "From Sweden," 10.

19. Report of the Special Rapporteur on the Promotion and Protection of the Right to Freedom of Opinion and Expression, Mr. Abid Hussein, UN Doc. E/CN.4/1998/64, January 28, 1998, paras. 12 and 14.

20. See, for instance, Resolution 1998/42, April 17, 1998, para. 2.

21. See, for instance, Special Rapporteur, 1999 Report, UN Doc. E/CN.4/1999/64, January 29, 1999, para. 12; 2000 Report, UN Doc. E/CN.4/2000/63, January 18, 2000, para. 42; and 2005 Report, E/CN.4/2005/64, para. 39.

22. Joint Declaration of the UN Special Rapporteur on Freedom of Opinion and Expression, the OSCE Representative on Freedom of the Media, and the OAS Special Rapporteur on Freedom of Expression, December 6, 2004.

23. UN Human Rights Committee, General Comment no. 34, Article 19, UN Doc. CCPR/C/GC/34 (September 12, 2011). See also UN Human Rights Committee views in Toktakunov v. Kyrgyzstan (1470/2006), CCPR/C/101/D/1470/2006 (2011).

24. See Article 19, "Open Development: Access to Information and the Sustainable Development Goals" (July 19, 2017), 6–9.

25. The other five that do not have access to information laws had a combined population in 2018 of about 1.2 million. See Worldometer, "Countries in the World by Population," http://www.worldometers.info/world-population/population-by-country. Accessed July 1, 2020.

26. Supreme Court of Justice, Chamber of Constitutional Affairs, judgment of March 21, 2014.

27. Venezuela, Supreme Court of Justice, judgments of June 15, 2010, and August 5, 2014. See Catalina Botero, "The Role of the Inter-American Human Right System," chapter 8, note 84, in this volume.

28. Recommendation no. R(81)19 on Access to Information Held by Public Authorities.

29. Recommendation no. R (2002)2, adopted on February 21, 2002, parts 3 and 4.

30. Council of Europe Convention on Access to Official Documents, adopted on November 27, 2008; opened for signature on June 18, 2009 (Council of Europe Treaty Series no. 205).

31. Parliamentary Assembly of the Council of Europe, opinion 270 (2008), paras. 5 and 9. Text adopted by consensus.

32. European Court of Human Rights, Társaság a Szabadságjogokért [Hungarian Civil Liberties Union] v. Hungary, application no. 37374/05, April 14, 2009, para. 26.

33. European Court of Human Rights Grand Chamber, *Magyar Helsinki*, para. 148.

34. See, for instance, the United Kingdom's intervention in *Magyar Helsinki*.

35. On April 30, 2019, the African Commission's special rapporteur issued a new draft Declaration of Principles on Freedom of Expression and Access to Information to better address the impact of the Internet and digital technologies on these rights. The African Commission is expected to adopt the new declaration in 2020.

36. The special rapporteur was assisted by the Human Rights Centre of the University of Pretoria, the Africa Freedom of Information Centre, Article 19, and the Open Society Justice Initiative, among others.

37. Mendel, *Freedom of Information*, 7; Article 19, "Open Development," 8; Maeve McDonagh, "The Right to Information in International Human Rights Law," *Human Rights Law Review* 13 (2013): 25.

38. This number was calculated from the figures provided on the Worldometer website, based on 2018 data from the United Nations Population Division estimates.

39. The Global Right to Information Rating, http://www.rti-rating.org, was developed by two leading RTI civil society organizations, the Centre for Law and Democracy, and Access Info Europe. See also Toby Mendel, "The Fiftieth Anniversary of the Freedom of Information Act: How it Measures up Against International Standards and Other Laws," *Communication Law and Policy* 21, no. 4 (2016): 468–476.

40. Human Rights Committee, General Comment no. 34, paras. 22–30; Joint Declaration of the Special Rapporteurs of the UN and OAS, and the OSCE Representative on Freedom of the Media (2004); Inter-American Model Law; Model Law for Africa; Council of Europe, Tromsø Convention, Article 3(2).

41. Human Rights Committee, General Comment no. 34, paras. 19 and 22; Joint Declaration of the Special Rapporteurs; Inter-American Court of Human Rights, *Claude Reyes*, paras. 77–78, 89, and 95.

42. This assessment is based on a review of indicators 2, 15, 19, 25, 29, 30, 35, and 44 of the Global Right to Information Rating.

43. International Court of Justice, Nicaragua v. United States.

44. See *Report of the Special Rapporteur on the Promotion and Protection of the Right to Freedom of Opinion and Expression*, United Nations Office of the High Commissioner for Human Rights, September 4, 2013 (A/68/362), paras. 18–19: "The right to seek and receive information is an essential element of the right to freedom of expression . . . and access to information is often essential for individuals seeking to give effect to other rights." See also Inter-American Court, *Claude Reyes*, para. 77; Council of Europe, Tromsø Convention, Article 2(1); African Commission on Human and Peoples' Rights, Declaration of Principles, principle 4(1).

45. Human Rights Committee, Toktakunov v. Kyrgyzstan; Inter-American Court, *Claude Reyes*, para. 77; African Commission on Human and Peoples' Rights, Declaration of Principles, principle 4(1).

46. European Court of Human Rights, *Magyar Helsinki*, paras. 156–170, especially 167–168. Note that the court protects the right to access information about oneself via the right to respect for private and family life.

47. Model Law for Africa, sections 1, 2(a), and 2(b).

48. This assessment is based on a review of indicators 8 and 9 of the Global Right to Information Rating.

49. Assessment of whether a constitution recognizes RTI as a fundamental right is based upon a review of constitutional excerpts posted on the Global Right to Information Rating, indicator 1. For the importance of a constitutional protection of RTI, see Kyu Ho Youm and Toby Mendel, "The Global Influence of the United States on Freedom of Information," in *Troubling Transparency: The History and Future of Freedom of Information*, ed. David E. Pozen and Michael Schudson (New York: Columbia University Press, 2018), 249–268, at 253.

50. S. P. Gupta v. Union of India (1982) AIR (SC) 149, at 232.

51. This conclusion is reached by assessing excerpts of laws that are used by the Global Right to Information Rating to justify the ratings for indicators 1–4.

52. See Youm and Mendel, "Global Influence," 249; Lamble, "United States FOI Laws," 53.

53. Five countries are members of the Commonwealth: Kenya, Malawi, Rwanda, Sierra Leone, and Tanzania. One country, South Sudan, has English as its official language.

54. China and Yemen limit RTI to citizens and to noncitizens from countries that grant reciprocal access rights. Nine of the twenty-one countries in Asia (Bangladesh, India, Indonesia, Nepal, Pakistan, the Philippines, Sri Lanka, Thailand, and Vietnam) and three of five countries in the Middle East (Iran, Jordan, and Yemen) with RTI laws limit the right to citizens only.

55. Toby Mendel, *Amending Access to Information Legislation: Legal and Political Issues* (Washington, DC: World Bank Group, 2011).

The Protection of Political Expression | **THREE**

NANI JANSEN REVENTLOW AND

JONATHAN MCCULLY

Political expression is indispensable for the functioning of any governed society. After all, at a very rudimentary level, it is how those who seek to govern a population communicate with the governed. In democratic societies, freedom of political expression is vital because it allows the public (*demos*) to have a say in how they are ruled (*krátos*). It also allows the electorate to understand the views of their representatives and promotes the accountability and public scrutiny of those in power.

There are, of course, different degrees to which political expression may be protected within a society. For instance, in a tyrannical regime, the only individual who may be afforded protection for their political speech may be the head of state and (perhaps) other members of the political elite. In flawed democracies, a certain level of criticism of politicians may be tolerated but discussion of official or national secrets may be forbidden. Therefore, trying to determine the existence of a global norm for political expression is no simple task.

This chapter will draw on the jurisprudence from international and regional human rights mechanisms, as well as comparative law, to propose the existence or emergence of four global norms of political speech:

1. political expression is to be given the highest protection on the hierarchy of speech rights;
2. the speech of elected representatives on the floor of the legislature needs to be free from the threat of legal action;
3. the media needs to be given access to the legislature to cover the activities of its members; and
4. the reputation of politicians cannot benefit from special protection but instead has a reduced level of protection compared to private individuals.

POLITICAL SPEECH: A HIGHER DEGREE OF PROTECTION

International law has recognized the central role that political expression plays in informing and educating the body politic and in holding the powerful to account. This is down to, among other things, the fact that the right to freedom of expression facilitates and strengthens individuals and institutions that are willing to criticize and scrutinize those in power. For instance, the European Court of Human Rights (ECtHR) has described the media as a "public watch-dog,"[1] and has stated that media freedom "affords the public one of the best means of discovering and forming an opinion of the ideas and attitudes of their political leaders."[2] In light of this, the ECtHR has stated that not only is it the task of the media to impart information and ideas on subjects of public or political interest but also the public has a right to receive such information and ideas.[3] The Inter-American Court of Human Rights (IACtHR) has recognized the indispensable role that freedom of expression plays in the establishment and maintenance of opposition and other influential organizations, such as political parties and trade unions.[4]

International and regional mechanisms have further observed that the right to freedom of expression is a vital means by which the public engages in the governance of their own country, and an important means by which they exercise democratic control over those in power.[5] For example, the United Nations Human Rights Committee (HRC) has observed, "It is the essence of [democratic] societies that its citizens must be allowed to inform themselves about alternatives to the political system/parties in power, and that they may criticize or openly and publicly evaluate their Governments without fear of interference or punishment."[6] The African Commission on Human and Peoples' Rights has likewise recognized that "freedom of expression is . . . vital to an individual's personal development, his political consciousness, and participation in the conduct of public affairs in his country."[7] In this way, the right to freedom of expression is crucial to the effective exercise of the public's right to vote in elections,[8] and therefore to the public's ability to effect political change in society.

In light of these considerations, it is perhaps unsurprising that political expression has been recognized as requiring a higher degree of protection under the right to freedom of expression compared to other forms of expression. This is a norm that has been adopted by international and regional courts and tribunals, including the HRC, the IACtHR, and the ECtHR.[9] It can also be found in the jurisprudence of domestic courts around the world.

In the United Kingdom, the House of Lords has distinguished between three types of expression: political, artistic, and commercial. As has been noted by Lady Hale in *Campbell v. MGN*, the jurisprudence "consistently attaches great importance to political expression and applies rather less rigorous principles to expression which is artistic and commercial."[10] Even in the United States, which is known for its relative free speech absolutism and content neutrality, the Supreme Court has recognized that political speech is an area in which the importance of First Amendment protection is "at its zenith."[11]

In Australia, which is an unusual constitutional democracy insofar as it does not have explicit protection for the right to freedom of expression in its constitution, the courts have demonstrated a commitment to giving stronger protection to political expression than to other forms of speech by reading into the constitution a limited right to freedom from laws that "burden freedom of communication about government or political matters."[12] This protection for political expression, to the exclusion of other forms of speech, has been justified on the basis that it is necessary to maintain Australia's constitutionally protected system of governance. In *Lange v. Australian Broadcasting Corporation*, the high court reasoned as follows:

> Communications concerning political or government matters between the electors and the elected representatives, between the electors and the candidates for election and between the electors themselves were central to the system of representative government, as it was understood at federation. While the system of representative government for which the Constitution provides does not expressly mention freedom of communication, it can hardly be doubted, given the history of representative government and the holding of elections under that system in Australia prior to federation, that the elections for which the Constitution provides were intended to be free elections . . . Furthermore, because the choice given by [the Constitution] must be a true choice . . . legislative power cannot support an absolute denial of access by the people to relevant information about the

functioning of government in Australia and about the policies of political parties and candidates for election.

The Australian example appears to support the proposition that systems of government require a certain amount of political expression to function and that, in turn, this requires the strongest protection available to speech in any society be given to this expression.

PRIVILEGE: PROTECTING SPEECH IMPARTED IN THE LEGISLATURE

Different terms have been adopted around the world to refer to legislatures, but a shared principle among these various legislatures is that of deliberation. The legislature is usually the deliberative body where legislation is introduced, debated, amended, and passed. Given its role in society, certain norms appear to have emerged around speech in the legislature, with the purpose of protecting free expression in this specific context. One of these norms is the legal recognition that expression imparted by representatives during the deliberative process is to be given immunity from legal sanction. This norm plays an important role in securing the independence of the legislature, while also allowing for political debate to flourish on its floor.

The principles underlying this norm can be found in the jurisprudence of international and regional human rights bodies. For instance, the HRC has recognized that it is "essential" that there be free communication between citizens, candidates, and elected representatives about public and political issues.[13] The ECtHR has similarly recognized that freedom of expression is "especially important" for elected politicians as they represent the electorate, draw attention to their preoccupations, and defend their interests. For this reason, the ECtHR has stated that any restrictions on the freedom of expression of elected representatives would call for the "closest scrutiny."[14] In *Karácsony and Szél v. Hungary*, the ECtHR considered a complaint made by members of a Hungarian opposition party who had been fined for having taken peaceful protest actions during sessions of parliament. In its judgment, the ECtHR found a violation of the right to freedom of expression and highlighted that "the speech and expressions of democratically elected parliamentary representatives deserve very high level of protection. . . . In the determination of the need to protect speech in Parliament, it must be borne in mind that not only authorized speech, which is expressed in the deliberation process, constitutes communication contributing to the public debate of eminently political issues in society."[15]

These free speech principles were in existence long before the European Convention, the International Covenant on Civil and Political Rights, or even international law itself. In classical Athens, prior to the demise of its system of direct democracy (*demokratia*), the free speech concepts of *isegoria* and *parrhesia* underpinned political life. The Greek term *isegoria* referred to the principle of giving equal opportunity for all male citizens of Athens to speak in the *ekklesia* (the assembly). This was complemented by the concept of *parrhesia*, which was the practice of open and frank discussion on the floor of the *ekklesia*. The concept of *parrhesia* recognizes that the ability to express oneself freely can assist the deliberative process in a democracy. One classical scholar has noted that to speak with *parrhesia* "was to confront, oppose, or find fault with another individual or a popular view in a spirit of concern for illuminating what is right and best."[16] This, in many political systems, can also describe the deliberative process of a legislature.

In modern parliamentary democracies, open and frank discussion on the floor of parliament is safeguarded through the legal principle of parliamentary privilege. This principle can be traced back to England in the Middle Ages,[17] but was first given statutory footing in Article 9 of England's Bill of Rights 1689, which stated that "freedom of speech and debates or proceedings in Parliament ought not to be impeached or questioned in any court or place out of Parliament."[18] This provision continues to apply today to protect a member of Parliament (MP) from being subjected to any civil or criminal penalty, in any court or tribunal, for what they have said in the course of proceedings in Parliament.[19] Language similar to Article 9 of the Bill of Rights 1689 can be found in the statutory definitions of this privilege in, among other jurisdictions, the United States, Seychelles, Zambia, Singapore, Malaysia, and Sri Lanka. The provision's language also can be found in legislation providing for the immunities and privileges pertaining to the East African Legislative Assembly, the supranational legislative organ of the East African Community. With different language, the constitutional law of the People's Republic of China similarly protects deputies to the National People's Congress from being "called to legal account for their speeches or votes at its meetings."[20]

In some jurisdictions, the privilege only protects actions or statements made within Parliament (such as Article 9 of England's Bill of Rights 1689 and its derivatives). In others, the protection of parliamentary privilege extends beyond the floor of the legislature and attaches to expressions made by elected representatives in performance of their other functions as well.[21] This is the position with regard to members of the European parliament, for example, who cannot be "subject to any form of inquiry, detention or legal proceedings in respect of opinions expressed or votes cast by them in *the performance of their duties*" (emphasis added).[22] The Court of Justice of the European Union has explained that parliamentary privilege depends "not on the place where the statement was made, but rather on its character and content." However, the court clarified that the "connection between the opinion expressed and parliamentary duties must be direct and obvious."[23] The Supreme Court of Brazil, in *Couto Filho v. Neves*, similarly considered the privilege enjoyed by councilors. The court said that the speech of councilors benefits from constitutional immunity where the speech was made within the jurisdiction of the relevant municipality, the speech concerned facts related to the councilor's mandate, and the speech was relevant to these facts.[24]

Despite these differences in approach, a global norm emerges from a commonality. The most comprehensive study of the domestic practice of parliamentary privilege was published in 1998, and found that all fifty-six countries surveyed provided protection to members of parliament against (at the very least) legal action resulting from an opinion expressed from the floor of the parliament or in committee.[25] In such circumstances, the parliamentarian speaking will be performing their fundamental duties. This narrow core of parliamentary privilege has been endorsed by the ECtHR in *A. v. United Kingdom*. In that case, the ECtHR considered the question of whether the form of parliamentary privilege adopted under Article 9 of England's Bill of Rights 1689, which left individuals without a remedy before the courts when they had been defamed or otherwise had their rights affected by statements made by MPs on the floor of the legislature, was consistent with the right to access a court and the right to respect for one's private life.[26]

The case concerned statements made by an MP during a debate on the subject of municipal housing policy. During his speech, the MP suggested that Ms. A., the applicant, was an antisocial neighbor, and he gave specific examples of her alleged behavior. The applicant disputed many of the allegations, which were later reproduced in newspaper articles. The allegations made against the applicant led to her being racially abused, and she and her family had to be rehoused because of the risk to their safety. The applicant was left with no judicial remedy because the statements were protected by parliamentary privilege, and she was told that abuse of parliamentary freedom of speech was a matter for internal self-regulation by Parliament.

The ECtHR reasoned that the restriction on the applicant's right to access a court and right to respect for her private life pursued the legitimate aim of "protecting free speech in Parliament and maintaining the separation of powers between the legislature and the judiciary." The ECtHR then turned to consider whether the parliamentary privilege was a proportionate restriction on these rights. In doing so, the ECtHR reasoned that the broader the immunity, the more compelling must be its justification in order for it to be compatible with the rights. In finding that the parliamentary privilege was a proportionate restriction on the applicant's rights to access a court and to respect for her private life, the ECtHR made reference to the fact that the immunity only attached to statements made in the course of parliamentary debates on the floor of the legislature. The ECtHR reasoned that, in this way, the immunity was "designed to protect the interests of Parliament as a whole as opposed to those of individual MPs."[27] In its judgment, the ECtHR appeared to endorse the norm at the heart of parliamentary privilege around the world, namely that information imparted on the floor of the legislature should be free from legal sanction or reproach.

ACCESS: THE MEDIA SHOULD BE ABLE TO REPORT ON THE ACTIONS OF THE LEGISLATURE

There have been several recent examples of the media being excluded from or hindered in reporting on what is happening in the legislature. In 2015, the media was barred from observing the parliament in Myanmar after photographs surfaced of a sleeping MP.[28] In 2016, the Ugandan parliament issued a directive that prevented journalists who were not graduates and had less than three years' experience from reporting on parliament.[29] Later that same year, new rules were introduced in Poland to restrict the number of journalists covering parliament and to limit the areas of parliament where recordings could take place.[30] Despite these concerning examples, it is noteworthy that prior to these restrictions, the default norm was that media outlets were provided some form of access to the legislature.

International and regional human rights bodies have recognized the vital role the media performs in scrutinizing the activities of elected representatives, and that the media has a right to report from parliament as long as they do not pose a reasonable risk to public order or safety. In *Gauthier v. Canada*, the HRC considered a complaint from a journalist who applied for and was refused membership to the Parliamentary Press Gallery, which was a private association tasked with administering the accreditation system for access to the precincts of the parliament of Canada. The state argued that this refusal did not place the complainant at a "significant disadvantage" because he could still rely on the televised broadcasts from parliament or observe proceedings from the public gallery, but this argument was rejected by the HRC. The HRC concluded that the refusal of accreditation to the complainant was a violation of his right to freedom of expression because the accreditation scheme had no safeguards against journalists being arbitrarily excluded from accessing parliamentary media facilities. In its decision, the HRC highlighted that "citizens, in particular through the media, should have wide access to information and the opportunity to disseminate information and opinions about the activities of elected bodies and their members." Nonetheless, the HRC did concede that, under certain circumstances, restrictions on access may be required to "ensure the effective operation of Parliament and the safety of its members."[31]

The balance that has to be struck between the media's access to the precincts of the legislature and the interest in protecting public order and public safety within those precincts was considered by the ECtHR in *Selmani v. Macedonia*. This case concerned the forcible removal of journalists from the gallery of the parliament of Macedonia following a disruption among elected representatives in the chamber below. When assessing whether this measure was necessary and proportionate for the purpose of "ensuring public safety and the prevention of disorder," the ECtHR assessed whether the decision to remove the journalists was based on a reasonable assessment of the risks posed by their continued presence, whether the journalists were still able to report on the incident in parliament, and the journalists' conduct. In its judgment, the ECtHR held that any attempt to remove journalists from parliament requires particularly strict scrutiny when they are exercising "their right to impart information to the public about the behaviour of elected representatives in Parliament and about the manner in which authorities handle disorder that occurs during Parliamentary sessions." The ECtHR also highlighted that the applicants' journalistic functions included the "obtaining [of] first-hand and direct knowledge based on their personal experience of the events unfolding in the [parliamentary] chamber."[32]

The importance of providing the media with access to the legislature and the facilities necessary in order to report on its activities has also been recognized at the national level. In some countries, such as Colombia, the principle of providing the media access to the legislature and the facilities (such as a special space) necessary to report from the legislature has been given statutory recognition.[33] In other countries, the media's access to the legislature has been jealously protected by the courts.

In Germany, the administrative court of Berlin repealed a yearlong ban on a journalist from entering the Bundestag. This ban was imposed because the journalist had breached the legislative house's rules by filming in the restrooms of the Reichstag, without prior authorization, in the course of an investigation into cocaine consumption. The court highlighted that this ban could not be imposed as a punishment, and that such a ban may only be imposed when the individual had breached the house rules and there was a real risk that they would breach the house rules again, in a comparable way.[34]

In *Primedia Broadcasting v. Speaker of the National Assembly*, the Supreme Court of Appeal of South Africa recognized the constitutional right of South Africans "to see and hear what happens in Parliament." This case was a constitutional challenge to the broadcasting rules and policies for the South African parliament. The case also challenged the constitutionality of the television broadcast feed being limited to the face of the Speaker of the parliament during a disturbance on the floor and the removal of MPs by the protection services. The Supreme Court of Appeal of South Africa stated that "the behaviour of MPs in Parliament is something which the public has the right to see and hear. It is political speech of the first order." The Supreme Court of Appeal went on to note that as most people cannot attend parliament, they rely on the media to exercise this right. The judgment went on to note that the right was not unlimited but could be restricted when it was "objectively reasonable" to do so. On this occasion, the restrictions imposed on broadcasts were not objectively reasonable because, among other things, the broadcasting of disorderly conduct caused no demonstrable harm.[35]

There is limited jurisprudence on the media's right to access the legislature. Nonetheless, taking the jurisprudence into account alongside the default norm adopted in many countries, it would appear that a global norm exists that the media should have access to the legislature to allow the public to see and hear what is taking place there. Furthermore, the media must be given the necessary facilities to allow it to carry out its role, and restrictions can only be imposed where there is a reasonable risk to public safety or the functioning of the legislature.

POLITICAL FIGURES AND REPUTATION: NO SPECIAL PROTECTIONS, BUT GREATER TOLERANCE

Historically, states have introduced and maintained laws that attempt to protect the reputations of political figures separately from, and more vigorously than, the protections afforded to ordinary individuals. These laws provide for offenses such as lèse-majesté,[36] *desacato*,[37] defamation of the head of state,[38] or undermining the authority of public officials.[39] Arguably, this special protection became something of a norm in itself. These laws remain on the statute books of many countries around the world and have been used to curtail speech ranging from criticism of government[40] to allegedly distasteful,[41] offensive,[42] or insulting[43] speech aimed at political leaders.

Nonetheless, there appears to be an emerging global norm at the international level that such laws offend the right to freedom of expression. This norm has gained traction before national courts but has yet to be fully internalized by national legislatures. Nonetheless, international and comparative jurisprudence would suggest a norm sea change in how the reputation of political figures are to be treated when they come into conflict with the right to freedom of expression.

International and regional mechanisms have clarified that the role performed by political figures does not necessarily deprive them of the treaty protections afforded to their rights, including their right to reputation.[44] However, it has been noted that some laws are premised on the assumption that certain political figures are beyond criticism or reproach due to their status, and therefore worthy of greater protections. In response, there has been a trend at the supranational level to find such laws incompatible with the right to freedom of expression because they amount to a disproportionate restriction on free speech.[45]

The ECtHR first considered this issue in *Colombani v. France*, a case that concerned the conviction of a newspaper editor and a journalist for "insulting a foreign head of State," namely the king of Morocco, in an article about drug trafficking. The prosecution of the offense of insulting a foreign head of state, which could only be taken at the request of the person who was allegedly insulted, followed special procedural rules that differed from those governing the prosecution of criminal defamation more generally. Unlike criminal defamation, the defendant's malicious intent had to be proved by the prosecution, and the defendant could not rely on a defense of truth. The latter difference was critical, as it meant that an individual could be prosecuted for defamatory remarks even when those remarks were factually true.[46] The ECtHR noted that the effect of this difference was to "confer a special legal status on heads of State, shielding them from criticism solely on account of their function or status, irrespective of whether the criticism is warranted. That . . . amounts to conferring on foreign heads of State a special privilege that cannot be reconciled with modern practice and political conceptions. Whatever the obvious interest which every State has in maintaining friendly relations based on trust with the leaders of other States, such a privilege exceeds what is necessary for that objective to be attained."[47]

The ECtHR found that the offense failed to meet any "pressing social need" in a democratic society and therefore violated the right to freedom of expression. However, the ECtHR was careful to highlight that it was the special protection afforded to foreign heads of state that was found to violate the right, and not the foreign head of state's right to use the standard procedure available to everyone to sue in defamation.[48] Subsequently, the ECtHR found that these findings on the subject of foreign heads of state applied with "even greater force" to a state's interest in protecting the reputation of its own head of state.[49]

Some case law from a number of common law countries indicates that there may be a certain degree of judicial acknowledgment of the norm that public figures should not have special protection for their reputations over and above ordinary citizens. One early example is the 1951 case of the Supreme Court of Canada, *R. v. Boucher*, which examined the sedition laws as they were applied in the eighteenth century. The Supreme Court noted that the sedition laws were problematic because they were premised on the idea that the government should enjoy a certain amount of immunity from criticism or reproach. The Supreme Court reasoned that "if we conceive of the governors of society as superior beings, exercising a divine mandate, by whom laws, institutions and administrations are given to men to be obeyed, who are, in short, beyond criticism, reflection or censure upon them or what they do implies either an equality with them or an accountability by them, both equally offensive."[50]

The Supreme Court also noted that the constitutional conception of governments changed during the nineteenth century and that this had necessitated a modified legal view of public criticism. As governments became democratically elected, they were then accountable to the public for their actions. This had an impact on the legal definition of sedition, which would later require a direct incitement to disorder and violence before an action could be prosecuted as seditious.[51]

This development can also be seen in a number of other countries that inherited the eighteenth-century laws on sedition from England but who later rejected the offense as unconstitutional. One notable example is Nigeria. In *State v. Ivory Trumpet Publishing Company*, the High Court of Nigeria considered whether prosecuting an individual under sedition laws for being critical of a state governor was reasonably justifiable in a democratic society in the interests of public safety or public order. The publication focused on the governor's financial dealings, suggesting he was paying party money without account. In its judgment, the high court noted the changes brought about by the 1979 Nigerian constitution, following which a governor was recognized as a politician, whereas before he did not have to stand for election following his assumption of office. The high court observed that, as a politician, the governor had no special immunity.[52] In 2017, the High Court of Kenya considered the constitutionality of a provision of the Kenyan Penal Code that created a criminal offense for "undermining the authority of a public official." The high court held that "it is no longer tenable to use laws that *prima facie*, are oppressive to the public for the sole purpose of protecting the dignity of public officers, thereby, violating people's right to freedom of expression."[53]

Despite these pertinent examples, the norm under international law that laws giving political figures special protection from public criticism or offense are unacceptable under the right to freedom of expression does not seem to have been fully internalized across the globe. For example, a 2016 study of the laws of fifty-seven Organization for Security and Co-operation in Europe states found that nine jurisdictions sanction defamation more harshly if the victim is a public official, and another fifteen states provide for criminal liability for various forms of insult against public officials. Twenty-four of the states provide a specific criminal offense where there has been defamation of the head of state, and eighteen states have special laws protecting foreign heads of state.[54]

Under international law, however, instead of being treated as figures who are beyond criticism or reproach, it has become a consistent principle that political figures should expect to be the subject of political debate and must tolerate a certain degree of harm that can be caused to their reputation in the process. This norm also appears to have gained a significant amount of acceptance by domestic courts around the world, suggesting an emerging norm countering the special status laws protecting the reputations of certain political figures.

The HRC has observed that "the value placed by the [International Covenant on Civil and Political Rights] upon uninhibited expression is particularly high in the circumstances of public debate in a democratic society *concerning figures in the public and political domain*."[55] The HRC has also indicated that those who hold high political office can legitimately be subject to public criticism and opposition.[56]

This principle has been further expanded upon by regional human rights courts. For instance, the African Court on Human and Peoples' Rights (ACtHPR) considered the level of protection that was to be afforded to the reputation of public figures in *Konaté v. Burkina Faso*.[57] This case considered the compatibility of Burkina Faso's criminal defamation laws, and their application and enforcement, with the right to freedom of expression. The applicant was the editor and founder of a newspaper that published three articles heavily criticizing the state prosecutor of Burkina Faso and implicating him in corruption. The applicant was convicted of "defamation," "public insult," and "insult" and received a one-year prison sentence and a fine of $3,000; his newspaper was also suspended for a period of six months.

When considering whether this conviction and sentence amounted to a violation of the right to freedom of expression, the ACtHPR considered the fact that the state prosecutor was a "public figure." The ACtHPR noted that the need for a limitation on the right to freedom of expression necessarily varied depending on whether the person was a public figure or not, and then went on to say that "people who assume highly visible public roles must necessarily face a higher degree of criticism than private citizens; otherwise public debate may be stifled altogether".[58]

This approach has also been adopted by the ECtHR and the IACtHR, both of which have recognized that the limits of acceptable criticism are wider for political figures because they inevitably and knowingly lay themselves open to close scrutiny of their every word and deed.[59] Both courts have recognized that this lower threshold of protection applies not only to politicians but also to those whose activities have entered the realm of public debate.[60] The ECtHR has further clarified that although an individual expressing themselves in a public debate concerning political or public figures must not overstep certain limits, they are permitted to rely on a degree of exaggeration, immoderation, or even provocation.[61]

The principle that politicians should expect and tolerate a greater degree of criticism because of their position in society appears to have been adopted by domestic courts around the world. In Botswana, it has been relied on by the court of appeal to lower the quantum of damages to be awarded to a politician in a defamation case.[62] In Brazil, it has been used to dismiss a politician's claim for damages for alleged harm to his personality rights by the use of a look-alike "dummy" in a protest.[63] In Russia, it can be found in the Resolution of the Plenum of the Supreme Court, which gives judges guidance on how to handle defamation cases.[64] In some jurisdictions, notably the United States,[65] South Korea,[66] and the Philippines,[67] this principle can be seen in the legal rule requiring politicians to meet a higher burden of proof (that is, "actual malice") before they can pursue defamation cases, suggesting a move away from special protections for the reputations of political figures and toward lesser protections for the reputations of political figures.

CONCLUSION

In this chapter, we have proposed the existence or emergence of four global norms of political speech, and it appears that the level of acceptance of these norms across the globe corresponds to the order in which they have been addressed in the chapter. Strongest is the first norm, that political expression is to be given the highest degree of protection under the right to freedom of expression, compared to other forms of speech; this norm is a prerequisite for governments—especially democratic governments—to be able to function, and it appears to have been widely accepted as such by international and national courts alike.

This is closely followed by the principle that the speech of elected representatives should be free from threat of legal action. While there is some level of variance concerning the scope of this protection, with some courts affording protection to all speech that takes place in the context of the representatives' exercise of their official duties, no matter the location, there is a core norm that, as a minimum, information imparted on the floor of the legislature should be free from legal sanction or reproach.

While international and national jurisprudence and legislation appear to demonstrate the existence of a default norm that the media needs to be given access to the legislature to cover legislative activities, the jurisprudence also shows that there is a degree of variance, and there are examples of international and national adjudicators indicating that there is scope for restrictions of this right of access to safeguard public safety or the functioning of the legislature.

The issue of special protection for the reputation of politicians shows the greatest contrast. There is evidence, based on national legislation, that a norm exists offering politicians and heads of state a greater degree of protection than regular individuals against critical speech. International jurisprudence shows the existence of a contrasting norm, however, according to which politicians' reputations enjoy a reduced level of protection compared to regular citizens, a norm that appears to be gaining traction in national courts as well. Here, the assessment would appear to be that there are two countering norms at play and that international and national jurisprudence seem to indicate stronger support for a reduced level of protection, despite national legislation adhering to the increased level of protection norm. Time will tell how these two standpoints will balance out against each other.

NOTES

1. European Court of Human Rights (ECtHR), Bladet Tromsø and Stensaas v. Norway, application no. 21980/93, para. 59.
2. ECtHR, Castells v. Spain, application no. 11798/85 (1992), para. 43.
3. ECtHR, Axel Springer AG v. Germany (No. 2), application no. 48311/10, para. 55.

4. Inter-American Court of Human Rights (IACtHR), Compulsory Membership in an Association Prescribed by Law for the Practice of Journalism, series A, no. 5 (1985), para. 70.

5. IACtHR, Herrera-Ulloa v. Costa Rica, series C, 107, para. 127.

6. United Nations Human Rights Committee (HRC), Adimayo M. Aduayom, Sofianou T. Diasso and Yawo S. Dobou v. Togo, communications nos. 422/1990, 423/1990, and 424/1990, UN documents CCPR/C/51/D/422/1990, 423/1990, and 424/1990 (1996), para. 7.4.

7. African Commission on Human and Peoples' Rights, *Media Rights Agenda & Others v. Nigeria*, communications nos. 105/93, 128/94, 130/94, 152/96, para. 54.

8. HRC, General Comment no. 34: Article 19 (Freedoms of Opinion and Expression), UN document CCPR/C/GC/34, September 12, 2011, para. 20.

9. See, for example, HRC, General Comment No. 34, para. 11; ECtHR, Surek v. Turkey, application no. 26682/95, para. 61; IACtHR, Ivcher-Bronstein v. Peru, series C 74, para. 155; and Herrera-Ulloa v. Costa Rica, para. 127.

10. United Kingdom, Campbell v. MGN Ltd., [2004] UKHL 22 (2004); [2004] 2 AC 457, para. 117.

11. United States, Meyer v. Grant, 486 U.S. 414 (1988), p. 425.

12. High Court of Australia, Lange v. Australian Broadcasting Corporation, [1997] HCA 25.

13. HRC, General Comment no. 34, para. 20.

14. ECtHR, Jerusalem v. Austria, application no. 26958/95, para. 36.

15. ECtHR, Karácsony and Szél v. Hungary, application nos. 42461/13 and 44357/13, para. 66–67.

16. Sara Monoson, *Plato's Democratic Entanglements: Athenian Politics and the Practice of Philosophy* (Princeton, NJ: Princeton University Press, 2000), 53.

17. See Hannes Kleineke, "The History of Parliament: Parliamentary Privilege in the Middle Ages," *History of Parliament*, http://www.historyofparliamentonline.org/periods/medieval/parliamentary_privilege_freedom_arrest_imprisonment.

18. Parliament of England, Bill of Rights 1689, Article 9.

19. Ex parte Watson, [1869] Queen's Bench Reports 573, p. 576.

20. United States Constitution, Article (1)(6), September 17, 1787; Seychelles National Assembly (Privileges, Immunities and Powers) Act 2011, section 3; Zambia National Assembly (Powers and Privileges) Act 1957, section 3; Singapore Parliament (Privileges, Immunities and Powers) Act 1962, section 5; Malaysia Houses of Parliament (Privileges and Powers) Act 1952, section 3; East African Legislative Assembly (Powers and Privileges) Act, 2003, section 3; constitutional law of the People's Republic of China, Article 75.

21. See, for example, Article 26 of the French constitution; Article 57(1) of the Austrian federal constitutional law; and Article 53 of the constitution of Brazil.

22. European Parliament, protocol no. 7 on the privileges and immunities of the European Union, *Official Journal of the European Union* C 326/1, Article 8.

23. Court of Justice of the European Union, Aldo Patriciello, case C-163/10, para. 30, 35.

24. Brazil, Couto Filho v. Neves, case no. 600.063 (February 25, 2015).

25. Robert Myttenaere, Report of Parliamentary Privilege, adopted at the Moscow Session, September 1998.

26. ECtHR, A. v. United Kingdom, application no. 35373/97.

27. A. v. United Kingdom, para. 77–78, 84–85.

28. "Images of Sleeping MPs Get Reporters Banned from Burma's Parliament," *Asian Correspondent*, May 28, 2015.

29. Esther Nakkazi, "Parliament Bars Reporting by Journalists with No Degree," *University World News*, January 29, 2016, https://www.universityworldnews.com/post .php?story=20160129115625851.

30. "Poland: Journalists Must Have Access to Parliament," Article 19, December 19, 2016, https://www.article19.org/resources/poland-journalists-must-have-access-to -parliament.

31. HRC, Gauthier v. Canada, communication no 633/1995, UN document CCPR/ C/65/D/633/1995 (1999), para. 13.5–6.

32. ECtHR, Selmani and Others v. Macedonia, application no. 67259/14., para. 69, 75–76, 84.

33. Ley 5 de 1992 por la cual se expide el Reglamento del Congreso; el Senado y la Cámara de Representantes, *Diario Oficial* no. 40.483 de 18 de junio de 1992.

34. VG Berlin, case no. 27 A 344/00, NJW 2002, 1063.

35. South Africa, Primedia Broadcasting v. Speaker of the National Assembly, [2016] ZASCA 142, para. 1, 28–30, 50.

36. See, for example, Thailand Criminal Code, section 112; or Criminal Code of the Netherlands, section 111.

37. See, for example, Penal Code of Venezuela, Articles 148 and 149.

38. See, for example, Criminal Code of Azerbaijan, Article 323; or German Criminal Code, Article 90.

39. See, for example, Penal Code of Botswana, section 134.

40. Jack Moore, "Canadian Arrested in Turkey for Insulting President Erdogan on Facebook," *Newsweek*, January 6, 2017, https://www.newsweek.com/canadian -arrested-turkey-insulting-president-erdogan-facebook-539293.

41. Media Report, "Conviction for Treason on the Internet: Contrary to Article 10 ECHR?" August 17, 2016.

42. Alison Smale, "Comedian's Takedown of Turkish President Tests Free Speech in Germany," *New York Times*, April 11, 2016, https://www.nytimes.com/2016/04/12/world/europe/jan-bohmermann-erdogan-neo-magazin-royale.html.

43. BBC, "Lese-Majeste Explained: How Thailand Forbids Insult of Its Royalty," October 6, 2017, https://www.bbc.com/news/world-asia-29628191.

44. HRC, General Comment no. 34, para. 38; ECtHR, Lingens v. Austria, application no. 9815/82, para. 42; Herrera-Ulloa v. Costa Rica, para. 127.

45. HRC, General Comment no. 34, para. 38.

46. ECtHR, Colombani and Others v. France, application no. 51279/99, para. 66.

47. Colombani and Others v. France, para. 68.

48. Colombani and Others v. France, para. 69–70.

49. ECtHR, Artun and Güvener v. Turkey, application no. 75510/01, para. 31, stating "That interest . . . could not serve as justification for affording the head of State privileged status or special protection vis-à-vis the right to convey information and opinions concerning him."

50. Canada, R. v. Boucher, [1951] S.C.R. 265, p. 285–286.

51. R. v. Boucher, p. 286.

52. Nigeria, State v. Ivory Trumpet Publishing Company Limited, [1984] 5 NCLR 736, p. 753.

53. Kenya, Robert Alai v. Attorney General and Director of Public Prosecution, petition no. 174 of 2016 (2017), para. 40.

54. Scott Griffen, *Defamation and Insult Laws in the OSCE Region: A Comparative Study* (Vienna: Organization for Security and Co-operation in Europe, 2017).

55. HRC, General Comment no. 34, para. 34 (emphasis added). See also HRC, Bodrožić v. Serbia and Montenegro, communication no. 1180/2003, UN Document CCPR/C/85/D/1180/2003 (2006), para. 7.2.

56. HRC, Rafael Marques de Morais v. Angola, communication no. 1128/2002, UN Document CCPR/C/83/D/1128/2002 (2005), para. 6.8.

57. African Court on Human and Peoples' Rights, Lohe Issa Konaté v. Burkina Faso, application no. 004/2013.

58. Konaté v. Burkina Faso, citing African Commission on Human and Peoples' Rights, Media Rights Agenda and Others v. Nigeria, communication nos. 105/93, 128/94, 130/94, 152/96, para. 74.

59. ECtHR, Oberschlick v. Austria (no. 2), application no. 20834/92, para. 59; Herrera-Ulloa v. Costa Rica, para. 129.

60. ECtHR, Nilsen and Johnsen v. Norway, application no. 23118/93, para. 52; IACtHR, Canese v. Paraguay, series C, no. 111, para. 103.

61. IACtHR, Ziembinski v. Poland (no. 2), application no. 1799/07, para. 44.

62. Botswana, Tsodilo Services (Pty) Ltd. v. Tibone (2011), 2 BLR 494 CA.

63. Brazil, Zachia v. Center of Professors of the State of Rio Grande do Sul, case no. 719.618 (2012).

64. Resolution of the Plenum of the Supreme Court of the Russian Federation of February 24, 2005, no. 3: "Political figures, by seeking to enlist public support, thereby agree to become an object of public political debate and criticism in the media."

65. New York Times Co. v. Sullivan, 376 U.S. 254 (1964), p. 273: "If judges are to be treated as 'men of fortitude, able to thrive in a hardy climate' . . . surely the same must be true of other government officials, such as elected city commissioners. Criticism of their official conduct does not lose its constitutional protection merely because it is effective criticism, and hence diminishes their official reputations."

66. Kyu Ho Youm, "The 'Actual Malice' of *New York Times Co. v. Sullivan*: A Free Speech Touchstone in a Global Century," *Communication Law and Policy* 19, no. 2 (2014): 185–210. See also Korean Supreme Court, September 2, 2011 judgment, 2010Do 17237.

67. Philippines, Vasquez v. Court of Appeals, 373 Phil. 238 (1999).

FOUR

International, Regional, and National Approaches to the Protection of Reputation and Freedom of Expression

PETER NOORLANDER

International norm setting on defamation has been driven by the interplay between the recognition that the right to freedom of expression, on the one hand, and the right to be protected against attacks on one's reputation, on the other, are fundamental human rights. Both are protected under international human rights law: the right to freedom of expression under Article 19 of the Universal Declaration of Human Rights,[1] Article 19 of the Covenant on Civil and Political Rights,[2] Article 13 of the American Convention on Human Rights,[3] and Article 10 of the European Convention on Human Rights;[4] and the right to be protected against attacks on one's reputation under Article 12 of the Universal Declaration of Human Rights, Article 17 of the Covenant on Civil and Political Rights, Article 11 of the American Convention on Human Rights, and Article 8 of the European Convention on Human Rights.[5] Each of these conventions also provides for reputational interests as a legitimate ground for restricting the right to freedom of expression, and this is how the majority of international norms and standards have developed, by examining the extent to which defamation laws can justifiably be used to restrict the right to freedom of expression, particularly—though not exclusively—in relation to the media.

Although defamation law dates back many centuries,[6] true international standard setting[7] really only started in earnest through a series of judgments of the European Court of Human Rights, in the 1980s and 1990s. The court's judgment in *Lingens v. Austria*[8] was particularly instrumental, laying a clear marker on the importance of the right to freedom of expression in political debate and in opening up space for criticism of elected politicians. In a judgment that continues to be cited to this day by courts around the world, the court pointed out that elected politicians "inevitably and knowingly [lay themselves] open to close scrutiny of [their] every word and deed [and must] consequently display a greater degree of tolerance."[9]

The *Lingens* judgment—like that other standard setter in the field of defamation law, the U.S. Supreme Court's judgment in *New York Times Co. v. Sullivan*[10]—concerned attempts by politicians and public officials to silence criticism of them. The courts in each case responded by emphasizing the duty, in a democratic society, incumbent on the media to provide such criticism, and the need for tolerance by politicians and elected officials. In the decades that followed, other courts around the world, as well as intergovernmental watchdogs such as the UN Special Rapporteur on Freedom of Opinion and Expression, have invoked the same rationale to build, layer by layer, a set of norms and standards to protect against the use of defamation laws to chill public debate. This has led to the emergence of global standards limiting the use of the criminal law to protect reputation, particularly on the part of politicians and public officials, stating that imprisonment is never a proportionate sanction for defamation and limiting other sanctions. This chapter provides an overview of these standards.

CRIMINAL DEFAMATION

There is wide divergence on the question of whether the criminal law is the right tool to protect reputation. Freedom of expression advocates point to the widespread—and ongoing—abuse of criminal laws in many countries to silence opposition voices; cases are often brought by powerful politicians, public servants, or business interests who wish to silence those who are critical of them.[11] Others point to the long-standing abuse-free existence of criminal defamation laws in many other countries.

At the global level, standard setting has been driven by the annual joint declarations issued by the global and regional special rapporteurs on freedom of expression appointed by the United Nations, the Organization for Security and Co-operation in Europe, the Inter-American Commission on Human Rights, and the African Commission on Human and Peoples' Rights.[12] This quartet's[13] first declarations noted the "abuse" of "restrictive defamation and libel laws" and "urged" states to review criminal defamation laws.[14] Seeing little or no change, and with ongoing abuse rampant, "including by politicians and other public figures," its 2002 joint declaration stated, simply and forcefully, "Criminal defamation is not a justifiable restriction on freedom of expression; all criminal defamation laws should be abolished and replaced, where necessary, with appropriate civil defamation laws."[15] This marked a principled stance from which the rapporteurs have not deviated.[16]

However, despite sustained civil society pressure, other international bodies have not joined the rapporteurs. The United Nations Human Rights Committee touched on the issue of criminal defamation in its 2011 General Comment no. 34, Article 19, on freedoms of opinion and expression. In the section on restrictions on political speech, the committee expresses particular concern over defamation laws that provided heightened protection to officials and politicians. But while it urges that "states parties should consider the decriminalization of defamation" and that "the application of the criminal law should only be countenanced in the most serious of cases," the committee stops short of calling for abolition.[17]

Several regional human rights watchdogs and intergovernmental bodies have adopted a similar stand, calling for an end to the abuse of criminal defamation laws but without calling for their outright abolition. The Inter-American Declaration of Principles on Freedom of Expression[18] cautions against heightened protection for public officials and politicians—a particular issue of concern in the Americas. The African Commission's Declaration of Principles on Freedom of Expression calls for the review of all criminal law restrictions on freedom of expression and the introduction of safeguards to prevent the abuse of all defamation laws.[19]

In Europe, the Parliamentary Assembly of the Council of Europe adopted a resolution, Towards Decriminalisation of Defamation, which calls on states to "guarantee that there is no misuse of criminal prosecutions for defamation" and to implement a series of safeguards to this end.[20] This call was endorsed by the Committee of Ministers of the Council of Europe, which in addition called on states to take a proactive approach with respect to defamation by aligning domestic legislation with the case law of the European Court of Human Rights, "with a view to removing all risk of abuse or unjustified prosecutions." The Committee of Ministers declined the call from the Parliamentary Assembly to develop detailed guidelines on defamation, stating that it considered this to be the responsibility of the European Court of Human Rights.[21]

International human rights courts have adopted a broadly similar stand. The European Court of Human Rights has held that "a criminal measure as a response to defamation cannot, as such, be considered disproportionate."[22] However, the court has also stated that, ordinarily, civil law measures should be sufficient to provide redress for any defamatory remarks and that criminal law should not be resorted to unless it is absolutely necessary, "for instance in the case of speech inciting to violence."[23] The European Court has, however, been inconsistent in applying this criterion, in some cases allowing seemingly innocuous cases of defamation to be handled through the criminal law while adopting a stricter stance in others. The Inter-American Court of Human Rights has adopted the same line,[24] cautioning in particular against the use of criminal defamation law to restrict criticism of politicians and public officials (through so-called *desacato* laws, which will be discussed in greater detail later).[25]

The African Court on Human and Peoples' Rights was asked, in its first ruling on a criminal defamation case, to go further and to declare that criminal defamation laws violate the right to freedom of expression. In a 6–4 ruling, the court declined, holding instead that "criminal sanctions . . . are subject to the criteria of necessity and proportionality."[26] The minority did opine that "criminalization of defamation is not justified,"[27] and litigation on the compatibility with the right to freedom of expression of Uganda's criminal defamation laws is pending at the East African Court of Justice.[28] The Economic Community of West African States (ECOWAS) Community Court of Justice, in its 2018 examination of the criminal libel and sedition laws of The Gambia, has gone the furthest, stating, "The existence of criminal defamation and insult or sedition laws are indeed inacceptable instances of gross violation of free speech and freedom of expression."[29] The court examined specifically the wording of the laws of The Gambia, criticizing "the restrictions and the vagueness with which these laws have been framed and the ambiguity of the mens rea,"[30] but it concluded that all criminal defamation laws violate the right to freedom of expression and directed The Gambia to decriminalize its criminal defamation laws.

With international human rights courts (except for the ECOWAS court) leaving the door ajar, it is little surprise that there is a divided picture with regard to national practice. Some states have heeded the call of the international rapporteurs on freedom of expression to decriminalize their defamation laws, and some national courts have held that criminal defamation laws are unconstitutional. In the Americas, under sustained pressure from the Inter-American

Commission and Court of Human Rights as well as the Special Rapporteur on Freedom of Opinion and Expression, Nicaragua, Panama, Argentina, and El Salvador partially repealed the crimes of libel and slander, while Mexico (at the federal level), Grenada, and Jamaica[31] went a step further and fully repealed their criminal defamation laws.[32] In Africa, courts in Kenya and Zimbabwe have declared that criminal defamation laws violate the right to freedom of expression.[33]

Interestingly (and unfortunately, unusually), the United Kingdom decriminalized its defamation laws in 2009 specifically to set a positive international precedent. Introducing the amendments in Parliament, Lord Bach stated that criminal defamation and associated offenses were "arcane [and] have largely fallen into disuse. They stem from a bygone age when freedom of expression was not seen as the right that it is today." Determined to set an international precedent, and perhaps mindful that many countries have "inherited" criminal defamation laws as one of many questionable colonial legacies, Lord Bach went on to state that "taking the initiative to abolish them will be a positive step . . . in challenging similar laws in other countries where they are used to suppress free speech."[34]

Thus far, not many have joined the United Kingdom; the majority of countries around the world retain criminal defamation laws on their statute books.[35] Most European countries retain criminal defamation laws,[36] and even in the United States, considered to have the strongest constitutional protection for freedom of speech of any country in the world, criminal defamation laws have been found to be constitutional, albeit under strict conditions.[37] Nor have all courts that have considered the issue ruled to decriminalize. The Constitutional Court of South Africa and the Supreme Court of India recently considered whether the criminal defamation laws of these countries contravened constitutionally protected right to freedom of expression and concluded that they did not.[38]

NO IMPRISONMENT OR OTHER DISPROPORTIONATE SANCTIONS

In contrast to the question of whether criminal defamation laws as such violate the right to freedom of expression, there is strong unanimity among national and international courts, intergovernmental watchdogs, and the vast majority of states that imprisonment for defamation is disproportionate and violates the right to freedom of expression. The special rapporteurs on freedom of expression have called for the abolition of "unduly harsh sanctions such as imprisonment, suspended sentences, loss of civil rights, including the right to practise journalism, and excessive fines."[39] Similarly, the UN Human Rights Committee has stated that "imprisonment is never an appropriate penalty [for defamation]."[40]

Although journalists still may be imprisoned for defamation in some countries,[41] this is usually met with widespread condemnation, and the majority of countries no longer impose imprisonment as a sanction—even when it is technically provided for in the statute books. No international human rights court has ever upheld a sanction of imprisonment. In *Cumpǎnǎ and Mazǎre v. Romania*, the European Court of Human Rights held that the "imposition of a prison sentence [for defamation] will inevitably have a chilling effect."[42] This is true even for suspended or conditional sentences, or when journalists have been pardoned. The court has held that "the chilling effect that the fear of such sanctions has on the exercise of journalistic freedom of expression is evident" and that this effect "works to the detriment of society as a whole."[43]

Though a cursory reading of leading international judgments, such as *Konaté v. Burkina Faso* and *Cumpǎnǎ and Mazǎre v. Romania*,[44] would suggest that human rights courts might permit imprisonment for some extreme forms of defamation, this would be to misunderstand the courts' intentions. As explained by judges Sophia Akuffo, Bernard Ngoepe, and Duncan Tambala in their Joint Separate Opinion in *Konaté*, "once a so-called criminal defamation amounts to say hate speech or incitement, it is no longer criminal defamation; it mutates into one of the already existing and well known specific crimes such as sedition or high treason."[45] Similarly, the European Court of Human Rights' dictum in *Cumpǎnǎ and Mazǎre* reserves imprisonment for "exceptional circumstances . . . where other fundamental rights have been seriously impaired, as, for example, in the case of hate speech or incitement to violence,"[46] indicating that imprisonment for regular defamation offenses that do not constitute hate speech—which would be nearly all cases—would violate the right to freedom of expression. The examples that the court provides are mentioned only because the laws of some countries conflate reputation with hate speech, treating the hate speech as a category of reputation.

Disproportionate sanctions exist under civil defamation laws as well, particularly in the form of damage awards. In his 2000 annual report, the UN Special Rapporteur on Freedom of Opinion and Expression recommended that "sanctions for defamation should not be so large as to exert a chilling effect on freedom of opinion and expression and the right to seek, receive and impart information."[47]

At the regional level, the European Court of Human Rights has produced a small body of jurisprudence on this specific issue. It has held that disproportionate damage awards violate the right to freedom of expression—even if what the media wrote was untrue and defamatory.[48] Not only must there be a relationship of proportionality between the damage done by the defamatory remarks and the damages awarded, but also regard must be given to the impact of the award on the journalist or media outlet concerned[49] as well as the wider chilling effect that a large damage award might have across a country. In *Timpul Info-Magazin and Anghel v. Moldova*, in which a media outlet had had to close down as the result of a fine imposed upon it, the court emphasized "its chilling effect on the applicant newspaper, and that its imposition was capable 'of discouraging open discussion of matters of public concern' . . . by silencing a dissenting voice altogether." Even modest financial penalties can have such an effect: in *Brasilier v. France* the court found that "the most moderate possible" award, of one franc, was disproportionate because of the chilling effect on freedom of expression. By the same token, the court has allowed large awards to be imposed against media companies when defamatory remarks have been particularly serious.[50] The Committee of Ministers affirmed these principles in its 2004 declaration on freedom of political debate in the media.[51] In 2009, the court clarified that the principles also extends to the amount in legal fees that a defendant in a defamation case may be ordered to pay, finding a cost award of £500,000 to be exorbitant.[52]

The jurisprudence of the other regional human rights courts is not as well developed, but it heads in the same direction. Thus, the African Court on Human and Peoples' Rights found a violation of the right to freedom of expression where a state could not show that, in setting the level of a defamation award, regard had been given to the financial situation of the media outlet concerned.[53] In *Tristan Donosco v. Panama*, which concerned criticism of a public official, the Inter-American Court of Human Rights held that any sanctions for defamation should not be excessive, and that the chilling effect of potential financial sanctions needs to be taken into account: "The fear of a civil penalty, [for example] a very steep civil reparation, may be . . . equally or more intimidating and inhibiting for the exercise of freedom of expression than a criminal punishment, since it has the potential to attain the personal and family life of an individual who accuses a public official, with the evident and very negative result of self-censorship both in the affected party and in other potential critics of the actions taken by a public official."[54]

Disproportionate nonfinancial sanctions, such as (temporary) suspension of a media outlet or barring a journalist from working (in countries where journalism is a regulated profession, in itself a contentious issue under international freedom of expression standards), are also frowned upon. The African Court on Human and Peoples' Rights has held that the suspension of a newspaper for defamation violated the right to freedom of expression.[55]

POLITICIANS, PUBLIC OFFICIALS, AND THE PUBLIC INTEREST

It is a long-held tenet of international human rights law that politicians, by virtue of having put themselves up for election to serve the people, should be open to higher levels of scrutiny than ordinary individuals. In one of the first defamation cases to come before it, the European Court held that:

> Freedom of the press . . . affords the public one of the best means of discovering and forming an opinion of the ideas and attitudes of political leaders. The limits of acceptable criticism are accordingly wider as regards a politician as such than as regards a private individual. Unlike the latter, the former inevitably and knowingly lays himself open to close scrutiny of his every word and deed by both journalists and the public at large, and must consequently display a greater degree of tolerance. No doubt Article 10 para. 2 enables the reputation of others to be protected, and this protection extends to politicians too, even when they are not acting in their private capacity; but in such cases the requirements of such protection have to be weighed in relation to the interests of open discussion of political issues.[56]

The case concerned the conviction for defamation of journalists who had published two articles discussing the participation of Austrians in atrocities committed during World War II. The articles criticized the chancellor, who would be retiring following recently held elections, for allegedly protecting former Nazis. The chancellor won a defamation judgment against the journalists. The European Court of Human Rights held that this violated the journalists' right to freedom of expression.

The judgment, and this paragraph in particular, often has been repeated in other judgments, and its spirit has become a staple of international human rights law. The European Court has since expanded this "heightened protection" to discussion of the functioning of public officials, those who have voluntarily entered the public realm,[57] and, more broadly, has crafted an overarching—and still developing—protection for expression on issues of public interest. The court has further clarified that in engaging in such debate, individuals are entitled to use a degree of exaggeration, immoderation, and provocation.[58]

At the global level, the joint declarations issued by the special rapporteurs on freedom of expression have repeatedly stressed that the abuse of defamation laws by politicians and other public figures needs to be ended,[59] and the UN Human Rights Committee's General Comment on Freedoms of Opinion and Expression states that "the value placed . . . upon uninhibited expression is particularly high in the circumstances of public debate in a democratic society concerning figures in the public and political domain."[60]

The inter-American human rights bodies have taken a strong line, focused in particular on the use of so-called *desacato* laws—criminal law provisions specifically designed to protect the reputation of politicians and public officials. The Inter-American Court of Human Rights has held that such laws are incompatible with the right to freedom of expression.[61] This has led to the abolition of *desacato* laws in Argentina, Chile, Costa Rica, Nicaragua, Panama, Paraguay, and Peru, as a direct result of pressure from the Inter-American Commission on Human Rights and, later, the Special Rapporteur on Freedom of Opinion and Expression appointed by the commission, and the Inter-American Court of Human Rights.[62] Taking note of these developments, the constitutional courts of Honduras, Guatemala, Brazil, and Bolivia have declared *desacato* laws unconstitutional; while Peruvian and Colombian courts have ruled the use of "ordinary" defamation laws to be unconstitutional if their purpose is to protect the honor of public officials.[63]

International human rights courts have held that the private life of politicians also can be open to public criticism. In the case of *Fontevecchia v. Argentina*, brought by a magazine that had been fined for reporting on an affair between the president and a congresswomen, which had resulted in the birth of a child and for both of whom the president had secured asylum in Paraguay, the Inter-American Court held that this "involved a person who held the highest elective public office in his country . . . and therefore was subject to greater scrutiny not only regarding his official activities or the exercise of official functions, but also regarding aspects that, in principle, could be linked to his private life but revealed matters of public interest." It followed that the reporting concerned a legitimate societal interest.[64] The European Court of Human Rights has ruled similarly, in the case of *Couderc and Hachette Filipacchi Associés v. France*, which concerned reporting on extramarital affairs and children of Prince Albert of Monaco.[65]

National courts in many countries follow the same line. Arguably, the European Court's decision in *Lingens*—that great hallmark of free speech—was itself heavily influenced by a comparative law brief submitted by the International Press Institute and Interights, which surveyed defamation laws in Europe and the United States and the value they place on open criticism of politicians.[66] In this sense, the jurisprudence is a beautiful example of a line of national decisions, led by the U.S. Supreme Court's seminal *New York Times Co. v. Sullivan* judgment, which influenced the European Court of Human Rights and, from there, branched out to influence other international and regional human rights courts before moving back down again to other national courts.

In spite of these pro-speech developments, laws to protect heads of state (including those of other countries) and monarchies remain on the statute books in a number of countries.[67] Sometimes referred to as lèse-majesté laws,[68] these are easily abused to restrict government critics. The European Court of Human Rights has on several occasions held that these laws violate the right to freedom of expression, but they appear to be hard to get rid of.[69] Even in reasonably well-established democracies such as the Netherlands, a proposal to abolish the country's lèse-majesté laws in early 2018 was met with strong opposition.[70]

CONCLUSIONS

As measured over the past thirty years, there is an unmistakable pro–freedom of expression trend in the defamation jurisprudence of international human rights courts and bodies. Driven by a balancing of the competing rights of freedom of expression and of privacy and the protection of reputation, and very mindful of the role played by the media in a democracy, this jurisprudence has sought to end the abuse of defamation laws, particularly by politicians and similar public figures. The jurisprudence has held that there should be no heightened protection for politicians and other public figures but that they should instead be open to a higher level of scrutiny, and that defamation laws should never restrict debate on issues of public interest. No sanctions should be imposed that are disproportionate or that would threaten the financial survival of the individual or media outlet concerned, even if reporting is found to have been defamatory; and no one should ever serve a prison sentence for a simple act of defamation. These are clear red lines that have been drawn and on which there is broad consensus.

The jurisprudence is rooted in decades of global norm setting on broader standards of democracy and the protection of freedom of expression as a core right underlying democracy, alongside the international practice of a number of influential lawyers, informed by academics with a comparative outlook and aided by the increased cross-border availability of judgments of influential courts. This has been particularly obvious in the common law world, where judges are traditionally more open to hearing wider arguments than purely statute-based ones, an approach that international human rights courts have also adopted. For example, UK-based and Harvard-educated barrister Lord Anthony Lester has spoken of how he has "used *Sullivan* a lot" and has had quite some success with that approach.[71] Indian Supreme Court judgments frequently read like treatises on comparative law,[72] and the European Court of Human Rights' judgment in *Lingens*, as mentioned, is suffused with the spirit of *Sullivan*, even if it didn't follow it expressly.

Nongovernmental organizations (NGOs) have been very influential as well, whether in cases such as *Lingens* and countless others or by working with the UN Special Rapporteur on Freedom of Opinion and Expression and other intergovernmental watchdogs to develop standards.[73] Over time, this cross-fertilization became very intentional; for example, the NGO Media Legal Defence Initiative pursued a multiyear strategy of first litigating potentially standard-setting defamation cases before the African Court of Human and Peoples' Rights and then using the judgments obtained there—such as in *Konaté v. Burkina Faso*[74]—in cases before national and regional courts to further establish and enforce the standard.

However, there remains divergence over the question of whether criminal defamation laws as such are compatible with the right to freedom of expression. At the international level, the special rapporteurs on freedom of expression established at the UN, the Organization of American States, the Organization for Security and Co-operation in Europe, and the African Union, which face, through their complaints mechanisms, almost daily allegations of abuse of criminal defamation laws, particularly by politicians and public officials, have urged the decriminalization of such laws. There has been strong follow-up to this in the Americas, but elsewhere the picture is divided: national courts and legislatures in many relatively well-established democracies either have not discussed the issue or, if they have, have maintained that there remains a need for criminal defamation laws. International human rights courts have left the door ajar, although the recent ECOWAS judgment has gone further, and the East African Court of Justice is considering the matter. Undeniably, there are also what can be referred to "persistent offenders"—countries where individuals are still imprisoned for defamation.[75] There are relatively few such countries,[76] and news of such imprisonment is often met with international protest, illustrating that these situations are very much the exceptions that confirm the rule.

Although this jurisprudential direction of travel is welcome for freedom of expression advocates, the impact of defamation laws continues to be felt—to the detriment of media and others reporting on issues of social interest, and therefore to the detriment of society as a whole. The main remaining issues are twofold, and related, namely the cost of defending a case, and the use of defamation and similar laws with no purpose other than to tie journalists and other critical voices up in legal proceedings for years on end, forcing them to incur costs. It is no longer just politicians and public officials who feature as claimants, and journalists are not the only defendants. Large corporations with deep pockets increasingly feature as claimants, and environmental and human rights NGOs have joined the ranks of defendants. International courts have begun to set some standards—the special rapporteurs on freedom of expression have flagged the cost of defending proceedings as an issue, and the European Court of Human Rights has ruled on cases where defendants have been saddled with truly astronomical fees—but standard-setting work remains to be done on this issue.

NOTES

1. Adopted as UN General Assembly Resolution 217, UN document A/RES/217(III), December 10, 1948.
2. Adopted as UN General Assembly Resolution 2200A (XXI), December 19, 1966.
3. Pact of San Jose, adopted November 22, 1969.
4. Council of Europe, European Treaty Series no. 5, November 4, 1950.
5. The African Charter on Human and Peoples' Rights does not protect the right to reputation, nor a right to privacy. It is worth noting that Article 8 of the European Convention on Human Rights does not name the protection of reputation but the European Court has interpreted serious attacks on reputation as engaging the right to privacy protected under Article 8. See A. v. Norway, application no. 28070/06, judgment of April 9, 2009, and subsequent decisions. Paragraph 64 states, "In order for Article 8 to come into play, the attack on personal honour and reputation must attain a certain level of gravity and in a manner causing prejudice to personal enjoyment of the right to respect for private life."
6. For a brief overview, and an interesting reminder that in most legal systems the protection of reputation has much deeper roots than does the right to freedom of expression, see Eric Barendt, "Libel and Invasion of Privacy," in *Freedom of Speech*, 2nd ed. (Oxford: Oxford University Press, 2005), 198–246, and the sources cited therein.
7. I refer here to the setting of human rights–based standards across large regions and multiple jurisdictions, and not merely limited to common law or other

like-minded countries. Although, of course, the common law of defamation developed across multiple jurisdictions prior to the 1980s, this was overwhelmingly driven by the English courts, and its spread was integral to the British colonial project. It was not driven by a human rights agenda—in fact, the colonial project ran counter to human rights.

8. European Court of Human Rights (ECtHR), Lingens v. Austria, application no. 9815/82, judgment of July 8, 1986. Case information on this and all other judgments handed down by national courts mentioned in this chapter is available at Columbia University, Global Freedom of Expression, "Case Law," https://globalfree domofexpression.columbia.edu/cases/.

9. Lingens v. Austria, para. 42. Columbia University, Global Freedom of Expression, shows that Lingens v. Austria has been cited in dozens of other cases. https:// globalfreedomofexpression.columbia.edu/cases/lingens-v-austria/.

10. United States, *New York Times Co. v. Sullivan*, 376 U.S. 254 (1964).

11. Of course, defamation laws serve to protect the reputational interests of all, including "ordinary" people. In the age of social media, when defamatory accusations are easily uttered and have a long afterlife, they serve an important purpose. But often, and particularly when it comes to commentary on matters of public interest, defamation laws disproportionately favor the rich and powerful, both in substance and in terms of who has access to the legal means to enforce them. This has been reported, for example, in Andrew Kenyon, *Defamation: Comparative Law and Practice* (Oxford: CRC Press, 2013), 109 (analyzing the types of defamation claimants in England, which has a particularly busy defamation practice).

12. Technically, the title of the Organization for Security and Co-operation in Europe (OSCE) mandate holder is Representative on Freedom of the Media. For the sake of brevity, I will refer to all as "special rapporteurs" throughout. From the perspective of tracking norm development, it is interesting to note that these joint declarations were very much driven by the freedom of expression organization Article 19, which saw this high-level norm development as crucial to the protection and promotion of the right to freedom of expression. For background, see Tony Mendel, "The UN Special Rapporteur on Freedom of Opinion and Expression: Progressive Development of International Standards Relating to Freedom of Expression," in *The United Nations and Freedom of Expression and Information: Critical Perspectives*, ed. Tarlach McGonagle and Yvonne Donders (Cambridge: Cambridge University Press, 2015), 235–268.

13. This initially was a trio: the African Commission on Human and Peoples' Rights appointed its rapporteur on freedom of expression in December 2004, through Resolution 71, adopted at its 36th Ordinary Session, November 23–December 7,

2004. This rapporteur was therefore absent from the first six editions of the joint declaration.

14. First Joint Declaration by the Rapporteurs for Freedom of Expression (1999); Joint Declaration about Censorship by Killing and Defamation (2000). All joint declaration are archived at the website of the OSCE Representative on Freedom of the Media, http://www.osce.org/fom/66176.

15. Joint Declaration on Freedom of Expression and the Administration of Justice, Commercialisation and Freedom of Expression, and Criminal Defamation (2002). Summarized at Organization of American States (OAS), "International Mechanisms for Promoting Freedom of Expression," http://www.oas.org/en/iachr/expression /showarticle.asp?artID=87&lID=1.

16. Upon taking office in 2005, the African Commission's special rapporteur adopted a statement, together with the OAS special rapporteur, joining in the condemnation of criminal defamation laws. See https://www.oas.org/en/iachr/expression /showarticle.asp?artID=394&lID=1. Subsequent joint declarations by all mandates, in 2010 and 2017, have affirmed the principled call to decriminalize defamation laws. See OAS, "Tenth Anniversary Joint Declaration: Ten Key Challenges to Freedom of Expression in the Next Decade" (2010), http://www.oas.org/en/iachr /expression/showarticle.asp?artID=784&lID=1; and OAS, "Joint Declaration on Freedom of Expression and 'Fake News,' Disinformation and Propaganda" (2017), http://www.oas.org/en/iachr/expression/showarticle.asp?artID=1056&lID=1.

17. Human Rights Committee (HRC), General Comment no. 34, Article 19, "Freedoms of Opinion and Expression," UN document CCPR/C/GC/34, September 12, 2011, para. 47.

18. Approved by the Inter-American Commission on Human Rights during its 108th Regular Session.

19. Declaration of Principles of Freedom of Expression in Africa, African Commission on Human and Peoples' Rights, 32nd session, October 17–23, 2002: Banjul, The Gambia.

20. Council of Europe, Parliamentary Assembly Resolution 1577, Towards Decriminalisation of Defamation (2007).

21. Council of Europe, reply adopted by the Committee of Ministers on June 11, 2008, at the 1,029th meeting of the ministers' deputies, doc. CM/AS(2008)Rec1814-final, para. 3–4.

22. ECtHR, Lindon, Otchakovsky-Laurens and July v. France, application nos. 21279/02 and 36448/02, judgment of October 22, 2007, para. 59.

23. ECtHR, Raichinov v. Bulgaria, application no. 47579/99, judgment of April 20, 2006, para. 50. See also ECtHR, Cumpănă and Mazăre v. Romania, application no. 33348/96, judgment of December 17, 2004, para. 115.

24. See Inter-American Court of Human Rights (IACtHR), Kimel v. Argentina, judgment of May 2, 2008, series C, no. 177; Ricardo Canese v. Paraguay, judgment of August 31, 2004, series C, no. 111; Herrera-Ulloa v. Costa Rica, judgment of July 2, 2004, series C, no. 107.

25. IACtHR, Palamara Iribarne v. Chile, series C, no. 135.

26. African Commission on Human and Peoples' Rights, Lohe Issa Konaté v. Burkina Faso, application no. 04/2013, judgment of December 5, 2014, para. 166.

27. Lohe Issa Konaté v. Burkina Faso, note 29, Joint Separate Opinion of Judges Sophia A. B. Akuffo, Bernard M. Ngoepe, and Duncan Tambala, December 5, 2014, para. 4.

28. Ronald Ssembuusi v. Attorney General of the Republic of Uganda, reference no. 16 (2014).

29. FAJ and others v. the Gambia, Economic Community of West African States Court of Justice, judgment of February 13, 2018, p. 40.

30. Ssembuusi v. Attorney General, p. 47.

31. See Nicaragua, law no. 641 of November 16, 2007, *La Gaceta* no. 232; Panama, law no. 26 of May 21, 2008, *Gaceta Oficial* 26.045; Argentina, law no. 26.551 of November 18, 2009, *Boletín Oficial* no. 31.790; El Salvador, decree no. 836 of December 7, 2011, *Diario Oficial* no. 299, vol. 393; Mexico, decree of April 13, 2007, *Diario Oficial de la Federación*; Grenada, Criminal Code (Amendment) Act 2012; and Jamaica, defamation act 2013.

32. This is described in detail in Catalina Botero, "The Role of the Inter-American Human Rights System in the Emergence and Development of Global Norms on Freedom of Expression," chapter 8 of this volume.

33. See, for example, recent decisions in Kenya, Jacqueline Okuta & Anor v. AG & Others, February 6, 2017; and Zimbabwe, Madanhire & Another v. AG, Constitutional Court, const. application no. CCZ 78/12, judgment of June 12, 2014

34. Hansard parliamentary reports, House of Lords, vol. 713, October 28, 2009, column 1173. https://publications.parliament.uk/pa/ld200809/ldhansrd/text/91028 -0003.htm.

35. The last global report dates from 2012, when Article 19 found that 174 countries retained criminal penalties for defamation, with twenty-one countries having fully decriminalized their defamation laws.

36. *Defamation and Insult Laws in the OSCE Region: A Comparative Study*, Organization for Security and Co-operation in Europe, March 7, 2017, http://www.osce.org /fom/303181.

37. United States, Garrison v. Louisiana, 379 U.S. 64 (1964).

38. India, Subramanian Swamy v. Union of India, Writ Petition (criminal) no. 184 of 2014, judgment of May 13, 2016; South Africa, S v. Hoho, Supreme Court of Appeal, case no. 493/05, judgment of September 17, 2008.

39. OSCE, *Tenth Anniversary Joint Declaration: Ten Key Challenges to Freedom of Expression in the Next Decade*, February 4, 2010, https://www.osce.org/fom/41439.

40. HRC, General Comment no. 34, para. 47

41. According to the Committee to Protect Journalists, in 2017, nineteen journalists were imprisoned on defamation charges, in Bangladesh, Ecuador, Egypt, Saudi Arabia, Somalia, Thailand, Turkey, and Uganda. See https://cpj.org/data/imprisoned /2017.

42. Cumpănă and Mazăre v. Romania, note 23, para. 116.

43. Cumpănă and Mazăre v. Romania, note 23, para. 114. This has become an oft-repeated dictum of the court. See, for example, Kudeshkina v. Russia, application no. 29492/05, judgment of February 26, 2009, para. 99; and Baka v. Hungary, application no. 20261/12, judgment of June 23, 2016, para. 167.

44. Konaté v. Burkina Faso, note 29; Cumpănă and Mazăre v. Romania, note 23.

45. Konaté v. Burkina Faso, note 29, Joint Separate Opinion, para. 4.

46. Cumpănă and Mazăre v. Romania, note 23, para. 115.

47. Report of the special rapporteur on access to information, criminal libel and defamation, the police and the criminal justice system, and new technologies, UN document E/CN.4/2000/63, para. 52.

48. ECtHR, Tolstoy Miloslavsky v. the United Kingdom, application no. 18139/91, July 13, 1995.

49. ECtHR, Steel and Morris v. the United Kingdom, application no. 68416/01, May 15, 2005 (ruling that a defamation award was disproportionate relative to the income of the defendants). See also ECtHR, Koprivica v. Montenegro, application no. 41158/09, November 22, 2011; Filipovic v. Serbia, application no. 27935/05, November 20, 2007; Tešić v. Serbia, application nos. 4678/07 and 50591/12, February 11, 2014.

50. ECtHR, Timpul Info-Magazin and Anghel v. Moldova, application no. 42864/05, November 27, 2007; ECtHR, Brasilier v. France, application no. 71343/01, April 11, 2006. See also ECtHR, Krone Verlag GmbH v. Austria, application no. 27306/07, June 19, 2012.

51. Council of Europe, Declaration on Freedom of Political Debate in the Media, adopted by the Committee of Ministers on February 12, 2004, at the 872nd meeting of the Ministers' Deputies.

52. ECtHR, MGN v. United Kingdom, application no. 39401/04, judgment of January 18, 2011.

53. Konaté v. Burkina Faso, note 29, para. 171.

54. IACtHR, Tristán Donoso v. Panama, judgment of January 27, 2009, para. 129.

55. Konaté v. Burkina Faso, note 29, para. 169.

56. Lingens v. Austria, application no. 9815/82, judgment of July 8, 1986, para. 42.

57. ECtHR, Nilsen and Johnsen v. Norway, application no. 23118/93, judgment of November 25, 1999, para. 52. For the corresponding development in the case law of the Inter-American Court of Human Rights, see Canese v. Paraguay, series C, no. 111, para. 103.

58. See, for example, Ziembinski v. Poland (no. 2), application no. 1799/07, judgment of July 5, 2016, para. 44.

59. For example, the 2002 declaration notes "the ongoing abuse of criminal defamation laws, including by politicians and other public figures"; the 2005 joint declaration states, "Criminal defamation laws intimidate individuals from exposing wrongdoing by public officials and such laws are therefore incompatible with freedom of expression"; and the 2010 joint declaration highlights as "particularly concerning" a "failure to require public officials and figures to tolerate a greater degree of criticism than ordinary citizens." Joint declarations are available at http://www.osce.org/fom/66176.

60. HRC, General Comment no. 34, para. 34.

61. IACtHR, Palamara Iribarne v. Chile, series C, no. 135.

62. As described by Botero-Marino, "The Role of the Inter-American Human Rights System."

63. See Honduras, Supreme Court of Justice, Chamber of Constitutional Affairs, judgment of May 19, 2005; Guatemala, Constitutional Court, judgment of February 1, 2006; Brazil, Supreme Court of Justice, Fifth Chamber, judgment of December 15, 2016; Bolivia, Constitutional Court, judgment of September 20, 2012; Peru, Supreme Court of Justice, Chamber of Criminal Affairs, judgment of June 18, 2010; Colombia, Supreme Court of Justice, Chamber of Criminal Affairs, judgment of July 10, 2013.

64. IACtHR, Fontevecchia and D'amico v. Argentina, series C, no. 238, para. 60, 62.

65. ECtHR, Couderc and Hachette Filipacchi Associés v. France, application no. 40454/07.

66. As argued by Dinah Shelton, "The Participation of Nongovernmental Organizations in International Judicial Proceedings," *American Journal of International Law* 88, no. 4 (1994): 611–642, at 635–636.

67. For instance, Article 323 of the Criminal Code of Azerbaijan; or Article 90 of the German criminal code.

68. For instance, section 112 of Thailand's criminal code; or section 111 of the Criminal Code of the Netherlands.

69. See, for instance, ECtHR, Colombani and Others v. France, application No. 51279/99; or ECtHR, Artun and Güvener v. Turkey, application no. 75510/01, para. 31, which holds, "That interest . . . could not serve as justification for affording the head of State privileged status or special protection vis-à-vis the right to convey information and opinions concerning him."

70. Daniel Boffey, "Dutch Divided Over Law Against Insulting the King," *Guardian*, February 5, 2018, https://www.theguardian.com/world/2018/feb/05/dutch-divided -over-law-against-insulting-the-king.

71. For instance, Anthony Lester, "Two Cheers for the First Amendment," *Harvard Law and Policy Review* 8, no. 1 (2014): 177–194, at 184.

72. A good example is India, Singhal v. Union of India, writ petition no. 167 (2012), on intermediary liability.

73. Article 19 deserves special notice in this regard, having originated the UN, the OAS, the OSCE, and the African Union rapporteurs' influential joint declarations. See note 12.

74. Konaté v. Burkina Faso, para. 166.

75. As documented, for example, by the Committee to Protect Journalists in its annual "prison census." For the latest tally, see Committee to Protect Journalists, "Imprisoned," https://cpj.org/imprisoned.

76. According to the Committee to Protect Journalists, in 2017, journalists were imprisoned for defamation in only nine countries: Bangladesh, Ecuador, Egypt, Morocco, Saudi Arabia, Somalia, Thailand, Turkey, and Uganda. https://cpj.org /data/imprisoned/2017/.

Is There a Global Norm for the Protection of Journalists' Sources?

FIVE

RICHARD DANBURY

People frequently provide journalists with information to report to the public. Some don't want their identity revealed.[1] This chapter is about the rules that protect journalists from being compelled to reveal the identities of such people. It examines whether there is a global norm that journalists' sources should be protected.

There are a number of reasons why such a norm might exist, but broadly stated it would facilitate information being widely dispersed in the public sphere when it is in the public interest for this to happen. However, there are also cogent and defensible reasons to reject such a norm, as a matter of principle. It can prevent people who have been defamed from receiving compensation, for instance, or it can inhibit investigations into terrorism, to select but two examples. Such reasons—among others—may amount to counternorms, to be balanced against a norm on journalistic source protection. Alternatively, they may provide rationales for individuals, organizations, or states to defy a norm of journalistic source protection, for good or ill. Further, or alternatively, they may describe the appropriate limits of any norm.

Given the fact that the existence of a norm is not clear-cut, to what extent can it be said that a global norm exists? This chapter seeks to answer that question, first by identifying what the characteristics of such a norm might be and then by examining a range of international, regional, and national hard and soft laws to evaluate whether they express these characteristics.[2] It demonstrates that the norm exists in a range of laws and rules in international bodies, regional courts and institutions, and national laws across the globe, and in some cases has existed for many years.

But, as will be demonstrated, these laws and rules differ in significant ways. There are significant differences in both the form and substance of the laws and rules of journalistic source protection, which means that similar actions by people will be affected in different ways in different countries and contexts. A source in Syria may not be protected in the same way as a source in the Sudan or in Australia, despite apparently receiving similar protection in law. This amounts to an important limitation on the notion that there is a homogenous global norm, applied equally everywhere with equal force. However, it should not be seen as undermining the notion that the core of a norm exists.

CHARACTERISTICS OF JOURNALISTIC SOURCE PROTECTION NORMS

Any analysis of a global norm of journalistic source protection needs to start by identifying what a norm of journalistic source protection looks like and distinguishing it from other, similar rules. Janice Brabyn has proposed a useful definition: "A jurisdiction has special protection against judicially compelled disclosure of the identity of news gatherers' confidential sources only when at least in some circumstances, notwithstanding satisfaction of all standard prerequisites for the granting of the relevant judicial order, including in particular relevance, good faith and reasonableness, news gatherers cannot be judicially compelled to disclose their confidential sources' identities."[3] Almost inevitably, the rationale for declining to compel the disclosure of such sources is that it is not in the wider, longer-term public interest so to do.

The attraction of this definition is that it describes what a norm looks like in basic structural terms and allows for differences in the form and substance of the norm in different national and international legal contexts. This chapter demonstrates that there are significant examples of such variations around the globe. For example, while the norm is commonly justified on public interest grounds, there are differences in the balances struck between the strength of this and other competing public interests and private rights in different jurisdictions, particularly in how proportionality tests determine these balances. This definition also allows for such variation.

GLOBAL NORMS

There is much evidence of a global norm of journalistic source protection of the type identified by Brabyn. This can be demonstrated by looking at international, regional, and national hard and soft law, relying on previous work in this area, notably by David Banisar and Julie Posetti.[4]

United Nations

A number of resolutions, reports, recommendations, statements, and comments issued by the various bodies of the United Nations recognize the importance of journalistic source protection. In 2012, for instance, the UN Human Rights Council issued its Resolution on the Safety of Journalists. In the third numbered paragraph, the council stressed "the need to ensure greater protection for all media professionals and for journalistic sources."[5]

In 2013, the United Nations Educational, Scientific and Cultural Organization General Conference issued a resolution on Internet-related issues, one of the recitals of which noted that "privacy is essential to protect journalistic sources, which enable a society to benefit from investigative journalism, to strengthen good governance and the rule of law, and that such privacy should not be subject to arbitrary or unlawful interference."[6]

Moving on to other UN documents, as far back as 1998, the Special Rapporteur on Freedom of Opinion and Expression observed in his report, "Independent and State-owned media contribute most effectively to the realization of the right to information in countries where there is a statutory presumption that journalists are not required to disclose their sources except in the most limited and clearly defined circumstances. Without such protection for both journalists and sources, the media's access to information and their ability to communicate that information to the public are likely to be compromised."[7] Similar points have been emphasized by subsequent rapporteurs. Frank La Rue, for example, emphasized the importance of source protection a number of times, notably in 2012.[8] These reports have been cited in national and regional courts.[9]

Other rapporteurs also have emphasized the importance of journalistic source protection. In 2008, the UN Special Rapporteur on Freedom of Opinion and Expression, the Organisation for Security and Co-operation in Europe (OSCE) Representative on Freedom of the Media, the Organization of American States Special Rapporteur on Freedom of Expression, and the African Commission on Human and People's Rights (ACHPR) Special Rapporteur on

Freedom of Expression and Access to Information issued a Joint Declaration on Defamation of Religions and Anti-Terrorism and Anti-Extremism Legislation. This contained an endorsement of the importance of respecting the confidentiality of journalistic sources in such contexts.[10]

Also worth highlighting is the 2011 General Comment no. 34 by the UN Human Rights Committee, which says that "states parties should recognize and respect that element of the right of freedom of expression that embraces the limited journalistic privilege not to disclose information sources."[11]

European Regional Bodies

Council of Europe

There are a number of instances of the organs of the Council of Europe recognizing the existence of a norm of journalistic source protection. In addition to taking the form of soft law—declarations, recommendations, and the like— they also are embodied in the case law of the judgments of the regional apex court of human rights, the European Court of Human Rights (ECtHR).

Judgments of the European Court of Human Rights

Judgments of the ECtHR on journalistic source protection are, in the words of Eric Barendt, "one of the few areas of freedom of expression law where European jurisprudence is more generous than that of the United States with regard to the exercise of the freedom."[12] Unlike the U.S. Supreme Court, the ECtHR has been unequivocal in its finding that journalistic source protection engages the protection of fundamental law guarantees and engages Article 10 of the European Convention on Human Rights. Additionally, source protection may engage other articles in the convention, notably Article 8 on the right to privacy.[13]

The leading case on the subject was heard in 1996. In Goodwin v. UK,[14] the court considered the United Kingdom's laws on journalistic source protection, in particular section 10 of the Contempt of Court Act 1981 as interpreted by the High Court and the Court of Appeal of England and Wales, and the House of Lords. The British courts had compelled a journalist to reveal the source of his story about the financial affairs of a private company, and the journalist appealed to the ECtHR. The court declared, in a passage that has been frequently cited elsewhere,[15] that "protection of journalistic sources is one of the basic conditions for press freedom. . . . Without such protection, sources may be deterred from assisting the press in informing the public on matters of public interest."[16]

The ECtHR has built on *Goodwin* and has developed a nuanced and detailed analysis of what "an overriding requirement in the public interest" may be, and therefore the conditions under which a journalist can be compelled to reveal their sources.[17] The framework under which these decisions are considered is the characteristic threefold test the ECtHR applies when assessing whether there has been a breach of the right of freedom of expression.[18] The court also, on occasion, affords states a margin of appreciation.

Millar and Scott have identified two limbs of protection that the European Court affords to journalistic source protection—substantive safeguards and procedural safeguards.[19] An example of a substantive safeguard is found in the case of *Tillack v. Belgium*, where the investigating authorities seized much of a journalist's working papers and tools. The ECtHR found that the journalist had been under suspicion because of "vague, unsubstantiated rumours," which had led to his material being seized; this was insufficient to justify such an action. The court also considered the amount of material taken (four mobile phones, a metal cabinet, and sixteen crates of papers) to be disproportionate. These two substantive failures on the part of authorities—the vagueness of the basis of action and the disproportionality of the action itself—led to an infringement of Article 10.

The court also mandates certain procedural safeguards that must be observed by authorities when seeking journalistic sources. An example can be found in *Sanoma Uitgevers v. Netherlands*.[20] The authorities in this case approached an investigating judge for an informal view about the balance between a journalist's rights to retain information and the police's right to demand it, rather than making a formal application to a court. The ECtHR found that "such a situation is scarcely compatible with the rule of law." Lack of independent oversight meant that there were inadequate safeguards in place to protect the journalist in question. A more formal process is required, the court has indicated, if an authority seeking disclosure of a journalistic source is not to infringe Article 10. Moreover, the court has indicated that such a formal review has to take place *before* rather than after any search or order for disclosure, as "review *post factum* ... cannot restore the confidentiality of journalistic sources once it is destroyed."[21]

Soft Law

The ECtHR's case law should be seen against the soft law that has emerged from the Council of Europe on the question of source protection. The earliest declaration from the council the author can find in relation to the norm was issued in 1994, at the Fourth European Ministerial Conference on Mass Media Policy in Prague, two years before the *Goodwin* case. The conference adopted the Resolution on Journalistic Freedoms and Human Rights. Principle 3(d) and 7(e) of the resolution emphasized the importance of protecting journalists' confidential sources.[22]

In 1996, the Committee of Ministers of the Council of Europe adopted a Recommendation on the Protection of Journalists in Situations of Conflict and Tension, and principle 5 echoed parts of the 1994 document.[23] The committee has continued to stress the importance of journalistic source protection over the following years, including in 2000, when it issued its Recommendation on the Right of Journalists Not to Disclose Their Sources of Information, devoted entirely to this subject. Importantly, the recommendation called for protection for institutional journalists but did not explicitly extend similar protection to others who perform a functionally similar task. The exclusivity of this was somewhat alleviated by principle 2 of the annex, which called for protection to be extended: "Other persons who, by their professional relations with journalists, acquire knowledge of information identifying a source through the collection, editorial processing or dissemination of this information, should equally be protected under the principles established herein."[24]

Subsequent to this, the Committee of Ministers has continued to emphasize the importance of journalistic source protection. In 2003, it did so in relation to criminal proceedings, and in declarations in 2005 and 2007 did so in relation to the fight against terrorism. The subject was returned to in 2014 and 2016.[25]

In 2008, the Parliamentary Assembly of the Council of Europe echoed the Committee of Ministers' views, adopting the Indicators for Media in a Democracy, paragraph 8.8 of which says "the confidentiality of journalists' sources of information must be respected." In 2011, the assembly also issued an important document devoted to this subject, *A Recommendation on the Protection of Journalists' Sources*. The assembly agreed with the approach of the Committee of Ministers on the question of who the immediate beneficiary of a right of source protection should be, as the recommendation says "non-journalists cannot benefit from the right of journalists not to reveal their sources."[26]

European Union

The institutions of the European Union have been less concerned with journalistic source protection than has the Council of Europe, but there is some recognition of this norm in both soft law and harder law. Indeed, as far ago as 1994, the European Parliament passed a regulation on the protection of journalists' sources, which emphasized the importance of source protection as a means of supplying information to the public and promoting administrative transparency.[27] And in 2014, the Council of the European Union issued *EU Human Rights Guidelines on Freedom of Expression: Online and Offline*, paragraph 31 of which says states should protect public interest journalistic sources, save (as a footnote explains) where there is an overriding requirement in the public interest in conformity with international human rights law.[28]

American Regional Bodies

Julie Posetti notes some expressions of the norm of journalistic source protection by regional American bodies. Most importantly, perhaps, in 1994 the Hemisphere Conference on Free Speech, instituted by the Inter American Press Association, adopted the Chapultepec Declaration, principle 3 of which says, in connection with freedom of information, that "no journalist may be forced to reveal his or her sources of information."[29] And in 2000, the Inter-American Commission on Human Rights (IACHR) approved the Declaration of Principles on Freedom of Expression. Principle 8 of this declaration provides that "every social commentator has the right to keep his/her source of information, notes, personal and professional archives confidential." Principle 8 was endorsed and emphasized in the IACHR's 2013 report *Violence against Journalists and Media Workers*.[30]

Interestingly, the IACHR explicitly extends the norm of source protection beyond institutional or professional journalists. This contrasts with the approach adopted by the Committee of Ministers of the Council of Europe.

African Regional Bodies

Posetti presents evidence that African regional bodies have endorsed the norm of journalistic source protection. In 2002, the ACHPR adopted a Declaration of Principles on Freedom of Expression in Africa. Declaration 15 is titled "Protection of Sources and Other Journalistic Material" and provides that "media practitioners shall not be required to reveal confidential sources of information . . . except in accordance with the following principles," and then sets out four tests, including those of necessity and proportionality.[31] The norm has also been recognized in the judgments of regional courts such as the East African Court of Justice (EACJ).[32] The EACJ held that a 2013 Burundian law[33] violated the provisions of the Treaty for the Establishment of the East African Community[34] because Article 20 of the law required journalists to disclose confidential sources of information where the information related to state security, public order, defense secrets, and the moral and physical integrity of a person or people. The EACJ, in reaching its decision, cited the ECtHR decision of *Goodwin v. UK*.[35]

NATIONAL LAWS

With regard to the domestic law of particular countries, there is widespread evidence of the existence of norms of journalistic source protection. In her study, Posetti reported, "Of the 121 Member States studied here, developments that impact on source protection in practice, or in potential, have occurred in 84 (69%) countries since 2007, the date of the Privacy International review of source protection laws. However, these changes were not evenly dispersed around the world."[36]

The national laws discussed here are grouped geographically, but geography can be misleading. Some threads can be identified that transcend geography. These track more closely to the legal family to which a country's laws are related. For example, as will be shown, the United Kingdom, South Africa, Hong Kong, and Singapore approach source protection in a similar way. This is not because of their positions on the globe but because—being common law countries—they are all influenced by an English case, *Hennessy v. Wright (no. 2)* heard in 1888.[37]

Sub-Saharan Africa

Posetti identifies Uganda,[38] Zimbabwe,[39] and Burundi (discussed earlier), among others, as having laws designed to protect journalistic sources, and such laws have been proposed in Mauritius.[40]

South Africa is an interesting example because of the long pedigree of its source protection laws. Such laws were affirmed in a relatively recent decision of the South Gauteng High Court.[41] Notably, in coming to this conclusion, the high court relied on a far older judgment. This was the 1910 case of *Spies v. Vorster*, in which the Supreme Court of South Africa held that a rule called the "newspaper rule" applied in the country. This is a common law rule dating from the late nineteenth century, which protects journalists from disclosing their source at a preliminary stage in defamation litigation. *Spies v. Vorster* shows that the norm of journalistic source protection was well established by the time it was heard. A hundred years ago, Henry Bale, chief justice of Natal, said that confidential relationships between newspaper editors and correspondents had "existed for generations."[42]

The Arab World

Norms of journalistic source protection have been noted by Posetti in Sudan, Algeria, and Syria.[43] Agnès Callamard has critiqued proposed laws of journalistic source protection that were—at the time of her writing—proposed in Iraq, and Article 19 undertook a similar task with regard to Tunisia.[44]

Asia and the Pacific

There are many instances of source protection being recognized in Asian and Pacific countries, but China, a country of enormous influence, does not protect journalistic sources in law.[45] This is in contrast to the position of the Special Administrative Region of Hong Kong, which provides a regimen for the special protection of journalistic material with features similar to the UK's Police and Criminal Evidence Act 1984.[46] Hong Kong case law has endorsed the importance of press freedom and source protection,[47] and the Court of the First Instance has declined to order the disclosure of footage of protests that was recorded by television news crews.[48]

In Australia, by 2016, six out of nine jurisdictions (Australian Capital Territory, New South Wales, Tasmania, Victoria, Western Australia, and the federal jurisdiction) had shield laws to protect journalistic sources.[49] In New Zealand, section 68 of the Evidence Act 2006 provides a qualified protection for journalists and their employers, which may be overcome by the order of a high court judge if certain tests are met. A journalist is defined by the section as "a person who in the normal course of that person's work may be given information by an informant in the expectation that the information may be published in a news medium." This enabled the High Court of New Zealand, in 2014, to find that a blogger qualified for journalistic source protection.[50]

In Singapore, the common law newspaper rule (mentioned earlier in relation to South Africa) has been disavowed,[51] but the Singapore Court of Appeal has found that the law nevertheless protects journalists' sources; it even extended this protection to a blogger—although the blogger was formerly an institutional journalist.[52] In Malaysia, the federal court has upheld the decision of a lower court in a defamation action that a journalist did not have to reveal his source.[53]

Europe

Journalistic sources are commonly protected in European jurisdictions. The jurisdiction with the longest pedigree of providing constitutional protection to the press is Sweden, which in 1766 passed the Freedom of the Press Act.[54] More modern source protection law can be found in chapter 3 of the 1949 Freedom of the Press Act and in chapter 3 of the 1991 Fundamental Law of Freedom of Expression, part of the Swedish constitution. They may not be waived by a journalist—indeed, if a journalist intentionally or negligently reveals the identity of a source against the source's wishes, the journalist may be imprisoned. Traditional publishers are covered by these protections, but those who publish news from new platforms—such as websites—need to apply for a "certificate of no legal impediment to publication" to benefit.[55]

Many other European countries have legal provisions that protect journalistic sources; examples include Norway,[56] Germany,[57] France,[58] Portugal,[59] Switzerland,[60] and Ireland.[61] The UK rules that protect journalists' sources can be traced back to the 1888 authority of *Hennessy v. Wright (no. 2)*, mentioned earlier, which established the "newspaper rule." The enduring influence of this on contemporary judgments in South Africa and Singapore has been noted. The rule provides a limited protection for journalists' sources and holds that a publisher will not be ordered to reveal their source during the pretrial stage of a defamation action.[62] There was some thought that the protection it afforded might be more extensive. But in 1981, the House of Lords, in *British Steel Corporation v. Granada Television*, confined the rule to interlocutory actions in defamation, and explicitly ruled out "the contention that newspapers enjoyed . . . a privileged position."

Concern that this precedent provided insufficient protection for journalists and their sources led to the passing of the current section 10 of the Contempt of Court Act 1981.[63] This provision, still in force, protects journalists from having to reveal their sources, unless it is necessary in the interest of justice, national security, the prevention of disorder, or the prevention of crime. However, section 10 has proved to be a relatively weak protection for British journalists, and the ECtHR has found on more than one occasion that British judges, using this provision, have been insufficiently protective of journalists' Article 10 rights.[64] This has led to the present position, in which UK judges interpret section 10 in line with the way the ECtHR interprets Article 10 in these questions.[65]

North America

The position in the United States has prompted extensive discussion. The basic position, though, is that, unlike the postitions of the ECtHR and Sweden, the U.S. Supreme Court has declined to find that journalistic source protection is a constitutional right derived from the First Amendment.[66] That said, some commentators—even some judges—are not convinced that this is the final word on the matter.[67] Nonetheless, a variety of U.S. states (thirty-seven, according to Posetti) have passed some type of shield laws to protect journalistic sources, and the passing of a federal shield law has been discussed.[68] Some states have extended source protection beyond institutional journalists, to include bloggers.[69] There also are other guidelines and regulations that seek to protect journalists' sources.[70]

The Canadian Supreme Court has likewise rejected the notion that protection of journalists' sources is a constitutional right.[71] It recognized that there could be an immunity, but said that this should be decided on a case-by-case basis.[72] However, in 2017, Canada passed the Journalistic Source Protection Act, which amends the Canada Evidence Act and "allows journalists to not disclose information or a document that identifies or is likely to identify a journalistic source unless the information or document cannot be obtained by any other reasonable means and the public interest in the administration of justice outweighs the public interest."[73] Mexico also has a shield law, which provides that a journalist can only reveal a source's identity with their consent.[74] Additionally, Posetti describes three Mexican states as having introduced protection for journalists' sources since this law was passed.[75]

South America and the Caribbean

David Banisar reported, in 2007, that "the recognition of protection of journalistic sources is generally respected in Latin America both at the regional and local levels. Most countries have adopted constitutional or legal protections which give a strong level of legal protection."[76] Discussing a few examples is useful.

In Brazil, anonymity is forbidden under Article 5(4) of the constitution, but Article 5(14) provides that "the confidentiality of the source shall be safeguarded, whenever necessary to the professional activity."[77] In Ecuador, the Organic Communications Law was passed in 2013, with a provision that protects journalistic sources. The law as a whole has been criticized in general, and commentators have found fault with the provision that protects sources.[78] The

Dominican Republic has also brought in source protection laws in Article 49(3) of a new constitution, but there are concerns that it has not proved to be effective.[79] Source protection laws also exist in Colombia, and here the Constitutional Court has delivered a judgment that upheld them.[80]

A GLOBAL NORM?

Origins and Contemporary Development

There have been confidential relationships between sources of information and the people who gather information for millennia, across many different cultures. In Europe, some confidential relationships have been protected for centuries, as legal norms that protect confidential relationships had arisen by the late sixteenth century.[81] These early rules protected lawyer–client confidentiality.

One specific class of confidential relationship between information supplier and gatherer concerns what we now call news. The process of gathering and disseminating news had evolved by the fifteenth century into professional networks that primarily served the needs of commerce and business.[82] With the introduction of printing into Europe, these networks expanded greatly, and in the sixteenth century they served a wider public. By the late seventeenth century, the mass production and dissemination of news was well established. More research is needed into the early days of mass journalism to know how early a norm of journalistic source protection developed, but it did not seem to evolve as early as other norms of confidentiality.

However, what we do know is that by the mid-eighteenth century, the first European laws to protect the press, Sweden's Freedom of the Press Act, were passed, followed by the First Amendment to the U.S. Constitution (though scholars dispute whether this was intended to protect the institution of journalism or the right of individuals to print their words). By the nineteenth century, some European countries had limited laws designed to protect journalistic confidences in some contexts;[83] indeed, by the early years of the twentieth century, a South African court recognized that norms to protect some aspects of journalistic confidentiality had "existed for generations" in the common law.[84]

By the late twentieth century, these norms had become conceived as related to, or extended from, fundamental rights guarantees, specifically the right to freedom of expression. In 1986, the OSCE Concluding Document of the Vienna Meeting linked respect for journalistic professional confidentiality with the

International Covenant on Civil and Political Rights and the Universal Declaration of Human Rights. In 1994, the Fourth Ministerial Conference of the Council of Europe, the European Parliament of the European Union, and the American Hemisphere Conference on Free Speech, in its Chapultepec Declaration, all made declarations about the importance of journalistic source protection.[85] In 1996, the European Court of Human Rights handed down its influential ruling in *Goodwin v. UK*, which recognized journalistic source protection as an aspect of Article 10 of the European Convention on Human Rights.[86] It is against this background that the laws described here have evolved.

Does a Norm Exist?

This very brief history and the survey that preceded it provide a cogent case that there is a global norm of journalistic source protection. It is clear that journalistic source protection concerns are reflected in a wide variety of different international, regional, and national laws across the globe. But there still can be room for doubt that there is a global norm. This is for at least two reasons. One problem with such a suggestion arises because there are differences in the nature and substance of the rules that protect journalistic sources. A second is that there are differences in how the norm is applied and enforced.

Differences in Scope

The first point can be rephrased by asking whether the differences that exist in the scope and strength of the laws described here undermine the case that there is a global norm. The better answer is that they do not. It will be useful to set out some of the major differences, before explaining why.

One significant difference in the scope of source protection norms concerns to whom they apply; another relates to the activity to which they apply.

WHOM DOES THE NORM COVER?

Some laws and rules confine protection to institutional journalists working for news organizations; others extend them to functional journalists—independent bloggers, nongovernmental organizations, and the like—who perform tasks similar to the tasks of institutional journalists. This latter approach is particularly evident in common law jurisdictions, which seem hesitant to afford special privileges of source protection to institutional journalists.[87] This can be seen in the UK's *British Steel Corporation v. Granada Television* decision, the U.S. decision of *Branzburg v. Hayes*, the Canadian decision of *R. v. National Post*, and the

New Zealand decision of *Slater v. Bloomfield.* Part of this wariness is conceptual—the concern being that institutional journalists should be conceived as merely utilizing the right of freedom of expression that is vouchsafed to every individual. That means it is inappropriate to consider them a "priestly class."[88] Another concern is that recognition as a special class may actually harm journalists and journalism.[89]

Others raise the difficulties of drawing a line: How does one legitimately distinguish an institutional journalist—who might write rubbish—from a blogger—who might be a valuable source of news and social commentary?[90] In the words of Millar and Scott, "It might be thought that the key issue today is whether the person is collating then disseminating information and ideas of public importance."[91] It would follow that the norm should be applicable to a wider group of people than institutional journalists. Connected to this is the question of how one can privilege institutional journalists without raising the specter of *licensing* journalists, which is to be avoided on the grounds that it permits the state an unacceptable amount of control over the flow of information.[92]

By contrast, other jurisdictions consider it appropriate to confine source protection rights to institutional journalists. The Committee of Ministers and Parliamentary Assembly of the Council of Europe, for example, recommends confining source protection laws to professional journalists,[93] and source protection laws in Sweden are somewhat confined in their application. This approach might tentatively be associated with civil law countries. The view here is that it is not objectionable per se for journalists to be subject to a registration scheme—such a scheme may, for example, be a means of ensuring professional journalistic standards. It does not necessarily lead to unacceptable control by the state over the flow of information; indeed, it may be a means of preventing unacceptable *private* control over the flow of information.[94]

Perhaps the traditional common law approach generates as many problems as it solves. Lines will still need to be drawn, and we will need to ask which bloggers deserve source protection rights and which do not. If we do not draw lines, then, as Clay Shirky puts the point: "If anyone can be a publisher, then anyone can be a journalist . . . If anyone can be a journalist, then journalistic privilege suddenly becomes a loophole too large to be borne by society."[95] If everyone is special, no one is special. In contrast, confining the protection to professional journalists, however they are defined, merely places the line in a different place—one that, moreover, as Frederick Schauer has argued, may be easier to determine.[96]

Connected to this is another issue: the question of who can waive the obligation to protect his or her source.[97] Some opinions in American courts have held that any privilege belongs to the reporter, not to the source. A consequence of this might be that the source cannot waive their right to be kept anonymous but the reporter can.[98] This may also be the position in the United Kingdom's interpretation of Article 10 of the European Convention on Human Rights,[99] but may not be the view of the European Court itself.[100] In any event, it is not true elsewhere. In Sweden, for example, as has been discussed, a journalist will commit a criminal offense if they intentionally or negligently name their source.[101] The Canadian Supreme Court considers the matter unresolved.[102]

WHAT ACTIVITY DOES THE NORM COVER?

The other differences of scope that exist in different source protection norms concern the activity the laws cover. Different jurisdictions have different rules about how far source protection laws should extend along the chain of activities that leads to a journalistic report—specifically, whether sources should be protected when the information they provide is used by the journalist for background as opposed to being used more directly in the reporting of a story. This is an issue that divides the U.S. Supreme Court from the ECtHR. In *Goodwin*[103] the ECtHR assumed, and the dissenting judges did not demur, that Article 10 was indeed engaged when a source provided information for background.[104] In contrast, the U.S. Supreme Court appears to distinguish between news gathering (the collection of news) and reporting (the communication of it) and suggests that the First Amendment does not cover source protection when information is collected for the purpose of news gathering.[105]

Differences in Strength

Another type of difference is the *strength* with which laws protect journalistic sources. The ECtHR sees source protection as an element of fundamental rights, and source protection is part of the constitutions of Brazil, Colombia, the Dominican Republic, and Sweden.[106] By contrast, the U.S. Supreme Court and the Canadian Supreme Court decline to treat journalistic sources as constitutionally protected but do protect them in statutory law. Those jurisdictions that provide constitutional law protection for source protection may be seen as protecting it in a stronger way than those that protect it by passing particular statutes.

A related but distinct difference in strength can be identified in the way in which courts approach specific dilemmas about whether to compel the revelation of a journalistic source. This difference derives from how judges reason, rather than from the formal classification of laws. Frederick Schauer distinguishes between courts that adopt a rule-based approach to resolving such dilemmas and those that adopt an act-balancing approach.[107] The difference between the two is that a rule-based approach lays more emphasis on the benefits that arise from source protection per se when it conflicts with other norms, because society benefits from the fact that journalistic source protection exists, even if, in particular cases, it may cause harm. In contrast, the act-balancing approach looks at the facts as they arise in the particular case and concentrates on how a dilemma should be resolved with reference to the balance of harm in the case in question. As an example of these types of judicial reasoning, George Hwang has described how the Singapore Court of Appeal has rejected a rule-based approach.[108]

Act-based approaches can chill journalistic freedom, as a journalist may not know in advance of a hearing whether the courts will protect his or her source in a particular instance. This uncertainty may inhibit a journalist from offering a source protection—or even from investigating a story in the first place.

Do the Differences Make a Difference?

It is evident that there are significant differences in the scope and strength of the laws of journalistic source protection. This raises the prospect that, if there is widespread formal recognition of a norm of source protection in name yet insufficient similarity in how sources should be protected in substance, it does not make sense to say a norm exists.

The better view is that there are sufficient commonalities in substance to say that there exists a global source protection norm. Confirmation of this can be found in the frequent existence of situations in which a legal rule exists that prevents an otherwise valid judicial order to compel disclosure of a journalist's source, on the grounds that it *is* a journalist's source. This, it will be remembered, is how Brabyn defined the norm. In other words, despite the differences identified here, the shared view across the jurisdictions surveyed is that it is appropriate for journalistic sources to be protected to some extent from the normal process of the law. The localized differences among jurisdictions relate to what that "extent" should be.

Enforcement

Nonetheless, there is a need for caution. The differences that have been identified indicate that great care is required, so that such a conclusion does not lead to the view that conduct is regulated by the norm in the same way throughout the world. The concern is that, while there may be formal rules, if no one follows them or they can be easily avoided, then it is doubtful whether a global norm can be said to exist. For instance, Posetti reports that "the laws in most of the Arab countries are in favor of source protection, yet in practice the matter is different"; despite the existence of such laws, journalists are sometimes required to reveal the identity of their sources under emergency laws, or on the premise of fighting terrorism.[109]

It is important to recognize that the adoption of a formal law of source protection may actually impede the adherence to a norm. This is because a country may be able to avoid international scrutiny and pressure by pointing to the fact that they have adopted a formal law, and they may claim that this law is a testament to their adherence to the norm of source protection, even while, in reality, they afford no—or no sufficient—protection to journalists and their sources on the ground. Adoption of a formal law, in other words, may provide a shield against diplomatic pressure or a smokescreen behind which a state can hide. It may help the state to resist pressure to encourage the recognition of a norm and to resist efforts to ensure that it actually does protect journalists and their sources.

The issue is not confined to the situation in the Middle East. Research by Judith Townend and this author indicates widespread instances of technology facilitating hidden circumvention of source protection laws in various jurisdictions, including in the Global North.[110] States hide behind the existence of formal laws of source protection, all the while acting in ways that breach journalistic confidentiality. This happens because, among other things, the technological protections available for sources have not kept pace with the ability of states and other actors to use technology to intercept or monitor communications. There are many examples of this having taken place.[111]

Do the Evasions Negate the Norm?

Do these points undermine the claim that there is a global norm? They establish that it is frequently not clear how, or to what extent, a journalist can expect to protect his or her source, even where there is a formal law of source protection. Where this happens, it makes no sense to assert that there is a substantive global norm. The most that can be said is that many states and international organizations pay lip service to a formal global norm.

However, the fact that the norm may not be observed and enforced does not necessarily mean that the norm does not exist. It may just mean that it exists but is being violated, and mere violation of a norm does not negate it. Whether a norm is or is not negated is a question of judgment, an assessment of whether the extent of violation is such that a norm has been sucked dry. This is a judgment that ideally should be based on empirical work, to find out how extensive any problems of enforcement are. Such empirical research is beyond the scope of this chapter. However, the author's view is that it is likely that the violations that undoubtedly exist are not so serious or of such an extent as to undermine the thesis that a global norm of journalistic source protection exists.

CONCLUSION

This chapter has demonstrated that legislators and judges across the globe have recognized that a norm of journalistic source protection can be of value to society. The chapter outlines the differences that exist in the scope, strength, and enforcement of laws that protect journalists' sources. But the conclusion is that these differences do not undermine the thesis that there is a global norm of journalistic source protection of the type identified at the beginning of the chapter.

Nonetheless, the last word should be a caveat: even while we recognize this development, it also is important to recognize that progress is not inevitable. As Monroe Price and Nicole Stremlau wrote in their 2018 global survey, "Throughout the globe, journalism-related source protection laws have been increasingly at risk of erosion, restriction and compromise in the digital era."[112]

NOTES

The author gratefully acknowledges the invaluable comments made by Dr. Judith Townend, Professor Monroe Price, and Dr. Agnès Callamard on earlier drafts of this chapter. He also has drawn on the illuminating discussion that took place at Columbia University in September 2017 as preparation for this book. Errors remain his own.

1. Sources may be confidential, where the journalist knows their identity, or anonymous, where he or she does not. The distinction is not relevant, though, to the current discussion.
2. Professional codes of ethics frequently contain provisions to protect journalists' sources, most notably principle 6 of the International Federation of Journalists'

Declaration of Principles on the Conduct of Journalists, https://www.ifj.org/media-centre/news/detail/category/europe/article/status-of-journalists-and-journalism-ethics-ifj-principles.html. See also Julie Posetti, *Protecting Journalism Sources in the Digital Age* (Paris: UNESCO, 2017).

3. Janice Brabyn, "Protection Against Judicially Compelled Disclosure of the Identity of News Gatherers' Confidential Sources in Common Law Jurisdictions," *Modern Law Review* 69 (2006): 902.

4. David Banisar, *Silencing Sources: An International Survey of Protections and Threats to Journalists' Sources* (London: Privacy International, 2007); and Posetti, *Protecting Journalism Sources.*

5. United Nations Human Rights Council, "Resolution on the Safety of Journalists," A/HRC/21/L.6 (2012), numbered para. 3.

6. United Nations Educational, Scientific and Cultural Organization (UNESCO), "Resolution on Internet-Related Issues: Including Access to Information and Knowledge, Freedom of Expression, Privacy and Ethical Dimensions of the Information Society," General Conference, 37th session, November 2013. See also UNESCO, *Outcome Document of the "CONNECTing the Dots: Options for Future Action" Conference*, March 3–4, 2015, 6.2, https://en.unesco.org/sites/default/files/234090e-1.pdf.

7. Abid Hussain, *Report of the Special Rapporteur, Mr. Abid Hussain, Submitted Pursuant to Commission on Human Rights Resolution 1997/26*, E/CN.4/1998/40 (1998), 17.

8. Frank La Rue, *Report of the Special Rapporteur on the Promotion and Protection of the Right to Freedom of Opinion and Expression*, A/HRC/20/17 (2012), 109. See also La Rue, *Report of the Special Rapporteur on the Promotion and Protection of the Right of Freedom of Opinion and Expression*, A/HRC/23/40 (2013), 52; and David Kaye, *Report of the Special Rapporteur on the Promotion and Protection of the Right to Freedom of Opinion and Expression*, A/HRC/29/32 (2015), 12.

9. For example, the special rapporteur's 2015 report was referred to in the European Court of Human Rights (ECtHR) case of Becker v. Norway, application no. 21272/12 (2017), 40.

10. Frank La Rue, Miklos Haraszti, Catalina Botero, and Faith Pansy Tlakula, "Joint Declaration on Defamation of Religions, and Anti-Terrorism and Anti-Extremism Legislation" (2008), 2.

11. United Nations Human Rights Committee, "General Comment no. 34," CCPR/C/GC/34 (2011), 45.

12. Eric Barendt, *Anonymous Speech: Literature, Law and Politics* (Oxford: Hart Publishing, 2016), 102.

13. Gavin Millar and Andrew Scott argue that other rights often add little to the Article 10 analysis, but can do so on occasion. See Millar and Scott, *Newsgathering: Law, Regulation and the Public Interest* (Oxford: Oxford University Press, 2016),

14. Goodwin v. UK (1996), 22 EHRR 123, application no. 17488/90 (1996).

15. See, for example, Inter-American Commission on Human Rights (IACHR), *Violence against Journalists and Media Workers: Inter-American Standards and National Practices on Prevention, Protection and Prosecution of Perpetrators*, OEA/Ser.L/V/II CIDH/RELE/INF.12/13 (2013), 52; Burundian Journalists Union v. Attorney General of the Republic of Burundi, reference 7 of 2013, East African Court of Justice (2013), May 15, 2015, 108; and Bosasa Operation (Pty.) Ltd. v. Basson & Another, [2012] ZAGPJHC 71, 29.

16. Goodwin v. UK, 39.

17. See European Court of Human Rights Press Unit, "Protection of Journalistic Sources," Factsheet, February 2019, http://www.echr.coe.int/Documents/FS_Journalistic_sources_ENG.pdf; Council of Europe, "The Protection of Journalistic Sources, a Cornerstone of the Freedom of the Press," Thematic Factsheet, May 2017, https://rm.coe.int/factsheet-on-the-protection-of-journalistic-sources-may2017/16807178d7; and George Nicolaou, "The Protection of Journalists' Sources," in *Freedom of Expression: Essays in Honour of Nicolas Bratza*, ed. Casadevall Josep et al. (Oisterwijk: Wolf Legal Publishers, 2012). A recent case (at the time of this writing), Becker v. Norway, affirmed the importance of journalistic source protection, with the ECtHR saying that it cannot be automatically removed by a source's own conduct and even extends when the identity of the source is known.

18. See, for example, Tillack v. Belgium (2012) 55 EHRR 25, application no. 20477/05, 60.

19. Millar and Scott, *Newsgathering*, chap. 3.

20. Sanoma Uitgevers Bv v. Netherlands, application no. 38224/03, September 14, 2010.

21. Telegraaf Media Nederland Landelijke Media B.V. and Others v. the Netherlands, application no. 39315/06, November 22, 2012, 101.

22. Council of Europe Council of Ministers, "Resolution no. 2: Journalistic Freedoms and Human Rights," 4th European Ministerial Conference on Mass Media Policy, Prague, December 7–8, 1994.

23. Council of Europe Committee of Ministers, "Recommendation on the Protection of Journalists in Situations of Conflict and Tension," recommendation R(96)4 (1996).

24. Council of Europe Committee of Ministers, "Recommendation on the Right of Journalists Not to Disclose Their Sources of Information," recommendation R(2000)7 (2000), definition (a).

25. Council of Europe Committee of Ministers, "Recommendation on the Provision of Information through the Media in Relation to Criminal Proceedings," Rec(2003)13 (2003); "Declaration on Freedom of Expression and Information in the Media in the Context of the Fight against Terrorism," adopted March 2, 2005; "Guidelines on Protecting Freedom of Expression and Information in Times of Crisis," CM/Del/Dec(2007)1005/5.3 (2007), 13–14; "Declaration on the the Protection of Journalism and Safety of Journalists and Other Media Actors," adopted on April 30, 2014, 9–11; "Recommendation on the Protection of Journalism and Safety of Journalists and Other Media Actors," CM/Rec(2016)4 (2016), appendix 2, 30, 38.

26. Council of Europe Parliamentary Assembly, "Indicators for Media in a Democracy," Resolution 1636 (2008), para. 8.8; "The Protection of Journalists' Sources," Recommendation 1950 (2011), 15.

27. European Parliament, "Resolution on the Confidentiality of Journalists' Sources and the Right of Civil Servants to Disclose Information," *Official Journal of the European Communities* 94/C/44/02, 34 (1994).

28. Council of the European Union, *EU Human Rights Guidelines on Freedom of Expression Online and Offline* (2014).

29. Inter American Press Association, Hemisphere Conference on Free Speech, "Declaration of Chapultepec," adopted March 11, 1994.

30. IACHR, "Declaration of Principles on Freedom of Expression" (2000), https://www.oas.org/en/iachr/expression/showarticle.asp?artID=26&lID=1; *Violence against Journalists*, 34–36.

31. African Commission on Human and Peoples' Rights, "Declaration of Principles on Freedom of Expression in Africa" (2002).

32. See, for instance, East African Court of Justice, Burundian Journalists Union v. Attorney General of the Republic of Burundi, https://www.eacj.org/?cases=burundi-journalists-union-vs-the-attorney-general-of-the-republic-of-burundi.

33. Burundi, law no. 1/11 (June 4, 2013), amending law no. 1/025 (November 27, 2003).

34. Specifically, Article 6(d), which relates to (among other things) adherence to the principles of democracy and the provisions of the African Charter on Human and Peoples' Rights, and 7(2), which relates to (among other things) maintenance of "universally accepted standards of human rights." Article 9 of the African Charter protects freedom of information and dissemination of opinions.

35. Burundian Journalists Union v. Attorney General of the Republic of Burundi, 108.

36. Posetti, *Protecting Journalism Sources,* 8. Some of the "developments" Posetti identifies are in fact detrimental to source protection, but Posetti's work does identify a wide variety of jurisdictions across the globe that recognize journalistic source protection.

37. Hennessy v. Wright (no. 2), [1888] 24 QBD 445n.

38. Uganda, Press and Journalist Act 2000. Much of the rest of this act has been criticized; see, for example, Article 19, *Memorandum on the Press and Journalist Act and the Press and Journalist (Amendment) Bill, 2000 of Uganda* (London: Article 19, 2010).

39. Constitution of Zimbabwe, Amendment (no. 20) Act 2013, section 61(2).

40. Geoffrey Roberston, "Media Law and Ethics in Mauritius" (2013), part 7.

41. Bosasa Operation (Pty.) Ltd. v. Basson & Another.

42. Spies v. Vorster, [1910] 31 NPD 205, 218. The point was also recognized in South African common law; see Upington v. Murray and St. Leger, Buch., [1877], 31.

43. Sudan, Press and Press Printed Materials Act 2009, s 27(1)(b); Algeria, Information Code 2012, Article 85; Syria, Legislative Decree 108/2011.

44. Agnès Callamard, "Protecting Journalists in Iraq," *Guardian*, August 28, 2009, https://www.theguardian.com/commentisfree/2009/aug/28/iraq-draft-law-journalist-protection; Article 19, "Tunisia: Press Regulation," https://www.article19.org/resources.php/resource/2944/en/tunisia:-press-regulation.

45. Posetti, *Protecting Journalism Sources*, 68, 73.

46. Interpretation and General Clauses Ordinance, Cap 1, s 84; Brabyn, "Protection Against Judicially Compelled Disclosure," 913.

47. Apple Daily Ltd v. Commissioner of the Independent Commission against Corruption (no. 2), [2000] 1 HKLRD 647.

48. Commissioner of Police v. Television Broadcast Ltd., [2016] HKEC 550.

49. Posetti, *Protecting Journalism Sources*, 71.

50. High Court of New Zealand, Slater v. Blomfield, [2014] NZHC 2221.

51. Singapore, Tullett Prebon (Singapore) Ltd. v. Spring Mark Geoffrey, [2007] SGHC 71, 21.

52. James Michael Dorsey v. World Sports Group Pte. Ltd., [2014] SGCA 4 (CA). This is an illuminating judgment and will be discussed again later, as it highlights the difference between the act-based and rule-based approaches that judges can take with regard to source protection.

53. Malaysia, Datuk Seri Tiong King Sing v. Datuk Seri Ong Tee Keat and Joseph Sipalan, March 7, 2016.

54. Banisar, *Silencing Sources*, 21.

55. Discussed in Posetti, *Protecting Journalism Sources*, 113–118.

56. As discussed in relation to Becker v. Norway.

57. Germany, German Code of Criminal Procedure 1987, as amended, section 53(5).

58. Among others, France, law no. 2010-1 of January 4, 2010, Concerning the Protection of Journalists' Secret Sources.

59. Portugal, Journalist's Statute (law no. 1/99), as amended, Article 11.

60. Switzerland, Swiss Criminal Code of December 21, 1937, as amended, Article 28a.

61. Ireland, Mahon Tribunal v. Keena and Kennedy, [2010] 1 IR 336, illuminatingly discussed in Ronan Ó Fathaigh, "Keena v. Ireland and the Protection of Journalistic Sources," *Irish Journal of European Law* 19, no. 1 (1016).

62. Hennessy v. Wright (no. 2).

63. Millar and Scott, *Newsgathering*, 3.19–20.

64. Financial Times v. United Kingdom, (2010) 50 EHRR 46, application no. 821/03.

65. See, for instance, Ashworth Hospital Authority v. Mirror Group Newspapers Ltd., [2002] UKHL 29, [2002] 1 WLR 2033, 38.

66. Branzburg v. Hayes, 408 U.S. 665 (1972).

67. See the concurring judgment of Judge Tatel in re Grand Jury Subpoena, Judith Miller, 438 F3d 1141 (DC Cir 2006) (2006); David A. Anderson, "Confidential Sources Reconsidered," *Florida Law Review* 61, no. 4 (2009); and Barendt, *Anonymous Speech*, 105.

68. See, for example, the Free Flow of Information Act of 2013, discussed by Posetti, *Protecting Journalism Sources*, 91.

69. O'Grady v. Superior Court, 139 Cal. App. 4th 1423 (2006).

70. Discussed, for example, in Brabyn, "Protection Against Judicially Compelled Disclosure," 912–913; Posetti, *Protecting Journalism Sources*, 88–94.

71. Canada, R. v. National Post.

72. For a discussion, see Barendt, *Anonymous Speech*, 107–108.

73. Canada, Journalistic Sources Protection Act 2017.

74. Mexico, Federal Penal Code, Law of Journalists' Professional Secrets, Federal District, June 7, 2006, as amended, Article 243 (3).

75. Posetti, *Protecting Journalism Sources*, 100.

76. Banisar, *Silencing Sources*, 81.

77. Brazil, Constitution of the Federative Republic of Brazil, 3rd ed. (2010).

78. Ecuador, Organic Communications Law (2013). See Alejandro Martínez, "Ecuador's Controversial Communications Law in 8 Points," *Journalism in the Americas* blog, Knight Center for Journalism in the Americas, University of Texas at Austin, June 20, 2013, https://knightcenter.utexas.edu/blog/00-14071-8-highlights-understand-ecuador%E2%80%99s-controversial-communications-law.

79. Dominican Republic, Constitution of the Dominican Republic (2010). See Posetti, *Protecting Journalism Sources*, 100.

80. Constitutional Court of Colombia, Judgment on Confidentiality of Sources, judgment T-298/09 (2009).

81. Berd v. Lovelace, 21 ER 33 (1576) Cary 62 (1576).

82. Andrew Pettegree, *The Invention of News: How the World Came to Know about Itself* (New Haven, CT: Yale University Press, 2014).

83. Hennessy v. Wright (no. 2).

84. South Africa, Spies v. Vorster, [1910] 31 NPD 205.

85. Council of Europe Council of Ministers, "Resolution no. 2: Journalistic Freedoms"; European Parliament, "Resolution on the Confidentiality of Journalists' Sources"; "Chapultepec Declaration," adopted by the Hemisphere Conference on Free Speech, Mexico City, March 11, 1994.

86. Goodwin v. UK, (1996) 22 EHRR 123, application no. 17488/90 (1996).

87. This approach is not confined to common law jurisdictions. See, for example, IACHR, "Declaration of Principles on Freedom of Expression," principle 8.

88. Per Branzburg v. Hayes, 704. See also Geoffrey Robertson and Andrew G. L. Nicol, *Media Law*, 5th ed. (London: Thomson/Sweet & Maxwell, 2007), 315; and William E. Lee, "The Priestly Class: Reflections on a Journalist's Privilege," *Cardozo Arts and Entertainment Law Journal* 23 (2006).

89. See, for example, David Lange, "The Speech and Press Clauses," *UCLA Law Review* 23 (1975), 107; W. W. Van Alstyne, "The Hazards to the Press of Claiming a Preferred Position," *Hastings Law Journal* 28 (1977): 769; and Robertson and Nicol, *Media Law*, 340.

90. This point was considered a significant reason for the U.S. Supreme Court to reject a claim that journalists should have special access to convicted prisoners, in Procunier v. Martinez, 416 U.S. 396, 94 S. Ct. 1800 (1974). The British House of Lords came to a different view in R. v. Home Secretary, Ex. P. Simms, [2000] 2 AC 115.

91. Millar and Scott, *Newsgathering*, 3.14. See also Benkler, *The Wealth of Networks: How Social Production Transforms Markets and Freedom*, chap. 7; or, for example, IACHR, "Declaration of Principles on Freedom of Expression," principle 8.

92. For a discussion of the rise of newspapers after the lapse of the acts licensing newspapers, and thereby journalists, see Will Slauter, "The Rise of the Newspaper," in *Making News: The Political Economy of Journalism in Britain and America from the Glorious Revolution to the Internet*, ed. Richard John and Jonathan Silberstein-Loeb (Oxford: Oxford University Press, 2015).

93. Despite this, the ECtHR has recognized that nongovernmental organizations can act as societal watchdogs, equivalent to journalists, and have extended to them journalistic protection as well as ethical duties of verification. See, for example, Medžlis Islamske Zajednice Brčko and Others v. Bosnia and Herzegovina, [2017] ECHR 608, application no. 17224/11.

94. "Licensing of Media Workers," Article 19, https://www.article19.org/pages/en/licensing-of-media-workers.html. Note, also, that outside the United States, broadcast journalist institutions are frequently subject to licensing and content

regulation. See Owen Fiss, "Why the State?," in *Democracy and the Mass Media*, ed. Judith Lichtenberg (Cambridge: Cambridge University Press, 1990).

95. Clay Shirky, *Here Comes Everybody* (London: Penguin, 2008), 71–72.

96. Frederick Schauer, "Towards an Institutional First Amendment," *Minneapolis Law Review* 89 (2005). Barendt suggests a positive rationale for affording institutional journalists special source protection rights; see Barendt, *Anonymous Speech* (chapter 5).

97. Brabyn, "Protection Against Judicially Compelled Disclosure," 904.

98. In re Grand Jury Subpoena (Judith Miller), 438 F3d 1138 (D.C. Cir. 2006) (2005), concurring judgment of Judge Taltel, 1177.

99. United Kingdom, R. v. Norman, [2016] EWCA Crim. 1564, 33.

100. Becker v. Norway.

101. Becker v. Norway, 32.

102. R. v. National Post, 44.

103. Goodwin v. UK. This strand is also present in other ECtHR cases. For example, it was attested to in Satakunnan Markkinapörssi Oy and Satamedia Oy v. Finland, Grand Chamber, June 27, 2017, 175; Selmani v. Former Yugoslav Republic of Macedonia, First Section, February 9, 2017, 75 (regarding a fight in a legislature, where the press bench was cleared); and Brambilla v. Italy, First Section, June 23, 2016 (regarding journalists eavesdropping on police radio). In Brambilla v. Italy, no breach was found, but see the concurring opinion of Judge Spano, 2.

104. Millar and Scott, *Newsgathering*, 3.07 and note 11, raise the possibility that the decision might have been different, had the UK government argued the point.

105. Branzburg v. Hayes, 681–682.

106. An argument can be advanced that the United Kingdom affords source protection of a constitutional nature, despite the UK not having a written constitution, on the grounds that case law has aligned the interpretation of section 10 of the Contempt of Court Act 1981 with Article 10 of the European Convention on Human Rights. The convention operates as a higher-order form of law in the UK, by virtue of the Human Rights Act (1998).

107. Frederick Schauer, "Who Decides?," in *Democracy and the Mass Media*, ed. Judith Lichtenberg (Cambridge: Cambridge University Press, 1990).

108. George Hwang, "Confidentiality of Journalists' Sources in Singapore: Silence Is Not Golden," in *Media Law and Policy in the Internet Age*, ed. Dorren Weisenhaus and Simon Young (Oxford: Hart Publishing, 2017).

109. Posetti, *Protecting Journalism Sources*, 65.

110. Judith Townend and Richard Danbury, *Protecting Sources and Whistleblowers in a Digital Age* (London: Information Law and Policy Centre, Institute of Advanced Legal Studies, 2017).

111. Some (through 2017) are set out in the time line available at Information Law and Policy Centre, "Source Protection Report and Resources," https://infolawcentre .blogs.sas.ac.uk/source-protection-report-2017.

112. Monroe Price and Nicole Stremlau, *World Trends in Freedom of Expression and Media Development: Global Report 2017/18* (Paris: UNESCO, 2018).

Intergovernmental Institutions and
International Actors as Norm Entrepreneurs

PART II

The Norm Entrepreneurship
of the United Nations

TARLACH MCGONAGLE AND

EMMANUEL VARGAS PENAGOS

The United Nations makes for a very interesting case study on the cultivation and promotion of global norms of freedom of expression. This is not because the UN has had unmitigated success in that regard (it hasn't!) but because it has succeeded in developing a diverse range of norms over the years, sometimes in the face of considerable ideological resistance and bureaucratic wrangling. It provides many examples of norm entrepreneurship and norm antipreneurship; norm cascades and norm trickles; norm bandwagons that have trundled forward into uncharted terrain and norm bandwagons that have simply gotten stuck in the mud.

This chapter begins with an overview of the UN system for the protection and promotion of the right to freedom of expression. It then explores the UN's norms of freedom of expression through a structure that reflects three broad phases in the development of freedom of expression and information at the UN. Each period "is denoted by its key features or aspirations: trail-blazing, consolidation and expansion, and the quest for coherence and consistency."[1] The trail-blazing period was characterized by the development and setting of norms. The period of consolidation and expansion was characterized by the interpretation, application, and widening of norms. The quest for coherence and consistency has emerged organically from the ongoing interpretation, application, and widening of norms. In parallel to these periods, UN norms have been—and continue to be—exported. The chapter will conclude with a reflection on the difficulty of gauging whether the UN's normative standards on freedom of expression have really been "internalized" at the global level. To this end, the uptake by regional human rights courts of UN standards on freedom of expression will be briefly examined.[2]

THE UN SYSTEM FOR FREEDOM OF EXPRESSION

The UN has developed an elaborate international system for the protection and promotion of human rights. Within that system, it is possible to discern a system for the protection and promotion of freedom of expression. That "system within a system" forms the backdrop to the present chapter.

The UN system for freedom of expression comprises principles and rights, as enshrined in treaty law and developed in jurisprudence; state reporting/monitoring mechanisms; political and policy-making standards; and specialized procedures or actors. But the system is not neat and tidy or symmetrical. Each of the instruments and mechanisms has its own objectives and emphases and/or mandates and working methods. Each has its place in the system due to the overall "unity of purpose and operation."[3] This system could even be described as a complex adaptive system. It is complex due to its composition of instruments and actors and the interplay between them, and it is adaptive to ever-changing internal political priorities and external political and sociocultural circumstances, at the national and international levels.

Figure 6.1 provides a visual representation of the main treaties that make up the UN system for the protection of freedom of expression, which will be introduced here. In penumbra of these treaties is a supplementary set of political standards,[4] and various intra-institutional bodies and actors that contribute on an ongoing basis to the development of the right to freedom of expression. These include specialized agencies of the UN, such as the UN Educational, Scientific and Cultural Organization (UNESCO), and specialized mandates, especially the UN Special Rapporteur on Freedom of Opinion and Expression. There is dynamic interplay between the treaties, the political standards, and the various institutional actors, which contributes to the realization of the right to freedom of expression in practice.

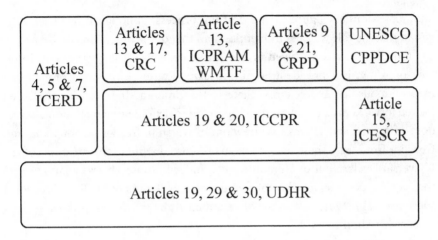

Figure 6.1 A visual representation of the main treaties that make up the United Nations system for the protection of freedom of expression.

Trailblazing

The fledgling UN organization was very conducive to norm entrepreneurship. The break with the League of Nations, compounded by the horrific crimes against humanity of World War II, engendered a new international order. Space opened up for political vision, leadership, and initiative, all of which could be channeled into norm-setting activities. Professor Raphael Lemkin epitomized such norm entrepreneurship. He coined the term "genocide"[5] and was centrally involved in the drafting of the Convention on the Prevention and Punishment of the Crime of Genocide. Indeed, such was the nature of his involvement and his incessant lobbying to have genocide recognized as an international crime that he has been referred to as "the father of the convention." John P. Humphrey has written, "Never in the history of the United Nations has one private individual conducted such a lobby."[6]

Other examples of norm entrepreneurship in the early days of the UN involved collective endeavors by groups of individuals, such as the drafting of the Universal Declaration of Human Rights. The key makers and shapers in the drafting process were John P. Humphrey (a Canadian who was the first director of the Division of Human Rights at the UN Secretariat), Eleanor Roosevelt (U.S. delegate to the UN and former first lady of the United States), and Charles Malik (Lebanese delegate to the UN). René Cassin (a French human rights lawyer) was another prominent figure in the drafting process, although it has been suggested that his role was less influential than that of the other three.[7]

Others were also involved in the drafting exercise. The posthumous influence of former U.S. president Franklin Delano Roosevelt is worthy of mention; in his famous "Four Freedoms" State of the Union address of 1941, Roosevelt looked forward to "a world founded upon four essential human freedoms": freedom of speech and expression, freedom of worship, freedom from want, and freedom from fear. These four freedoms resonate loudly in the preamble of the Universal Declaration of Human Rights. Indeed, Roosevelt was adamant that the four freedoms should be enjoyed universally. Drafts of his Four Freedoms speech reveal how he deliberately strengthened the references in the speech to "everywhere in the world."[8]

It is beyond the scope of this chapter to mention all of the personalities involved in the various drafting processes that we will discuss.[9] Instead, the emphasis will be on the institutional aspects and dynamics of norm entrepreneurship.

Conference on Freedom of Information

The UN's first foray into norm setting with respect to freedom of expression (or freedom of information, to use the institutional jargon of the day) could be described as an example of "norm implosion," or a norm bandwagon that got stuck in the proverbial mud.

In one of its earliest resolutions, the UN General Assembly affirmed the fundamental importance of freedom of information, famously describing it as the "touchstone" of all other human rights.[10] The main purpose of the resolution was to call for an international conference on freedom of information, which was held in Geneva in the spring of 1948. John P. Humphrey, as director of the UN's Division of Human Rights, was at the helm.

The concrete output of the conference comprised three draft conventions (most notably a draft Convention on Freedom of Information), draft articles on freedom of information for inclusion in the International Bill of Rights, and forty-three resolutions on different aspects of freedom of information.[11] As such, the conference was regarded at the time as "a great success"[12] and afterwards as a "high point in the United Nations discussions of freedom of information."[13] However, the high expectations raised by the conference failed to be realized in its political aftermath.[14] Although the text of the draft convention had been agreed upon in Geneva in 1948, it was not opened for signature and ratification then and there. Instead, a political decision was made to refer all three draft conventions to the Economic and Social Council for "study," and to all governments invited to the conference for "comments."[15] The council would then "examine" the draft conventions "in light of" governmental comments before submitting them to the UN General Assembly for approval, prior to opening them for signature by states. It was thought that such a step would lend greater "prestige and authority" to the draft conventions.[16]

However, according to Humphrey, this strategy backfired badly. The step to seek extra validation meant that the adoption of the draft conventions was postponed. This gave opponents of the draft Convention on Freedom of Information (in particular) time to mobilize, and Cold War politics then quickly froze any prospect of progress toward its adoption and ratification.

The conference's centerpiece, the draft Convention on Freedom of Information, was never adopted, and most of its resolutions failed to achieve any lasting impact. In this sense, the 1948 conference can be described as an example of norm implosion inasmuch as the content of the norms had been agreed upon but the extra political step of consultation nipped the prospect of norm expansion in the bud. It would be unfair, however, to regard the conference as a total failure. It did, after all, provide the drafters of the Universal Declaration of Human Rights (UDHR) and the International Covenant on Civil and Political Rights (ICCPR) with texts for freedom of expression provisions that were very close to the formulas that were ultimately adopted.[17]

Universal Declaration of Human Rights

December 10, 1948, is widely heralded as the day on which the foundation stone of modern international human rights law was laid. The UN General Assembly's adoption of the UDHR on that date was undoubtedly a momentous achievement. While the adoption of the declaration was historic, its initial importance was primarily (and merely) symbolic.[18] It was a political declaration itemizing a range of human rights that should collectively become a common standard of achievement for all peoples and nations. It created moral rather than legal obligations for states.

The drafters of the UDHR appreciated the historical significance of the achievement, but they also appreciated the enormity of the task that they had set in the text of the UDHR—to progressively but ultimately secure the universal realization of all the rights that it enumerated.

A parsing of the preamble of the UDHR reveals its gritty determination to categorically reject and prevent the repetition of the "disregard and contempt for human rights [that] have resulted in barbarous acts which have outraged the conscience of mankind." The UDHR was intended to lay the foundations for "a world in which human beings shall enjoy freedom of speech and belief and freedom from fear and want has been proclaimed as the highest aspiration of the common people." It was also intended as "a common standard of achievement for all peoples and all nations, to the end that every individual and every organ of society, keeping this declaration constantly in mind, shall strive by teaching and education to promote respect for these rights and freedoms and by progressive measures, national and international, to secure their universal and effective recognition and observance, both among the peoples of Member States themselves and among the peoples of territories under their jurisdiction."

The drafters of the UDHR can be regarded as a very particular type of norm entrepreneurs—real trailblazers, who blended together creativity and advocacy at the drafting table, in the corridors of power and in salons.[19] Their task to develop a new norm was explicit, and it gave them a legitimacy and a novelty of purpose rarely enjoyed by later norm entrepreneurs within the UN system. They were not encumbered by the need to build on, dismantle, or overcome preexisting norms. The tabula rasa nature of their drafting exercise meant that they could expend their energies on developing creative endeavors rather than facing down resistant forces. This gave them room to think outside of boxes instead of having to cram their ambitions and ideas into preexisting, normative boxes.

Already referenced in the preamble, the right to freedom of expression is enshrined in UDHR Article 19, which is the best-known free expression provision in any international instrument. There is great power in the succinct, simple formulation of the right: "Everyone has the right to freedom of opinion and expression; this right includes freedom to hold opinions without interference and to seek, receive and impart information and ideas through any media and regardless of frontiers."

This crisp formulation creates a sense of boundless potential and élan, but Article 19 must be read in conjunction with Articles 29 and 30 of the UDHR. Article 29 refers to the duties and responsibilities that govern the exercise of the rights enumerated in the declaration, while Article 30 is a prohibition of abuse of rights clause, designed to prevent any provisions in the declaration from being invoked in a manner contrary to its letter or spirit.

UDHR Article 19 is without a doubt the firmest foundation stone in the UN's normative architecture for the protection of freedom of expression (see figure 6.1). A drawn-out drafting process to complete the International Bill of Rights (comprising the UDHR, ICCPR, and International Covenant on Economic, Social and Cultural Rights) followed; it lasted until 1966, which was a very lengthy interlude for such an urgent project. Be that as it may, once the normative cogs finally started turning, they did so firmly.

The first UN treaty to reference and take cognizance of UDHR Article 19 was the International Convention on the Elimination of All Forms of Racial Discrimination (ICERD). ICERD trammels the scope of the right to freedom of expression in order to pursue its driving aim, the prevention of racial discrimination. ICERD has been widely perceived as an outlier among other international human rights treaties that contain provisions governing the relationship between freedom of expression and hate speech, because ICERD Article 4 creates more far-reaching obligations for states parties than comparable provisions in other treaties.[20]

CONSOLIDATION AND EXPANSION

If Article 19's relationship with ICERD appears essentially corrective, its relationship with other UN treaties is clearly more constructive and creative. UDHR Article 19 was the blueprint for ICCPR Article 19. The latter is a more seasoned version of the former. ICCPR Article 19 also integrates the special duties and responsibilities governing the exercise of the right, as well as certain permissible limitations on the right. It reads:

1. Everyone shall have the right to hold opinions without interference.
2. Everyone shall have the right to freedom of expression; this right shall include freedom to seek, receive and impart information and ideas of all kinds, regardless of frontiers, either orally, in writing or in print, in the form of art, or through any other media of his choice.
3. The exercise of the rights provided for in paragraph 2 of this article carries with it special duties and responsibilities. It may therefore be subject to certain restrictions, but these shall only be such as are provided by law and are necessary:
   (a) for respect of the rights or reputations of others;
   (b) for the protection of national security or of public order (ordre public), or of public health or morals.

Article 19 should be read in conjunction with Article 20—its would-be "fourth paragraph"[21] or "*lex specialis.*"[22] Article 20 limits the right to freedom of expression by requiring states parties to the covenant to prohibit by law propaganda for war as well as advocacy of different types of hatred "that constitutes incitement to discrimination, hostility or violence."[23]

With its more detailed provisions and its legally binding character, ICCPR Article 19 built on the foundation stone of UDHR Article 19, and it appears to have surpassed its progenitor in respect of the influence it has had on new norm setting. It has served both as a source of inspiration and as a model for many comparable provisions in other treaties. For instance, Article 13 of the Convention on the Rights of the Child (CRC), adopted in 1989,[24] and Article 13 of the 1990 International Convention on the Protection of the Rights of All Migrant Workers and Members of Their Families[25] are almost carbon copies of ICCPR Article 19. CRC Article 13 omits the reference to "special duties and responsibilities" that is central in ICCPR Article 19, and Article 13 of the convention on migrant workers essentially merges ICCPR Articles 19 and 20 into one article.

Beyond these important steps in the consolidation of the Article 19s of UDHR and ICCPR as the leading normative standard for freedom of expression across the UN, institutional attention inevitably began to seek out new frontiers for the norm. New treaties provided an ideal opportunity to stretch the still-growing normative standard in different directions. Such strategic stretching was intended to apply the general norm in a way that would reflect situational specificities with respect to different themes or groups of beneficiaries.

In the CRC, as already mentioned, Article 13 is the hard-core freedom of expression provision. Article 17, however, develops specific emphases of the right to freedom of expression of children. It acknowledges and explores the instrumental role of the media in providing particular types of content that are necessary or suitable for children. Recognizing the important function of the mass media, it calls on state parties to:

(a) encourage the mass media to disseminate information and material of social and cultural benefit to the child . . .;

(b) encourage international cooperation in the production, exchange and dissemination of such information and material from a diversity of cultural, national, and international sources;

(c) encourage the production and dissemination of children's books;

(d) encourage the mass media to have particular regard to the linguistic needs of the child who belongs to a minority group or who is indigenous; and

(e) encourage the development of appropriate guidelines for the protection of the child from information and material injurious to his or her well-being . . .

The explicit textual emphases in CRC Article 17 are clearly too specific for inclusion in the articulation of the general norm for freedom of expression in

Article 19 of ICCPR. Yet those emphases are important attempts to tailor the right to freedom of expression (and in particular the right to seek and receive information and ideas) to the specific situation and needs of children and thereby to allow them to exercise their right to freedom of expression in an effective manner. Article 17 seeks to tread the fine line between the *freedom* of children to access diverse information and material (including online material) and the *protection* they need from information and material that could harm them.[26]

It is conceivable that, in the fullness of time, the Human Rights Committee might have developed similar emphases in its views on individual communications and/or in its concluding observations on state reports. However, inserting these specific provisions into the CRC provided a direct pretext to develop children's right to freedom of expression in a structured way. It puts different aspects of this right, as exercised by children, on a firmer legal footing and makes the normative development of the right less contingent on chance. This approach catalyzes processes of norm expansion by rolling out a generic right to freedom of expression in a specific context and spelling out its implications for a particular group—children.

The drafters of the Convention on Rights of Persons with Disabilities (CRPD), adopted in 2006, engaged in similar strategic norm expansion. They saw opportunities to harness contemporary technological capabilities so that individuals with disabilities could exercise their rights to freedom of expression and access to information in an effective manner. CRPD Article 9, entitled "Accessibility," thus requires states parties to the convention to take appropriate measures to, among other things:

2(f) promote other appropriate forms of assistance and support to persons with disabilities to ensure their access to information;

2(g) promote access for persons with disabilities to new information and communications technologies and systems, including the Internet;

2(h) promote the design, development, production and distribution of accessible information and communications technologies and systems at an early stage, so that these technologies and systems become accessible at minimum cost.

These positive state obligations flow from the general norm on freedom of expression, but again, they are too specific in their orientation for neat inclusion in a terse general articulation of the right to freedom of expression and information. Nevertheless, their explicit enshrinement in the CRPD is likely to provide a valuable impetus for states to take active measures toward ensuring that those with disabilities can exercise their rights to freedom of expression and information in an effective manner.

CRPD Article 21, "Freedom of Expression and Opinion, and Access to Information," is even more detailed. It reads:

> States Parties shall take all appropriate measures to ensure that persons with disabilities can exercise the right to freedom of expression and opinion, including the freedom to seek, receive and impart information and ideas on an equal basis with others and through all forms of communication of their choice . . . , including by:
>
> (a) providing information intended for the general public to persons with disabilities in accessible formats and technologies appropriate to different kinds of disabilities in a timely manner and without additional cost;
>
> (b) accepting and facilitating the use of sign languages, Braille, augmentative and alternative communication, and all other accessible means, modes and formats of communication of their choice by persons with disabilities in official interactions;
>
> (c) urging private entities that provide services to the general public, including through the Internet, to provide information and services in accessible and usable formats for persons with disabilities;
>
> (d) encouraging the mass media, including providers of information through the Internet, to make their services accessible to persons with disabilities;
>
> (e) recognizing and promoting the use of sign languages.

This provision is again informed by the specific needs of persons with disabilities, concerning their ability to enjoy the rights to freedom of expression and information, especially insofar as their enjoyment of those rights is predicated on, or facilitated by, communications technologies. As Jack Balkin has observed, "Where the exercise of a liberty depends upon technology, access to that technology largely determines the substantive liberty of the actor."[27] This observation is particularly apposite for persons with disabilities. CRPD Article 21 points up the need for information and communications technology to be suited to the needs of persons with disabilities, otherwise their right to freedom of expression and information is unlikely to be effective in practice.[28]

THE QUEST FOR COHERENCE AND CONSISTENCY

The three broad phases in the development of freedom of expression and information norms at the United Nations, announced at the start of this chapter, are not always linear. While the trailblazing phase clearly came first, the phase of consolidation and expansion overlaps to an extent with the quest for coherence and consistency in the interpretation of relevant UN norms. In both phases, the development, adoption, and reliance on general comments and general recommendations by various UN treaty bodies have been instrumental.

General comments or general recommendations focus on specific themes or treaty provisions and are usually the leading source of interpretive guidance for the treaty in question. General comments or recommendations typically reflect the accumulated experience and expertise of treaty bodies on their subject matter. They can also serve to update or modernize treaty bodies' approaches to the themes or treaty provisions they address. Several general comments or recommendations have made very significant contributions to the interpretation and wider understanding of UN norms on freedom of expression. These include the Human Rights Committee's General Comment no. 34 on ICCPR Article 19, "Freedom of Opinion and Expression" (2011);[29] General Recommendation no. 35, "Combating Racist Hate Speech," from the Committee on the Elimination of Racial Discrimination (2013); and the CRPD's General Comment no. 2 on CRPD Article 9, "Accessibility" (2014).

General Comment no. 34 hauled the Human Rights Committee's approach to the right to freedom of expression into the digital age.[30] It dwells on the interplay between the right to freedom of expression and other rights guaranteed by the ICCPR, and it clarifies—in detail—the scope and content of the right. It also pays considerable attention to permissible limitations on the exercise of the right and the (strict) criteria that govern those limitations.

Similarly, the drafting of General Recommendation no. 35 afforded the Committee on the Elimination of Racial Discrimination the opportunity to modernize and clarify its approach to racist hate speech.[31]

The modernization impulse provided by the Committee on the Rights of Persons with Disabilities' General Comment no. 2 on accessibility is less pronounced that those of General Comment no. 34 and General Recommendation no. 35 because, as was explained earlier in this chapter, the text of the CRPD is already modern in its outlook. Nevertheless, General Comment no. 2 provides useful elucidation of the specific details of CRPD Article 9, in terms of its scope and substance and its relation to other articles in the convention.

As discussed, UNESCO and the UN Special Rapporteur on Freedom of Opinion and Expression maneuver strategically in the penumbra of UN treaty-based norms on freedom of expression and engage extensively with those norms.[32] Their work raises awareness and promotes wider understanding of, and reliance on, those norms and thus contributes to their consolidation and internalization by states. The annual declarations adopted jointly by the UN special rapporteur and corresponding mandate holders in other regional human rights systems are of particular value in this regard.[33]

It should also be noted that specialized UN mandates are increasingly contributing to norm internalization in the area of freedom of expression. Given the multifaceted nature of freedom of expression, the right is often relevant to the work of other specialized mandates. Relevant statements and other work of those specialized mandates, independently or jointly with the Special Rapporteur on Freedom of Opinion and Expression, can highlight particular aspects of the right to freedom of expression and recall the importance of the norms that address those aspects.[34]

The pursuit of coherence and consistency—the lodestars of normative processes—can gather momentum from norm bandwagon effects, but often they also have to overcome "antipreneurial" resistance. The controversial "defamation of religions" campaign provides a good illustration of such resistance.[35] Between 1999 and 2010, a campaign headed by the Organisation of the Islamic Conference (now the Organisation of Islamic Cooperation) led to a series of (annual) resolutions on the topic "Combating Defamation of Religions" in the (former) UN Commission on Human Rights and its successor, the UN Human Rights Council. The ostensible aim of the resolutions was clear: to curb (harsh) criticism of religions, particularly of Islam. As Agnès Callamard and Sejal Parmar detail in chapter 11 of this volume, a shift of focus and of "institutional dynamics" in 2011 occasioned a departure from "defamation of religions" to a "new approach" to the underlying concerns of the series of earlier resolutions.[36] The new approach was characterized by its overt grounding in international human rights norms, in particular the right to freedom of expression, and contemporary interpretations of those norms.

The Combating Defamation of Religions campaign can be described as antipreneurial, because it sought to achieve particular political ends by disregarding and deviating from existing UN legal norms on freedom of expression. Paradoxically, the new approach that replaced the central focus on defamation of religions demonstrated the strength and resilience of the UN's norms on freedom of expression in practice.

EXPORTING FREEDOM OF EXPRESSION NORMS

The process of internalizing norms is anything but straightforward. It is neither linear nor self-propelling. It is not even self-evident that norms ultimately will be internalized by states. Norms need to be steered and embraced before they become internalized. All this makes it very difficult to gauge whether the UN's normative standards on freedom of expression really have been "internalized" at the global level. One way to try to gauge this is to consider the extent to which regional human rights courts rely on those norms.

Over the years, in its case law on the right to freedom of expression, the European Court of Human Rights has occasionally referred to the texts of settled UN norms, such as UDHR Article 19 and ICCPR Article 19.[37] Such references have been made to note UN approaches to (various aspects of) the right to freedom of expression and/or to provide support for the court's own approach to freedom of expression pursuant to ECHR Article 10.[38] In its recent case law on the right to freedom of expression, the court has continued to refer intermittently to settled UN norms,[39] but it has found it instructive to also refer to evolving interpretations of UN norms, in particular as set out in General Comment no. 34.[40] It referred to General Recommendation no. 35 for the first time in 2018.[41]

Council of Europe bodies other than the European Court of Human Rights also refer to UN norms on freedom of expression, including General Comment no. 34. For instance, the Committee of Ministers referred to General Comment no. 34 in its recommendation to member states on the protection of journalism and the safety of journalists and other media actors.[42]

Similar usage of UN norms on freedom of expression can be seen in the case law of the Inter-American Court of Human Rights.[43] Awareness of relevant UN norms has been present from the court's very first decision regarding freedom of expression[44] and on through landmark judgments such as *Claude Reyes et al. v. Chile*, which concerned access to public information,[45] to more recent judgments.[46] General Comment no. 34 has also been cited.[47] References to UN instruments and other relevant documents regarding freedom of expression are more visible in the work done by the Inter-American Commission on Human Rights, especially by its special rapporteur on freedom of expression. Such relationship can be evidenced in the Declaration of Principles of Freedom of Expression, a bedrock for this right in the Americas.[48]

The African Court of Human Rights' jurisprudence on freedom of expression is nascent and very limited, yet it too draws on relevant UN norms, for reasons similar to those of the other regional human rights courts. In its 2014 groundbreaking judgment regarding criminal defamation, *Lohé Issa Konaté v. the Republic of Burkina Faso*, the court devoted significant attention to UN norms, especially ICCPR Article 19.[49] The free speech guarantees provided by the UDHR and ICCPR have also been highlighted in the case law of the African

Commission on Human and Peoples' Rights and in the 2002 Declaration of Principles on Freedom of Expression in Africa.[50]

The congruence of UN norms on freedom of expression and equivalent regional standards is borne out by the limited but increasingly numerous references to the UN norms by regional courts and intergovernmental bodies. This demonstrates that UN norms do have a benchmarking function at the regional level. The extent to which UN norms are referenced and followed at the regional level can be a good indicator of norm internalization in those regions where formalized intergovernmental human rights systems are in place. On the other hand, as a result of that very congruence, it is also plausible that regional human rights courts may see only limited added value in having recourse to UN norms and thus may be inclined to invoke those norms only to elucidate or to reinforce the specific regional norms or to supplement them in specific ways.

Yet an examination of the approach taken by regional human rights courts reveals very little about the approach of states. Thus, another way to gauge the internalization of UN free expression norms is to try to measure their penetration into national legal systems. This, too, is a complicated and challenging exercise. The first question is whether the UN norms have undergone constitutional incorporation. This will depend on various factors, including whether a state has a monist or a dualist legal system and whether it even has a (written) constitution. The date of adoption and/or the dates of relevant amendments to the constitution can broaden or narrow the possibilities for a constitution to reference international norms; more recent constitutions have the benefit of drawing on well-known, older international standards. It is also pertinent to ask whether the spirit of the UN norms has been captured or the letter of the norms has been replicated.

Another key consideration concerns whether and/or how constitutional or superior courts have invoked UN norms in the past and their openness to do so in the future. Much will ride on the national judiciary's level of awareness of relevant UN norms. Whether or not a state belongs to a (well-developed) regional system of human rights protection can also affect the internalization dynamic. This gamut of questions goes far beyond the scope of the present chapter, but it should be flagged as a focus for future research.[51]

CONCLUSION

This chapter set out to give an overview and analysis of norm establishment and entrepreneurship in the area of freedom of expression within the United

Nations. The overview and analysis are necessarily limited in scope, but it is hoped that they provide useful general groundwork for more detailed research on the normative ambitions, roles, and impact of specific treaties, bodies, and actors within the UN system. The overview and analysis highlight a variety of treaty-driven and other dynamics, which merit specific and separate consideration but also, importantly, general consideration from the perspective of the broader, complex, adaptive normative UN system as a whole. The internalization of relevant UN norms is an ongoing challenge, within the UN system and beyond, but the documented examples provide evidence of progress in that regard and grounds for cautious confidence that this progress will continue.

Today's world has largely become "a global village of precedent,"[52] where technology, information, and knowledge (resources) and advocacy are combining to facilitate the global dissemination of the UN's freedom of expression norms. But even with enhanced opportunities for their dissemination, there are no guarantees that these norms will be fully and faithfully implemented across the globe. Their prospects of being internalized at the national level depend on constitutional, legislative, political, and judicial openness to them and a willingness to be guided by them.

It should be an institutional imperative for the United Nations to promote these norms or, more specifically, to promote awareness of their content and of the importance of implementing them at the national level. This is a task not only for the formal custodians of relevant treaties but also for other institutional actors who operate in the interstices of treaty law, responding to and intervening in specific cases, recalling the relevance and primacy of the internationally accepted norms.

Other stakeholders should lend helping hands, too. More mapping of the complicated trajectories of norm internalization by states is needed to enhance our understanding and ability to assess and strengthen the normative cycle. There is a clear need to conduct more extensive and systematic research on norm internalization by states, combining appropriate comparative law and policy tracking and other research methods to those ends.

NOTES

1. Tarlach McGonagle, "The Development of Freedom of Expression and Information Within the UN: Leaps and Bounds or Fits and Starts?," in *The United Nations and Freedom of Expression and Information: Critical Perspectives*, ed. Tarlach

McGonagle and Yvonne Donders (Cambridge: Cambridge University Press, 2015), 1–51, at 1.

2. In many ways, this entire volume, particularly parts 1 and 2, testifies to the internalization of the UN norms.

3. The phrase "unity of purpose and operation" is borrowed from Thomas I. Emerson, who used it in his treatise on the system of freedom of expression that has been built on the First Amendment of the U.S. Constitution. Emerson, *The System of Freedom of Expression* (New York: Random House, 1970), 4.

4. The term "political standards" covers a range of political instruments, such as declarations, recommendations, and resolutions, as well as (major) policy documents.

5. Raphaël Lemkin, "Genocide," in *Axis Rule in Occupied Europe: Laws of Occupation, Analysis of Government, Proposals for Redress* (Washington, DC: Carnegie Endowment for International Peace, 1944), 79–95.

6. John P. Humphrey, *Human Rights and the United Nations: A Great Adventure* (New York: Transnational Publishers, 1984), 54.

7. Samuel Moyn, *The Last Utopia: Human Rights in History* (Cambridge, MA: Belknap Press of Harvard University Press, 2010), 65. Compare this, however, with the 1968 Nobel Peace Prize award ceremony speech acknowledging René Cassin's contribution to the drafting process.

8. Franklin D. Roosevelt, "The Four Freedoms," State of the Union message, January 6, 1941. For details and photos of the successive drafts with Roosevelt's handwritten revisions of the text, see "FDR and the Four Freedoms Speech," National Archives, Franklin D. Roosevelt Presidential Library and Museum, https://fdrlibrary.org/four-freedoms.

9. See Humphrey, *Human Rights*; Moyn, *Last Utopia*; M. A. Glendon, *A World Made New: Eleanor Roosevelt and the Universal Declaration of Human Rights* (New York: Random House, 2001); and J. H. Burgers, "The Road to San Francisco: The Revival of the Human Rights Idea in the Twentieth Century," *Human Rights Quarterly* 14 (1992): 447–477.

10. United Nations General Assembly, Resolution 59(1), December 14, 1946.

11. See also *Final Act of the United Nations Conference on Freedom of Information*, Geneva, Switzerland, March 23–April 21, 1948. United Nations Digital Library, https://digitallibrary.un.org/record/3806839?ln=en.

12. Humphrey, *Human Rights*, 53.

13. S. P. López, *Freedom of Information*, Report by the Rapporteur on Freedom of Information, UN ECOSOC, Official Records, 16th Session, Supp. no. 12 (New York: United Nations, 1953), 11.

14. Seminar on Freedom of Information, organized by the UN in cooperation with the Government of Italy, Rome, April 7–20, 1964, document no. ST/TAO/HR/20, 16, para. 58.

15. United Nations Conference on Freedom of Information, Resolution no. 43.

16. Humphrey, *Human Rights*, 53.

17. William A. Schabas, ed., *The Universal Declaration of Human Rights: The Travaux Préparatoires* (Cambridge: Cambridge University Press, 2013); Marc J. Bossuyt, ed., *Guide to the "Travaux Préparatoires" of the International Covenant on Civil and Political Rights* (Dordrecht, Germany: Martinus Nijhoff, 1987), 373–402.

18. Yet, of the fifty-eight member states of the UN at the time, forty-eight voted for the resolution proclaiming the Universal Declaration of Human Rights, eight abstained, and two failed to vote or abstain.

19. Humphrey underlines the importance of "diplomatic cocktail parties" at the UN around that time and points out that they offered a valuable setting in which diplomats could "convey informally a suggestion or opinion which his government is still unprepared to advance officially." Humphrey, *Human Rights*, 61–62.

20. See Agnès Callamard and Sejal Parmar, "Norms in Conflict: The Restraints on the Emergence of a Free Speech Norm," chapter 11 of this volume; and Tarlach McGonagle, *Minority Rights, Freedom of Expression and of the Media: Dynamics and Dilemmas* (Belgium: Intersentia, 2011), 280–290.

21. K. J. Partsch, "Freedom of Conscience and Expression, and Political Freedoms," *The International Bill of Rights: The Covenant on Civil and Political Rights*, ed. Louis Henkin (New York: Columbia University Press, 1981), 227; Manfred Nowak, *U.N. Covenant on Civil and Political Rights—CCPR Commentary*, 2nd rev. ed. (Kehl: N. P. Engel, 2005), 477; UN Human Rights Committee (HRC), "Prohibition of Propaganda for War and Inciting National, Racial or Religious Hatred," General Comment no. 11, Article 20, July 29, 1983; and HRC, "Freedoms of Opinion and Expression," General Comment no. 34, Article 19, UN Doc. CCPR/C/GC/34 (September 12, 2011).

22. HRC, "Freedoms of Opinion and Expression," para. 51.

23. See also Callamard and Parmar, "Norms in Conflict."

24. However, Article 13 of the Convention on the Rights of the Child omits references to the right to hold opinions without interference or to the duties and responsibilities that go hand in hand with the exercise of the right to freedom of expression. Compare to the International Covenant on Civil and Political Rights (ICCPR), Articles 19(1) and (3).

25. United Nations General Assembly, Resolution 45/158, December 18, 1990.

26. See Lucy Smith, "Convention on the Rights of the Child: Freedom of Expression for Children," in *The United Nations and Freedom of Expression and Information:*

Critical Perspectives, ed. Tarlach McGonagle and Yvonne Donders (Cambridge: Cambridge University Press, 2015), 145–170.

27. Jack M. Balkin, "Some Realism about Pluralism: Legal Realist Approaches to the First Amendment," *Duke Law Journal* 1990, no. 3 (1990): 406.

28. See Eliza Varney, "Convention on the Rights of Persons with Disabilities: Ensuring Full and Equal Access to Information," in *The United Nations and Freedom of Expression and Information: Critical Perspectives*, ed. Tarlach McGonagle and Yvonne Donders (Cambridge: Cambridge University Press, 2015), 171–207.

29. See Michael O'Flaherty, "International Covenant on Civil and Political Rights: Interpreting Freedom of Expression Standards for the Present and the Future," in *The United Nations and Freedom of Expression and Information: Critical Perspectives*, ed. Tarlach McGonagle and Yvonne Donders (Cambridge: Cambridge University Press, 2015), 55–88.

30. General Comment no. 34 replaced the committee's earlier General Comment no. 10 on ICCPR Article 19, which dated from 1983.

31. Patrick Thornberry, "International Convention on the Elimination of All Forms of Racial Discrimination: The Prohibition of 'Racist Hate Speech,'" in *The United Nations and Freedom of Expression and Information: Critical Perspectives*, ed. Tarlach McGonagle and Yvonne Donders (Cambridge: Cambridge University Press, 2015), 121–144. For an overview and analysis of how the Committee on the Elimination of Racial Discrimination has applied General Recommendation no. 35 since its adoption, see Tarlach McGonagle, "General Recommendation No. 35 on Combating Racist Hate Speech," in *Eliminating Racial Discrimination: 50 Years of the International Convention on the Elimination of All Forms of Racial Discrimination 1965*, ed. David Keane and Annapurna Waughray (Manchester University Press, 2017), 246–268.

32. Of course, as we have seen, the United Nations Educational, Scientific and Cultural Organization also forms part of that treaty-based normative framework (as discussed). See Sylvie Coudray, "UNESCO: Freedom of Expression, Information, and the Media," in *The United Nations and Freedom of Expression and Information: Critical Perspectives*, ed. Tarlach McGonagle and Yvonne Donders (Cambridge: Cambridge University Press, 2015), 208–234; and Toby Mendel, "The UN Special Rapporteur on Freedom of Opinion and Expression: Progressive Development of International Standards Relating to Freedom of Expression," in the same volume, 235–268.

33. Many chapters in the present volume reference the importance of joint declarations.

34. See, for instance, David Kaye et al., "Time to End Global Crisis of Impunity for Crimes Against Journalists," Office of the High Commissioner for Human Rights, October 31,

2018. The statement was released by seven UN experts ahead of the International Day to End Impunity for Crimes Against Journalists, November 2, 2018.

35. See Sejal Parmar, "Uprooting 'Defamation of Religions' and Planting a New Approach to Freedom of Expression at the United Nations," in *The United Nations and Freedom of Expression and Information: Critical Perspectives*, ed. Tarlach McGonagle and Yvonne Donders (Cambridge: Cambridge University Press, 2015), 373–427; and McGonagle, *Minority Rights*, 363–375.

36. Parmar, "Uprooting 'Defamation of Religions,'" 373–427.

37. See, for example, European Court of Human Rights (ECtHR), Müller and Others v. Switzerland, May 24, 1988, series A, no. 133; and Jersild v. Denmark, September 23, 1994, series A, no. 298.

38. See Antoine Buyse, "Tacit Citing: The Scarcity of Judicial Dialogue between the Global and the Regional Human Rights Mechanisms in Freedom of Expression Cases," in *The United Nations and Freedom of Expression and Information: Critical Perspectives*, ed. Tarlach McGonagle and Yvonne Donders (Cambridge: Cambridge University Press, 2015), 443–465, at 449–454.

39. ECtHR, Magyar Helsinki Bizottság v. Hungary, Grand Chamber, no. 18030/11, November 8, 2016.

40. Bizottság v. Hungary; Ahmet Yildirim v. Turkey, no. 3111/10, ECHR (2012); Youth Initiative for Human Rights v. Serbia, no. 48135/06, June 25, 2013.

41. ECtHR, Savva Terentyev v. Russia, no. 10692/09, August 28, 2018.

42. Recommendation CM/Rec(2016)4 of the Committee of Ministers of the Council of Europe to member states on the protection of journalism and the safety of journalists and other media actors, adopted on April 13, 2016.

43. See Buyse, "Tacit Citing," 454–456.

44. IACtHR, "Compulsory Membership in an Association Prescribed by Law for the Practice of Journalism," American Convention on Human Rights, Articles 13 and 29, Advisory Opinion OC-5/85 of November 13, 1985, series A, no. 5.

45. IACtHR, Claude Reyes et al. v. Chile, judgment of September 19, 2006 (Merits, Reparations and Costs), series C, no. 151.

46. See, for example, IACtHR, Gomes Lund et al. (Guerrilha do Araguaia) v. Brazil, judgment of November 24, 2010 (Preliminary Objections, Merits, Reparations and Costs), series C, no. 219.

47. See, for example, IACtHR, Granier et al. v. Venezuela, judgment of June 22, 2015 (Preliminary Objections, Merits, Reparations and Costs), series C, no. 293.

48. Organization of American States, "Declaration of Principles on Freedom of Expression," http://www.oas.org/en/iachr/expression/showarticle.asp?artID=26.

49. African Court on Human and Peoples' Rights, *Lohé Issa Konaté v. Burkina Faso*, application no. 004/2013, December 5, 2014.

50. African Commission on Human and People's Rights, Kenneth Good v. Republic of Botswana, 313/05; and "Resolution on the Adoption of the Declaration of Principles on Freedom of Expression in Africa," Resolution 62(32) (2002), principle 2.

51. The authors conducted a cursory search for examples of constitutional incorporation and judicial referencing. The results of this exploratory search suggested great variety of constitutional provisions guaranteeing freedom of expression and, namely, a range in whether those provisions bear evidence of having been directly or indirectly influenced by UN norms. The results also suggested that while national constitutional and superior courts do—to varying degrees—refer to Article 19 of the Universal Declaration of Human Rights and to Article 19 of the ICCPR in their jurisprudence, references to General Comment no. 34 are so far less prevalent (the general comment was adopted only in 2011).

52. Kevin Boyle, untitled address, Human Rights Centre, University of Essex, December 8, 1999.

On "Balancing" and "Social Watchdogs"

SEVEN

The European Court of Human
Rights as a Norm Entrepreneur for
Freedom of Expression

JAN OSTER

The European Court of Human Rights (ECtHR, or the "Strasbourg Court") has significantly contributed to the development of European standards related to freedom of expression and information, and to the domestication and internalization of these standards by national actors and institutions—to the emergence of international norms. To explain the ECtHR's contribution, this chapter adopts Martha Finnemore's and Kathryn Sikkink's three-stage process of a norm's "life cycle": norm emergence through a norm entrepreneur, followed by a norm cascade and norm internalization.[1]

THE EUROPEAN COURT OF HUMAN RIGHTS
AS A NORM ENTREPRENEUR

Finnemore and Sikkink might not have envisaged the ECtHR as a norm entrepreneur within the meaning of their theoretical framework, which largely refers to private actors and organizations of civil society.[2] This concept typically would apply to nongovernmental organizations that frequently submit substantial third-party interventions to the court.[3] However, the court cannot be compared with a domestic legislator or adjudicator as a mere addressee, or recipient, of norm entrepreneurship, either. In the inchoate post-Westphalian network of states and nonstate entities, national and international law, as well as "hard law" and "soft law," the ECtHR can best be described as a "transnational" court, without which norms may not have regionalized on pan-European level.[4] As such, the ECtHR infers norms in the form of rules and principles based on the human rights codified in the European Convention on Human Rights (ECHR) and on the rights entrusted to the court's supervision.[5] Particularly relevant for the purposes of this chapter is ECHR Article 10, which protects freedom of expression.

However, the Strasbourg Court's norms on freedom of expression cannot be fully understood without knowing the limits of the court's norm entrepreneurship. It is inherent in international human rights conventions that they are subsidiary to the national protection of human rights.[6] The ECHR is no exception. Article 35(1) provides that the Strasbourg Court may only deal with an application after all domestic remedies have been exhausted. In other words, the convention states are initially responsible for securing human rights. The court's task is thus not to take the place of the national authorities but rather to *review*, under the ECHR, the decisions they have rendered.[7]

As an international court, the Strasbourg Court grants a certain margin of appreciation to the domestic authorities. This is because the domestic authorities might be in a better position to assess the factual circumstances of a case (for example, if they conclude that a particular expression threatens national security)[8] or to make normative evaluations concerning issues that require knowledge of local sensitivities (for example, where "morals,"[9] the right to respect for private life[10] or "religious feelings"[11] of members of a particular community are at stake). Unfortunately, the Strasbourg Court's case law on the breadth of the margin of appreciation is not always consistent.[12] In any case, even where states enjoy a margin of appreciation, the exercise of their discretion goes hand in hand with the court's supervision.[13] In particular, the margin of appreciation is limited where restrictions on speech relating to a matter of public concern are at issue.[14]

The more this margin of appreciation is limited, the stricter the scrutiny the ECtHR applies with regard to the legal and factual circumstances of an application. A narrow margin of appreciation therefore leads to a higher degree of harmonization of norms on a pan-European level; a broad margin of appreciation maintains fragmentation of norms. The margin of appreciation is thus not only the determining factor for the Strasbourg Court's norm entrepreneurship within the theoretical framework of Finnemore and Sikkink but also the fulcrum for the difference between universalism and pluralism of human rights protection in Europe.

REGIONAL NORMS ON FREEDOM OF EXPRESSION

The regional norms enacted by the ECtHR concern the theoretical foundation, the "balancing" methodology, and the doctrine of freedom of expression.

Theory

In the seminal decision *Handyside v. United Kingdom*, the ECtHR established, and has since reiterated: "Freedom of expression constitutes one of the essential foundations of [a democratic] society, one of the basic conditions for its progress and for the development of every man. Subject to [ECHR Article 10(2)], it is applicable not only to 'information' or 'ideas' that are favourably received or regarded as inoffensive or as a matter of indifference, but also to those that offend, shock or disturb the State or any sector of the population. Such are the demands of that pluralism, tolerance and broadmindedness without which there is no 'democratic society.' "[15]

In cases following *Handyside*, the court replaced the term "development of every man" with "each individual's self-fulfilment."[16] The Strasbourg Court has thus positioned its freedom of expression theory[17] on both the consequentialist argument from democracy[18] and the liberal argument from individual autonomy and self-fulfillment.[19] In the court's jurisprudence, the argument from democracy becomes most visible in cases involving criticism of public figures and other contributions to matters of public importance (as will be evident in the section on doctrine).

Methodology

Once the Strasbourg Court has established that there has been an interference with freedom of expression, the court "balances" freedom of expression with conflicting rights and interests on an ad hoc basis. According to Article 10(2) of the ECHR, interferences with freedom of expression are allowed if such limitations are prescribed by law (principle of legality), pursue a legitimate aim (principle of legitimacy), and are necessary in pursuit of this aim (principle of proportionality). In particular, where conflicting human rights are at stake, such as freedom of expression and the right to respect for private life, the

Strasbourg Court does not afford dominance to freedom of expression but treats it as a right with value equal to the human rights of others.[20]

Doctrine

Most important for legal practice are the contributions of the Strasbourg Court to the development of substantive pan-European freedom of expression norms. A few non-exhaustive examples should be highlighted here, distinguished as the scope and content of freedom of expression, on the one hand, and the limits thereof, on the other hand.

First, the ECtHR regularly emphasizes the importance of contributions on matters of public concern to a democratic society. The more a publication pertains to a matter of public concern, the stronger the protection it deserves in the balancing exercise. Although the Strasbourg Court has never expressly defined what "public interest" actually is, its case law provides a broad range of precedents. It involves not only speech on political matters[21] and matters of public administration,[22] but also, for example, on businesses,[23] criminal offenses and their prosecution,[24] the protection of animals,[25] historical debates,[26] and sports-related issues.[27]

The ECtHR has also significantly contributed to pan-European standards on the right of access to information, although such a right is not expressly included in ECHR Article 10. To be sure, the court is still reluctant to conceptualize freedom of information as an intrinsic right, that is, as a right of access to information to be granted without the applicant having to demonstrate a particular interest in, or purpose of doing something with, the information that is requested.[28] This is different in the European Union, where Article 42 of the EU Charter of Fundamental Rights and—with some reservations—Article 15(3) of the Treaty on the Functioning of the European Union grant such an unconditional right.

However, after some evolutionary steps,[29] the Grand Chamber clarified the court's principles of access to information in the 2016 decision *Magyar Helsinki Bizottság v. Hungary*. Accordingly, ECHR Article 10 does not, in principle, "confer on the individual a right of access to information held by a public authority nor oblige the government to impart such information to the individual." But such a right or obligation may arise, inter alia, "in circumstances where access to the information is instrumental for the individual's exercise of his or her right to freedom of expression, in particular 'the freedom to receive and impart information' and where its denial constitutes an interference with that right."[30] This is the case if the gathering of the information is a relevant preparatory step for contribution to a public debate, the information itself is of public interest, and the applicant is a journalist or an organization contributing to the discussion of public affairs.[31]

This leads to another set of pan-European freedom of expression norms, namely those concerning the privileged protection of the journalistic media. The court regularly emphasizes that "although the press[32] must not overstep certain bounds, regarding in particular protection of the reputation and rights of others, its duty is nevertheless to impart—in a manner consistent with its obligations and responsibilities—information and ideas on all matters of public interest. Not only does the press have the task of imparting such information and ideas; the public also has a right to receive them. Were it otherwise, the press would be unable to play its vital role of 'public watchdog.' "[33]

Freedom of expression and media freedom are overlapping concepts, but they are not coextensive.[34] In subjective terms, freedom of expression applies to everyone, whereas media freedom only protects "the media" (as we will discuss later, in the "Outlook" section). In objective terms, media freedom affords particular privileges to the media that do not apply to freedom of expression in general: the media speech privilege and the protection of the media as an institution. The media speech privilege includes the idea that a person or institution, by virtue of being media and acting as media, is governed by a different set of factors concerning the intensity of protection when issuing a publication, compared to freedom of expression afforded to private individuals or to nonmedia entities. The fact that an impugned statement is "media speech," rather than speech by any other individual or institution, adds to the burden of justifying its restrictions.[35]

In addition, media freedom provides privileged protection to the media that goes beyond protection of media publications. This institutional protection of the media guarantees rights that are not directly related to the content of a publication or the way in which it is presented but are related to the media in its news gathering, editorial, or distribution processes, or even to the mere existence of an independent media. The institutional protection of the media includes, for example, the independence of public broadcasters,[36] the protection of journalistic research and investigation,[37] and the confidentiality of journalistic sources[38] and journalistic communication.[39]

The media thus has a right to keep its sources confidential. But to what extent are the sources themselves protected, especially those who expose misconduct at their workplace? The court has already exercised considerable norm entrepreneurship on the protection of such whistle-blowers. Since its seminal 2008 decision in *Guja v. Moldova*, the court has established several factors to be taken into account when balancing the interests of the public in receiving information, the whistle-blower's freedom of expression interest, and the public or private[40] employer's interest in keeping information confidential. These factors are the extent to which the information is of public concern; whether the whistle-blower was the only person, or part of a small group of people, who were aware of the occurrences at their workplace; whether any other effective means to remedy the wrongdoing was available to the whistle-blower; the accuracy of the information disclosed; whether the damage inflicted upon the employer's interest outweighs the interest of the public in having the information revealed; whether the sanction was proportionate; and the motive behind the actions of the reporting employee or civil servant.[41]

But the court's norm entrepreneurship is not limited to the content of freedom of expression; it necessarily includes norms on the limits thereof. This is the case, for example, with regard to "hate speech." The court regularly justifies prohibitions of attacks on the underlying values of the ECHR—equality, anti-discrimination, tolerance, and democracy—or even excludes such speech from ECHR Article 10 protection altogether by virtue of Article 17. Such attacks may consist of expressions of racism, anti-Semitism, or Islamophobia.[42] This jurisprudence reflects the idea that free speech should not be granted to those who aim to eliminate the freedom of others. In short, intolerance should not be tolerated.[43]

Related to this point is another pan-European norm established by the ECtHR that limits the exercise of freedom of expression: the court regularly finds laws prohibiting the denial of the Holocaust to be justified.[44] This doctrine is met with a refusal in U.S. scholarship, where robust skepticism about what is perceived as "governmentally declared truths" prevails.[45] However, according to the Strasbourg Court, the denial of the Holocaust is not only to be considered a negation of a clearly and legally established historical fact but also an incitement to hatred against the Jewish community, and it may thus legitimately be interfered with by virtue of the "rights of others" justification in ECHR Article 10(2).[46]

Finally, the ECtHR has significantly contributed to European norms on the protection of privacy as a limit to freedom of expression. For the ECtHR, the fact that speech relates to a public figure is, as such, not sufficient to grant strong freedom of expression protection, because not all speech on public figures is necessarily speech on a matter of public concern. Since its seminal decision in *von Hannover v. Germany (no. 1),*[47] involving tabloid reporting on the private life of the Princess of Monaco, the ECtHR has regularly expressed its repugnance for sensational and lurid news "intended to titillate and entertain, which

[is] aimed at satisfying the curiosity of a particular readership regarding aspects of a person's strictly private life," serving only to "entertain" and not to "educate."[48]

NORM CASCADE AND NORM INTERNALIZATION

According to Finnemore and Sikkink, a norm cascade occurs when norms reach a "tipping point," or critical mass of state endorsements. This process can be followed by a norm internalization, in which norms "become so widely accepted that they are internalized by actors and achieve a 'taken-for-granted' quality that makes conformance with the norm almost automatic."[49] The "cascading" and "internalization" of ECtHR norms is, in the first place, provided for in the ECHR itself. According to Article 46(1), the convention states "undertake to abide by the final judgment of the court in any case to which they are parties." In the case of a violation of the ECHR, the court may afford just satisfaction to the injured party (Article 41). The judgment's enforcement is supervised by the Committee of Ministers (Article 46[2]).

The cascading and internalization of the Strasbourg Court's decisions is thus largely a top-down promulgation of norms, forcing the convention states to readjust their standards of balancing freedom of expression with conflicting rights. This has worked both ways: it has led partly to stronger freedom of expression protection and partly to stronger protection of conflicting rights, in particular the right to respect for private life, as detailed in Article 8, with its subcategories of privacy and reputation.[50]

An example of stronger freedom of expression protection is the development of the "qualified privilege" defense in the English tort of defamation. Before 1999, a publisher who could not prove the truth of a defamatory statement had a qualified privilege defense only if they were under a public or private duty to report certain information to another individual who had a personal interest in the information concerned (the duty and interest test).[51] This excluded statements that were made to the general public, such as by newspaper or broadcasting.[52] In 1998, the British Parliament adopted the Human Rights Act (c42), incorporating into UK law the rights contained in the ECHR. In 1999, the House of Lords then issued the seminal decision in *Reynolds v. Times Newspapers*. In *Reynolds*, Lord Nicholls explained, "Freedom of expression will shortly be buttressed by statutory requirements. Under . . . the Human Rights Act 1998, expected to come into force in October 2000, the court is required, in relevant cases, to have particular regard to the importance of the right to freedom of expression. The common law is to be developed and applied in a manner consistent with article 10 [of the ECHR], and the court must take into account relevant decisions of the [ECtHR]."[53] With a view to this "new legal landscape," as Lord Steyn put it, Lord Nicholls established ten non-exhaustive criteria to balance freedom of expression with the right to respect for one's reputation, including the extent to which the subject matter is a matter of public concern and the steps taken by the publisher to verify the information.[54]

Although *Reynolds* was still a far cry from the robust free speech protection afforded by the U.S. Supreme Court in *New York Times Co. v. Sullivan*,[55] it significantly expanded the qualified privilege defense for the media against defamation claims,[56] thus expanding the media's freedom of expression protection.[57] The internalization of ECtHR norms thus did occur both indirectly, through legislative changes, namely the adoption of the Human Rights Act 1998, and directly, through a national court adjusting its decisions. Although section 4 of the 2013 Defamation Act subsequently codified the qualified privilege defense and abolished the "*Reynolds* defense," *Reynolds* will remain influential on the interpretation of section 4.[58]

An example of stronger protection for rights conflicting with freedom of expression relates to the right to privacy. Before the enactment of the Human Rights Act 1998, English law lacked an express privacy tort. However, since 1998, English courts have significantly expanded the equitable claim for "breach of confidence" to accommodate the ECHR Article 8 right to respect for privacy, thus restricting the media's right to report on the private lives of celebrities.[59] Similarly, the ECtHR's *von Hannover (no. 1)* decision on privacy protection of public figures induced German courts to abandon the concept of a "public figure par excellence." Just as with the *Reynolds* defense, the internalization of ECtHR norms took place through national courts adjusting their decisions.

But the court's persuasive authority goes beyond the ECHR's contracting states. Domestic supreme courts and international adjudicators are in a constant judicial dialogue when interpreting the provisions of the constitutions or human rights treaty they supervise. This dialogue includes informal personal interchanges, institutionalized discourses, and references in judicial decisions. Informal personal interchanges may take place in the academic sphere, for example, within the framework of conferences and guest lectureships, such as the Global Constitutionalism Seminar at Yale Law School. "Institutionalized discourses" involve public forums expressly dedicated to the exchange on constitutional and human rights-related matters. For example, the Council of Europe's Venice Commission, which mainly consists of judges and academics, advises Council of Europe member states on democracy, human rights, and the rule of law.[60] An example of intercontinental judicial dialogue was the June 2016 workshop involving the ECtHR and the African Court on Human and Peoples' Rights (ACtHPR).[61]

Such judicial dialogue eventually manifests itself in references in judicial decisions. For example, the Inter-American Court of Human Rights (IACtHR), when deciding on privacy issues or on conflicts between freedom of the media and religious freedom, regularly refers to the Strasbourg Court.[62] In turn, the Inter-American Court's approach to freedom of access to information seems to serve as a role model for the increasingly generous ECtHR case law on freedom of information.[63] The ACtHPR frequently refers to the ECtHR[64] and also to the IACtHR.[65]

Finally, domestic supreme courts or constitutional courts also frequently refer to each other, including to the U.S. Supreme Court.[66] However, these references are not necessarily mutual, and often are one-sided. More recently established courts are more likely to refer to seasoned courts than vice versa. The reason for this is arguably that more traditional courts are often located in more maturely developed democracies, that they naturally possess a larger body of case law, and that they operate with more refined legal doctrines.[67] This would explain, for example, the early German Federal Constitutional Court references to the U.S. Supreme Court, the ACtHPR references to the IACtHR, and references by both the African Court and the Inter-American Court of Human Rights to the European Court.

Most significant, however, has been the introduction of human rights into the legal order of the European Union and its predecessors by the European Court of Justice (now known as the Court of Justice of the European Union, or the "Luxembourg Court"). When introducing human rights protection into the system of European economic integration, the Luxembourg Court has regularly referred to the ECHR and the case law of the ECtHR.[68] Long before the EU Charter of Fundamental Rights entered into force in 2007, the court developed case law on, for example, freedom of expression,[69] freedom of assembly,[70] freedom of the press,[71] freedom of broadcasting,[72] and media pluralism[73] by reference to ECHR Article 10 and/or the case law of the ECtHR. Regrettably, the Luxembourg Court's human rights jurisprudence has never reached the analytical depths of the Strasbourg Court's.[74]

NORM "ANTIPRENEURS"

According to Alan Bloomfield, emerging norms may struggle to establish themselves due to the contestation, conflicts, or competition of "antipreneurs."[75] This phenomenon applies no less to the ECtHR than to the "classical" norm entrepreneurs as envisaged by Finnemore and Sikkink, albeit under different circumstances. The main antipreneurs against norms generated by the ECtHR are the convention states themselves. This seems to confirm the realist school of thought, according to which states' material interests or "hard power" will determine whether norms emerge, are consolidated, and are internalized. However, one has to be careful to avoid an overly simplified dichotomy along the lines of "ECtHR versus convention states." Instead, it is suggested that one should distinguish more carefully between an "internal contestation" and an "external contestation."

An internal contestation is to be understood as a contestation, conflict, or competition within the system itself. Within the system of the norm entrepreneurship of the ECtHR, an internal contestation takes place, first, within the court proceedings. The convention states are the respondents to applications from people, organizations, or groups claiming to be the victim of a human rights violation. Within this system, the states inevitably struggle for the maintenance of the status quo, a finding of a nonviolation of human rights. But this does not mean that the states contest norm entrepreneurship of the ECtHR as such. On the contrary, in scenarios such as *von Hannover (no. 1)*, in which two conflicting human rights are at stake, the convention state even argues for the adoption of a norm in favor of the human right the convention state sees itself defending (in the *von Hannover* case, freedom of expression). If the Strasbourg Court decides against the state—that is, if it finds a human rights violation—the convention state has the right to ask for a referral to the Grand Chamber, just as the applicant would have if the court had found a nonviolation (ECHR Article 43). This contestation of the ECtHR's norm entrepreneurship takes place within the system provided by the ECHR itself and thus should not give rise to any concerns.

Furthermore, even criticism following a final ECtHR decision should be regarded as internal contestation, if it remains within the boundaries of a reasonable public or academic debate. For example, the *von Hannover (no. 1)* decision and the subsequent abolition of the "public figure par excellence" in German legal doctrine have, to put it mildly, not been universally welcomed in German media law scholarship.[76] However, the obligation of Germany to implement the court's decision has never been called into question. And even the announcement by domestic supreme courts of "red lines," or core aspects of domestic public policy that have to be considered when implementing ECtHR decisions,[77] can be regarded as a judicial dialogue that operates within the system provided by the convention.

In contrast to an internal contestation, an external contestation of the ECtHR's norm entrepreneurship puts the system as such into question. Clearly, such an external contestation has not yet taken place with regard to a norm related to freedom of expression, but it would not be inconceivable, either. Moreover, the external contestation of other norms may have a devastating effect on the cascade and internalization of freedom of expression–related norms as well, which is why a few non-exhaustive examples for external contestations shall be identified here.

An external contestation would be the refusal of a convention state to implement a decision of the ECtHR. For example, the execution of ECtHR judgments by states has reached an all-time low in recent decisions by the Russian Constitutional Court to refuse to implement ECtHR judgments found to be in violation of the Russian constitution.[78] Another external contestation consists of the announcement of measures that would openly contradict the convention. An example would be President Erdoğan's vow to reinstate the death penalty in Turkey,[79] which would be incompatible with the convention.[80] The ultimate external contestation is the threat to withdraw from the convention altogether. Unfortunately, the United Kingdom itself, which ranks among its ancestry some of the greatest champions of liberty, frequently flirts with this option.[81] Calls for withdrawal from the ECHR have been particularly vocal since the Strasbourg Court declared the blanket ban on British prisoners' right to vote contrary to the ECHR,[82] and following the court's prohibition on deporting suspected terrorists to countries where they would face human rights violations.[83]

These examples should not conceal the fact that convention states have largely been compliant with the court's decisions, although the Strasbourg Court's formal enforcement mechanisms—apart from expulsion from the Council of Europe—are limited.[84] However, the influence of the convention will ultimately depend on the convincing force of the ECtHR's judgments, the political will within the convention states to implement them, and the extent to which the system of mutual respect and peer pressure makes convention states abide by the rules.

OUTLOOK

The Strasbourg Court's "mission" as norm entrepreneur for freedom of expression is far from being accomplished, and it is unlikely that it ever will be. The Internet, in particular, has brought up new questions for which the court still has to develop principled answers. The following two questions are certainly among those in which the ECtHR's norm entrepreneurship will be much in demand.

As has been demonstrated, the ECtHR grants privileged protection to the journalistic media. This raises the question as to what the "media" actually is. To what extent does this concept also encompass publishers who have not undertaken journalistic education and who are not affiliated to a news organization, such as bloggers? The Strasbourg Court has never provided a succinct definition of its notion of media. However, the court's more recent case law suggests a functional, rather than formal, understanding of media. The freedoms and privileges of the media do not apply only to professional journalists, as is suggested by the court's earlier case law and by Council of Europe documents.[85] Rather, the court's more recent decisions, including the judgment in *Magyar Helsinki Bizottság v. Hungary*, mentioned previously, indicate that the court extends the media's privileges, and also its enhanced duties and responsibilities, to anyone who regularly contributes to matters of public concern and abides by certain standards of conduct, such as nongovernmental organizations and other "social watchdogs."[86] However, a clarification of the court's principles in this regard, particularly with a view to the requirements that have to be fulfilled in order to qualify as a public or social watchdog, would be desirable.

Another challenge to the court's norm entrepreneurship concerns the liability of Internet intermediaries. Articles 12–15 of the EU's e-commerce directive provide certain immunities for Internet intermediaries—access providers and host providers—that merely disseminate third-party information. However, since the EU is not a member to the ECHR,[87] the Strasbourg Court may not scrutinize the correct interpretation of the e-commerce directive, but it may give a ruling on whether the outcome of a domestic court's application of those provisions was reconcilable with ECHR Article 10.

In *Delfi v. Estonia*, for instance, the court decided that a news portal may be held liable for readers' insulting contributions to its comments section. The court identified the following aspects as relevant for its analysis: the context of the comments, the liability of the actual authors of the comments, the measures applied by the applicant company to prevent or remove defamatory comments, and the consequences of the domestic proceedings for the applicant company.[88] Yet the Joint Concurring Opinion to *Delfi* remarked that the court "should have stated more clearly the underlying principles leading it to find no violation of [ECHR] Article 10," having left "the relevant principles to be developed more clearly in subsequent case law."[89] This is certainly true for the liability not only of news portals but also of online social media platforms in which people comment on topics that have not been brought up by the service provider (such as

Facebook, Twitter, and so forth).[90] Whichever path the Strasbourg Court takes, norm antipreneurship complaining about either "collateral censorship"[91] or the lack of protection of personality rights online will be unavoidable.

NOTES

This contribution builds on, and further expands, ideas I developed in my book *Media Freedom as a Fundamental Right* (Cambridge: Cambridge University Press, 2015).

1. Martha Finnemore and Kathryn Sikkink, "International Norm Dynamics and Political Change," *International Organization* 52, no. 4 (1998): 887–917, at 895.
2. Finnemore and Sikkink, "International Norm Dynamics," 899–901.
3. According to the European Convention on Human Rights (ECHR), Article 36. As an example, see Magyar Helsinki Bizottság v. Hungary (2016), application no. 18030/11, para. 104–116.
4. See Jan Oster, *European and International Media Law* (Cambridge: Cambridge University Press, 2017), 20–22.
5. On the distinction between "rules" and "principles," see Ronald Dworkin, *Taking Rights Seriously* (London: Duckworth, 1977), 22–31.
6. For further references, see Jan Oster, *Media Freedom as a Fundamental Right* (Cambridge: Cambridge University Press, 2015), 118.
7. Handyside v. United Kingdom (1976), application no. 5493/72, para. 49–50; Sunday Times v. United Kingdom (no. 1) (1979), application no. 6538/74, para. 59.
8. Compare Sürek v. Turkey (no. 1) (1999), application no. 26682/95, para. 61; Şener v. Turkey (2000), application no. 26680/95, para. 40; Erdoğdu v. Turkey (2000), application no. 25723/94, para. 62.
9. Handyside v. United Kingdom, 48; European Commission on Human Rights, Hoare v. United Kingdom (1997), application no. 31211/96, para. 1.
10. Mosley v. United Kingdom (2011), application no. 48009/08, para. 108.
11. See, for instance, Otto-Preminger-Institut v. Austria (1994), application no. 13470/87, para. 50; Wingrove v. United Kingdom (1996), application no. 17419/90, para. 58; İ.A. v. Turkey (2005), application no. 42571/98, para. 25.
12. See Steven Greer, "'Balancing' and the European Court of Human Rights: A Contribution to the Habermas-Alexy Debate," *Cambridge Law Journal* 63, no. 2 (2004): 412, 425; Helen Fenwick and Gavin Phillipson, *Media Freedom under the Human Rights Act* (Oxford: Oxford University Press, 2006), 82–86; Ignacio de la Rasilla del Moral, "The Increasingly Marginal Appreciation of the Margin-of-Appreciation Doctrine," *German Law Journal* 6, no. 7 (2006): 611; Valya Filipova, "Standards of

Protection of Freedom of Expression and the Margin of Appreciation in the Jurisprudence of the European Court of Human Rights," *Coventry Law Journal* 17, no. 2 (2012): 64; and Oster, *Media Freedom as a Fundamental Right*, 119–123.

13. See, for example, *Éditions Plon v. France* (2004), application no. 58148/00, para. 42; Egeland and Hanseid v. Norway (2009), application no. 34438/04, para. 48.

14. See, for instance, Lingens v. Austria (1986), application no. 9815/82; Flux v. Moldova (no. 1) (2006), application no. 28702/03, para. 32.

15. Handyside v. United Kingdom, para. 49. This principle is reiterated in, among many other decisions, Sunday Times v. United Kingdom (no. 1), para. 65; Lingens v. Austria, para. 41; and Axel Springer AG v. Germany (no. 1) (2012), application no. 39954/08, para. 78.

16. See, for instance, Lindon, Otchakovsky-Laurens and July v. France (2007), application nos. 21279/02 and 36448/02, para. 45; Frankowicz v. Poland (2008), application no. 53025/99, para. 38.

17. See Oster, *Media Freedom as a Fundamental Right*, 13–23.

18. See, in particular, Alexander Meiklejohn, *Free Speech and its Relation to Self-Government* (New York: Harper Brothers, 1948); Meiklejohn, "The First Amendment Is an Absolute," *Supreme Court Review* (1961): 245; Robert H. Bork, "Neutral Principles and Some First Amendment Problems," *Indiana Law Journal* 47, no. 1 (1971): 1; Cass R. Sunstein, "Free Speech Now," *University of Chicago Law Review* 59 (1992): 255, 263; and James Weinstein, "Participatory Democracy as the Central Value of American Free Speech Doctrine," *Virginia Law Review* 97, no. 3 (2011): 633.

19. See Vincent Blasi, "The Checking Value in First Amendment Theory," *American Bar Foundation Research Journal* (1977): 521, 545; C. Edwin Baker, "Scope of the First Amendment Freedom of Speech," *UCLA Law Review* 25 (1978): 964, 996; Thomas M. Scanlon, "Freedom of Expression and Categories of Expression," *University of Pittsburgh Law Review* 40 (1979): 519, 533; Martin H. Redish, "The Value of Free Speech," *University of Pennsylvania Law Review* 130 (1982): 591, 593; Robert C. Post, "Meiklejohn's Mistake: Individual Autonomy and the Reform of Public Discourse," *University of Colorado Law Review* 64 (1993): 1109; Vanessa Moore, "Free Speech and the Right to Self-Realization," *UCL Jurisprudence Review* 12 (2005): 95; and C. Edwin Baker, "Autonomy and Hate Speech," in *Extreme Speech and Democracy*, ed. Ivan Hare and James Weinstein (Oxford: Oxford University Press, 2009), 139.

20. See Hachette Filipacchi Associés ("Ici Paris") v. France (2009), application no. 12268/03, para. 41; Mosley v. United Kingdom, para. 111; and Von Hannover v. Germany (no. 2) (2012), application nos. 40660/08 and 60641/08, para. 106.

21. See, for instance, Lingens v. Austria (1986), para. 42; Feldek v. Slovakia (2001), application no. 29032/95, para. 74; and Gutiérrez Suárez v. Spain (2010), application no. 16023/07, para. 26.

22. See, for example, Thorgeir Thorgeirson v. Iceland (1992), application no. 13778/88; Nilsen and Johnsen v. Norway (1999), application no. 23118/93, para. 44; and Kasabova v. Bulgaria (2011), application no. 22385/03, para. 56.

23. See, for example, Steel and Morris v. United Kingdom (2005), application no. 68416/01.

24. See, for instance, White v. Sweden (2006), application no. 42435/02, para. 29; and Salumäki v. Finland (2014), application no. 23605/09, para. 54.

25. See, for example, Bladet Tromsø and Stensaas v. Norway (1999), application no. 21980/93; PETA Deutschland v. Germany (2012), application no. 43481/09, para. 47; and Animal Defenders International v. United Kingdom (2013), application no. 48876/08, para. 102.

26. See, for example, Feldek v. Slovakia, para. 80; and Karsai v. Hungary (2009), application no. 5380/07, para. 35.

27. See, for example, Société de Conception de Presse et d'Edition et Ponson v. France (2009), application no. 26935/05, para. 55.

28. See Oster, *European and International Media Law*, 59–64.

29. See Leander v. Sweden (1987), application no. 9248/81; Matky v. Czech Republic (2006), application no. 19101/03; Társaság a Szabadságjogokért v. Hungary (2009), application no. 37374/05; Youth Initiative for Human Rights v. Serbia (2013), application no. 48135/06; and Österreichische Vereinigung zur Erhaltung, Stärkung und Schaffung eines wirtschaftlich gesunden land- und forstwirtschaftlichen Grundbesitzes v. Austria (2013), application no. 39534/07.

30. Magyar Helsinki Bizottság v. Hungary (2016), para. 156, 161, and 166.

31. Magyar Helsinki Bizottság v. Hungary, para. 158.

32. The court extends the protection afforded to the press to audiovisual media; see Jersild v. Denmark (1994), application no. 15890/89, para. 31; and Radio France and others v. France (2004), application no. 53984/00, para. 33.

33. Axel Springer AG v. Germany (no. 1), para. 79; von Hannover v. Germany (no. 2), para. 102. See also, for example, Sunday Times v. United Kingdom (no. 1), para. 65; Bladet Tromsø and Stensaas v. Norway, para. 62; and Times Newspapers Ltd. v. United Kingdom (nos. 1 and 2) (2009), application nos. 3002/03 and 23676/03, para. 40.

34. See Oster, *Media Freedom as a Fundamental Right*, 48.

35. Oster, *Media Freedom as a Fundamental Right*, 48–51.

36. See, for example, Manole and others v. Moldova (2009), application no. 13936/02, para. 98.

37. See, for example, Cumpănă and Mazăre v. Romania (2004), application no. 33348/96, para. 96; and Dammann v. Switzerland (2006), application no. 77551/01, para. 52.

38. See, for example, Goodwin v. United Kingdom (1996), application no. 17488/90, para. 39; and Sanoma Uitgevers B.V. v. Netherlands (2010), application no. 38224/03, para. 50.

39. See, for example, Roemen and Schmit v. Luxembourg (2003), application no. 51772/99, para. 57; and Nagla v. Latvia (2013), application no. 73469/10, para. 95.

40. See Heinisch v. Germany (2011), application no. 28274/08.

41. Guja v. Moldova (2008), application no. 14277/04. See also, for example, Bucur and Toma v. Romania (2013), application no. 40238/02, para. 101.

42. See, for example, Norwood v. United Kingdom (2004), application no. 23131/03, p. 4; Pavel Ivanov v. Russia (2004), application no. 35222/04, p. 4; Nachova and others v. Bulgaria (2005), application nos. 43577/98 and 43579/98, para. 145; Timishev v. Russia (2005), application nos. 55762/00 and 55974/00, para. 56; Leroy v. France (2009), application no. 36109/03, para. 27; and Aksu v. Turkey (2012), application nos. 4149/04 and 41029/04, para. 44.

43. See Karl Popper, *The Open Society and Its Enemies* (1945; repr. London: Routledge, 2002), chapter 7, note 4.

44. Lehideux and Isorni v. France (1998), application no. 55/1997/839/1045, para. 47; Garaudy v. France (2003), application no. 65831/01.

45. See, for example, Russell L. Weaver, Nicholas Delpierre, and Laurence Boissier, "Holocaust Denial and Governmentally Declared 'Truth': French and American Perspectives," *Texas Tech University Law Review* 41 (2009): 495; and Steven G. Gey, "The First Amendment and the Dissemination of Socially Worthless Untruths," *Florida State University Law Review* 36 (2008): 1. On the "distrust of government" as a free speech rationale, see Frederick Schauer, *Free Speech: A Philosophical Enquiry* (Cambridge: Cambridge University Press, 1982), 81, 148, 162–163.

46. Lehideux and Isorni v. France, para. 47; Garaudy v. France.

47. Von Hannover v. Germany (no. 1) (2004), application no. 59320/00.

48. Mosley v. United Kingdom (2011), para. 114 and 131. See also, for example, Hachette Filipacchi Associés ("Ici Paris") v. France, para. 40; MGN Ltd. v. United Kingdom (2011), application no. 39401/04, para. 143; Alkaya v. Turkey (2012), application no. 42811/06, para. 35.

49. Finnemore and Sikkink, "International Norm Dynamics," 895, 901, 904.

50. On reputation as a subcategory of ECHR Article 8, see Chauvy and others v. France (2004), application no. 64915/01, para. 70; Radio France and others v. France (2004), application no. 53984/00, para. 31; and Print Zeitungsverlag GmbH v. Austria (2013), application no. 26547/07, para. 31.

51. Toogood v. Spyring [1834] 1 CR M & R 181. Also see, for instance, Davies v. Snead [1870] LR 5 QB 608; Adam v. Ward [1917] AC 309 (334); Turner v. MGM [1950] 1 All ER 449; Blackshaw v. Lord [1984] QB 1; and Regan v. Taylor [2000] 1 All ER 307.

52. See, for example, London Artists v. Littler [1968] 1 All ER 1075.

53. Reynolds v. Times Newspapers Ltd. [2001] 2 AC 127, 200.

54. Reynolds v. Times Newspapers Ltd., 205.

55. New York Times Co. v. Sullivan, 376 U.S. 254 (1964).

56. It has never been expressly clarified whether only the professional media or also private individuals may invoke the Reynolds defense. The explanatory notes to the Defamation Act 2013 (para. 33) now express that the public interest defense in section 4 shall also apply to private individuals. See also Hourani v. Thomson and others [2017] EWHC 432 (QB), para. 165.

57. See also Jameel v. Wall Street Journal Europe [2006] UKHL 44.

58. See, for example, Economou v. de Freitas [2016] EWHC 1853 (QB), para. 160; Alastair Mullis and Andrew Scott, "Worth the Candle? The Government's Draft Defamation Bill," *Journal of Media Law* 3 (2011): 1, 4–5; and Mullis and Scott, "Tilting at Windmills: The Defamation Act 2013," *Modern Law Review* 77 (2014): 87, 90.

59. See Campbell v. MGN [2004] UKHL 22; and OBG Ltd. and others v. Allan and others [2007] UKHL 21.

60. Council of Europe, Venice Commission, http://www.venice.coe.int.

61. "European Court of Human Rights and African Court Start Week-Long Joint Workshop to Exchange Judicial Experiences in Arusha," African Court of Human and People's Rights, June 23, 2016, http://en.african-court.org/index.php/news /press-releases/item/83-european-court-of-human-rights-and-african-court-start -week-long-joint-workshop-to-exchange-judicial-experiences-in-arusha.

62. See, for example, Inter-American Court of Human Rights, "Advisory Opinion on Compulsory Membership in an Association Prescribed by Law for the Practice of Journalism," [1985] OC-5/85, para. 69; Ivcher-Bronstein v. Peru, [2001] Case 11.762, para. 152; Herrera-Ulloa v. Costa Rica, [2004] Case 12.367, para. 113 and 126; and Eduardo Andre Bertoni, "The Inter-American Court of Human Rights and the European Court of Human Rights: A Dialogue on Freedom of Expression Standards," *European Human Rights Law Review* (2009): 332, 348–352.

63. See Magyar Helsinki Bizottság v. Hungary, para. 146, referring to the seminal Inter-American Court of Human Rights case on access to information, Claude Reyes et al. v. Chile, [2006] Case 12.108.

64. See, for example, African Court on Human and People's Rights, Alex Thomas v. United Republic of Tanzania (2015), application no. 005/2013, para. 97; Actions pour la Protection des Droits de l'Homme (APDH) v. the Republic of Côte d'Ivoire (2016), application no. 001/2014, para. 64; Wilfred Onyango Nganyi and 9 others v. United Republic of Tanzania (2016), application no. 006/2013, para. 136. See also African Commission on Human and Peoples' Rights, Huri-Laws v. Nigeria (2000), application no. 225/98, para. 41.

65. See, for example, Alex Thomas v. United Republic of Tanzania (2015), para. 98.

66. See, for example, the reference to Palko v. Connecticut, 302 U.S. 319, 327 (1937) (Cardozo J) in the seminal decision on freedom of expression in German Federal Constitutional Court, "Lüth," [1958] Case no. 1 BvR 400/51; Supreme Court of Canada, R. v. Morgentaler, [1988] 1 S.C.R. 30, referring, inter alia, to Roe v. Wade, 410 U.S. 113 (1973), and to German Federal Constitutional Court, "Abortion decision," [1975] Case no. 1 BvF 1, 2, 3, 4, 5, 6/74.

67. See Luís Roberto Barroso, "Here, There, and Everywhere: Human Dignity in Contemporary Law and in the Transnational Discourse," *Boston College International & Comparative Law Review* 35 (2012): 331, 343–344; and Oster, *Media Freedom as a Fundamental Right*, 5–6.

68. Nold v. Commission, Case C-4/73 (1974), para. 13.

69. The Society for the Protection of Unborn Children Ireland Ltd. v. Grogan and others, Case C-159/90 (1991), para. 31.

70. Schmidberger v. Austria, Case C-112/00 (2003), para. 20.

71. Familiapress v. Heinrich Bauer Verlag, Case C-368/95 (1997), para. 25–26.

72. ERT v. DEP and others, Case C-260/89 (1991), para. 41; TV 10 SA v. Commissariaat voor de Media, Case C-23/93 (1994), para. 24.

73. Stichting Collectieve Antennevoorziening Gouda and others v. Commissariaat voor de Media, Case C-288/89 (1991), para. 23; Commission v. Netherlands, para. 30, Case C-353/89 (1991).

74. See, for example, Google Spain SL and Google Inc. v. AEPD and Costeja González, Case C-131/12 (2014), where the court—unlike the advocate general—did not even mention the EU Charter of Fundamental Rights, Article 11 ("Freedom of Expression").

75. Alan Bloomfield, "Norm Antipreneurs and Theorising Resistance to Normative Change," *Review of International Studies* 42, no. 2 (2016): 310.

76. For English-language scholarship, see, for example, Dieter Dörr and Eva Aernecke, "A Never Ending Story: *Caroline v. Germany*," in *The Right to Privacy in the Light of Media Convergence*, ed. Dieter Dörr and Russell L. Weaver (Berlin: de Gruyter, 2012), 114–124, which also provides further references to literature in German.

77. See, for example, German Federal Constitutional Court, [2004] Case 2 BvR 1481/04 "Görgülü"; and House of Lords, R. v. Special Adjudicator ex p. Ullah, [2004] UKHL 26, para. 20 (per Lord Bingham of Cornhill).

78. See Natalia Chaeva, "The Russian Constitutional Court and Its Actual Control Over the ECtHR Judgement in Anchugov and Gladkov," *EJIL:Talk!* (blog), *European Journal of International Law*, April 26, 2016, https://www.ejiltalk.org/the-russian-constitutional-court-and-its-actual-control-over-the-ecthr-judgement

-in-anchugov-and-gladko/; and "Russia: Constitutional Court Backs Selective Justice," *Human Rights Watch*, April 19, 2016, https://www.hrw.org/news/2016/04/19/russia-constitutional-court-backs-selective-justice.

79. See Hanna Yusuf, "Erdoğan Vows to Reinstate Death Penalty as Referendum Opponents Face 'Attacks and Imprisonment,'" *Independent*, March 19, 2017, http://www.independent.co.uk/news/world/politics/recep-tayyip-erdo-an-death-penalty-turkey-referendum-merkel-nazi-vote-a7638151.html.

80. Article 1 of Protocol no. 6 to the convention ("Abolishing the Death Penalty in Peacetime"); Article 1 of Protocol no. 13 ("Abolishing the Death Penalty in all Circumstances").

81. See, for example, Will Worley, "Theresa May 'Will Campaign to Leave the European Convention on Human Rights in 2020 Election,'" *Independent*, December 29, 2016, http://www.independent.co.uk/news/uk/politics/theresa-may-campaign-leave-european-convention-on-human-rights-2020-general-election-brexit-a7499951.html.

82. Article 3 of the First Protocol to the ECHR; Hirst v. United Kingdom (no. 2) (2005), application no. 74025/01.

83. Othman (Abu Qatada) v. United Kingdom (2012), application no. 8139/09.

84. Bernadette Rainey, Elizabeth Wicks, and Clare Ovey, *The European Convention on Human Rights*, 6th ed. (Oxford: Oxford University Press, 2014), 64. On the ECHR's "control system," see the 14th Protocol to the ECHR (Council of Europe Treaty Series no. 194).

85. See Sürek and Özdemir v. Turkey (1999), application nos. 23927/94 and 24277/94, para. 63; Şener v. Turkey (2000), application no. 26680/95, para. 42; Wizerkaniuk v. Poland (2011), application no. 18990/05, para. 68; Kaperzyński v. Poland (2012), application no. 43206/07, para. 70; Council of Europe, Recommendation no. R (2000) 7 on the right of journalists not to disclose their sources of information, the appendix of which states, "For the purposes of this Recommendation . . . the term 'journalist' means any natural or legal person who is regularly or professionally engaged in the collection and dissemination of information to the public via any means of mass communication"; and Recommendation CM/Rec(2011)7, "On a New Notion of Media," appendix, para. 38.

86. See Fatullayev v. Azerbaijan (2010), application no. 40984/07, para. 95; Růžový panter, o.s. v. Czech Republic (2012), application no. 20240/08; Braun v. Poland (2014), application no. 30162/10; Magyar Helsinki Bizottság v. Hungary, para. 164. For a general overview and reference to the academic debate, see Oster, *European and International Media Law*, 9–12.

87. See Court of Justice of the European Union, Opinion 2/13.

88. Delfi AS v. Estonia (2015), application no. 64569/09, para. 143.
89. Delfi AS v. Estonia, Joint Concurring Opinion of Judges Raimondi, Karakas, De Gaetano, and Kjølbro, para. 8.
90. See Delfi AS v. Estonia, para. 116.
91. See Delfi AS v. Estonia, Joint Dissenting Opinion.

The Role of the Inter-American
Human Rights System in the Emergence
and Development of Global Norms
on Freedom of Expression

EIGHT

CATALINA BOTERO-MARINO

The inter-American system for the protection of human rights of the Organization of American States (OAS) has promoted and developed important regional standards for the protection of the right to freedom of expression, some of which have the potential to become global norms on the matter. The objective of this chapter is to explain the key actors and institutions in the process of emergence and consolidation of these standards, the specific dynamics of this process, and some of the impacts that these standards have had on other human rights protection systems.

THE KEY ACTORS AND INSTITUTIONS IN THE EMERGENCE AND CONSOLIDATION OF THE INTER-AMERICAN STANDARDS ON FREEDOM OF EXPRESSION

The Inter-American Human Rights System as Norms Builder

The inter-American system, unlike the current European system, has two entities to protect and promote human rights, including freedom of expression.

These are the Inter-American Commission on Human Rights (IACHR)[1] and the Inter-American Court of Human Rights.[2]

Until the end of the twentieth century, the IACHR and the Inter-American Court were the only entities that protected freedom of expression in the inter-American system. During this period, the IACHR produced a single thematic report on freedom of expression and decided on a few cases on this matter.[3] The Inter-American Court, in turn, only issued two advisory opinions on this right.[4] In this context, it was hardly possible to speak of the existence of true inter-American standards on the subject. This lack of legal development is explained by the fact that during the first two decades of the American Convention on Human Rights, the inter-American system was in an incipient process of institutional development and had to focus all of its efforts on the atrocities committed in the region in the past decades. In fact, during the first years of implementation of the American Convention, both the IACHR and the Inter-American Court had to deal with the massacres, forced disappearances, and torture that characterized the dictatorships and armed conflicts of many of the states in the region.[5]

However, at the end of the 1990s and the beginning of this century, thanks to impetus from human rights and journalist organizations, the media, and some states that had engaged in their transition to democracy, the two entities of the inter-American system began to give special attention to the right to freedom of expression. It is sufficient to briefly mention three fundamental decisions of that period in order to understand the importance that the region gave to freedom of expression at the turn of the century: the IACHR's creation of the Office of the Special Rapporteur for Freedom of Expression, in 1997; the issuance of the Declaration of Principles on Freedom of Expression of the IACHR, in 2000;[6] and the issuance of the OAS Inter-American Democratic Charter, in 2001, according to which freedom of expression is one of the *"essential components of the exercise of democracy"* (emphasis mine).[7] The Office of the Special Rapporteur, which began its work in 1998, became, for more than fifteen years, the only permanent rapporteur headed by an independent expert, elected by IACHR commissioners. As will be explained, this office has been a key player in the promotion of regional standards on freedom of expression.

With the adoption of these three decisions, the two main obstacles to the development of the right to freedom of expression in the inter-American system were resolved: while the Office of the Special Rapporteur reinforced the technical capacity of the IACHR, the Declaration of Principles and the Inter-American Democratic Charter gave freedom of expression a privileged place in the democracies of the region. Thereafter, an exponential increase in the creation of regional standards on freedom of expression began. Between 2001 and 2017, the Inter-American Court of Human Rights—thanks to the cases sent by the IACHR—issued a total of twenty-three judgments directly related to this right, corresponding to a little more than 10 percent of all rulings produced during this period. For its part, the IACHR approved dozens of admissibility, merits and thematic reports on the matter. And finally, the Office of the Special Rapporteur produced a total of nineteen annual reports that comprehensively analyze the situation of freedom of expression in all the states of the region, and more than thirty thematic reports that develop particular aspects of the right to freedom expression.[8]

Other Norms Builders Working Alongside the Inter-American System

In addition to the entities of the inter-American system, other actors and institutions have been instrumental in developing regional standards on freedom of expression. First, the political entities of the OAS—in particular, the General Assembly—have played a role in the adoption of treaties, declarations, and resolutions, which include the main inter-American norms on freedom of expression, such as the American Declaration of the Rights and Duties of Man (1948), the American Convention on Human Rights (1969), the Inter-American Democratic Charter (2001),[9] the Model Inter-American Law on Access to Public Information (2010),[10] and other resolutions that have been vital for the consolidation of the right of access to information in the region.[11]

Second, the importance of what we might call "transitional governments" of the last two decades of the twentieth century and the beginning of the new millennium is unquestionable. Governments that sought to advance democracy after the military dictatorships of the Southern Cone, such as in Argentina and Chile, were fundamental because they proposed and succeeded in electing to the Inter-American Court and to the IACHR human rights experts particularly sensitive to freedom of expression.[12] These governments respectfully abided by all the decisions of the IACHR and the Inter-American Court in the area of freedom of expression, reforming in response their legal frameworks, policies, and practices on the matter. Argentina, for example, repealed the crime of *desacato* (contempt) following the IACHR's recommendations in the case of *Verbitsky v. Argentina*.[13] Chile, for its part, welcomed the Inter-American Court's decision in the case of *Olmeda Bustos v. Chile* to repeal the norm of its constitution that authorized prior censorship.[14] In turn, the governments of Mexico and Peru, which at the beginning of the twenty-first century were undergoing a process of democratic reconquest, played a fundamental role in the regional recognition of the right of access to information as a fundamental right. These states prompted the first access laws in the region, long before the Inter-American Court ruled on this matter.[15]

Third and finally, it is important to highlight the role played by civil society organizations. Nongovernmental organizations have been responsible for bringing to the inter-American system particular cases of violation of inter-American standards on freedom of expression.[16] They have established channels of direct communication with commissioners and judges and, in many cases, have been responsible for the emergence of new regional standards. For example, the so-called Grupo Oaxaca of Mexico played a decisive role in the promulgation of the Mexican law of access to information in 2002, and later was able to influence, through Judge García Ramírez, the decision of the Inter-American Court case of *Claude Reyes et al. v. Chile* (2006).[17] Another example is the Center for Legal and Social Studies in Argentina and the Committee to Protect Journalists, which managed to give a remarkable boost to the IACHR's campaign to decriminalize criminal defamation in the region. Furthermore, the Committee to Protect Journalists, the Inter American Press Association, and other local organizations played an essential role in the inter-American system in the fight against impunity for crimes committed against journalists.

Actors Working Against the Inter-American System

Notwithstanding the aforementioned developments, the creation of inter-American standards on freedom of expression has not been a linear or harmonic process, nor has it been without contradictions. Since its inception, the process has encountered fierce opposition from states in the region with less democratic development, and from some political bodies of the OAS that have been influenced by them. One of the most serious episodes of confrontation in the inter-American system came in 1999, when Peruvian president Alberto Fujimori attempted to circumvent the jurisdiction of the Inter-American Court a few months after the IACHR had filed a petition in *Ivcher Bronstein v. Peru*.[18] The episode was, however, finally resolved shortly after, in 2000, when Fujimori was removed from his official position and had to leave office.

Another serious episode of confrontation occurred between 2009 and 2010, led by the government of Venezuela. Since 2003, the IACHR and the Office of the Special Rapporteur have been reporting on various violations of freedom of expression in Venezuela, such as arbitrary imposition of criminal and administrative sanctions against journalists and the media, acts of violence committed against them, refusal to renew Venezuelan cable television network Radio

Caracas Televisión Internacional's operating license, and the continued hostile statements of then President Hugo Chávez against independent media, among others. In 2009 and 2010, the special rapporteur published two reports detailing the situation in Venezuela.[19] In 2009, the Inter-American Court condemned the state of Venezuela in three different cases in relation to violations of freedom of expression.[20] In response to the intervention of the inter-American system, the Venezuelan government began a smear campaign against the IACHR and the Inter-American Court. The episode finally led to the denunciation of the American Convention by the state of Venezuela, in September 2012.

A third confrontation took place in 2012 and featured the Ecuadorian government. Between 2011 and 2012, the Office of the Special Rapporteur denounced, through its annual reports and press releases, various cases of violation of freedom of expression in Ecuador, including the imposition of criminal sanctions against journalists and millionaire civil rulings against media companies, the arbitrary use of official publicity, the interruption of the transmission of television programs critical of the government, and the concentration of media ownership in the hands of the national government, among others.[21] In 2012, the Ecuadorian government went to the Permanent Council of the OAS, proposing a package of reforms to the IACHR, which had the objective of technically and economically asphyxiating the Office of the Special Rapporteur.[22] These reforms were long discussed but finally rejected, thanks to the strong opposition of governments such as Mexico, Uruguay, and Costa Rica. Although the Ecuadorian government's strategy against the special rapporteur failed on such occasion, in 2015 it elected to the Inter-American Court Judge Patricio Pazmiño, whose political independence has been seriously questioned.

THE PROCESS OF THE EMERGENCE, DEVELOPMENT, AND INTERNALIZATION OF INTER-AMERICAN STANDARDS ON FREEDOM OF EXPRESSION

As previously mentioned, over the past twenty years the inter-American system has developed different regional standards on freedom of expression. From a methodological point of view, the system has applied a three-part test (called, in some rulings, the proportionality test) to evaluate restrictions on freedom of expression. The application of this test is based on the idea that in matters of public interest the right to freedom of expression enjoys special and enhanced protection. From the material point of view, the jurisprudence has set important standards that revolve around five central themes:[23]

1. The special protection of public interest speech and, in particular, the restriction of criminal law as a means to limit this type of speech.[24]
2. The recognition of the right of access to information as a fundamental right of universal character and the application of a strict test of proportionality against any type of restriction that seeks to impose itself.[25]
3. The prohibition of all forms of prior censorship.[26]
4. The prohibition of all forms of "indirect censorship," that is, the use of apparently legitimate powers and/or state resources to reward social media or journalists based on their coverage or editorial line.[27]
5. The state's obligation to prevent, protect, and seek justice in the face of acts of violence committed against journalists.[28]

Of the inter-American standards mentioned, those related to the first two themes are the ones that have received the greatest reception in the region. Therefore, to explain the emergence and consolidation of regional standards on freedom of expression in the inter-American system, I will turn my attention to case studies of the special protection of public interest speech and of the right of access to information.

Although each standard has had its own development and has been characterized by unique dynamics, it can be said that there is a common pattern that is repeated in both cases and that it is relevant to describe. The process of the emergence of a regional standard usually begins when a group of citizens or a nongovernmental organization identifies a problem related to freedom of expression and makes claims that transcend the domestic scope. In some cases, these claims are directly received by the states and become an impetus—a good practice—that motivates the entities of the inter-American system into developing standards around this topic.[29] In other cases, the claims are rejected internally and, in this way—after exhaustion of domestic resources—they reach the regional forum.[30]

Thanks to this process, the Office of the Special Rapporteur is able to identify the problem—usually through its monitoring work or through direct communications with social organizations, journalists, or the media—and to determine whether it is a relevant issue that must be prioritized by the system. To that end, the Office of the Special Rapporteur takes into account whether it is a problem that affects the right to freedom of expression in the region in general or, despite its singularity, is extremely serious.

Once the problem is identified and prioritized, the special rapporteur begins a phase of "laying the groundwork," which consists of creating a conceptual framework around the previously identified problem, with the dual objective of drawing the attention of the states and bodies of the OAS, and preparing the arguments that may serve as the basis for a possibly contentious case. For the preparation of these reports, the Office of the Special Rapporteur usually refers to comparative law, to the obiter dicta of previous judgments of the IACHR and the Inter-American Court, and to decisions (legislative or judicial) of the OAS member states.

The next phase is strategic litigation. To this end, the Office of the Special Rapporteur selects and puts forward to the bodies of the inter-American system a case that reflects the problems identified. Having the IACHR recognize a standard has always been considered of crucial importance to the inter-American system in view of the fact that a significant number of states (parties to the American Convention) consider that the decisions of the IACHR have a value equivalent to the decisions of their respective supreme or constitutional courts. Although the OAS General Assembly has urged member states to accept the recommendations made by the IACHR,[31] in some states, these recommendations are understood as "soft law" or relevant doctrine.

Following the obtaining of a ruling from the IACHR comes the phase of internalization of the standard in the domestic legal systems of the region, which can be achieved through legislative and/or constitutional reforms or through jurisprudential developments. In this phase, the work of the Office of the Special Rapporteur is again crucial, as they perform visits and write annual reports, encouraging the incorporation of these standards into domestic law.

The following subsections describe in detail the process of the emergence, consolidation, and internalization of inter-American standards related to the protection of public interest speech and the right of access to information.

Case Study No. 1: The Standard of Special Protection of Public Interest Speech and the Restriction on Criminal Law as a Means to Limit this Type of Speech

At the beginning of the 1990s, many countries in Latin America and the Caribbean sanctioned with imprisonment anyone who, by any means, offended the honor or reputation of a public official. *Desacato*, as this crime is called, differs from criminal defamation in two respects: the victim is a public official, and the penalty for *desacato* is greater than that foreseen for ordinary defamation crimes. *Desacato* continued to exist at the beginning of the 1990s as an inheritance from Latin America's authoritarian past.

The IACHR noticed this situation when it reviewed the *Verbitsky v. Argentina* case in 1992, thanks to the strong momentum of civil society organizations in Argentina and to the relationship that journalist Horatio Verbitsky had with the IACHR commissioners. The case was resolved amicably when, in 1993, Argentina removed the crime of *desacato* from its criminal code.[32] Having identified the problem, and accompanied by the political momentum of Argentina, chapter 5 of the IACHR's 1994 annual report publicly denounced the crime of *desacato* as incompatible with Article 13 of the American Convention. In the opinion of the IACHR, *desacato* undermined the most basic democratic principle, according to which public officials should always be subject to public scrutiny. To support its position, the IACHR relied on jurisprudence from the European Court of Human Rights.[33] In its report, the IACHR also warned that at least fourteen states in the region consecrated *desacato*, and recommended its repeal altogether. As a result of the report, Paraguay repealed this crime in 1997.[34]

In 1998, the Office of the Special Rapporteur published its first annual report, and from that moment on it vindicated the position of the inter-American system against the use of criminal law as a means to restrict public interest speech.[35] Following the example set by the IACHR in 1994, the Office of the Special Rapporteur made an assessment of the criminalization of *desacato* in the region and again declared it incompatible with the right to freedom of expression. In 2000, the IACHR approved the Declaration of Principles on Freedom of Expression, which expressly states, "Laws that penalize offensive expressions directed at public officials, generally known as 'desacato laws,' restrict freedom of expression and the right to information." Shortly after, Costa Rica and Peru[36] removed the crime of *desacato* from their criminal codes.

While all this occurred, three different cases on criminal restrictions on freedom of expression and special protection of public interest speech were being processed within the IACHR: the *Herrera-Ulloa*, *Ricardo Canese*, and *Palamara Iribarne* cases.[37] The third case was especially interesting because Palamara Iribarne had been condemned precisely for *desacato*. The three cases were decided by the IACHR, between 2002 and 2003, and then by the Inter-American Court, between 2004 and 2005. In the judgment handed down in the *Palamara Iribarne* case (2005), the Inter-American Court explicitly acknowledges that *desacato* crimes are incompatible with the American Convention and that the use of criminal law as a means to restrict public interest speech is unnecessary and disproportionate in a democratic society.

As a result of these three rulings, Panama, Chile, and Nicaragua repealed the crime of *desacato* from their criminal codes.[38] Likewise, the constitutional courts of Honduras, Guatemala, and Bolivia declared the crime of *desacato* unconstitutional based on the jurisprudence of the Inter-American Court.

More recently, the Brazilian Supreme Court of Justice stated that the crime of *desacato* is inapplicable as it is incompatible with the American Convention.[39]

The Office of the Special Rapporteur has always been aware that simply repealing the crime of *desacato* is not sufficient to protect public interest speech, as criminal defamation (such as libel or slander) can also be used to suppress this kind of speech. For this reason, since its first annual report, the Office of the Special Rapporteur has been recommending, in addition to repealing *desacato*, the repeal of criminal defamation offenses in matters of public interest.[40] The same standard had been recognized in the Declaration of Principles on Freedom of Expression, principle 10 of which further establishes that the application of civil penalties as a means of protecting the honor of public officials is, in any case, subject to the standard of actual malice.

Throughout its reports, the special rapporteur continued to advocate the repeal of defamation crimes, until finally the Inter-American Court recognized in three different cases that criminal law is a disproportionate means of restricting public interest speech.[41] In this context, Nicaragua,[42] Panama,[43] Argentina,[44] and El Salvador[45] partially repealed the crimes of libel and slander. In Peru[46] and Colombia,[47] the highest criminal courts, citing jurisprudence of the Inter-American Court, decided that defamation crimes, despite being in principle constitutional, are disproportionate when used to protect the honor of public officials. Mexico (at the federal level),[48] Grenada,[49] and Jamaica[50] went a step further and completely repealed criminal defamation crimes from their criminal codes. In turn, the Mexican Supreme Court of Justice of the Nation stated that in those states where slander or libel had not been repealed, these crimes cannot be used to criminalize criticism of officials, since this type of criticism is of public interest and therefore is subject to special protection.[51]

Following the repeal of the crime of *desacato* in eleven countries in the region, and of defamation in nine, most of them influential countries on regional policy, a new inter-American standard on freedom of expression appeared to be in the process of consolidation. Unfortunately, in Venezuela and Ecuador, national courts have been prosecuting and convicting journalists for publicly criticizing the president and other public officials. As a result of these cases, the IACHR and the Office of the Special Rapporteur have issued important pronouncements, which, as mentioned, have generated a strong political reaction from the governments of both states.[52]

In 2013, in the midst of clashes between the governments of Venezuela and Ecuador and the entities of the inter-American system, the Inter-American Court of Human Rights issued a ruling on the *Mémoli v. Argentina* case, which is perhaps one of the most criticized in inter-American jurisprudence.[53] It authorizes, for the first time in its jurisprudence, the application of criminal penalties to public interest speech, based on a remarkably restrictive definition of public interest speech. Although the Inter-American Court recognizes that such speech deserves special protection, it defines public interest speech as speech that refers to "public officials" but not that which refers to individuals who administer public goods. This regression in the jurisprudence of the Inter-American Court seems to have been the result of pressure from the governments of Ecuador and Venezuela on the inter-American system.

In 2019, in *Álvarez Ramos v. Venezuela*, the court established, in a much more categorical way than any previous decision, that it is disproportionate to use criminal law to punish those who critique public officials' performance of duties.[54] However, it restricts public interest speech, which requires special protection, to speech that refers to the performance of public duties by officials. This approach leaves out speech that is evidently of public interest, such as speech referring to the use of public goods or public resources by private individuals. For this reason, despite the ruling's progress in opposing the use of criminal defamation for speech against public officers, the protection of public interest speech more broadly continues to be at risk.

Case Study No. 2: The Standard of the Right to Access Information

The Office of the Special Rapporteur first addressed in detail the right of access to information in its 2001 annual report.[55] In this report, the Office of the Special Rapporteur held that Article 13 of the American Convention protects the right of all persons to access information held by the state. The report, however, expressed concern that only seven countries in the region had some kind of legal regulation to exercise this right, and it warned that this "culture of secrecy" represented a "danger to the constitutional democratic system."

The problem with the right of access to information had attracted the attention of the special rapporteur, thanks to the work of the Oaxaca Group from Mexico, resulting in the approval of the Federal Law on Transparency and Access to Public Government Information (2002)—undoubtedly the most pioneering and revolutionary law of access to information in the region.[56] At the same time, similar laws were passed in Panama and Peru, with the difference being that none of them established the creation of an independent and specialized entity for the defense of this right.[57] The following year, thanks to the intervention of the governments of Mexico and Peru, the OAS General Assembly approved Resolution 1932, which, in addition to recognizing the right of access to information as an indispensable requirement for the functioning of democracy, entrusted the Office of the Special Rapporteur with the task of including in its annual reports an assessment of the situation of this right in the region.[58]

In compliance with the mandate of the General Assembly, the Office of the Special Rapporteur presented, in its 2003 Annual Report, a much deeper analysis on the subject.[59] Based on obiter dicta of the Inter-American Court and the IACHR, the Office of the Special Rapporteur made a deliberate effort to demonstrate that Article 13 of the American Convention protects the right of access to information. The 1999 report by the UN special rapporteur on the promotion and protection of the right to freedom of opinion and expression, which had previously recognized that the right of access to information was protected by Article 19 of the International Covenant on Civil and Political Rights, was crucial in this process.[60]

Simultaneously, the Office of the Special Rapporteur brought before the IACHR the case of *Claude Reyes et al. v. Chile*, which had originally been submitted by a Chilean civil society organization and concerned access to information on environmental issues.[61] The IACHR ruled on the case in 2005, and subsequently so did the Inter-American Court, in 2006. In its ruling, the court recognized that Article 13 of the American Convention protects the fundamental right of access to information held by the state, without the need to demonstrate a particular interest, and that any restriction on this right should be provided for by law, pursue a legitimate purpose, and be necessary for the attainment of that purpose.[62] Many of the arguments and normative sources used by the Inter-American Court had already been used by the special rapporteur in her 2003 report and were based on the same philosophy that had inspired the Mexican law on access to information. It was no coincidence that Mexican judge, Sergio García Ramírez, was, at the moment of the decision, the president of the Inter-American Court.

Following the judgment of *Claude Reyes*, Chile reformed its legal framework and established a reinforced system of guarantees on the right of access to information.[63] In turn, the Chilean Constitutional Court, in 2007, recognized that in Chile there is a fundamental right of access to information.[64] At the same time, Honduras,[65] Nicaragua,[66] Guatemala,[67] and Uruguay[68] enacted laws on access to information. Following this first wave, in 2010, the OAS General Assembly—with the impetus of Mexico and Peru—approved the Model Inter-American Law on Access to Public Information,[69] and that same year, the Inter-American Court, in the case of *Gomes Lund et al. v. Brazil*,[70] reiterated the precedent of *Claude Reyes*. This resulted in a second wave of access to information laws in El Salvador,[71] Brazil,[72] Colombia,[73] Argentina,[74] and Paraguay.[75] Additionally, the highest constitutional courts in Colombia,[76]

Guatemala,[77] El Salvador,[78] Mexico,[79] Paraguay,[80] Costa Rica,[81] and Argentina,[82] with explicit reference to the *Claude Reyes* case, recognized that the right of access to information is a fundamental universal right governed under the "principle of maximum disclosure."

After the recognition of the right of access to information in twenty-four countries in the region—most of them also influential countries on regional policy—a new inter-American standard on freedom of expression seems to have been consolidated. In addition, the Inter-American Court, in the case of *Omar Humberto Maldonado et al. v. Chile* (2015), once again reiterated the precedent of *Claude Reyes*, clarifying, however, that in order to guarantee the operation of truth commissions in transitional justice processes, certain restrictions on the right of access to information could be justified.[83]

In its annual reports, the Office of the Special Rapporteur has reiterated the fundamental nature of this right and the absolute exceptional nature of any restriction that may be imposed on it. However, the process of developing the right to access to information has encountered strong opposition from Venezuela, where the Supreme Court of Justice has systematically denied the exercise of this right, on the grounds that it compromises the efficiency of public administration, and that its exercise is subject to the accreditation of a particular interest.[84]

THE VIRTUOUS CIRCLE BETWEEN INTER-AMERICAN STANDARDS ON FREEDOM OF EXPRESSION AND THOSE OF OTHER HUMAN RIGHTS SYSTEMS: A FEW EXAMPLES

In this last section, we will briefly look at some examples that suggest the existence of what could be called a virtuous circle among the different international systems for the protection of human rights, privileging those demonstrating the influence of the inter-American system on other human rights systems. Although the congruences among these systems are not necessarily proof of the process of emergence of global norms, they reflect a trend in this direction that is important to highlight.

The Congruence Between the Inter-American System's Jurisprudence and the Jurisprudence of Other International Human Rights Tribunals

The inter-American standard of protection on the right of access to information—and in particular the judgment of the Inter-American Court in the case of *Claude Reyes* (2006)—has had a certain impact on the jurisprudence of the European

Court of Human Rights. In the case of *Magyar Helsinki v. Hungary* (2016), the European Court, citing the precedent of *Claude Reyes*, decided that Article 10 of the European Convention on Human Rights protects the right of access to information, so that any restriction of this right—like any other restriction on freedom of expression—is subject to the three-part test or necessity test.[85] Previously, in the case of *Stoll v. Switzerland* (2007), the European Court had ruled that a journalist's conviction for the publication of confidential information constituted a disproportionate restriction on freedom of expression. As a basis for that decision, the European Court considered that "the disclosure of state-held information should play a very important role in a democratic society," citing the IACHR's application before the Inter-American Court in the case of *Claude Reyes*.[86]

The inter-American standard of special protection of public interest speech—and in particular the judgments of the Inter-American Court in the cases of *Herrera-Ulloa* (2004), *Ricardo Canese* (2004), and *Palamara Iribarne* (2005)[87]—have also had some impact on the jurisprudence of the African Court on Human and Peoples' Rights. In the case of *Lohé Issa Konaté v. Burkina Faso* (2013), the African Court established that only in absolutely exceptional cases is it permissible to use criminal laws as a method to restrict freedom of expression, and in particular to restrict public interest speech. Citing the Inter-American Court, it stated that "states should use these laws only as a last resort and [reject] imprisonment for defamation, considering it as disproportionate and in violation of freedom of expression."[88]

The Congruence Between the Reports of the OAS Special Rapporteur and General Comment No. 34 (2011) of the United Nations Human Rights Committee

In 2010, the Office of the Special Rapporteur published two reports in which it systematized and developed the most important inter-American standards on freedom of expression. In its first report, *Inter-American Legal Framework of the Right to Freedom of Expression*, and its second, *The Right of Access to Information in the Inter-American Legal Framework*, the Office of the Rapporteur studied the content, meaning, and scope of the right to freedom of expression and access to information in the inter-American system.[89] Shortly after these reports were published, the Office of the Special Rapporteur sent them to the United Nations Human Rights Committee as part of this entity's consultation process toward the formulation of a new General Comment on Article 19 of the International Covenant on Civil and Political Rights.

The following year, in 2011, the committee published General Comment no. 34 (2011).[90] Although—following common practice—General Comment no. 34 omits references to sources exogenous to the universal system, the influence of the reports of the OAS special rapporteur seems clear, as do, consequently, the legal doctrine and jurisprudence that these reports standardized. Among other things, both documents acknowledge that the right of access to information is a universal fundamental right, protected by the right to freedom of expression; that state authorities have an obligation to clearly present "the reasons for any denial of access to information"; and that states are required to have effective resources to challenge decisions to deny information.[91]

The Congruence Between the Report *Violence Against Journalists and Media Workers* (2013) and Recommendation CM/Rec (2016)4 (2016)

In 2013, the Office of the Special Rapporteur published the report *Violence against Journalists and Media Workers*.[92] In its report, the Office of the Rapporteur extensively develops the doctrine according to which states have the triple obligation to prevent, protect, and seek justice in cases of violence against journalists.[93] The obligation of prevention, according to the special rapporteur, entails, among other things, educating the population and the authorities, adopting a public discourse that contributes to preventing this type of violence and that omits any stigmatization,[94] and "the obligation to respect the right of journalists to reserve their sources."[95] The obligation to protect, for its part, consists, among other things, of the duty to implement special protection measures in favor of journalists at risk because of their professions.[96] Finally, the obligation to seek justice includes the duty to investigate, prosecute, and punish those responsible for any act of violence against journalists.[97] For the Office of the Special Rapporteur, this duty involves having autonomous and specialized authorities,[98] protecting judicial operators involved in the investigation and prosecution stages,[99] and addressing different situations, such as the existence of armed conflicts[100] or gender discrimination.[101]

Recommendation CM/Rec(2016)4 was adopted by the Committee of Ministers of the Council of Europe in 2016, and it indicates the obligations of the states of the European Union when acts of violence are committed against journalists. The committee begins by pointing out that European states have the obligations that had previously been identified by the OAS special rapporteur in its report of 2013.[102] In relation to the obligation of prevention, the committee maintains that public officials should avoid discourses that endanger the safety of journalists and should respect the confidentiality of their sources. In relation to the obligation of protection, it establishes that states have the obligation to adopt special measures in situations of "imminent and real risk" for journalists, as already set out by the OAS special rapporteur.[103] In relation to the obligation to seek justice, the Committee of Ministers' approach is largely modeled on that of the special rapporteur's report. It considers that this obligation implies, among other things, the duty to have autonomous and specialized authorities;[104] to protect judges, prosecutors, and witnesses;[105] and to use a differential approach, taking into account situations of special conflict[106] as well as practices of gender discrimination.[107]

There is a final element that seems necessary to highlight. This is the significant influence that the joint declarations of the special rapporteur on freedom of expression have had on all of the OAS special rapporteur's reports since 1999—including the ones mentioned in this chapter—and the important role of Article 19 in prompting and pushing forward these declarations.

NOTES

I would like to thank my colleagues Julián Niño and Salomé Gómez for their invaluable support in the production of this chapter. I would also like to thank the Global Freedom of Expression project at Columbia University, which allowed us to have reliable and updated information on the process of internalization of inter-American standards on freedom of expression.

1. The Inter-American Commission on Human Rights (IACHR) was the first human rights protection entity of the inter-American system. At the time of its creation, in 1959, it did not really have powers to effectively protect human rights. Since the implementation of the American Convention on Human Rights in 1978, the IACHR has the triple function of monitoring and reporting on the human rights situation throughout the region; deciding, based on a "quasi-jurisdictional" contentious process, on specific cases of violation of these rights that have occurred in any of the thirty-four states of the Organization of American States (OAS); and submitting to the Inter-American Court of Human Rights (IACtHR) those cases in which the states involved have refused to follow their recommendations, provided that such states have recognized the jurisdiction of the court.

2. The Inter-American Court of Human Rights was created in 1978, with the implementation of the American Convention on Human Rights. It has the dual function of issuing advisory opinions on the interpretation of the American Convention on Human Rights and the American Declaration of the Rights and Duties of Man,

and deciding on particular cases of human rights violations filed by the IACHR. The Inter-American Court, unlike the IACHR, has no jurisdiction over all the states of the OAS but only over those who, in addition to having ratified the American Convention, have explicitly recognized their jurisdiction. To date, twenty-one states of the OAS have recognized the jurisdiction of the IACtHR. The list of these states is available at OAS, Department of International Law, "Multilateral Treaties," http://www.oas.org/dil/treaties_B-32_American_Convention_on_Human_Rights_sign.htm.

3. Inter-American Commission on Human Rights, *Report on the Compatibility of "Desacato" Laws with the American Convention on Human Rights*, Annual Report 1994, chap. 5, OEA/Ser.L/V/II.88, Doc. 9 rev, February 17, 1995. The list of the most important cases related to freedom of expression decided by the IACHR is available at OAS, "Merits Reports or Applications Before the Inter-American Court," http://www.oas.org/en/iachr/expression/jurisprudence/decisions_iachr_merit.asp.

4. IACtHR, *Compulsory Membership in an Association Prescribed by Law for the Practice of Journalism*, American Convention on Human Rights, Articles 13 and 29, Advisory Opinion OC-5/85 of November 13, 1985, series A, no. 5; IACtHR, *Enforceability of the Right to Reply or Correction*, American Convention on Human Rights, Articles 14(1), 1(1), and 2, Advisory Opinion OC-7/86 of August 29, 1986, series A, no. 7.

5. Catalina Botero-Marino, *A Hemispheric Agenda for the Defense of Freedom of Expression*, 2009 Thematic Report of the OAS Special Rapporteur for Freedom of Expression, OEA/Ser.L/V/II, CIDH/RELE/INF. 4/09, February 25, 2009, para. 1–11.

6. OAS, "Declaration of Principles on Freedom of Expression," approved by the IACHR in October 2000, http://www.oas.org/en/iachr/expression/showarticle.asp?artID=26&lID=1.

7. OAS General Assembly, Resolution 1 (28-E/01), September 11, 2001.

8. The list of merits reports on the right to freedom of expression of the IACtHR is available at OAS, "Merits Reports or Applications before the Inter-American Court," http://www.oas.org/en/iachr/expression/jurisprudence/decisions_iachr_merit.asp. The list of judgments on the right to freedom of expression of the IACtHR is available at OAS, "Decisions and Judgments of the Inter-American Court," http://www.oas.org/en/iachr/expression/jurisprudence/si_decisions_court.asp. The list of judgments of the IACtHR is available at Inter-American Court of Human Rights, "Decisions and Judgments," http://www.corteidh.or.cr/cf/Jurisprudencia2/busqueda_casos_contenciosos.cfm?lang=en. The reports on the right to freedom of expression from the special rapporteur are available at OAS,

"Annual Reports," http://www.oas.org/en/iachr/expression/reports/annual.asp, and "Thematic Reports," OAS, http://www.oas.org/en/iachr/expression/reports/thematic .asp.

9. OAS General Assembly, Resolution 1 (28-E/01), September 11, 2001.

10. OAS General Assembly, Resolution 2607 (40-O/10), June 8, 2010.

11. OAS General Assembly resolutions 1932 (33-O/03); 2057 (34-O/04); 2121 (35-O/05); and 2252 (36-O/06), among others.

12. Among them, it is necessary to emphasize Argentine commissioner Juan Méndez (2000–2003) and Mexican judge Sergio García Ramírez (2004–2009), who were decisive in the decriminalization of *desacato* and the consolidation of the right of access to information in the region, respectively.

13. See IACtHR, report no. 22/94 (Friendly Settlement), case no. 11.012 (Verbitsky v. Argentina), September 20, 1994; law 24.198 of May 12, 1993, *Boletín Oficial* no. 27.652, p. 1 (Argentina).

14. See IACtHR, Olmedo Bustos et al. v. Chile (*The Last Temptation of Christ*), Merits, Reparations and Costs, Judgment of February 5, 2001, IACHR series C, no. 73; law No. 19742 of August 8, 2001, *Diario Oficial* no. 37.046, p. 2 (Chile).

15. Mexico, Federal Law on Transparency and Access to Public Government Information of June 11, 2002, *Diario Oficial*, June 11, 2002; Peru, law no. 27.806, August 2, 2002, *Diario Oficial El Peruano*, p. 227.605.

16. Among them are the notable organizations the Committee to Protect Journalists, the Inter American Press Association, and Human Rights Watch.

17. IACtHR, Claude Reyes et al., v. Chile, Merits, Reparations and Costs, Judgment of September 19, 2006, IACHR series C, no. 151.

18. This case involved journalist Baruch Ivcher Bronstein, who had been deprived of his Peruvian citizenship after making statements critical of the government. In the IACHR's view, this constituted a form of "indirect censorship," contrary to freedom of expression. See IACtHR, Ivcher Bronstein v. Peru, Merits, Reparations and Costs, Judgment of February 6, 2001, IACHR series C, no. 74.

19. Catalina Botero-Marino, *Venezuela*, 2009 Country Report of the OAS Special Rapporteur for Freedom of Expression, OEA/Ser.L/V/II, doc. 51, December 30, 2009; Botero-Marino, *Venezuela*, 2010 Country Report of the OAS Special Rapporteur for Freedom of Expression, OEA/Ser.L/V/II, doc. 5, March 7, 2011.

20. IACtHR, Ríos et al. v. Venezuela, Preliminary Objections, Merits, Reparations and Costs, Judgment of January 28, 2009, IACHR series C, no. 194; Perozo et al. v. Venezuela, Preliminary Objections, Merits, Reparations and Costs, Judgment of January 28, 2009, IACHR Series C, No. 195; Usón Ramírez v. Venezuela, Preliminary Objections, Merits, Reparations and Costs, Judgment of November 20, 2009, IACHR series C, No. 207.

21. Catalina Botero-Marino, *Ecuador*, 2011 Annual Report of the OAS Special Rapporteur for Freedom of Expression, chap. 2(B)(9), OEA/Ser.L/V/II, Doc. 69, December 30, 2011.

22. The reform package sought to prevent the Office of the Special Rapporteur from publishing annual reports separate from those of the IACHR, to prevent the rapporteur from being financed through sources external to the OAS, and to create a "code of ethics" for the rapporteur.

23. Recently, the entities of the Inter-American System, especially the Office of the Special Rapporteur, have begun to develop new standards around other issues, such as the state's obligation to promote and ensure pluralism and diversity in the media and freedom of expression online. See IACtHR, Granier et al. (Radio Caracas Televisión) v. Venezuela, Preliminary Objections, Merits, Reparations and Costs, Judgment of June 22, 2015, IACHR series C, no. 293 (on pluralism); and Edison Lanza, *Standards for a Free, Open and Inclusive Internet*, 2016 Thematic Report of the OAS Special Rapporteur for Freedom of Expression, OEA /Ser.L /V/II, IACHR/RELE/ INF.17 /17, March 15, 2017.

24. IACtHR, Kimel v. Argentina, Merits, Reparation and Costs, Judgment of May 2, 2008, IACHR Series C, No. 177.

25. IACtHR, *Claude Reyes*.

26. IACtHR, *Olmedo Bustos*.

27. IACtHR, *Ivcher Bronstein*.

28. IACtHR, Velez Restrepo and family members v. Colombia, Preliminary Objections, Merits, Reparations and Costs, Judgment of September 3, 2012, IACHR series C, no. 248.

29. In this way, for example, the inter-American standard that recognizes the right of access to information as a fundamental right has been consolidated. See case study 2.

30. In this way, for example, it was possible to consolidate the inter-American standard that prohibits all forms of prior censorship. See IACtHR, *Olmedo Bustos*.

31. OAS, Resolution 1917 (33-O/03).

32. Argentina, law 24.198 of May 12, 1993, *Boletín Oficial* no. 27.652.

33. European Court of Human Rights (ECtHR), judgments of July 8, 1986 (*Lingens v. Austria*) and April 23, 1992 (*Castells v. Spain*).

34. Paraguay, law no. 1.160 of November 26, 1997 (criminal code).

35. Santiago Cantón, *Laws on Contempt, Compulsory Membership and the Murder of Journalists*, 1998 Annual Report of the OAS Special Rapporteur for Freedom of Expression, chap. 4.

36. Costa Rica, law no. 8.224 of March 13, 2002, *La Gaceta* no. 65; Peru, law no. 27.975 of May 28, 2003, *Diario Oficial El Peruano*, p. 244.983.

37. IACtHR, Herrera-Ulloa v. Costa Rica, Preliminary Objections, Merits, Reparations and Costs, judgment of July 2, 2004, IACHR series C, no. 107; Ricardo Canese v. Paraguay, Merits, Reparations and Costs, judgment of August 31, 2004, IACHR series C, no. 111; Palamara Iribarne v. Chile, Merits, Reparations and Costs, judgment of November 22, 2005, IACHR series C, no. 135.

38. Panama, law no. 22 of June 29, 2005, *Gaceta Oficial* 25.336; Chile, law no. 20.048 of August 22, 2005, *Diario Oficial* no. 38.250; Nicaragua, law no. 641 of November 16, 2007, *La Gaceta* no. 232.

39. Honduras, Supreme Court of Justice, Chamber of Constitutional Affairs, judgment of May 19, 2005; Guatemala, Constitutional Court, judgment of February 1, 2006; Bolivia, Constitutional Court, judgment of September 20, 2012; Brazil, Supreme Court of Justice, Fifth Chamber, judgment of December 15, 2016. Case information on this and all other judgments handed down by national courts mentioned in this chapter is available at Columbia University, Global Freedom of Expression, https://globalfreedomofexpression.columbia.edu/casos/?lang=es (in Spanish).

40. Santiago Cantón, *Evaluation of the State of Freedom of Expression in the Hemisphere*, 1999 Annual Report of the OAS Special Rapporteur for Freedom of Expression, chap. 2.

41. IACtHR, Kimel v. Argentina; Tristán Donoso v. Panama, Preliminary Objections, Merits, Reparations and Costs, Judgment of January 27, 2009, IACHR Series C, No. 193; Usón Ramírez v. Venezuela.

42. Nicaragua, law no. 641 of November 16, 2007, *La Gaceta* no. 232.

43. Panama, law no. 26 of May 21, 2008, *Gaceta Oficial* 26.045. See Supreme Court of Justice, judgment of April 11, 2014.

44. Argentina, law no. 26.551 of November 18, 2009, *Boletín Oficial* no. 31.790. See also Supreme Court of Justice, judgment of June 24, 2008.

45. El Salvador, Decree No. 836 of December 7, 2011, *Diario Oficial* no. 299, vol. 393.

46. Peru, Supreme Court of Justice, Chamber of Criminal Affairs, judgment of June 18, 2010.

47. Colombia, Supreme Court of Justice, Chamber of Criminal Affairs, judgment of July 10, 2013.

48. Mexico, decree of April 13, 2007, *Diario Oficial de la Federación*, April 13, 2007.

49. Grenada, Criminal Code (Amendment) Act 2012.

50. Jamaica, Defamation Act 2013.

51. Mexico, Supreme Court of Justice, judgment of June 17, 2009.

52. OAS Special Rapporteurship for Freedom of Expression, press release no. 96/11 (Revista Sexto Poder v. Venezuela), August 31, 2011; press release no. 93/15 (La Nación, Tal Cual et al. v. Venezuela), August 24, 2015. IACHR, precautionary

measure no. 406/11 (Palacio et al. v. Ecuador), February 21, 2012; precautionary measure no. 30–14 (Villavicencio v. Ecuador), March 24, 2014; report no. 66/2015 (Admissibility), case no. 1436-11 (Palacios v. Ecuador), October 27, 2015.

53. IACtHR, Mémoli v. Argentina, Preliminary Objections, Merits, Reparations and Costs, judgment of August 22, 2013, IACHR series C, no. 265

54. IACtHR, Álvarez Ramos v. Venezuela, Preliminary Objections, Merits, Reparations and Costs, judgment of August 30, 2019, IACHR series C, no. 380.

55. Santiago Cantón, *Report on the Action with Respect to Habeas Data and the Right of Access to Information in the Hemisphere*, 2001 Annual Report of the OAS Special Rapporteur for Freedom of Expression, chap. 3.

56. Mexico, Federal Law on Transparency and Access to Public Government Information of June 11, 2002, *Diario Oficial*, June 11, 2002.

57. Panama, law no. 6 of January 22, 2002, *Gaceta Oficial* no. 24.476; Peru, law no. 27.806 of August 2, 2002, *Diario Oficial El Peruano*, p. 227.605.

58. OAS General Assembly, Resolution 1932 (33-O/03), June 10, 2003.

59. Eduardo Bertoni, *Report on Access to Public Information in the Hemisphere*, 2003 Annual Report of the OAS Special Rapporteur for Freedom of Expression, chap. 4.

60. Abid Hussein, Report of the Special Rapporteur on the Promotion and Protection of the Right to Freedom of Opinion and Expression, UN Doc. E/CN.4/1999/64, January 29, 1999, para. 12.

61. The European Court of Human Rights, in the case of Guerra et al. v. Italy (judgment of February 19, 1998), had already recognized the existence of a right of access to information on environmental issues. However, this court held that the right of access arose not from Article 10 of the European Convention on Human Rights but from Article 8.

62. IACtHR, *Claude Reyes*, para. 88–91.

63. Chile, law no. 20.285 of August 11, 2008, *Boletín Oficial*, August 20, 2008.

64. Chile, Constitutional Court, judgment of August 9, 2007.

65. Honduras, decree no. 170-2006 of December 30, 2006, *La Gaceta*, December 30, 2006.

66. Nicaragua, law no. 621 of May 16, 2007, *La Gaceta* no. 118, June 22, 2007.

67. Guatemala, decree no. 57-2008 of October 23, 2008, *Diario de Centro América* no. 45, vol. 285.

68. Uruguay, law no. 18.381 of October 17, 2008, *Diario Oficial*, November 7, 2008.

69. OAS General Assembly, Resolution 2607 (40-O/10), June 8, 2010.

70. IACtHR, Gomes Lund et al. ("Guerrilha do Araguaia") v. Brazil, Preliminary Objections, Merits, Reparations and Costs, judgment of November 24, 2010, IACHR series C, no. 219, para. 196–199.

71. El Salvador, decree no. 534 of December 2, 2010, *Diario Oficial* no. 70, vol. 391.

72. Brazil, law no. 12.527 of November 18, 2011, *Diário Oficial da União*, November 18, 2011.

73. Colombia, law no. 1.712 of March 6, 2014, *Diario Oficial* no. 49.084.

74. Argentina, law no. 27.275 of September 14, 2014, *Boletín Oficial* no. 33.472, p. 1.

75. Paraguay, law no. 5.282 of September 18, 2015, *Registro Oficial* no. 180, September 19, 2014.

76. Colombia, Constitutional Court, judgment T-511 of June 18, 2010.

77. Guatemala, Constitutional Court, judgment of November 30, 2010.

78. El Salvador, Supreme Court of Justice, Chamber of Constitutional Affairs, judgment of December 5, 2012.

79. Mexico, Supreme Court of Justice, judgment of February 6, 2013.

80. Paraguay, Supreme Court of Justice, judgment of October 15, 2013

81. Costa Rica, Supreme Court of Justice, Chamber of Constitutional Affairs, judgment of March 21, 2014.

82. Argentina, Supreme Court of Justice, judgments of December 4, 2012, and March 26, 2014.

83. IACtHR, Omar Humberto Maldonado Vargas et al. v. Chile, Merits, Reparations and Costs, judgment of September 2, 2015, IACHR series C, no. 300.

84. Venezuela, Supreme Court of Justice, judgments of June 15, 2010, and August 5, 2014.

85. ECtHR, judgment of November 8, 2016 (Magyar Helsinki Bizottság v. Hungary), para. 146.

86. ECtHR, judgment of December 10, 2007 (Stoll v. Switzerland), para. 111.

87. IACtHR, Herrera-Ulloa v. Costa Rica, Preliminary Objections, Merits, Reparations and Costs, judgment of July 2, 2004, IACHR series C, no. 107; Ricardo Canese v. Paraguay, Merits, Reparations and Costs, judgment of August 31, 2004, IACHR series C, no. 111; Palamara Iribarne v. Chile, Merits, Reparations and Costs, judgment of November 22, 2005, IACHR series C, no. 135.

88. African Commission on Human and Peoples' Rights, judgment of December 5, 2014 (Lohé Issa Konaté v. Burkina Faso), para. 59.

89. Catalina Botero-Marino, *Inter-American Legal Framework of the Right to Freedom of Expression*, 2009 Annual Report of the OAS Special Rapporteur for Freedom of Expression, OEA/Ser.L/V/II, Doc. 51, December 30, 2009, chap. 3; Botero-Marino, *The Right of Access to Information in the Inter-American Legal Framework*, 2009 Annual Report, chap. 4.

90. Human Rights Committee, *General Comment no. 34: Article 19 (Freedoms of Opinion and Expression)*, CCPR/C/GC/34, September 12, 2011.

91. See Human Rights Committee, *General Comment no. 34*, para. 19; 2009 Annual Report, *Marco*, para. 26.

92. Catalina Botero-Marino, *Violence Against Journalists and Media Workers: Inter-American Standards and National Practices on Prevention, Protection and Prosecution*, 2013 Thematic Report of the OAS Special Rapporteur for Freedom of Expression, OEA/Ser.L/V/II, CIDH/RELE/INF. 12/13, December 31, 2013.

93. Botero-Marino, *Violence Against Journalists*, para. 31

94. Botero-Marino, *Violence Against Journalists*, para. 34

95. Botero-Marino, *Violence Against Journalists*, para. 52

96. Botero-Marino, *Violence Against Journalists*, para. 62.

97. Botero-Marino, *Violence Against Journalists*, para. 104.

98. Botero-Marino, *Violence Against Journalists*, para. 176.

99. Botero-Marino, *Violence Against Journalists*, para. 186.

100. Botero-Marino, *Violence Against Journalists*, para. 227.

101. Botero-Marino, *Violence Against Journalists*, para. 250.

102. Committee of Ministers of the Council of Europe (CMCE), *On the Protection of Journalism and Safety of Journalists and Other Media Actors*, Recommendation CM/Rec(2016)4, April 13, 2016, para. 2.

103. CMCE, *On the Protection of Journalism*, para. 9

104. See CMCE, *On the Protection of Journalism*, para. 20; and Botero-Marino, *Violence against Journalists*, para. 176.

105. See CMCE, *On the Protection of Journalism*, para. 22; and Botero-Marino, *Violence against Journalists*, para. 186.

106. See CMCE, *On the Protection of Journalism*, para. 14; and and Botero-Marino, *Violence against Journalists*, para. 227.

107. See CMCE, *On the Protection of Journalism*, para. 2(17); and Botero-Marino, *Violence against Journalists*, para. 250.

The African Human Rights System   **NINE**

A New Actor of Normative Integration

CATHERINE ANITE

This chapter explores the extent to which the African human rights system has adopted, incorporated, and expounded global freedom of expression norms. The first part examines the extent to which the legal framework of the system provides adequate protection for freedom of expression. It also evaluates the nature of legal norms advanced by the African Commission's Special Rapporteur on Freedom of Expression and the African court, and their similarities with norms in other contexts. The chapter then assesses the contribution of African subregional courts in advancing freedom of expression norms. The chapter will show that despite being the most recently established regional human rights mechanism, the African human rights system has steadily integrated freedom of expression standards and has urged member states to conform their legislation to international standards. It has gradually emerged as a frontline defender and promoter of freedom of expression, with its decisions having a positive trickle-down effect in national systems.

THE AFRICAN REGIONAL HUMAN RIGHTS SYSTEM, AN EMERGING ACTOR IN PROMOTING INTERNATIONAL STANDARDS OF FREEDOM OF EXPRESSION

The African Charter on Human and Peoples' Rights

The conversation in Africa to adopt a human rights convention was initiated in the 1960s,[1] but only yielded results in 1981, when the General Assembly of the Organisation of African Union (now the African Union) adopted the African Charter on Human and People's Rights.[2] The charter came into force on October 21, 1986, following ratification by an absolute majority of the Organisation of African Unity member states.[3] Today, with the exception of South Sudan, all African states have ratified the charter.[4]

The right to freedom of expression is provided for under Article 9 of the African Charter, which states that every individual has the right to receive information and "the right to express and disseminate his opinions within the law." Other relevant provisions include the charter preamble, which reaffirms member states' adherence to principles of human rights under the African system and the United Nations. In addition, Articles 2 and 28 of the charter emphasize that freedom of expression is guaranteed to all, without distinction, and Article 27(2) provides that "the rights and freedoms of each individual shall be exercised with due regard to the rights of others, collective security, morality and common interest."

The AU has further committed to protecting freedom of expression through the 2007 African Charter on Democracy, Elections and Governance, which provides under Article 27(8) that "in order to advance political, economic and social governance, State Parties shall commit themselves to . . . promoting freedom of expression, in particular, freedom of the press and fostering a professional media."

Although Article 9 of the African Charter explicitly provides for the enjoyment of freedom of expression without interference from state or nonstate actors, as in the Universal Declaration of Human Rights (UDHR), Article 9(2) makes no mention of enjoying the right "regardless of frontiers" or the right to seek information. It also introduces a clawback clause requiring enjoyment of the right to be "within the law," which could be understood to mean national laws rather than international or regional laws.

The African Commission on Human and Peoples' Rights

The African Commission was established under Article 30 of the African Charter and became operational on November 2, 1987.[5] As the first human rights enforcement and monitoring body created under the charter, it consists of eleven members chosen from among African personalities, known for their high morality, integrity, impartiality, and competence in matters of human and peoples' rights and who serve in their personal capacity.[6] It meets twice a year and has so far considered 298 complaints, ten of which are related to violations of freedom of expression.[7]

The role of the commission is multifaceted. In addition to adjudicating human rights disputes filed by individuals against states, it also interprets provisions of the African Charter at the request of a state party, an institution of the Organisation of African Union, or an African organization recognized by the African Union.[8]

The commission is a quasijudicial body whose decisions on human rights matters are regarded as "opinions," and it has been critiqued as being a powerless institution because of the recommendatory status of its findings, among other reasons.[9] Indeed, in the early years following its establishment, the commission faced various challenges, including underfunding and lack of political independence, which undermined its ability to deliver its mandate. However, through the repeated pressure of nongovernmental organizations (NGOs), it has gradually established itself as a far more solid regional human rights body than originally anticipated. This can be seen in the commission's adoption of resolutions condemning human rights violations in states such as Côte d'Ivoire, the Democratic Republic of Congo, Ethiopia, Somalia, South Africa, Sudan, The Gambia, Uganda, Zimbabwe, and the like.

The commission has adopted several resolutions on a range of human rights topics, such as the abolition of the death penalty, respect for human rights in the fight against terrorism, migration and human rights, respect for economic and social rights, respect for the rights of women, and respect for human rights defenders.[10]

The active participation of civil society groups and individuals in filing cases before the commission has bolstered its effectiveness and resulted in robust jurisprudence promoting freedom of expression and access to information rights. In 2002, following active campaigning and substantive drafting by various NGOs and experts, the commission adopted a Declaration of Principles on Freedom of Expression. The principles, although not binding on states parties to the African Charter, provide guidance, understanding, and

appreciation of freedom of expression as a right. They demand that states parties to the African Charter take positive measures to promote diversity in
expression, specifically access to communication by vulnerable groups like
women, children, refugees, and linguistic and cultural groups, and adopt an
Afrocentric approach to expression through the promotion and protection of
African voices, using local languages, including in courts. They also emphasize the independence of broadcast media, advocating for the transformation
of government-controlled broadcasters into public service broadcasters. The
declaration calls on African states to align their privacy and defamation laws
with international standards and to promote tolerance of criticism by public
figures.[11]

Various African countries have referenced the declaration while drafting
freedom of expression, access to information, and broadcast laws. However,
with the development of Internet rights, there was a need to expound and
modify the declaration to protect freedom of expression, access to information, and privacy online. In this regard, the African Commission's newly
appointed rapporteur for freedom of expression initiated the process of revising and amending the declaration during the April 2018 Ordinary Commission Session, forming a reference group comprising individual experts and
NGOs working to improve freedom of expression issues on the continent.[12]
The group, which included organizations such as the Kenya ICT [information
and communications technology] Action Network, the Collaboration on
International ICT Policy in East and Southern Africa, Article 19, Media Rights
Agenda, and Media Foundation for West Africa, has discussed various issues
concerning Internet governance and digital rights to be considered in the
revised declaration, and it formed a technical drafting team to produce the
draft amended declaration by mid-October 2018, before public consultations
commenced. In April 2020, the African Commission published the revised
declaration, which includes principles on Internet access, intermediaries, surveillance, and privacy rights.[13]

Other ongoing initiatives to improve Internet rights in Africa include the
African Declaration on Internet Rights and Freedoms,[14] a continent-wide initiative which aims to promote human rights standards and principles of openness
in Internet policy formulation and implementation, to address violations of
online rights by governments. An annual forum on Internet freedom in Africa
convenes various Internet governance and online speech experts working to
improve a wide range of digital rights in Africa.[15] In Southern Africa, the Media
Institute of Southern Africa is campaigning for the adoption of cyber laws that

are in line with human rights principles. Nigeria's digital rights and freedoms bill, which now awaits presidential assent is another example of a privately pushed initiative led by Paradigm Initiative to protect free speech online at a national level.[16]

Jurisprudence on Freedom of Expression by the African Commission

The commission has become an increasingly important actor in terms of integrating global freedom of expression norms onto the African human rights system. The African Court and subregional courts have relied significantly upon its decisions, thus allowing for harmonization across various regional institutions and the emergence of a coherent interpretation and application of legal norms related to freedom of expression.

The first and crucial step taken by the commission was to "neutralize the claw-back clauses" [of Article 9 of the charter] as part of its ruling in *Constitutional Rights Project, Civil Liberties Organisation and Media Rights Agenda v. Nigeria.*[17] The complaint, filed against Nigeria in 1993, concerned decrees by the military government that fined newspaper owners and provided for a seven-year imprisonment term of editors for owning, publishing, or printing unregistered newspapers. The decrees also banned circulation of newspapers and barred courts from "questioning the validity of any of the decrees." The commission found that Nigeria had violated freedom of expression under Article 9 and asked that the government take the necessary steps to conform their laws to the charter. The commission emphasized that international human rights standards must always prevail over contradictory national law, as doing otherwise would defeat any international standards, rendering the right illusory.[18] The commission also recognized the significance of public participation, stating, "Freedom of expression is a basic human right, vital to an individual's personal development, his political consciousness and participation in the conduct of public affairs in his country."[19] It contrasted other international human rights instruments with the African Charter, explaining that the charter does not contain a derogation clause, and in this regard, limitations on the rights and freedoms cannot be justified by emergencies or special circumstances, and must be in conformity with the charter.[20] The commission found the government liable, holding that its actions subjected journalists and newspapers to self-censorship and unjustifiably denied the public information.[21]

This stance was further reflected in the *Jawara* case,[22] where the commission stated that politically motivated harassment and intimidation of journalists deprived them of "their rights to freely express and disseminate their opinions, as well as the public, of the right to information." By the time the commission pronounced itself in 1998, the magazines had resumed operations and editors had been released from prison. Nevertheless, the decision established the importance of freedom of expression even in times of emergency.

The commission has largely reflected the three-part test, provided for under Article 19(3) of the International Covenant on Civil and Political Rights, according to which limitations to freedom of expression must be necessary and set in law, with a stronger reference to Article 10(2) of the European Convention of Human Rights, which demands that restrictions must be necessary in a democratic society.[23] The commission's jurisprudence is reflected in principle 2(2) of the Declaration of Principles on Freedom of Expression, according to which restrictions must be "provided by law, serve a legitimate interest and be necessary and in a democratic society." In the context of national security, the commission insisted that "the legitimate exercise of human rights does not pose dangers to a democratic state governed by the rule of law."[24]

The commission has made strong pronouncement on standards regarding criticism against public figures, primarily echoing the criteria laid down by the European Court of Human Rights in the landmark case of *Lingens v. Austria*.[25] In *Kenneth Good v. Botswana*, the commission stated, "A higher degree of tolerance is expected when it is a political speech and an even higher threshold is required when it is directed toward the government and government officials."[26]

The commission, however, is not explicit in barring criminal prosecutions against journalists on grounds of public interest except in very exceptional circumstances involving serious attacks on individuals' rights. For instance, in *John D. Ouko v. Kenya*, it provided that "if opinions are contrary to laid down laws, the affected government official has the right to seek redress in a court of law. Herein lies the essence of the law of defamation."[27] This is a position reflected in the majority of countries on the continent. Hence, in 2009, the Constitutional Court of Uganda dismissed a petition filed by journalists in an attempt to decriminalize criminal defamation. In the case of *Joachim Buwembo & 3 Others v. Attorney General of Uganda*, the court ruled that defamatory statements do not enhance public knowledge and development, but rather stifle and retard it, and that the press would be doing a disservice to the public by publishing defamatory libels.[28] In light of the standard set by the African Court in the Konaté case (to be discussed) and the move to decriminalize defamation in some African countries, the commission may be inclined to shift its position in the future, allowing criminal prosecutions and sanctions for defamatory speech.

Special Rapporteur on Freedom of Expression and Access to Information

In 2004, the African Commission established the Office of the Special Rapporteur on Freedom of Expression to monitor the situation of freedom of expression and compliance in member states by analyzing their media regulatory environment, conducting investigative missions, and making appropriate recommendations to the African Commission.[29] The rapporteur has, in partnership with civil society organizations, played a key role in advancing the right to access information.

In November 2007, primarily at the urging of civil society organizations, the commission expanded the mandate of the Special Rapporteur on Freedom of Expression to also include access to information (ATI). In 2010, the African Commission passed a resolution inviting the special rapporteur to begin the process of drafting a model law on access to information, which was adopted in April 2013. It provided "detailed and practical content to the legislative obligations of member states to the African Charter with respect to the right of access to information," in line with international standards.[30] The special rapporteur's advocacy efforts resulted in critical milestones—by November 2017, "twenty-one countries—nearly 40 percent of the African Union's member states—had RTI [right to information] laws on the books, and bills were pending in a half dozen additional countries."[31] The rapporteur also successfully advocated for the African Union to name September 28 as an annual day to commemorate the international right to information in Africa.[32] Additionally, in 2016, with the support of NGOs and individual experts, the special rapporteur embarked on a process to develop guidelines on access to information and elections in Africa, which now await adoption by the commission. The draft guidelines advocate for proactive disclosure of information during elections, citing inspiration from Articles 19 of the UDHR and the International Covenant on Civil and Political Rights (ICCPR), and the UN Human Rights Committee's General Comment no. 34 on freedom of expression.[33]

The rapporteur has also been a strong advocate for the repeal of criminal defamation and insult laws, pushing for the adoption of a resolution by the commission in 2010 urging states parties to the charter to repeal such laws.[34] This eventually led to the establishment of a decriminalization of defamation campaign in 2012.[35] Today, Zimbabwe,[36] Burkina Faso,[37] Kenya,[38] Lesotho,[39] and

The Gambia have repealed their laws. Other countries, such as Liberia, have committed to doing the same.[40]

The rapporteur also has filed amicus briefs in the East African Court of Justice to provide guidance on international standards on freedom of expression in a criminal defamation case.[41]

The African Court on Human and Peoples' Rights and Its Role in Globalizing the Right to Freedom of Expression

In 1998, the AU adopted a Protocol to the African Charter on Human and Peoples' Rights, establishing the African Court on Human and Peoples' Rights, which came into force on January 25, 2004.[42] Beginning in the early 1990s, international and national NGOs, in particular the International Commission of Jurists, had called for the establishment of an African court for human rights with binding powers, to complement the work of the African Commission. By 1993, they had drafted a protocol to that effect.[43] In June 1994, in the immediate aftermath of the Rwandan genocide, the Assembly of Heads of States of the African Union requested a meeting of experts to identify the means to enhance the efficiency of the commission, including through the establishment of an African Court.[44]

The jurisdiction of the African Court, stipulated under Article 3 of the protocol, extends to all cases and disputes submitted to it concerning the interpretation and application of the African Charter, the protocol to the charter, and any other relevant human rights instruments ratified by the member states of the African Union. The African Court is also mandated to provide, at the request of the AU, its member states, or African organizations recognized by the AU, advisory opinions on any legal matter relating to the charter or other relevant human rights instruments, provided that the subject matter of the opinion is not related to a matter being examined by the African Commission.[45] The decisions of the court are binding, as opposed to those of the commission, which only has powers to make recommendations.[46] The court, which began its official operations in November 2006, moved to Arusha, Tanzania, in August 2007, received its first application in 2008, and delivered its initial judgment in 2009. As of the end of July 2020, it has finalized one hundred cases.[47]

One key limitation of the court is that individuals and NGOs can only access it if their states have ratified the Protocol to the African Charter and have deposited declarations recognizing its competence.[48] So far, only thirty countries have ratified the protocol, and of those, only nine have submitted the declaration. These include Benin, Burkina Faso, Côte d'Ivoire, Ghana, Mali,

Malawi, Tanzania, Tunisia, and The Gambia.[49] The other notable challenge is that neither the protocol nor the charter have laid down any procedures for withdrawal. This presented a hurdle in 2016, when Rwanda opted to withdraw.[50] The court, relying on jurisprudence from the European Court of Human Rights and the Inter-American Human Rights Court, allowed Rwanda to withdraw its declaration one year from the date of notice, adding that the withdrawal has no legal effect on cases involving Rwanda pending before the court.[51] Unfortunately, in December 2019, Tanzania became the second country to withdraw from the court, despite having the highest number of cases filed.[52] As Tanzania is the host of this court, its withdrawal is alarming and sets a negative tone. Benin and Cote d'Ivoire withdrew in March and April 2020, respectively.[53]

Unlike the African Commission, which allows robust participation from individuals and NGOs in bringing cases before it, the process of depositing a declaration has hampered the court's progress in developing jurisprudence.

In order to encourage more countries to ratify the protocol and submit the declaration permitting individuals and NGOs direct access, the African Court, through its judges and registry, embarked on twenty-nine sensitization missions throughout the continent to raise awareness about the court and to encourage ratification of the protocol and submission of the declaration. This effort registered success in countries like Benin, Chad, Egypt ,and Tunisia, which submitted protocols, demonstrating that with gentle guidance and better understanding of the system, some African states are willing to commit to the African human rights system.

The court can also be accessed by the African Commission through a referral, by states parties to the protocol filing complaints against other states parties, or by African intergovernmental organizations.[54] The commission so far has not referred any matter on freedom of expression to the court for determination; neither has a state's party to the protocol or intergovernmental organizations filed any complaint against other states parties on violation of freedom of expression.

The Konaté Case, a Precedent with Normative Value

The African Court made significant clarifications on the parameters of the right to freedom of expression under Article 9 of the African Charter, while delivering its most significant judgment on freedom of expression, in December 2014. When deciding cases, the court relies on the provisions of the African Charter and any other relevant human rights instruments ratified by the states concerned.[55] Like the commission, the court also refers to international human rights instruments, and regional and global norms.

A seminal freedom of expression decision is *Lohé Issa Konaté v. the Republic of Burkina Faso*,[56] in which the court held that criminal defamation should only be used as a last resort and within the context of what is necessary in a democratic society. While this is not the first time a court in Africa had ruled that criminal defamation was rarely necessary and proportionate, it was significant nevertheless that the African Court had reached this finding. The case is presented in detail in the final section of this volume. For the purpose of this chapter, a few dimensions will be highlighted.

First, in reaching its decision, the court relied extensively on the interpretations of the African Commission,[57] in addition to regional and international standards and jurisprudence, thus strengthening legal integration across regions and within Africa.

Second, this approach did not prevent the African Court from strengthening the protection that the commission had afforded to freedom of expression thus far. In evaluating the degree of protection of individuals, the court stated that limitations must vary depending on whether the person is a public figure or not, finding that a prosecutor is a public figure and, as such, must be more exposed than an ordinary individual to severe criticisms.[58] This differs from the African Commission jurisprudence in *Zimbabwe Lawyers for Human Rights & Associated Newspapers of Zimbabwe v. Zimbabwe*, which had placed judicial officers on a higher pedestal, protecting them from public criticism.[59]

The court emphasized that, with respect to dishonouring or tarnishing the reputation of public figures like judicial officers, the laws of states parties to the African Charter and the ICCPR should not provide more severe sanctions than those relating to similar offenses against ordinary individuals.[60]

The court also rejected Burkina Faso's claim that Konaté did not qualify as a journalist because he did not have a press card and his newspaper was not registered with the administrative and tax authorities. The court pointed out that the national court had already convicted him as a journalist and therefore his de facto status was already accepted, despite administrative lapses. Furthermore, the court insisted that Article 9 of the covenant guarantees the right to freedom of expression to anyone, regardless of whether they are a journalist. This finding upholds standards in protection of journalists' rights already set by courts in Latin America, Europe, and other jurisdictions. As analyzed by Matt Duffy, this made it clear to the government that they do not have the authority to determine who is a journalist, which in turn could create an important foundation for other cases arguing against the licensing of journalists.[61]

Burkina Faso was then directed to amend its defamation laws and ensure that the sanctions meet the test of necessity and proportionality, in accordance with its obligations under the African Charter and international human rights instruments. The government of Burkina Faso complied by repealing custody in favor of fines for criminal defamation, in September 2015.

It is also worth noting that in their dissenting judgment, four of the eleven judges found that Konaté's conviction and sentence conflicted with Article 9 of the African Charter and other human rights instruments and was therefore invalid from the onset. They stated that criminal defamation is an unjustified restriction of freedom of expression and should not be acceptable under any circumstances.[62] Prior to the hearing of the case, Konaté had also sought provisional measures, seeking his immediate release from prison or, alternatively, access to adequate medical care. The court declined to grant his immediate release on the grounds that it would adversely affect the consideration of the substantive case. However, it ordered Burkina Faso to grant him access to all necessary medical care to avoid irreparable harm, and to report to court on the implementation of the order within fifteen days of its issuance.[63] The dissenting judges, however, disagreed with this position on several grounds, including the fact that failure to release the applicant would cause irreparable harm because personal freedom cannot be compensated by monetary damages.[64]

As highlighted by Hawley Johnson in chapter 18 of this volume, the African Court's *Konaté* decision has been cited by applicants or defendants in Angola, Lesotho, Mozambique, Nigeria, Tanzania, The Gambia, and Uganda, as well as in India. The High Court of Kenya, in its ruling on *Okuta v. Attorney General* went a step further than *Konaté* and declared the offense of criminal defamation under section 194 of the Kenyan Penal Code to be unconstitutional.[65] The Economic Community of West African States (ECOWAS) Community Court of Justice in West Africa relied on it to find The Gambia in violation of freedom of expression rights in February 2018, and it has been referenced in a criminal defamation case, *Ronald Ssembuusi v. the Attorney General of Uganda*, filed in the East African Court of Justice.

SUBREGIONAL HUMAN RIGHTS SYSTEMS

The East African Court of Justice

The East African Court of Justice was established under Article 9 of the Treaty for the Establishment of the East African Community, as a mechanism to resolve disputes arising within the six-member states and to "ensure the adherence to law in the interpretation and application of and compliance with this Treaty."[66] Article 6(d) lists fundamental principles intended to guide the court: "good governance including adherence to the principles of democracy, the rule of law, accountability, transparency, social justice, equal opportunities, gender equality, as well as the recognition, promotion and protection of human and peoples' rights in accordance with the provisions of the African Charter on Human and Peoples' Rights."

In principle, the court lacks an explicit mandate to hear cases involving human rights violations, since the heads of state of the East African Community countries have not concluded the protocol conferring a human rights mandate, under Article 27(2).[67] Still, it has addressed such cases, beginning with *Katabazi v. Secretary General of the East African Community*, determining that it "will not abdicate from exercising its jurisdiction of interpretation under Article 27(1) merely because the reference includes allegations of human rights violation."[68] This is a significant move on the part of the court, and it strengthens judicial independence.

In July 2013, the Burundi Journalists Union filed a reference in the court arguing that provisions of their 2013 press law violated fundamental and operational principles of the East African Community principles of democracy, rule of law, accountability, transparency, and good governance as protected by Articles 6(d) and 7(2) of the Treaty for the Establishment of the East African Community.[69]

The court found no justification for Article 19 of the Burundi press law, prohibiting disseminating "information on the stability of the currency, offensive reports on public or private persons, information that may harm the credit of the State and national economy, and records of diplomatic activity and scientific research." In its finding, it emphasized that citizens of any democratic state should be entitled to information that informs their choices in matters of governance, and that the restrictions embodied in the Burundian law unduly denied that right. It held that the prohibition was unreasonable, irrational, and not proportional to the objectives.[70]

In nullifying Article 20 of the press law provision requiring journalists to disclose their sources of information on grounds of state security, public order, defense secrets, and the moral and physical integrity of persons, the court reasoned that the way of dealing with state secrets is by enacting other laws to deal with the issue and not by forcing journalists to disclose their confidential sources. The court also stated that the obligation to disclose a source on grounds of moral or physical integrity is unreasonable and that privacy laws are sufficient to address this.[71] It adopted the reasoning of the European Court in *Goodwin v. UK* and affirmed the fundamental importance of freedom of expression in a democracy, reasserting the essential right of journalists to protect their confidential sources of information as one of the basic conditions of press freedom.[72]

The court however found no violation of the right to free press in the mandatory accreditation of foreign journalists, stating that this requirement is purely technical and administrative and that it is a reasonable and justifiable limitation, since freedom of the press is not absolute.[73] It found it necessary to sustain the provisions on the right of reply and correction and stated that these are compatible with the treaty because journalists are required to publish accurate information and, in the event that they do not, a party prejudiced by such inaccurate reporting is entitled to a right of reply.[74]

Burundi heeded to the court's order to amend its press law, by enacting a new press law (1/015) in May 2015, which provided for protection of sources under Article 16. However, its implementation has been moot following an attempted coup in 2015, civil unrest, and serious human rights violations, including allegations of crimes against humanity,[75] violations of freedom of expression, the closure of media outlets, and closure of civil society organizations. In September 2017, the Council of Ministers met to discuss a new draft bill that would introduce new restrictions on the practice of journalism.

The Burundi Journalists Union decision widely quoted comparative jurisprudence on freedom of expression norms from the European Court,[76] the African Commission,[77] and national courts.[78] It has paved the way for challenges to a number of restrictive media laws. In a 2018 judgment issued against the government of Tanzania in a newspaper shutdown case, the court emphasized that freedom of the press and freedom of expression are essential components of democracy, finding that the shutdown order was unlawful and did not meet the test for reasonability, rationality, and proportionality, as previously laid down.[79] In March 2019, the court found several provisions of Tanzania's Media Services Act, including those on sedition and criminal defamation, to be in violation of Articles 6(d) and 7(2) of the treaty, as they failed to meet all the thresholds under the three-part test, ordering Tanzania to take all necessary measures to conform their laws to the treaty.[80]

Journalists in Uganda currently await the court's verdict in *Ssembuusi v. the Attorney General of Uganda*, a case challenging the justifiability of criminal defamation laws. For the first time in its history, the court has admitted both the UN and AU special rapporteurs on freedom of expression and access to information and twenty freedom of expression organizations as amici curiae in the case, to provide expert interpretation on international freedom of expression standards. As of this writing, the final hearing is still pending. Perhaps the outcome will go beyond adopting the standards set by the majority decision in the Konaté case and state that criminal defamation is indeed an unjustifiable restriction on freedom of expression.

The Community Court of Justice of the Economic Community of West African States

The ECOWAS Community Court of Justice was established in 1991 by the member states of ECOWAS to ensure the observance of law and principles of equity and to interpret the treaty and other legal instruments adopted by the ECOWAS members. The court, created under Articles 6 and 15 of the amended Treaty of the Economic Community of West African States, issues binding decisions on individuals, corporate entities, and institutions of member states.[81] It is governed by a protocol, regulations, and addendums to these documents, stipulating composition, jurisdiction, powers, and various legal procedures.[82]

The court's mandate includes determination of human rights violations within member states and making declarations on the legality of regulations, directives, decisions, and other subsidiary legal instruments adopted by ECOWAS. In February 2018, the court delivered a landmark freedom of expression decision in a case filed by five applicants, including exiled journalists, alleging unlawful detention, arrests, and violations of freedom of expression and journalists' rights by the government of The Gambia. In *Federation of African Journalists and 4 others v. The Gambia*, the court found provisions on criminal defamation, sedition, and false news under Gambian laws were overly broad, amounted to censorship on publication, and thus constituted inacceptable instances of gross violations of freedom of expression. The court added that ambiguity causes a chilling effect and therefore restrictions on expression must be couched in the narrowest possible terms.[83] It also noted that the impugned laws were disproportionate and unnecessary in a democratic society, concluding that they violated Article 9 of the African Charter and Articles 19 of the ICCPR and UDHR. The arrest and detention of journalists for doing their work was also found to be unlawful.

Moving one step further than the African Court, the ECOWAS court directed The Gambia to decriminalize defamation, sedition, and false news in accordance with international standards on freedom of expression and its obligations under the African Charter. In its reasoning, the court relied on the African Court's *Konaté* decision; jurisprudence from the European Court, the Inter-American Court, and the UN Human Rights Committee; and a host of comparative global norms and jurisprudence from various domestic courts.

CONCLUSION

Despite being the newest of the regional systems, the African human rights mechanism is progressively buttressing global freedom of expression standards on the continent, as reflected in their jurisprudence and policy framework. Several countries have adopted access to information laws as advocated for by the special rapporteur, while others, such as Kenya, The Gambia, and Lesotho, have repealed restrictive criminal defamation laws. However, more effort is required to popularize and strengthen the system through concerted awareness raising[84] and training of civil society actors, law societies, and the media, as well as state authorities such as the judiciary, human rights commissions, and parliaments, to bridge the connection with domestic courts and policy makers. This will lead to a unified assimilation of their jurisprudence and standards within domestic jurisprudence and policies.

The East African Court of Justice has embarked on a process of sharing its decisions with civil society, judiciaries, law societies, and state agencies of its member states, while the ECOWAS court has partnered with the Pan African Lawyers Union to popularize and track the status of implementation of its decisions. Non-enforcement of decisions by states is perhaps the biggest challenge facing the regional systems; therefore, such efforts, including the African Court's sensitization missions, may contribute to states' willingness to fulfill their human rights obligations. In addition, focus should also be placed on advocacy efforts to encourage states to submit declarations allowing them to access the African court.

NOTES

1. This protracted process included the 1961 adoption by African jurists of the "Law of Lagos" declaration, which implored African governments to establish a human rights system on the continent with a treaty putting in place a court and a commission. See International Commission of Jurists, "African Conference on the Rule of Law, Lagos, Nigeria, January 3–7, 1961: A Report on the Proceedings of the Conference," https://www.icj.org/conferencia-africana-sobre-el-imperio-de-la-ley-lagos-nigeria-3-7-de-enero-de-1961-informe-sobre-los-trabajos-de-la-conferencia/.

2. *African (Banjul) Charter on Human and People's Rights*, adopted June 27, 1981, OAU Doc. CAB/LEG/67/3 rev. 5, 21 I.L.M. 58 (1982), entered into force October 21, 1986. https://www.achpr.org/public/Document/file/English/banjul_charter.pdf.

3. African Commission on Human and Peoples' Rights (ACHPR), "History of the African Charter," https://www.achpr.org/hotac.

4. ACHPR, "Ratification Table," https://www.achpr.org/ratificationtable?id=49.

5. See ACHPR, "About ACHPR," http://www.achpr.org/about/.

6. African Charter, Article 31(2).

7. See Institute for Human Rights and Development in Africa, African Human Rights Case Law Analyser, http://caselaw.ihrda.org.

8. African Charter, Article 45(1).

9. Frans Viljoen, "From a Cat into a Lion? An Overview of the Progress and Challenges of the African Human Rights System at the African Commission's 25-Year Mark," *Law, Democracy, and Development* 17 (2013): 299.

10. International Federation for Human Rights (FIDH), "Guiding Notes on the African Court," 24 (2010).

11. ACHPR, "Declaration of Principles on Freedom of Expression in Africa," adopted by the commission on October 23, 2002, https://www.right2info.org/resources /publications/instruments-and-standards/africa_declaration-of-principles-on -freedom-of-expression-in-africa.

12. ACHPR, "Press Release on the Election of a New Bureau, and Allocation of Special Mechanisms and States Parties among the Members of the Commission," November 2017, https://www.achpr.org/pressrelease/detail?id=74.

13. ACHPR, "Press Release on the Publication of the Declaration on Principles of Freedom of Expression and Access to Information in Africa," April 17 2020.

14. See African Declaration, "African Declaration on Internet Rights and Freedoms," http://africaninternetrights.org.

15. See Forum on Internet Freedom in Africa, "About FIFAfrica," https://cipesa.org /fifafrica/#about-fifafrica.

16. See Adeboye Adegoke and Tomiwa Ilori, "The Digital Rights and Freedom Bill: The Leap and the Hurdles," Digital Rights and Freedom Bill Archives, Paradigm Initiative, https://paradigmhq.org/tag/digital-rights-and-freedom-bill/.

17. ACHPR, *Constitutional Rights Project, Civil Liberties Organisation and Media Rights Agenda v. Nigeria*, Communication nos. 140/94, 141/94, 145/95, https://www .achpr.org/public/Document/file/English/achpr26_140.94_141.94_145.95_eng .pdf.

18. ACHPR, *Constitutional Rights Project*, para. 66, 73.

19. ACHPR, *Media Rights Agenda, Constitutional Rights Project v. Nigeria*, Communication nos. 105/93, 130/94, 128/94, and 152/96, October 31, 1998, para. 54. http://www .worldcourts.com/achpr/eng/decisions/1998.10.31_Media_Rights_Agenda_v _Nigeria.htm.

20. ACHPR, *Media Rights Agenda*, para 67.

21. ACHPR, *Media Rights Agenda*, para 38.

22. ACHPR, Sir Dawda K. Jawara v. The Gambia, Communication nos. 147/95–149/96, May 11, 2000, para. 65.

23. Zimbabwe Lawyers for Human Rights & Associated Newspapers of Zimbabwe v. Zimbabwe; Egyptian Initiative for Personal Rights and Interights v. Egypt 2, *Human Rights Law Reports* (2011), para. 240–256.

24. Amnesty International v. Sudan, 1999, para. 79.

25. European Court of Human Rights, *Lingens v. Austria*, application no. 9815/82, July 8, 1986, para. 43.

26. ACHPR, communication no. 313/05, May 26, 2010, para. 198.

27. ACHPR, communication no. 232/99, November 6, 2000, para. 28.

28. Constitutional Court of Uganda, reference no. 1/2008, para. 10 and 20, p. 18.

29. ACHPR, "Special Rapporteur on Freedom of Expression and Access to Information," https://www.achpr.org/specialmechanisms/detail?id=2.

30. ACHPR, *Model Law on Access to Information for Africa* (2013). https://www.achpr.org/legalinstruments/detail?id=32.

31. Sandra Coliver, "The Right of Access to Information Held by Public Authorities: Emergence as a Global Norm," chapter 2 in the present volume.

32. ACHPR, Resolution 222 (51) 2012, May 2, 2012.

33. United Nations Human Rights Committee, General Comment no. 34, CCPR/C/GC/34, September 12, 2011.

34. ACHPR, Resolution 169 (48)10, November 24, 2010.

35. Decriminalisation of Expression (DOX), "The Campaign," http://www.doxafrica.org/the-campaign.

36. Madhanire and Mtashazi v. the Attorney General, CCZ 2/14 Const. Application no. CCZ 78/12) [2014] ZWCC 2 (June 12, 2014).

37. Media Foundation for West Africa, "Burkina Faso: Major Boost for Press Freedom—Media Offences Decriminalised," February 12, 2016, http://www.mfwa.org/country-highlights/burkina-faso-major-boost-for-press-freedom-media-offences-decriminalised.

38. Jacqueline Okuta & another v. Attorney General & 2 others, [2017] eKLR. http://kenyalaw.org/caselaw/cases/view/130781.

39. Peta v. Minister of Law, Constitutional Affairs and Human Rights, and others, CC 11/2016 [2018] LSHCONST 251, May 18, 2018.

40. Executive Mansion, "President Sirleaf Signs Table Mountain Declaration; Second African Head of State to Do So," press release, July 21, 2012, http://emansion.gov.lr/2press.php?news_id=2261&related=7&pg=sp.

41. East African Court of Justice (EACJ), Ronald Ssembuusi v. the Attorney General of Uganda, reference no.16 of 2014. See Hadijah Nakitendde, "UN, AU Join Fight to

Challenge Uganda's Defamation Law," *The Sunrise*, July 31, 2015, http://www.sunrise
.ug/news/201507/un-au-join-fight-to-challenge-ugandas-defamation-law.html.

42. *Protocol to the African Charter on Human and Peoples' Rights on the Establishment of an African Court on Human and Peoples' Rights*, Articles 1 and 2, adopted June 1998 by OAU members, in Ouagadougou, Burkina Faso. https://guide-humanitarian-law.org/m/filer_public/7e/3d/7e3deb16-a761-405a-b8eb-d570a83ad89d/006-_protocol_on_the_establishment_of_an_african_court_on_human_and_peoples_rights.pdf.

43. For an account of how the court came about, and the role of nongovernmental organizations, see Gina Bekker, "The African Court on Human and People's Rights: Preserving State Interests," *Journal of African Law* 51, no. 1 (2007): 151–172.

44. Bekker, "African Court," 163–164

45. *Protocol to the African Charter*, Articles 3 and 4.

46. *Protocol to the African Charter*, Article 30. See also African Court on Human and Peoples' Rights, Rules of Court, Rule 61(5).

47. See African Court on Human and People's Rights, "Contentious Matters," https://www.african-court.org/en/index.php/cases/2016-10-17-16-18-21.

48. Article 5 and 34(6) of the protocol and rule 33 of the Rules of Court allow the court to receive complaints and/or applications submitted to it either by the ACHPR, state parties to the protocol, or African intergovernmental organizations.

49. See ACHPR, "Republic of Tunisia Signs African Court Declaration to Allow NGOs and Individuals to Access the Human and Peoples' Rights Court Directly," April 18, 2017, http://en.african-court.org/index.php/news/press-releases/item/145-republic-of-tunisia-signs-african-court-declaration-to-allow-ngos-and-individuals-to-access-the-human-and-peoples-rights-court-directly; ACHPR, "The Gambia Becomes the Ninth Country to Allow NGOs and Individuals to Access the African Court Directly," November 23, 2018, https://www.african-court.org/en/index.php/news/press-releases/item/257-the-gambia-becomes-the-ninth-country-to-allow-ngos-and-individuals-to-access-the-african-court-directly.

50. See Ministry of Justice of the Republic of Rwanda, "Clarification," http://www.minijust.gov.rw/fileadmin/Documents/Photo_News_2016/Clarification2.pdf.

51. African Court, Ingabire Victoire Umuhoza v. Republic of Rwanda, Ruling on Withdrawal of Declaration, application 003/2014, June 3, 2016, para. 56–69. www.african-court.org/en/index.php/56-pending-cases-details/867-app-no-003–2014-ingabire-victoire-umuhoza-v-republic-of-rwanda-details.

52. See Amnesty International, "Tanzania: Withdrawal of Individual Rights to African Court Will Deepen Repression," December 2, 2019, https://www.amnesty.org/en/latest/news/2019/12/tanzania-withdrawal-of-individual-rights-to-african-court-will-deepen-repression/.

53. African Court on Human and People's Rights, "Declarations Entered by Member States," https://www.african-court.org/en/index.php/basic-documents/declaration-featured-articles-2. Accessed August 26, 2020.

54. *Protocol to the African Charter*, Article 5.

55. *Protocol to the African Charter*, Article 7.

56. Lohé Issa Konaté v. the Republic of Burkina Faso, application no. 004/20135, case no. 004/2013, December 2014.

57. For instance, Malawi African Association and Others v. Mauritania

58. *Malawi*, para. 155.

59. ACHPR, *Zimbabwe Lawyers for Human Rights & Associated Newspapers of Zimbabwe v. Republic of Zimbabwe*, Communication no. 284/03, April 3, 2009, para. 91. https://ihrda.uwazi.io/en/document/578cfbxdgx9?page=9.

60. *Konaté*, para. 156.

61. Matt J. Duffy, "Konaté v. Burkina Faso: An Analysis of a Landmark Ruling on Criminal Defamation in Africa," *Journal of International Media & Entertainment Law* 6, no. 1: 7.

62. ACHPR, *Konaté*, Separate Opinion, para. 4–5. http://en.african-court.org/images/Cases/Dissenting-Separate%20Opinions/Joint_Separate_Opinion_of_Judges_Sophia_A._B._AKUFFO_Bernard_M._NGOEPE_and_Duncan__TAMBALA.pdf.

63. ACHPR, Lohé Issa Konaté v. Burkina Faso, application no. 004/2013, Order of Provisional Measures, October 4, 2013, para. 18–23. http://en.african-court.org/images/Cases/Orders/Order%20for%20Provisional%20Measures%20Appl.004-2013%20Lohe%20Konate%20v%20Burkina%20Faso%20-%20Engl.pdf.

64. ACHPR, Joint Dissenting Opinion of Judges Augustino Ramadhani, Duncan Tambala, and Elsie N. Thompson on Order for Provisional Measures, October 4, 2013. http://en.african-court.org/images/Cases/Orders/Appl.004-2013_joint_dissenting_opinion.pdf.

65. Nani Jansen Reventlow and Catherine Anite, "Kenyan Court Knocks Down Criminal Defamation, Safeguards Freedom of Expression," CyberLaw Clinic, Harvard Law School, February 8, 2017. https://blogs.harvard.edu/cyberlawclinic/2017/02/08/kenyan-court-knocks-down-criminal-defamation-safeguards-freedom-of-expression.

66. East African Community treaty, Article 23. The treaty entered into force on July 7, 2000. Member states include Burundi, Kenya, Rwanda, South Sudan, Tanzania, and Uganda.

67. Article 27(2): "The Court shall have such other original, appellate, human rights and other jurisdiction as will be determined by the Council at a suitable subsequent date. To this end, the Partner States shall conclude a protocol to operationalize the extended jurisdiction."

68. EACJ, Katabazi and 21 Others v. Secretary General of the East African Community and Another, reference no. 1 of 2007 [2007] EACJ 3, November 1, 2007.

69. EACJ, Burundi Journalists Union vs. Attorney General of the Republic of Burundi, reference no. 7 of 2013. https://eacj.org/wp-content/uploads/2015/05/Reference-No .7-of-2013-Final-15th-May-2c-2015-Very-Final.pdf.

70. *Burundi Journalists Union*, para. 95–99.

71. *Burundi Journalists Union*, para. 109–110.

72. *Burundi Journalists Union*, para. 108.

73. *Burundi Journalists Union*, para. 91–92.

74. *Burundi Journalists Union*, para. 103–106.

75. See UN Human Rights Council, reports of the Commission of Inquiry on Burundi, A/HRC/36/54, A/HRC/36/54/Corr.1, A/HRC/39/63.

76. European Court of Human Rights, Lingens v. Austria, application no. 9815/82 (1986); Christine Goodwin v. the United Kingdom, application no. 28957/95 (2002), http://hudoc.echr.coe.int/sites/eng/pages/search.aspx?i=001-60596.

77. ACHPR, Scanlen and Holderness v. Zimbabwe, communication no. 297/05 (2005); Law Offices of Ghazi Suleiman v. Sudan, communication no. 228/099 (2003); Kenneth Good v. Botswana, communication no. 313/05 (May 31, 2010).

78. Kenya, Cord v. Kenya, H.C. Petition No. 628 of 2014; South Africa v. Sunday Times Newspaper, (2) SA 221 (1994); New York Times Co. v. United States (Pentagon Papers), 403 U.S. 713 (1971).

79. Mseto & Hali Halisi Publishers Ltd. v. the Attorney General of Tanzania, reference no. 7 of 2016, para. 47, 67.

80. EACJ, First Instance Division, reference no. 2 of 2017, para. 83–103.

81. Economic Community of West African States (ECOWAS), Revised Treaty, adopted on July 24, 1993, at Cotonou. http://www.ecowas.int/wp-content/uploads/2015/01 /Revised-treaty.pdf.

82. Protocol A/P1/7/91, July 6, 1991; supplementary protocol A/SP.1/01/05, January 19, 2005; supplementary protocol A/SP.2/06/06, June 14, 2006; regulation of June 3, 2002; and supplementary regulation C/REG.2/06/06, June 13, 2006.

83. ECOWAS court, Federation of African Journalists and 4 others v. The Gambia, suit no. ECW/CCJ/APP/36/15, judgment no. ECW/CCJ/JUD/04/18, p. 40–41.

84. Rachel Murray and Debra Long, *The Implementation of the Findings of the African Commission on Human and Peoples' Rights* (Cambridge: Cambridge University Press, 2015), 90.

Globalizing the Battle Against Impunity TEN

JOEL SIMON AND ELISABETH WITCHEL

When press freedom groups began a campaign against impunity, they set out to gain justice in individual cases of journalists murdered for their work. Did a global norm evolve in the process?

Among the rights guaranteed by the Universal Declaration of Human Rights, Article 19, is notable for its elegance and simplicity. It states, "Everyone has the right to freedom of opinion and expression; this right includes freedom to hold opinions without interference and to seek, receive and impart information and ideas through any media and regardless of frontiers."[1] It would seem elemental that this right cannot be exercised in practice when those who express critical views are systematically murdered with impunity. Yet between 1992 and 2020, 870 journalists were murdered in direct reprisal for their work. Each of these killings was more than a murder; it was an effective form of censorship that deprived whole societies of essential information and protected powerful figures from the scrutiny that would make them accountable to the people.

Beginning in the mid-1990s in Latin America, a coalition of journalists and freedom of expression organizations set out to achieve justice for their slain colleagues and to fight the scourge of violent censorship. The strategy was to confront governments with their failure in these emblematic cases. Over more than two decades, these efforts spread to other regions, coalesced, and strengthened, to the point that today there is a global normative standard expressed through a series of resolutions and legal decisions that urges governments to prioritize investigations into and prosecutions of the killings of journalists, in order to safeguard and protect the right to free expression.

In the past decade, some of these dynamics played out in Pakistan, a country that has seen an explosion of independent media as well an explosion in violence against the press. From 2006 to 2016, twenty-four journalists were killed, according to research carried out by the Committee to Protect Journalists (CPJ).[2] One of the victims was Wali Khan Babar, a young television reporter, who was gunned down on the streets of Karachi in January 2011.

Babar had been reporting on crime and corruption for the popular television news channel GEO TV news, in Pakistan's largest city. His work put him at odds with the Muttahida Qaumi Movement, a political party that wielded immense power in Karachi at the time. Investigations into the killing of journalists in Pakistan have rarely progressed past an initial phase, and few expected Babar's case to play out differently especially since Babar's killers seemed to be professional and well organized. Prosecutors appeared outgunned—literally. At least five people connected to the investigation of the crime were murdered, including an eyewitness and two policemen.

Babar's case, however, proved to be an example not of how to subvert justice but of how to advance it despite seemingly insurmountable obstacles. National and international pressure mounted over Babar's case. His colleagues at GEO TV kept a steady media spotlight on the investigation and prosecution, while Pakistan's press freedom groups campaigned vigorously for justice. International freedom of expression groups echoed their message. In 2012, Pakistan was chosen as a focus country of the United Nations Plan of Action on the Safety of Journalists and the Issue of Impunity, putting the country at the center of a new global effort to stop violence against the press.[3] In 2013, CPJ published a detailed report on impunity in Pakistan, written by noted investigative reporter Elizabeth Rubin. The report probed the Babar killing, highlighting the failure of the investigation.[4]

The immense pressure surrounding the case led the government to relocate the trial from Karachi to an antiterrorism court in another district, where the Muttahida Qaumi Movement had less reach. (Most of the suspects were linked to the organization.) Then, on March 1, 2014, six men were convicted. Four were given life sentences, and two suspects who were at large were sentenced to death in absentia. It was the first local journalist's murder in Pakistan to see justice. Several weeks later, a CPJ delegation visited Pakistan and met with then Prime

Minister Nawaz Sharif. He agreed that steps should be taken to ensure it would not be the last, acknowledging that Pakistan's record of impunity had damaged the country's international reputation.[5] The meeting was a stark contrast to far chillier receptions CPJ had received in Pakistan in the past.

Around the world, four out of five murders of journalists are unsolved,[6] meaning that those who seek to censor information through violence are overwhelmingly successful. In many cases, investigations fail because those who carry out the crimes are connected to officialdom and are able to exert influence over the political and judicial systems. The killers of journalists often take advantage of conflict, instability, or institutional weaknesses to wage violence against those who expose or criticize their actions. From Mexico to Somalia, the pattern is the same: where journalist killings go unpunished, violence repeats, and a cycle takes hold.[7]

The convictions in the Babar killing suggest that the cycle can be disrupted, even in one of the most hostile of media environments. It starts with detecting and documenting the pattern of killing and speaking out. Not only do Pakistani journalists and civil society today routinely decry attacks on the media, but also the killing of a journalist can have global resonance that in turn influences government behavior. In 2013, one of the killers of reporter Ayub Khattak was also brought to justice. The situation for the media in Pakistan is still dire, but the media murder rate has declined in the last several years, according to CPJ research.

The developments in Pakistan are also telling of the extent to which countering impunity in attacks against the media has moved from the realm of journalist rights campaigning toward the beginnings of an international norm. A growing range of actors—from states historically antagonistic to journalist rights to the United Nations Security Council—increasingly accept that when a single killing of a journalist goes unpunished, the repercussions severely compromise media freedom. This failure in turn threatens global development, transparency, and even security. Many states acknowledge that they can no longer tolerate or abet impunity when journalists are assaulted but must increase their political will and take measures to address failures of justice. These behavioral standards are far from universally embraced, but they have been integrated into a variety of international frameworks.

Creating a norm was not the goal of CPJ or other groups that have campaigned against impunity. The priority, shared by other activists and many journalists around the world who had lost friends and colleagues, was to lower the high rates of violence against journalists through prosecutions—prosecutions that might be achieved if enough pressure was exerted on the leadership in those countries, through documentation, public awareness, international pressure, and legal action. Over time, these strategies generated the building blocks of a global normative shift that now sees states bearing responsibility for high rates of violence against journalists, through their failure to prosecute these cases. A fragile global consensus has emerged among international bodies, freedom of expression nongovernmental organizations (NGOs), and even among individual governments on the need and some of the ways to counter this impunity.

BACK TO THE BEGINNING

The battle against impunity began as a regional initiative focused on Latin America more than twenty years ago. In 1995, the Inter American Press Association (IAPA), an organization of leading newspaper publishers from throughout the Americas, began a systematic effort to track the killings of journalists in the region. They also sought to investigate each murder (sometimes by immediately deploying investigative reporters to the scene of the crime), raise awareness through national media campaigns, and confront political leaders about their failure to solve the crimes. The IAPA's Impunity Project, which was underwritten by the Miami-based Knight Foundation, also relied on the regional human rights mechanisms, notably the Inter-American Commission on Human Rights (IACHR) of the Organization of American States, to compel recalcitrant governments to move investigations forward and to provide protection for at-risk journalists. The effort had some striking successes. From 1995 to 2016, governments in seventeen countries prosecuted suspects in 126 journalists' killings in Latin America, according to IAPA statistics. At least 136 people were jailed, most of them hired killers.[8]

Underpinning the work of IAPA and other Latin American press freedom fighters is the region's legacy of airing and seeking redress for a broad range of human rights violations. As countries like Argentina, Chile, and Peru sought to confront their authoritarian pasts, holding violators to account through national courts, truth commissions, and the Inter-American Court evolved as a key model for promoting human rights. Combating impunity in this context went far beyond individual cases to establishing a climate conducive to healthy, peaceful democratic societies.

From 1998 to 2004, Alberto Ibargüen, then publisher of the *Miami Herald*, served as the chairman of the IAPA's anti-impunity campaign. In 2005, Ibargüen was selected as president of the Knight Foundation. Ibargüen also had been on the board of the Committee to Protect Journalists. In his new role as head of the

Knight Foundation, Ibargüen recognized that it might be possible to replicate on a global level some of the successes that the IAPA had achieved. In discussions with CPJ, Ibargüen agreed that if the organization could bring together the relevant expertise, including that of the IAPA, then the Knight Foundation would fund a pilot project to test the viability of a global effort to combat impunity.

Since its founding in 1981, CPJ had campaigned for justice when journalists were killed around the world. Indeed, some of these killings made international headlines, like the 1986 assassination of Colombian editor Guillermo Cano in Bogotá and the 1992 killing of ABC News correspondent David Kaplan by sniper fire in Sarajevo, Bosnia. While there was plenty of outrage in both cases, there were no systematic global efforts to demand justice. That changed with the murder of *Wall Street Journal* reporter Daniel Pearl, kidnapped and murdered by Al Qaeda militants in Pakistan in 2002. Intense international pressure—notably from the United States—forced Pakistan to carry out a rigorous investigation that eventually led to the conviction of four of his killers. Of course, Pearl's profile as an international correspondent was not typical—most journalists who are killed are local reporters working in their own country. But his case showed the importance of international attention, and also highlighted what's possible with political will.

Pearl's horrific murder raised global awareness about the changing landscape for journalists' safety. This need for a more comprehensive analysis into media deaths dovetailed with improvements in technology available to groups like CPJ. Since 1992, CPJ had published annual case lists and descriptions of journalists killed in the line of duty. In 2004, the organization began a major project to code all the data and enter it into a comprehensive database (cpj.org /killed), which yielded some surprising conclusions. For example, the majority of journalists killed in connection to their work around the world were specifically targeted for murder. A relatively small proportion were killed in cross fire. Those murdered had not covered frontline conflict but rather human rights, corruption, business, crime, and politics. And perhaps most disturbing, in more than 85 percent of those murders, the killers got away with the crime, a percentage that fluctuated over the next decade as new murders were perpetrated in far higher numbers than convictions took place, before finally dropping to 81 percent in 2019. Where there were convictions, they were usually of paid assassins, not of the masterminds.

Reports on journalist killings compiled by other international groups, such as Reporters Without Borders and the International Federation of Journalists, suggested a similar breakdown, and this consensus helped fuel global awareness about the nature of the risk. The data, in turn, compelled governments and international bodies like the United Nations to recognize the scope of the problem, as the phrase "Nine out of ten journalists murdered around the world are killed with impunity" became a global maxim.[9]

The data also revealed recurring patterns of violence when impunity is unaddressed. Killing with impunity is concentrated in a relatively small number of states. For example, in the decade from 2007 through 2016, 80 percent of all unsolved killings of journalists around the world took place in only twelve countries. Government and military officials are considered the leading suspects in more than a quarter of the cases in this same period. Based on this combination of information, CPJ and other groups argued that, regardless of who might be behind these crimes, the existence of impunity points to a systemic problem that states must address. Surprisingly, many countries with high rates of impunity were democracies whose leaders cared about their country's international reputation, an opening for effective advocacy.

In 2006, CPJ began to develop a global campaign based on widespread consultations with journalists from around the world and leading press freedom organizations. At the end of the process, CPJ identified two countries—Russia and the Philippines—where strategies similar to the ones deployed in Latin America by the IAPA could be effective. Both countries were among the most murderous for journalists, according to CPJ research. Both had abysmal records for bringing the killers to justice.

THE PILOT

The Philippines and Russia were selected for the pilot because both had serious levels of violence against journalists. They also were chosen because of the contrast they represented. In many ways, the situation in the two countries could not have been more different.

In the mid-2000s, the Russian economy was booming and the government was firmly in control. The media, once rambunctious, had largely been tamed, through a series of politicized lawsuits and hostile takeovers that had brought the broadcast networks under the influence of the Kremlin. The government, enjoying widespread popular support, was highly resistant to both international and domestic pressure.

The Philippines, on the other hand, was home to a vital and critical national press. It had a long history of independence but also a dark underside. In the provinces, many journalists worked under the sway of local political bosses, who paid them to engage in reckless denunciations of their rivals. Even though President Gloria Macapagal Arroyo had handily won her second term as president, in 2004, she was hemmed in by powerful military and regional political bosses. The criminal justice system in the Philippines was barely functional, with regional courts overburdened and underfunded.

In February 2008, CPJ joined forces with the Open Society Institute, the Bangkok-based Southeast Asian Press Alliance, and the Manila-based Center for Media Freedom and Responsibility to cosponsor an international conference on "Impunity and Press Freedom" in the Philippines. The conference, which took place in the Peninsula Hotel in Manila, brought together nearly two hundred participants, including representatives of the Philippine government, to discuss the issue of impunity and to seek solutions.

At the end of the two-day event, CPJ and the Freedom Fund for Filipino Journalists announced they would be joining forces in a campaign against impunity in the Philippines and that this would be part of a global effort. The Freedom Fund is an association of press freedom groups, publishers' associations, and individual media outlets dedicated to supporting journalists who are victims of attacks.

One of the lessons of the IAPA campaign in Latin America was that the issue of impunity must be humanized by highlighting individual cases. Initially, in the Philippines, the crusading investigative journalist Marlene Garcia-Esperat would be at the center of the calls for justice. Garcia-Esperat, a columnist from the volatile island of Mindanao, had been gunned down in front of her family in March 2005. At the time, Garcia-Esperat had already earned a national reputation in the Philippines for her fearless work exposing corruption. The heinous nature of her killing garnered enormous public sympathy. Garcia-Esperat's personal friend, lawyer Nena Santos, spearheaded the legal quest for justice, with support from the Freedom Fund, and their efforts helped produce convictions against three gunmen. A middleman who had turned state's witness had fingered two agriculture officials, whose corruption Garcia-Esperat had exposed, as the masterminds in the killings.[10]

Meanwhile, in Russia the campaign focused on Anna Politkovskaya, who had been gunned down outside her Moscow apartment in October 2006. Politkovskaya, a reporter with the fiercely independent Moscow newspaper *Novaya Gazeta*, had reported on human rights abuses in Chechnya and attacked President Vladimir Putin personally for indifference, ineptitude, incompetence, and cruelty. She had been honored internationally, and so her murder resonated around the world. But Vladimir Putin, responding to reporter's question while on a visit to Dresden, Germany, soon after her murder, reportedly declared that

Politkovskaya's "influence on political life in the country was extremely insignificant in scale. . . . She was known in journalist and human rights circles, but her influence on political life in Russia was minimal."[11]

For Politkovskaya's friends and colleagues, Putin's words were more than just a jab. Many assumed they would be interpreted by prosecutors and other high officials in Russia as a signal that the president wanted a perfunctory inquiry, not a real effort to find the killers of a journalist whom he viewed as a personal enemy. In fact, Politkovskaya was the thirteenth journalist to be murdered since Putin had come to power in 2000, and at the time there had not been a single conviction. This record of impunity was producing fear and self-censorship among Russian journalists, undermining efforts to report on a variety of controversial issues, from corruption to human rights abuses.

A month after the Politkovskaya murder, hundreds of leading journalists from the United States and around the world gathered in the grand ballroom in New York's Waldorf Astoria hotel for the annual Committee to Protect Journalists gala. Even as four courageous journalists received awards, Politkovskaya's recent murder cast a pall over the evening. Paul Steiger, CPJ chairman and at the time the managing editor of the *Wall Street Journal*, asked guests at the dinner to sign a petition calling on Russian authorities to prosecute the killers of journalists. In January 2007, a CPJ delegation led by Steiger traveled to Moscow to deliver the signed petition. The documents were handed to Ella Pamfilova, chairwoman of the Russian Human Rights Council, who promised to deliver them personally to President Putin. A representative from the Russian foreign ministry told the delegation that investigators were examining members of the Chechen police as possible suspects in the Politkovskaya murder. That news made headlines, especially after the Russian authorities denied that they had made the statement.

The CPJ visit to Moscow was part of a global constellation of outrage that eventually seemed to wear Putin down, and now the president delivered a new message. "The problem of the persecution of journalists is a very acute problem both for our country and for many other countries. And we acknowledge our responsibility in this," Putin said, before hundreds of journalists who had assembled for his annual press conference in early 2007, shortly after the CPJ mission. "I recall not only Anna Politskovkaya—she was quite a sharp critic of the authorities and that is a good thing. I recall other journalists as well, including Paul Khlebnikov."[12] Klebnikov, an American of Russian descent, was the editor of *Forbes* Russia. He was shot dead outside his Moscow office in July 2004.

Politkovskaya's case began to move. In August 2007, Russian prosecutors announced the arrest of ten suspects. Another victory against impunity followed later that year, when five members of a criminal gang in the Republic of Tatarstan were convicted of carrying out the 2000 murder of *Novaya Gazeta* reporter Igor Domnikov. These were the first convictions in a journalist's killing since Vladimir Putin had come to office.

This early stage of the campaign targeted national leaderships, using emblematic cases to rally domestic political pressure. Engagement with or support for local actors, such as national freedom of expression groups and media, were key to achieving this. Though concentrating an international spotlight on an issue that previously had been of concern largely to national stakeholders played an important role in eliciting responses from high political levels, it was only later that impunity came to be defined in global terms.

THE IMPUNITY INDEX

As the impunity campaign focused on country-level actions in the Philippines and Russia, a significant question emerged: How could progress, both on a national and an international level, be measured? And could an objective barometer of impunity be used as a means of goading recalcitrant governments toward action?

After consulting a variety of experts, including statisticians, CPJ developed a formula. We looked at a ten-year period and included only those countries with at least five unsolved murders. We defined "unsolved" generously—these were killings in which there had not been a single conviction. Recognizing that the murder of a journalist would have a different impact in a country like Mozambique, which has a tiny press corps concentrated in the capital, than in Brazil or India, where the media is both enormous and diverse, we sought to find a way to weight our findings. Since it was impossible to determine the size of the press corps in any given country, we used population figures. We divided the number of unsolved murders by the size of the population to come to an objective figure based on careful research—a number that governments couldn't challenge. We called it the Impunity Index.

CPJ launched the first Impunity Index at a press conference at the United Nations. Participants talked about the overall impact of impunity, the fear it engendered, and the toll it takes in terms of self-censorship and public accountability. Renowned Filipino journalist Sheila Coronel spoke about the failure of the Philippines government to win convictions. "The justice system is compromised," she said. "Judges are corrupt or afraid to prosecute the killers or they are under the sway of powerful patrons—police and law enforcement agencies are in the same situation and, in some cases, the killings have been by rogue policemen or rogue military officers."[13]

With the launch of the Impunity Index, the basic elements of the campaign were now in place. CPJ created an advisory board of experts, including Ricardo Trotti from the IAPA, and internally appointed an impunity campaign coordinator, Elisabeth Witchel (the coauthor of this chapter), to oversee the effort. CPJ developed a link on its website outlining the campaign and its goals and enlisted then CPJ board member Christiane Amanpour of CNN to record a video highlighting the issue.

CPJ distributed the Impunity Index to officials at the World Bank and the International Monetary Fund and encouraged them to begin using it as a yardstick for measuring democratic development. CPJ met with Ban Ki-moon, the UN secretary-general at the time, and asked him to speak out about the issue. CPJ staff coordinated their efforts with many colleagues on the international and domestic level, and in a relatively short period the word "impunity" entered the press freedom lexicon. The next step was turning the growing public awareness into action.

While CPJ saw the Impunity Index as a global tool, it also hoped the index would energize the two pilot campaigns in Russia and Philippines. In Manila, the Freedom Fund for Filipino Journalists hired lawyers to file legal appeals and worked closely with the public prosecutor, the late Leo Dacero, an important ally in the pursuit of justice, to protect witnesses at risk. Along with the National Union of Journalists of the Philippines, they kept up public pressure. CPJ and other press freedom groups spoke up in international circles—including in the U.S. Congress and the United Nations—to ensure that the issue of impunity for the killers of journalists was a regular feature in foreign aid discussions. In Russia, CPJ began working with reporters on the ground in Moscow to lay the groundwork for a major report on impunity, to be released the following year.

In March 2009, CPJ released its second annual Impunity Index, this time in Manila. The release was timed to coincide with the fourth anniversary of the killing of Marlene Garcia-Esperat.

Surprised by the level of public attention, the Arroyo government sought to downplay the findings. A presidential spokesman texted the press corps, calling the index "a bit of exaggeration." The message backfired when, instead of quelling media coverage, the text sparked a new round of attention that highlighted the data.[14]

The release of the Impunity Index also received attention in the Russian media, including on many widely read websites. CPJ followed the 2009 index up with a detailed seventy-two-page report entitled *Anatomy of Injustice*, which chronicled the failure of Russian authorities to achieve justice in the killing of seventeen journalists since Putin first came to power in 2000. A CPJ delegation presented the research in Moscow in September 2009.

Anatomy of Injustice, which included contributions from a variety of Russian and international experts, identified incompetence, secrecy, conflicts of interest, corruption, and political interference as the primary impediments to successful prosecutions. "Let us be perfectly plain," wrote CPJ board member and author Kati Marton in the preface. "Any state that turns a blind eye—or worse—toward the assassination of reporters cannot call itself a democracy. When journalists are threatened, democracy itself is threatened. Along with the rule of law, an independent judiciary, and an autonomous civil society, free media is one of the essential pillars of a healthy society. Remove one, and the whole structure may collapse."[15]

Immediately following the Moscow press conference, the CPJ delegation met with a team of eleven investigators looking into the murders. The meeting was contentious at times, but compared with previous responses, the mere fact that the Russian government was willing to engage was an encouraging sign.

IMPUNITY BECOMES A GLOBAL ISSUE

As CPJ built its global campaign, press freedom communities in countries besieged with violence and impunity waged their own battles at the national level. These ultimately coalesced into a joint movement spearheaded by IFEX, a 120-member umbrella group of freedom of expression organizations. In a 2008 survey, IFEX members named impunity as their top concern, and at the 2009 General Meeting in Oslo, it was agreed that impunity would be a joint priority.[16] "Standing by while journalists and other free expression advocates are being silenced, sending funeral wreaths, and having family members terrorized was just not an option," reflected IFEX Executive Director Annie Game in a blog post for CPJ.[17] Later that year, events in the Philippines would give new urgency to the effort.

On November 23, 2009, gunmen ambushed a caravan escorting political candidate Esmael "Toto" Mangudadatu as he prepared to file papers to run for provincial governor. The attackers slaughtered fifty-eight people, among them thirty journalists and two media workers. The bodies were dumped in predug mass graves. The Maguindanao massacre, as it is known, represented the largest number of journalists murdered in a single attack since CPJ began keeping track in 1992.

In April 2010, five months after the massacre, CPJ, in partnership with IFEX, convened a two-day Impunity Summit in New York City. Some forty journalists and freedom of expression advocates from around the world, including Russia, the Philippines, Pakistan and Colombia, came to share strategies and identify joint actions. "It is essential that the battle to stop journalists' murders and end impunity have a common cause and group identity," argued Trotti, who presented IAPA's work at the summit, "such as has occurred in other social causes—the fight against AIDS, breast cancer, or global warming, among others."[18] Participants at the summit agreed to launch an international day to end impunity. IFEX members subsequently chose the anniversary of the Maguindanao massacre to mark the occasion. For the next three years, November 23 was transformed into a day of remembrance, advocacy, and protest.

That the NGO community and media were focused on the fight against impunity was not altogether surprising, since journalists in all regions suffered from this common problem. But what moved the ball forward was the extent to which intergovernmental bodies took up the issue. Just over a year after the summit, the United Nations Educational, Scientific and Cultural Organization (UNESCO) began consultations on what would become the UN Plan of Action for the Safety of Journalists and the Issue of Impunity, a pivotal point in the adoption of impunity into the international agenda.

In March 2012, the Intergovernmental Council of UNESCO's International Programme for the Development of Communication, charged with strengthening news media in developing countries, debated the adoption of the draft Plan of Action. The plan called for greater coordination between UN agencies as well as promotion of legislation and mechanisms to protect journalists and prosecute their killers. It emphasized multistakeholder collaboration among the media, civil society, state actors, and intergovernmental bodies.[19]

Some member states—Pakistan, India, and Brazil being among the more vocal—expressed reluctance to move ahead, and the plan was not formally endorsed at that meeting.[20] Journalists in Brazil and Pakistan were appalled by this reticence and took to their keyboards, calling out their governments for delaying a crucial opportunity to act against killers of journalists.[21] In Brazil, the association of investigative journalists called ABRAJI, which had been pushing for action against impunity since the 2002 murder of award-winning investigative journalist Tim Lopes, issued a strong statement that was widely covered in the Brazilian press. The government swiftly changed its stance and declared its support for the plan.[22] Shortly afterwards, in April, the UN Chief Executive Board for Coordination, the main instrument of support for the coordinating role of the United Nations intergovernmental bodies on social, economic, and related matters, adopted the plan.[23]

Journalists traditionally are reluctant to put themselves at the center of the story. So efforts to spur international media into action were critical to raising the visibility of the impunity issue. From 2012 to 2015, the Centre for Freedom of the Media, based at the University of Sheffield, organized a series of events on impunity, including two symposiums cohosted by the BBC to promote involvement by media companies in the UN Plan of Action.[24] In February 2013, colleagues of Marie Colvin and Remy Ochlik, both killed in Syria in 2012, launched "A Day Without News," a traditional and social media blitz to bring attention to fallen colleagues and the need for more investigation into their deaths.

UNESCO was not the only UN forum to take up the issue around this time. Since 2012, the United Nations Human Rights Council, an intergovernmental body responsible for the promotion and protection of all human rights, has passed no less than four resolutions on the safety of journalists. The resolutions affirmed the impact of impunity and called on states to ensure accountability.[25]

In 2012, the UN Human Rights Committee, a body of legal experts, issued General Comment no. 34 on Article 19 of the International Covenant on Civil and Political Rights, identifying prosecution following attacks against journalists as a fundamental step to upholding the right to freedom of expression. All attacks against those who practice freedom of expression should be "vigorously investigated in a timely fashion, and the perpetrators prosecuted," the comment reads.[26]

That same year, the UN special rapporteurs on extrajudicial, summary, or arbitrary executions and the promotion and protection of the right to freedom of expression made impunity in targeted attacks against journalists the subject of their reports and called on states to implement mechanisms to protect journalists and promote justice.[27] Since then, the rapporteurs have continued to promote justice in journalist killings, with the rapporteur on extrajudicial, summary, or arbitrary executions taking the unprecedented step of conducting an independent inquiry into the 2018 murder of *Washington Post* columnist Jamal Khashoggi at the Saudi Arabian embassy.

In 2013, the issue gained traction outside UNESCO and the Human Rights Council. The UN Security Council hosted two debates focused on the safety of journalists and impunity, featuring testimony from award-winning Somali journalist Mustafa Haji Abdinur, who told the council members he was called "a dead man walking" because of the dangers of reporting in Mogadishu. Associated Press executive editor and CPJ board member (now board chair) Kathleen

Carroll answered the question of why the world's leaders should care about threats against journalists, noting, "An attack on a journalist is a proxy for an attack on the people, an attack on their right to information about their communities and their institutions."[28]

The next step came in November 2013, when the Permanent UN Mission of Greece drafted what would become United Nations General Assembly Resolution 68/163, Safety of Journalists and the Issue of Impunity. Prior to the assembly's review, IFEX members, including CPJ, hit the phones hard, contacting missions to urge them to support the resolution. It was subsequently adopted by consensus.

The resolution describes the absence of justice for victims as "one of the main challenges to strengthening the protection of journalists." It calls on states to "ensure accountability through the conduct of impartial, speedy, and effective investigations into all alleged violence against journalists and media workers falling within their jurisdiction." Governments are further charged to "bring the perpetrators of such crimes to justice and to ensure that victims have access to appropriate remedies." Finally, the resolution calls on states to dedicate the resources necessary to investigate and prosecute attacks against journalists and for the UN secretary-general to report to the General Assembly on the implementation of the resolution and the UN Plan of Action.[29]

Much of the language echoes the Human Rights Council's resolutions that came before it, but the General Assembly took the additional step of establishing the International Day to End Impunity for Crimes Against Journalists, though it proclaimed the date November 2, in remembrance of Claude Verlon and Ghislaine Dupont, two French journalists killed in Mali that year, rather than the November 23 anniversary of the Maguindanao massacre.[30] The United Nations General Assembly would pass another four resolutions on the safety of journalists and the issue of impunity by the end of 2019.[31] In less than a decade, what had started out as a series of disconnected, nationally focused efforts had become an international, UN-backed campaign.

Most of the UN resolutions and proclamations make a case that press freedom is a keystone to other global objectives. A free press facilitates transparency and the free flow of information for development. The expression of diverse views bolsters peace building and the exposure of human rights violations, government corruption, and crime. The consensus that combating impunity is critical to promoting the essential work of journalists has situated the issue within broader global objectives. "Safety and impunity issues are part of a wider ecology, which requires a complex set of interventions to address," said Guy Berger, director of UNESCO's Division for Freedom of Expression and Media Development.[32]

One recent manifestation of this is the inclusion of journalist safety in the UN's Sustainable Development Goals indicators. The UN's 2030 Agenda for Sustainable Development, adopted in late 2015, includes seventeen goals to "mobilize efforts to end all forms of poverty, fight inequalities and tackle climate change."[33] Goal 16 calls on states to promote a just, peaceful and inclusive society, with effective and accountable institutions. The Inter-agency and Expert Group on SDG Indicators, which drafted a series of objectives and measures around each goal, included data on journalist killings as a measure of a state's success in meeting goal 16.[34]

In an effort to push some of these commitments toward concrete actions, a global coalition of 120 nongovernmental organizations spearheaded by Reporters without Borders came together under the #ProtectJournalists banner to call on the UN to appoint a special representative for the safety of journalists. In a May 2017 meeting with representatives from the campaign, United Nations Secretary-General António Guterres committed to opening a direct channel of communication through which groups may refer urgent cases.[35]

Regional courts have provided legal underpinnings to the arguments taking hold in international forums. In its 2001 analysis of Hector Félix Miranda v. Mexico, the Inter-American Commission on Human Rights concluded that through its lack of investigation into the 1988 killing of Félix, a well-known Tijuana-based columnist, the Mexican state had "to the detriment of Hector Félix Miranda and that of every citizen—violated the right to freedom of expression."[36] More recently, in 2015, the African Court on Human and Peoples' Rights found that Burkina Faso had violated the right of the freedom of expression of journalists because its failure to prosecute the killers of investigative reporter Norbert Zongo, whose body was found in a burned-out car in December 1998, "caused fear and worry in media circles."[37] Another decision, Hydara v. Gambia, made by the court of the Economic Community of West African States in 2014, held that not only did The Gambia inadequately investigate the 2006 shooting of editor Deyda Hydara but also systematic impunity has had a chilling effect on journalists attempting to exercise the right to freedom of expression.[38] In 2018, the European Court of Human Rights ruled in the Politkovskaya case that Russia "had failed to take adequate investigatory steps to find the person or persons who had commissioned the murder."[39]

Other interventions by regional bodies in response to killings of journalists have escalated as well. For example, widespread concerns over Malta's response to the 2017 assassination of Daphne Caruana Galizia pushed the Council of Europe to appoint a special rapporteur to monitor the official investigation and the broader circumstances behind her death. Caruana Galizia was a prominent journalist and blogger who was reporting on high-level corruption in Malta when she was killed by a car bomb that exploded near her house.

This integration throughout the international system of the principles behind the impunity campaign raised international pressure and also rendered a fundamental change in the framing of the issue. The battle dynamics shifted somewhat, from activists and journalists versus governments to a global struggle in which states are invited to join—and, through their international obligations, states have committed, at least on paper, to taking part in this struggle. The challenge remains of how to leverage this new paradigm for effective action.

PUSHING FOR STATE-LEVEL ACTION

Creating change on a national level has been far more complex and fraught than winning international attention. Political will to aggressively tackle impunity is generally weak. Over time, however, the combination of domestic political pressure and concern for a country's international standing have begun to alter how states publicly regard and respond to journalist killings.

One modest measure of improvement has been responses by states to an accountability mechanism that exists within UNESCO. In 2006, UNESCO began requesting that states provide information on the judicial status of cases of killed journalists. For years, the response rates were worryingly low—less than 40 percent, indicating a high level of apathy. For several years, freedom of expression groups and UNESCO's press freedom division worked to raise awareness of this process and of the need for states to participate. In the 2017 report, the response rate had increased to over 70 percent.[40]

Meanwhile, the Impunity Index has served as an effective naming and shaming tool. Some of the countries that appeared on the first edition of the index in 2008 remain mired in conflict, including Iraq and Somalia. In more recent years, Syria and South Sudan have climbed in the rankings. At the same time, impunity in countries that are not at war and that moreover have robust democracies has remained deeply entrenched. Examples include Mexico, India, Brazil, and of course, the Philippines.[41]

For these governments, appearing in an index alongside conflict-ravaged states is an embarrassment. On more than one occasion, the index has elicited high-level public statements claiming that CPJ has distorted its findings. As in the Philippines, the transparent and clear methodology has allowed CPJ to push against such claims.[42] Since CPJ first began publishing the index, eleven repeat offender countries—meaning countries that CPJ identified as sustaining among the highest levels of impunity worldwide over time—prosecuted one or more suspects in at least one case, an indication that international pressure has brought some change.

Year on year, changes in the index are not dramatic, but over time it conveys an important narrative. The countries that have deteriorated the most are Mexico and Somalia. The most extreme positive shift is Colombia, which has gone from being among the worst countries in the world for impunity to falling off the index altogether. Colombia's "progress" is representative of the issue's many complexities. While the government did successfully convict the perpetrators in a small number of cases, its overall record of addressing impunity is poor. In at least thirty-seven murders recorded in the CPJ database since 1992, no one has been convicted. The improvement in Colombia's standing on the index is derived from a decline in new journalist murder cases over the past ten years, attributable to the end of the decades-long conflict and the implementation of a national protection mechanism.[43] However, another, more worrying factor behind Colombia's data is self-censorship, which essentially means that because of violence, journalists are not pursuing dangerous but vital stories.[44]

Increasingly, governments appear pressed to take at least a rhetorical stand against impunity. Leaders in Brazil, Pakistan, Somalia, and other countries have made public commitments to hold perpetrators to account and have followed these up with a small number of prosecutions.[45]

In some countries, governments have employed measures such as the establishment of special prosecutors, task forces, and commissions in response to pressure from media and freedom of expression groups. In Serbia, the government agreed to a proposal by journalists to establish a commission to investigate outstanding media murders. The commission, which includes Serbian police and security agents as well as journalists and media association representatives, reopened older unsolved cases. Its work has led to the prosecution of suspects in the 1999 murder of Slavko Ćuruvija, founder and editor of Serbia's first private daily newspaper. Kosovo and Montenegro have established similar commissions.[46]

Where impunity is fed by corruption, collusion, or a lack of resources on the part of local and provincial authorities, bringing in teams from the capital can be effective. Brazil mobilized a federal task force whose work led to the conviction of a suspect in the murders of journalist Rodrigo Neto and photographer Walgney Assis de Carvalho.[47] In Mexico, freedom of expression groups successfully campaigned over many years to federalize crimes against free expression, to pressure the congress to pass a constitutional amendment in 2013 that gives federal authorities broader jurisdiction to prosecute crimes against freedom of expression, and to establish a special prosecutor's office for crimes against freedom of expression.

For the most part, the results of these considerable political efforts have been largely disappointing. FEADLE, as the special prosecutor's office is known, has a miserable record.[48] Mexico remains one of the most dangerous places in the world to be a journalist, with nearly fifty journalists murdered because of their work and an additional sixty killings in which the motive is so far unconfirmed by CPJ. Nearly all the murders were carried out with full or partial impunity. Following a meeting with a CPJ delegation in May 2017, President Enrique Peña Nieto fired the head of FEADLE and appointed a new special prosecutor. Three weeks later, Javier Valdez Cárdenas, one of Mexico's leading journalists and a 2011 winner of CPJ International Press Freedom Award, was gunned down outside his office in Culiacán. The case would go on to become the first prosecution under the federal program when, in February 2020, one of the killers was convicted in a federal court. Though this represents a breakthrough on impunity in Mexico, justice is only partial. The killers' sentence of fourteen years and eight months came about through an abbreviated trial, the Mexican equivalent of a plea bargain.

In the Philippines, even the administration of President Rodrigo Duterte, who is openly hostile to the media,[49] has taken action to address the country's deplorable impunity ratings by launching the Presidential Task Force on Media Safety, which monitors and supports investigations into attacks against journalists.

Though there are many concerns among journalists and freedom of expression advocates around the implementation of national mechanisms, the emergence of such mechanisms can be viewed as testament that impunity is being taken up at state levels with some degree of political commitment. More and more countries are looking to develop models to improve investigations and prosecutions of journalist killings.[50] Some of these may never concretize, but the states' professed interest in putting measures in place, combined with the evolution of how leaders broach the issue, indicate that the global perspective is starting to translate to the local level. What is clear is that how some states comport themselves on the issue has changed. Whether the objective of the anti-impunity movement—to discourage attacks against journalists through prosecutions—has been met is less clear.

WHERE THE ISSUE STANDS NOW

In June 2017, diplomats, journalists, and representatives from UN agencies and freedom of expression groups convened in Geneva to review the first five years of the UN Plan of Action on the Safety of Journalists and the Issue of Impunity. In an editorial written in advance of the meeting, coauthors Alice Bah Kuhnke, Sweden's minister of culture and democracy, and Irina Bokova, UNESCO director-general, summarized what might be considered a norm in progress: "We cannot accept impunity for serious crimes [against journalists], which, in addition to being tragic in themselves, threaten to weaken societies by curbing peoples' right to free expression and information."[51]

Without a doubt the correlation between combating impunity and protecting a fundamental human right has been incorporated into dialogue within the international community. Efforts to combat impunity in violence against journalists are supported not only by the media community but also by national and international civil society groups and by intergovernmental bodies. There is a growing body of international documents, including a UN General Assembly consensual resolution, soft law, and court decisions, backing these tenets, along with an international day recognizing the issue. More importantly, state behavior is also showing signs of being influenced, with the establishment of mechanisms, legislation, and even a rise in convictions.

Nonetheless, impunity is still an unknown or downplayed problem in too many quarters. On the ground, progress toward justice is slow and uneven. The Philippines and Russia experiences bear this out. Justice in Garcia-Esperat's case has extended only to the hired guns. The alleged masterminds managed to challenge the murder charges against them, fend off arrest warrants, and eventually return to work at a government office. When the devastating news of the Maguindanao massacre broke, the freedom of expression community, unable to let such an atrocity stand, shifted its focus. Despite international attention, constant monitoring by national media freedom groups, and support given to the prosecution by several private attorneys, that case against the massacre suspects moved glacially. More than ten years and three presidents later, convictions were finally levied in late 2019. At least eighty suspects, however, are still at large.

At the same time, it must be noted there have been convictions in at least three other cases in recent years. One of those cases, the assassination of environmental journalist and activist Gerardo Ortega, has followed nearly the same pattern as Garcia-Esperat's case. Ortega also attacked corruption and had criticized local officials over an illegal mining project in the Philippines' Palawan province. On January 24, 2011, he was shopping in a busy area when he was shot in the back of the head. Public pressure swiftly mounted over the case and, as with Garcia-Esperat's murder, the gunman and other accomplices were convicted. Two politicians, former Palawan governor Joel Reyes and his brother, Mario Reyes, a former mayor in the same province, have been charged with commissioning the murder. Their trial is still pending.

In Russia, justice in Politkovskaya's case has also followed a rocky path. Most of the initial suspects arrested were released. Three went to trial but were acquitted in 2009. Eventually, six suspects would be sentenced for Politkovskaya's murder, but authorities have never identified the mastermind, as highlighted by the 2018 European Court of Human Rights ruling.

In the past decade, there have been convictions in four cases in Russia— those of Anna Politkovskaya, Anastasia Baburova, Malik Akhmedilov, and Igor Domnikov. Perhaps more importantly, the number of murders has dramatically dropped. Since 2010, six journalists were murdered in Russia, compared with twenty journalists' murders that took place during the previous decade. The prosecutions, as well as the unwanted international attention impunity campaigning brings when a journalist is killed, may be a deterrent to murder. But this is not proven. Meanwhile, less blunt means of repression, such as politically motivated legal harassment, have become more prevalent, and perhaps more effective, in the Philippines and Russia. Nonfatal assaults receive far less attention, and these continue unabated.[52]

When CPJ launched its impunity campaign in 2006, the theory of change was that public advocacy would pressure the authorities to investigate murders and that these investigations would lead to convictions. The increased likelihood of punishment would slow the pace of killing. More than a decade later, the evidence for this correlation is mixed. On the one hand, rates of targeted killings have dropped off in many countries that have been the focus of intensive campaigning. It may be that international pressure has changed the political calculus for those hostile to the press, upping the cost of inaction for governments. On the other hand, drops in violence also may be attributed to the end of conflict, to political changes, or to security improvements.

Sri Lanka, for example, had been on CPJ's Impunity Index since 2008 and fell off in 2016. Despite the fact that no one has been convicted in any journalist killing, a combination of pressure and political change has improved the safety environment for journalists. As in Colombia, journalists were targets in the decades-long civil war that has now come to an end. In early 2015, shortly after taking office, Sri Lanka's President Maithripala Sirisena pledged to address impunity. "The new Government will revive all the suppressed cases and hold proper, impartial and justifiable investigations," President Sirisena promised.[53] Several suspects were arrested for their involvement in two of the country's best-known cases, the 2009 murder of editor Lasantha Wickramatunga and the 2010 disappearance of cartoonist Prageeth Eknelygoda. Efforts soon dropped off, however, and are unlikely to be reinvigorated, given Sirisena's defeat in 2019 by Gotabaya Rajapaksa, brother to the former president, under whose leadership the attacks took place.

With pockets of progress, impunity rates are starting to drop worldwide—as of the end of 2019, they hovered at 81 percent when factoring in the Maguindanao massacre convictions, which accounts for thirty cases. The year 2019 also saw the lowest number of journalist murders that CPJ has ever recorded for a year, ten, but the decline has not been a steady one. In 2016, nineteen journalists were murdered for their work; the number for 2017 was eighteen, compared to fifty recorded in 2015. The number surged to thirty-six in 2018—the year eight journalists were killed in a double bombing in Kabul, four were murdered in a U.S. newsroom, and Jamal Khashoggi was assassinated—before falling in 2019.

Looking at individual countries, there simply haven't been enough convictions to draw a link to levels of violence. In the Philippines, it is too soon to gauge the impact of the Maguindanao convictions, leaving the experience of Brazil as the best indicator, and it does not tell a persuasive story so far. Brazil, after its initial hedging around the UN Action Plan, has emerged as one of the few countries that has backed its expressed commitments with significant numbers of prosecutions. Since 2013, suspects have been convicted in seven cases of journalist murders in Brazil. Yet at least sixteen journalists have been murdered for their work in Brazil in the same time period, though none were killed in 2019. Worldwide, journalist murders have dipped and surged. More time and more successful convictions may indeed indicate a clear shift in the ground for journalists in Brazil and elsewhere and may more conclusively validate CPJ's theory of change, but the data is not yet there. Meanwhile, the 2020 emergence of the worldwide COVID-19 epidemic has given rise to unprecedented challenges for fighting impunity and upholding press freedom.

Like crime itself, impunity and threats to journalists can never be entirely eliminated. For friends, family members, and colleagues, the fight for justice is often all that is left to keep alive the voices of those who have been silenced. After investigative reporter Pavel Sheremet was killed by a car bomb in June 2016, in Kiev, his mother pleaded, "Make sure Pavel did not die in vain. Keep fighting." This is the moral imperative, but the fight against impunity has also moved beyond the battle for individual justice. Over the past two decades, it has helped to create structures in which the affirmative obligation of governments to protect free expression and freedom of the press by combating violence against the media has been strengthened and reinforced. Ensuring that these efforts coalesce into an enduring global norm is the work ahead.

NOTES

1. UN General Assembly, Universal Declaration of Human Rights (217 A) (Paris, 1948).
2. Committee to Protect Journalists (CPJ), "Pakistan," May 4, 2005, https://cpj.org /killed/asia/pakistan/.
3. United Nations Educational, Scientific and Cultural Organization (UNESCO), *Implementation Strategy 2013–2014: UN Plan of Action on the Safety of Journalists and the Issue of Impunity*, http://www.unesco.org/new/fileadmin/MULTIMEDIA /HQ/CI/CI/pdf/official_documents/Implementation_Strategy_2013-2014_01.pdf.
4. Elizabeth Rubin, *Roots of Impunity: Pakistan's Endangered Press and the Perilous Web of Militancy, Security, and Politics*, CPJ special report, May 23, 2013, http:// www.cpj.org/reports/2013/05/pakistan-roots-impunity/.
5. Kati Marton, "Mission Journal: Hope in Pakistan," CPJ, March 21, 2014, https://cpj .org/blog/2014/03/mission-journal-hope-in-pakistan.php.
6. See CPJ online database of killed journalists, https://cpj.org/killed. UNESCO and other organizations have published similar findings.
7. Committee to Protect Journalists, *The Road to Justice: Breaking the Cycle of Impunity in the Killing of Journalists*, special report, October 2014, https://cpj.org/reports /2014/10/the-road-to-justice-killing-journalists-impunity.php.
8. Ricardo Trotti, director of the Inter-American Press Association Impunity Project, pers. comm., June 28, 2017.
9. The phrase "Nine out of ten journalists are killed with impunity," or variations reflecting the same trend, is repeatedly cited by the United Nations and freedom of expression groups. Some examples include UNESCO's International Day to End Impunity for Crimes against Journalists 2017; United Nations, "Secretary General's Message on the International Day to End Impunity," November 2, 2017, https:// www.un.org/sg/en/content/sg/statement/2017-11-02/secretary-generals-message -international-day-end-impunity-crimes; the International Federation of Journalists' End Impunity Campaign 2017; and the IFEX No Impunity Campaign, launched in November 2015, https://ifex.org/noimpunity/.
10. Madeline Earp and Mayuri Mukherjee, "In Garcia-Esperat Murder, a Twisting Path to Justice," Committee to Protect Journalists, March 24, 2010, https://cpj.org /blog/2010/03/philippine-impunity-in-garcia-esperat-murder.php; "Marlene Esperat," Center for Media Freedom and Responsibility, November 19, 2011, http://cmfr

-phil.org/endimpunityinph/resources-for-the-idei-blog-action-day-on-november
-21/cases-of-killings/marlene-esperat/.

11. Steven Lee Myers, "In a Very Risky Place to Gather News, a Familiar Story," *New York Times*, October 11, 2006, http://www.nytimes.com/2006/10/11/world/europe /11russia.html.

12. President of Russia, "Transcript of Press Conference with the Russian and Foreign Media," February 1, 2007, http://en.kremlin.ru/events/president/transcripts/24026.

13. United Nations, "Press Conference by Committee to Protect Journalists on New Impunity Index," April 30, 2008, http://www.un.org/press/en/2008/080430_Simon .doc.htm.

14. See examples of media coverage: "Palace Downplays CPJ Report on State of RP Press," *ABS-CBN News*, March 23, 2009, https://news.abs-cbn.com/nation/03/23 /09/palace-downplays-cpj-report-rp-state-press; "CPJ to Palace: Impunity in RP No Exaggeration," *GMA News*, March 24, 2009, https://www.gmanetwork.com /news/news/nation/153961/cpj-to-palace-impunity-in-rp-no-exaggeration/story/.

15. Kati Marton, preface to *Anatomy of Injustice: The Unsolved Killings of Journalists in Russia*, Committee to Protect Journalists, special report, September 2009, 6. https://cpj.org/reports/2009/09/anatomy-injustice-russian-journalist-killings.

16. Maureen James, head of funding and strategy development, IFEX, pers. comm., July 4, 2017.

17. Annie Game, "After UN Resolution on Impunity, More Work to Be Done," Committee to Protect Journalism, December 3, 2013, https://cpj.org/blog/2013/12/after -un-resolution-on-impunity-more-work-to-be-do.php.

18. Ricardo Trotti, "Fighting Impunity with Solidarity, Unity, and a Symbol," Committee to Protect Journalists, April 20, 2010, https://cpj.org/blog/2010/04/fighting -impunity-with-solidarity-unity-and-a-symb.php.

19. UNESCO, *UN Plan of Action on the Safety of Journalists and the Issue of Impunity*, CI-12/CONF.202/6, http://www.unesco.org/new/fileadmin/MULTIMEDIA/HQ /CI/CI/pdf/official_documents/UN-Plan-on-Safety-Journalists_EN_UN-Logo .pdf.

20. Elisabeth Witchel, "Brazil, Pakistan, India Fail Test on Journalist Murders," Committee to Protect Journalists, April 17, 2012, https://cpj.org/blog/2012/04/brazil -pakistan-india-fail-impunity-journalist-murders.php.

21. "Brasil bloqueia plano da ONU contra mortes dejornalistas," *Folha de S. Paolo*, April 1, 2012, www1.folha.uol.com.br/poder/2012/04/1070045-brasil-bloqueia -plano-da-onu-contra-mortes-de-jornalistas.shtml.

22. Veridiana Sedeh, "Brazilian Experience: Investigative Journalists Struggle to Enhance Journalists' Safety," *BBC Blogs*, October 17, 2012, https://www.bbc.co.uk /blogs/collegeofjournalism/entries/77ea9397-199b-3508-b95e-50ffba1eba37.

23. UNESCO, "UN Approves Common Strategy on Safety of Journalists," April 18, 2012, http://www.unesco.org/new/en/communication-and-information/resources /news-and-in-focus-articles/all-news/news/un_approves_common_strategy_on _safety_of_journalists.

24. William Horsley, "BBC to Host Global Editors' Meeting on Life-and-Death Issues," BBC Blogs, September 21, 2012, http://www.bbc.co.uk/blogs/collegeofjournalism /entries/d66e81d5-8916-30ee-8a57-797d8a832899; "Making the Protection of Journalists a Reality: Time to End Impunity," Centre for Freedom of the Media, University of Sheffield, January 21, 2014, http://www.cfom.org.uk/2014/01/making-the -protection-of-journalists-a-reality-time-to-end-impunity.

25. UN General Assembly, "Safety of Journalists," A/HRC/RES/21/12, Human Rights Council, 21st Session, October 9, 2012, Geneva; "Safety of Journalists," A/HRC/ RES/27/5, Human Rights Council, 27th Session, October 2, 2014, Geneva; "Safety of Journalists," A/HRC/33/L.6, Human Rights Council, 33rd Session, September 26, 2016, Geneva.

26. UN Human Rights Committee, General Comment no. 34, Article 19 (Freedoms of Opinion and Expression), CCPR/C/GC/34, September 12, 2011, para. 23. http:// www2.ohchr.org/english/bodies/hrc/docs/gc34.pdf.

27. Christof Heyns, "Report of the Special Rapporteur on Extrajudicial, Summary or Arbitrary Executions," A/HRC/20/22, Human Rights Council, 20th Session, April 10, 2012, Geneva, https://undocs.org/A/HRC/20/22; Frank La Rue, "Report of the Special Rapporteur on the Promotion and Protection of the Right to Freedom of Opinion and Expression," A/HRC/20/17, Human Rights Council, 20th session, June 4, 2012, Geneva.

28. Mustafa Haji Abdinur and Kathleen Carroll spoke at the first debate, "Protection of Civilians in Armed Conflict," UN Security Council, July 17, 2013; the second event took place on December 13, 2013. The Security Council has adopted two resolutions on safety of journalists: Resolution 1738 (2006), adopted on December 23, 2006, which highlights attacks against journalists in conflict zones; and Resolution 2222, adopted on May 27, 2015, which condemns attacks against journalists and impunity.

29. UN General Assembly, "The Safety of Journalists and the Issue of Impunity," A/RES/68/163, February 21, 2014, para. 23–24, 26. Adopted by the General Assembly on December 18, 2013. https://www.un.org/en/ga/search/view_doc.asp?symbol=A /RES/68/163 paras 23, 24, 26.

30. General Assembly, "Safety of Journalists," para. 21.

31. UN General Assembly, Resolution A/RES/69/185, in 2014; Resolution A/RES/70/162 (Safety of Journalists and the Issue of Impunity), in 2015; Resolution A/C.3/72/L.35/ Rev.1, in 2017; and Resolution A/RES/74/157, in 2019.

32. Quoted in Committee to Protect Journalists, "Building Pressure, Enforcing Compliance," in *Road to Justice*, chapter 5.

33. UN Sustainable Development Goals, "The Sustainable Development Agenda," http://www.un.org/sustainabledevelopment/development-agenda/.

34. UN Sustainable Development Goals, "SDG Indicators: Global Indicator Framework for the Sustainable Development Goals and Targets of the 2030 Agenda for Sustainable Development," goal 16, indicator 16.10.1, https://unstats.un.org/sdgs/indicators/indicators-list.

35. "UN Secretary-General Opens Channel of Communication on Safety of Journalists," Reporters without Borders, May 24, 2017, https://rsf.org/en/news/un-secretary-general-opens-channel-communication-safety-journalists.

36. Inter-American Commission on Human Rights, Hector Félix Miranda v. Mexico, para. 66.

37. African Court on Human and Peoples' Rights, Joint Declaration of Judges Gérard Niyungeko, Fatsah Ouguergouz, El Hadji Guisse, and Kimelabalou Aba, March 28, 2014.

38. Community Court of Justice, ECOWAS, judgment, Hydara v. Gambia, ECW/CCJ/APP/30/11, (2014), 4, 10.

39. European Court of Human Rights, "Investigation of Journalist Anna Politkovskaya's Murder Failed to Look Properly into Who Commissioned the Crime," press release, July 17, 2018, https://rm.coe.int/echr-followup-on-alert-investigation-of-journalist-anna-politkovskaya-/16808c5846.

40. UNESCO, "Percentage of Member States that Responded to UNESCO's Request for Information on the Safety of Journalists, 2013–2017," https://en.unesco.org/sites/default/files/percentage_of_member_states_that_responded_to_unescos_request_for_information_2013-2017.jpg.

41. Elisabeth Witchel, "Getting Away with Murder," Committee to Protect Journalists, https://cpj.org/reports/2018/10/impunity-index-getting-away-with-murder-killed-justice-3/.

42. Peter Nkanga, "Nigeria's Impunity Ranking: The Facts Don't Lie," Committee to Protect Journalists, May 3, 2013, https://cpj.org/2013/05/nigerias-impunity-ranking-the-facts-dont-lie/.

43. John Otis, "One Province Illustrates Colombia's Struggle with Impunity," Committee to Protect Journalists, https://cpj.org/2014/02/attacks-on-the-press-colombia-analysis.php; CPJ, "Measuring Progress Against Stubborn Reality," in *Road to Justice*, chapter 2.

44. "Colombia: Freedom of the Press 2016," Freedom House (2017), https://freedomhouse.org/report/freedom-press/2016/colombia.

45. Andrew Downie, "Amid Rising Violence in Brazil, Convictions in Journalists' Murders Are Cause for Optimism," Committee to Protect Journalists, February 29, 2016, https://cpj.org/blog/2016/02/amid-rising-violence-in-brazil-convictions-in-jour.php; "Prime Minister Pledges Justice, Security for Journalists in Pakistan," Committee to Protect Journalists, March 19, 2014, https://cpj.org/2014/03/prime-minister-pledges-justice-security-for-journa.php; Tom Rhodes, "As Impunity Reigns in Somalia, President Takes Note," Committee to Protect Journalists, December 4, 2012, https://cpj.org/blog/2012/12/as-impunity-reigns-in-somalia-president-takes-note.php.

46. Larry Kilman, *An Attack on One Is an Attack on All: Successful Initiatives to Protect Journalists and Combat Impunity* (Paris: UNESCO, 2017). http://unesdoc.unesco.org/images/0025/002504/250430e.pdf.

47. "Halftime for the Brazilian Press," Committee to Protect Journalists, May 2014, https://cpj.org/reports/2014/05/halftime-for-brazilian-press-censorship-violence-vicious-cycle-of-impunity.php.

48. "No Excuse: Mexico Must Break Cycle of Impunity in Journalists' Murders," Committee to Protect Journalists, May 2017, https://cpj.org/reports/2017/05/no-excuse-mexico-impunity-journalist-murder.php.

49. Shawn Crispin, "Mission Journal: Duterte Leads Tri-Pronged Attack on Press Amid Condemnation of Controversial Policies," Committee to Protect Journalists, July 5, 2018, https://cpj.org/blog/2018/07/mission-journal-duterte-leads-tri-pronged-attack-o.php.

50. Examples of such countries include Pakistan, Paraguay, and others. See "UNESCO and NORCAP Help Advance Pakistani Legislation on Safety of Journalists and Access to Information," UNESCO, December 7, 2016, http://www.unesco.org/new/en/communication-and-information/resources/news-and-in-focus-articles/all-news/news/unesco_and_norcap_help_advance_pakistani_legislation_on_safe/; and "Paraguay Signs Pioneering Commitment to Journalists' Safety," UNESCO, November 28, 2016, https://en.unesco.org/news/paraguay-signs-pioneering-commitment-journalists-safety.

51. Alice Bah Kuhnke and Irina Bokova, "Ending Impunity for Crimes against Journalists," *Huffington Post*, June 28, 2017, https://www.huffingtonpost.com/entry/ending-impunity-for-crimes-against-journalists_us_5953d30de4b0f078efd98687.

52. See, for instance, "Independent Journalist Yulia Latynina Flees Russia Following Attacks," Committee to Protect Journalists, September 11, 2017, https://cpj.org/2017/09/independent-journalist-yulia-latynina-flees-russia.php.

53. President Maithripala Sirisena speaking at ceremony at Sri Lanka Bar Association to award a prize to human rights activist Sandya Eknelygoda, wife of missing journalist Prageeth Eknelygoda, May 31, 2015, as reported in media.

Conflicts, Competition, Antiglobalization | **PART III**

ELEVEN

*The Restraints on the Emergence
of a Global Free Speech Norm*

AGNÈS CALLAMARD

AND SEJAL PARMAR

There are certain free speech issues about which normative consensus has not been—and may never be—reached. These issues are, instead, subjects of intense and ongoing contestation, if not outright conflicts, which are manifested in legislative debates, through judicial opinions, on the streets, as well as in the hallways of the United Nations. Some conflicts are recent, having been driven by the information technology revolution, such as those over the role and responsibilities of states and private companies with regard to the regulation of online content.[1] Other normative conflicts are older, even though they have been subsequently affected and shaped by the advent of the Internet. These have accompanied the development of the normative system of human rights law established under the auspices of the United Nations after World War II, though their roots often stretch further back in time, to before 1945.

This chapter focuses on one major normative conflict, which concerns the regulation of so-called hate speech. As part of an immense and wide-ranging scholarship on such speech,[2] commentators have tended to ascribe the absence of a common norm on the regulation of hate speech to the contrast between, on the one hand, the First Amendment to the U.S. Constitution, which is considered as presenting an "absolutist" and "exceptionalist" position toward free speech, and, on the other hand, the free speech protections of other national jurisdictions and of regional human rights systems, notably the system of the European Convention on Human Rights (ECHR), where the protection of freedom of expression is not prioritized over but rather is balanced against other rights.[3]

This chapter shifts the emphasis beyond the prevailing preoccupation with the European and American positions on hate speech and the contrasts between the two. We argue that the emergence of a global norm on hate speech has been hindered by two key, interrelated factors, which warrant greater attention. The first concerns the tensions between classical rationales for freedom of expression and the embeddedness of the principles of equality and nondiscrimination in the international human rights system. These, in turn, inform the second factor, which is the range of overlapping though inconsistent normative meanings attached to hate speech and associated concepts under international and regional treaty law, as well as national laws, and their authoritative interpretations.

We acknowledge that normative convergence, but also confusion, has been further compounded by the role played by Internet platforms in tackling online hate speech under their content moderation policies,[4] but consideration of the role of such platforms as norm influencers goes beyond the scope of this chapter. Rather, our focus is to map the key normative drivers of dissonance and divergence on hate speech across jurisdictions, with their deep philosophical roots as fundamental inhibitors of the rise of global norms on this critical aspect of freedom of expression. In doing so, we elaborate upon the valiant attempts to develop soft norms to mitigate normative conflicts over hate speech, notably from within the UN human rights system, which for various reasons have historically failed to gain sufficient traction. It is likely that the effects of the normative tensions on hate speech will continue to be felt and will inhibit the emergence of normative consensus around such speech, despite significant recent international developments in the realm of hate speech, notably the UN Strategy and Plan of Action on Hate Speech, which provides a very broad and nonlegal definition of "hate speech,"[5] and the landmark report of the UN Special Rapporteur on Freedom of Opinion and Expression, David Kaye, on the role and responsibilities of social media platforms with respect to hate speech.[6]

THEORETICAL UNDERPINNINGS

Leading constitutional law textbooks and monographs dealing with the subject of freedom of speech regularly begin by setting out the classical philosophical justifications for the right.[7] The justifications serve to not only show that "speech has attractive values, but that it has a rationale that justifies the high level of protection of free expression even if, in particular cases, a specific speech may bring more harm than good."[8] Such rationales have played an important role in the emergence and consolidation of free speech jurisprudence in the constitutional courts of liberal democracies, while suggesting that, more than any other right, freedom of expression warrants validation.[9]

Three principal justifications for freedom of expression are regularly identified, with the first two being viewed as consequentialist arguments.[10] First, there is the argument that free speech is necessary for the discovery or confirmation of "truth."[11] This libertarian vision of free speech, which is particularly compelling in the United States, was most famously taken up in *Abrams v. United States* by Justice Holmes, who asserted, "The best test of truth is the power of the thought to get itself accepted in the marketplace of ideas."[12] Second, there is the argument that free speech is necessary for the existence of a genuine democracy, or, in the words of Alexander Meiklejohn, the "program of self-government."[13] This justification for freedom of expression has been particularly influential in many jurisdictions around the world, and it explains the high level of protection given to political speech. The third and broadest argument is that freedom of expression is essential for individual self-development, self-fulfillment, and self-realization.[14] This conceives censorship as a denial of human autonomy and an undermining of human dignity.[15]

These justifications may be seen as complementary, though more often than not they have competed with one another for dominance in a judgment or policy decision. Indeed, jurisprudential and scholarly reflections often imply that there is a *choice* between those free speech justifications, based on arguments about "truth," democracy, or dignity. Divergences in the combination and relative emphasis lead to differences in positions on the applicable level of protection afforded to speech, and it certainly helps to explain the formidable challenges in identifying a coherent and robust philosophical basis for a global norm on hate speech to take root, and thus it also helps to explain the ongoing normative conflicts in the area of freedom of expression.

Moreover, the third justification for freedom of expression, based on self-development and autonomy, has been the least considered and least fleshed out in jurisprudence, policy documents, and scholarly works, including in the United States. The effect of the relative lack of emphasis upon this third rationale is a sense that it is less compelling as a basis for the positive exercise of free speech than truth- and democracy-based rationales. Its relegation behind these other dominant justifications has resulted in the undermining of a more holistic vision of the values underpinning freedom of expression.

The relationship between freedom of expression and dignity is further complicated by the fact that "dignity," together with the connected concept of equality, is in practice mostly invoked as a limitation of freedom of expression rather than as a possible basis for its positive exercise. Indeed, dignity and equality are frequently presumed to be on a collision course with the right,[16] "as an external constraint on free speech rather than an internal justification."[17] This is exemplified by the assertion of the European Court of Human Rights in *Erbakan v. Turkey* that while "tolerance and respect for the equal dignity of all human beings constitute the foundations of a democratic, pluralistic society . . . as a matter of principle it may be considered necessary in certain democratic societies to sanction or even prevent all forms of expression which spread, incite, promote or justify hatred based on intolerance."[18] In jurisdictions that have placed heightened emphasis on human dignity and equality—such as Germany, Israel, South Africa, and also the European Court of Human Rights—the scope of protection accorded to the right of freedom of expression tends to be narrower than in those that emphasize "truth" or democracy-based arguments and fear the "chilling effect" on political speech and the abuse by governments of vague speech restrictions, notably the United States.[19] As Andras Sajó has written, "Where dignity serves as a common underlying value of the legal system, speech that is seen as offensive to dignity will always rank second."[20] In this regard, the Camden Principles, driven by the nongovernmental organization Article 19, stand as one of the few formulations that recognizes the interdependent and mutually reinforcing nature of the equality of human dignity and freedom of expression.[21]

The sense that the recognition of dignity leads to limitations upon freedom of expression is also entrenched in international human rights law itself. On the one hand, as early as 1946, at its very first session, the UN General Assembly adopted Resolution 59(1), which states, "Freedom of information is a fundamental human right and . . . the touchstone of all the freedoms to which the United Nations is consecrated."[22] Two years later, the Universal Declaration of Human Rights (UDHR) was adopted, stating in its preamble that "the advent of a world in which human beings shall enjoy freedom of speech and belief and freedom from fear and want has been proclaimed as the highest aspiration of the common people."[23]

On the other hand, the international system is undeniably invested in dignity and in the principles of equality and nondiscrimination as its dominant values. From its very beginning, the entire international human rights framework proceeds from the claim contained in Article 1 of the UDHR that "all human beings are born free and equal in dignity and rights."[24] Article 2 of the UDHR goes on to declare that all the rights contained in the UDHR are for "everyone . . . without distinction of any kind such as race, color, sex, language, religion, political or other opinion, national or social origin, property, birth or other status." Both the International Covenant on Civil and Political Rights (ICCPR) and the International Covenant on Economic, Social and Cultural Rights[25] start with an assertion that the rights contained therein "derive from the inherent dignity of the human person."[26]

The right to equality and nondiscrimination find expression across many of the subsequent provisions in the International Bill of Rights on equality before the law, equality of men and women, equal right to a fair hearing, equality before courts and tribunals, equal rights as to marriage, equal access to public services, equal suffrage, equal pay, equal access to higher education, equal protection of children as minors and of minority rights, and the right to equality and nondiscrimination expressed in Article 26 of the ICCPR.[27] It is thus not surprising that international human rights law has largely framed the protection of freedom of expression in relation to other rights, including equality and nondiscrimination. These provide the basis for permissible restrictions on freedom of expression under Article 19(3) of the ICCPR and are also the reason for the inclusion of the prohibition of incitement on the grounds of nationality, race, or religion in Article 20(2) of the ICCPR. Moreover, the principle of equality has spurred the development, adoption, and ratification of many international human rights treaties on certain equality issues and declarations; the establishment of related treaty bodies, as well as other human rights bodies; numerous special procedures mechanisms; and the necessary allocation of resources for the Office of the High Commissioner for Human Rights, including for its long-standing and ongoing thematic focus on the promotion of equality and the combating of discrimination as a "pillar" of its program of work.[28]

NORMATIVE FRAMEWORKS ON HATE SPEECH AND INCITEMENT

An International Conundrum

The Convention on the Prevention and Punishment of the Crime of Genocide,[29] the International Convention on the Elimination of All Forms of Racial Discrimination (ICERD),[30] and the ICCPR all convey the notion that freedom of speech is not absolute and may be limited in certain circumstances, including when it undermines the right to equality and nondiscrimination. But they offer different approaches to the kind of hate speech that may and must be restricted, and the conditions for such limitations. Indeed, in a number of ways, the standards presented by these treaties contradict each other, thus contributing to the opacity and uncertainty of international law on the issue, engendering normative confusion, and preventing international convergence upon a single norm.

Article 4 of ICERD focuses on *racial* hate speech and identifies four distinct hate speech offenses punishable by law, while Article 19 of the ICCPR does not directly identify the kind of speech that may be restricted but only the conditions under which a speech may be permissibly restricted.[31] Article 19 allows states parties to restrict speech, provided the so-called three-part test is met, but it does not require them to do so. Article 20 of the ICCPR, on the other hand, prohibits certain expressions altogether. This provision places an obligation upon governments to prohibit by law "any advocacy of national, racial or religious hatred that constitutes incitement to discrimination, hostility or violence." Article 20 is in many ways an anomaly within the ICCPR: it is the only provision in the treaty that imposes a limitation on the exercise of any right (freedom of expression), and, in doing so, it requires states parties to "prohibit by law" certain forms of speech.[32]

A comparison of these three articles highlights a range of difficulties in, if not the impossibility of, finding a convergent norm regarding hate speech. First, there is the legal problem of ensuring that there is compatibility between Article 19 and Article 20 of the ICCPR. It took more than twenty years for the Human Rights Committee to clearly establish this compatibility, in its 2000 decision in Ross v. Canada, when it stated that "restrictions on expression which may fall within the scope of Article 20 must also be permissible under Article 19, paragraph 3, which lays down requirements for determining whether restrictions on expression are permissible."[33] In its most recent authoritative interpretation of Article 19 of the ICCPR, General Comment no. 34, the committee stated, "Articles 19 and 20 are compatible with and complement each other. The acts that are addressed in article 20 are all subject to restriction pursuant to article 19, paragraph 3. As such, a limitation that is justified on the basis of article 20 must also comply with article 19, paragraph 3."[34]

If the question of compatibility between the two provisions within the ICCPR has finally been resolved, the same cannot be said of the relationship between them, on the one hand, and Article 4 of the Committee on the Elimination of Racial Discrimination (CERD), on the other. First, Article 4 of the CERD recommendation focuses exclusively on racist hate speech, while Article 20 of the ICCPR includes at least three types of such speech, including that driven by national origin and religion. Second, Article 4 specifically calls for the criminalization of hate speech, in contrast with Article 20, which demands prohibition by law—an important distinction. CERD's General Recommendation 15 recalls the "mandatory character" of the article and states that its implementation requires not only the enactment of appropriate legislation but also the effective enforcement of such.[35] The Human Rights Committee, on the other hand, has stopped short of requiring criminalization of incitement, limiting itself to demanding an appropriate sanction.[36] Thirdly, and most controversially, while Article 20 limits the prohibition of advocacy that incites, Article 4 identifies four categories of misconduct: dissemination of ideas based upon racial superiority or hatred, incitement to racial hatred, acts of violence against any race or group of persons of another color or ethnic origin, and incitement to such acts. By requiring that states "declare an offence punishable by law all dissemination of ideas based on racial superiority or hatred," Article 4 establishes an offense strikingly different from that of incitement. General Recommendation 14 of CERD affirms that "the prohibition of the dissemination of all ideas based upon racial superiority or hatred is compatible with the right to freedom of opinion and expression."[37] By so stating, CERD positions freedom of speech as an obstacle to the realization of the rights that it is seeking to protect and promote, in particular the right to be protected from discrimination.

Regional Patchworks

Regional treaties have further muddied the normative framework as far as hate speech and incitement are concerned, while regional courts and other human rights bodies have failed to bring any kind of normative clarification or convergence. The American Convention on Human Rights (ACHR) is the only regional instrument that explicitly requires governments to make advocacy of hatred an offense punishable by law. Article 13(5) states, "Any propaganda for war and any advocacy of national, racial, or religious hatred that constitute incitements to lawless violence or to any other similar action against any person or group of persons on any grounds including those of race, color, religion, language, or national origin shall be considered as offenses punishable by law."

The obligations flowing from this provision, however, are quite different from those that are found in Article 20 of the ICCPR. First, the threshold required for an expression to be prohibited is that is must incite "lawless violence," suggesting that incitement to *lawful* violence is acceptable. Second, in contrast with Article 20 of the ICCPR, incitement to hostility or discrimination is not prohibited. The *travaux préparatoires* indicate that the U.S. delegation was instrumental in negotiating the final wording, largely based on the standard put forward by the United States Supreme Court in *Brandenburg v. Ohio*.[38] Since the Inter-American Court on Human Rights has not yet been presented with the opportunity to interpret the ACHR's restriction on hate speech, there is a dearth of authoritative interpretation on the provision.

In contrast, neither the ECHR, nor the African Charter on Human and Peoples' Rights include a specific prohibition of hate speech or incitement, such as that contained in Article 20 of the ICCPR. There is therefore no specific and direct obligation placed on states parties to these treaties to legislate against hate speech or incitement. To date, there is no case law under the African regional instruments dealing with the prohibition of incitement to national, racial, or religious hatred, or with hate speech.[39]

The European Court of Human Rights (ECtHR) has developed a significant jurisprudence on hate speech or incitement, but it has not necessarily delivered a consistent position, or one that is consistent enough to mitigate international and national divergences. According to Louis-Léon Christian's in-depth and extensive review of the ECtHR's jurisprudence from 2011, the court "has understood hate speech to consist, subject to the appropriate restrictions, of 'all forms of expression which spread, incite, promote or justify . . . hatred based on intolerance, including religious intolerance' but has not, however, committed itself to a definitive definition."[40]

The ECtHR has approached and assessed hate speech and incitement through two distinct "convention lenses." The first and most commonly applied one has been to determine whether state restrictions on hate speech or incitement meet the three-part test applicable to limitations on freedom of expression under Article 10 of the ECHR. The second has been to proceed from the position that the speech in question is excluded from the protection of Article 10 of the ECHR entirely, because it comes within the scope of Article 17 of the ECHR. This provision states, "Nothing in this Convention may be interpreted as implying for any State, group or person any right to engage in any activity or perform any act aimed at the destruction of any of the rights and freedoms set forth herein or at their limitation to a greater extent than is provided for in the Convention."[41] In addition, the ECtHR has tended to employ a case-by-case approach, relying in part on its margin of appreciation doctrine, from which it has been particularly difficult to extract clear and strong standards and principles, which could provide guidance.[42] The opportunities for stronger judicial integration through regional jurisprudence thus have not been forged.

National Patchworks

A third factor related to the absence of clarity regarding a global norm on hate speech is the extraordinary broad range of laws, as well as significant inconsistencies in their interpretation, both across and within countries, and vague ad hoc legal reasoning, often lacking in conceptual discipline or rigor.[43] In Europe, Louis-Leon Christian found that contrary to the general trend toward harmonization across European jurisprudence, "the practical action taken against hate speech appears to have been extremely complex, variable and, ultimately, vague," while "the punishment of hate speech is covered by a vast range of national laws that differ in nearly every State."[44] In sub-Saharan Africa, national laws vary as widely, while the limited case law to date is restricted to a few countries, including South Africa, Rwanda, and Kenya.[45]

The region of Latin America is equally diverse. States there have adopted criminal laws that prohibit hate speech or discriminatory speech in widely differing ways—from banning dissemination of ideas based on racial supremacy (Ecuador), to criminalizing incitement to violence (Bolivia), to including a prohibition of incitement to discrimination in anti-discrimination legislation (Brazil's Law 7716/89).[46] Similarly to the situation in Africa, there has been limited jurisprudence on the issue, a situation attributed by some to a rejection of a punitive response to hate speech[47] and by others to a limited understanding about the content and extension of hate speech regulations, with other speech restrictions on the basis of reputation being preferred.[48]

The one country that stands out, for both its position on hate speech and its consistency over time, is the United States. In the seminal case of *Brandenberg v. Ohio*, the Supreme Court held that speech can only be prohibited if it is "directed at inciting or producing imminent lawless action" and it is "likely to incite or produce such action."[49] The United States' approach prohibits "viewpoint discrimination"[50] and thus subjects even the most racist or anti-Semitic speech to the very high standard of strict scrutiny and protection.[51] This position is not without its detractors, including within the United States itself, largely on the grounds that it gives insufficient attention to dignity and equality.[52] But the approach has, to date, held up well in spite of the internal critiques, the quasi-universal rejections by other countries, the passage of time, and technological revolutions.[53]

Soft International Norms

How can the pressing challenge of normative dissonance and divergence in the realm of hate speech be addressed? One approach to this question is to turn to soft law norms. With regard to one kind of hate speech, that grounded on religious hatred, three normatively significant events took place between March 2011 and November 2012 that resulted in a political consensus, albeit an unstable one, as well as specific legal and policy approaches upon which global norms might be credibly constructed.[54]

First among these normative developments was the Rabat Plan of Action on the Prohibition of Advocacy of National, Racial or Religious Hatred that Constitutes Incitement to Discrimination, Hostility or Violence, which was initiated in response to debates on "defamation of religion" and adopted in November 2012.[55] Drafted by international experts, the Rabat Plan of Action sought to clarify the scope of state obligations under Article 20 of the ICCPR on the prohibition of incitement to violence, hostility, and discrimination.[56] Apparently drawing on all three classical justifications of freedom of expression, the Rabat Plan of Action insists that freedom of expression plays a crucial role in allowing vibrant public debates and ensuring democracy, while highlighting the interdependence of freedom of expression and freedom of religion. It states "free and critical thinking in open debate is the soundest way to probe whether religious interpretations adhere to or distort the original values that underpin religious belief."[57] It recommends that domestic legal frameworks on incitement to hatred be guided by express reference to Article 20 of the ICCPR and that a high threshold be sought for assessing restrictions to freedom of expression. And it offers a six-part threshold test to determine whether speech meets this threshold.

The Rabat Plan of Action "is a highly significant, if not critical, 'turning point' in the understanding and implementation of international law on freedom of expression and incitement to hatred," for reasons linked to its context, the clarity of the legal interpretation and policy recommendations, and the legitimacy of the drafting and discussion process.[58] In the intervening years, the Rabat Plan of Action has been widely referenced by a range of actors, particularly within the UN human rights system, but also beyond.[59] More specifically, it has been relied and expanded upon through other related processes and texts produced under the auspices of the United Nations[60] and referenced by a diversity of UN human rights bodies, including the Human Rights Council and General Assembly,[61] special procedures mechanisms,[62] and treaty bodies.[63] Noting its "impressive" mark upon the UN system, former High Commissioner Zeid Ra'ad Al Hussein observed, in December 2017, that within the previous five years the Rabat Plan of Action had been referred to in more than 120 UN documents by states, civil society organizations, and human rights mechanisms.[64]

Furthermore, the Rabat Plan of Action, particularly its six-part threshold test, has been reinforced through numerous references in the seminal report of Special Rapporteur David Kaye on social media platforms and hate speech[65] and also in the approach taken toward the implementation of the UN Strategy and Plan of Action on Hate Speech, including the UN Guidance Note on Addressing and Countering COVID-19 Related Hate Speech, which was published in May 2020.[66] Moreover, the Rabat Plan of Action has been drawn upon in civil society organizations' advocacy and standard-setting work.[67] All of this has certainly served to build up the status of the Rabat Plan of Action as *the* leading global soft law instrument on incitement to hatred.

Second, in March 2011, after more than a decade of acrimonious debates and intensive lobbying in Geneva and in capitals over resolutions on combating "defamation of religions," the Human Rights Council adopted Resolution 16/18, Combating Intolerance, Negative Stereotyping and Stigmatization of, and Discrimination, Incitement to Violence, and Violence against, Persons Based on Religion or Belief.[68] Resolution 16/18 was a breakthrough, since it meant that the principal organ of the UN human rights system was no longer mandating the implementation of domestic laws and policies restricting speech on the grounds that such speech constituted blasphemy. Similarly worded resolutions subsequently have been adopted by the Human Rights Council and the General Assembly. Since 2011, states have driven the so-called Istanbul Process with the aim of implementing Resolution 16/18.

Third, during its 102nd session, in July 2011, the Human Rights Committee adopted General Comment no. 34 on Article 19 of the ICCPR (freedom of opinion and expression), which states that "prohibitions of displays of lack of respect for a religion or other belief system, including blasphemy laws, are incompatible with the Covenant," unless they qualify as prohibitions on incitement under Article 20(2) of the ICCPR.[69] The distinct significance of the Human Rights Committee's general comment, however, lies in its status as the authoritative interpretation of the ICCPR.

This concentration of international soft law standards in 2011 and 2012 has not thus far resulted in building global normative consensus. Notwithstanding its impact within the UN human rights system, the Rabat Plan of Action received insufficient attention from other key actors, particularly the most influential states, the media, and civil society organizations at the subnational level.[70] While the Rabat Plan of Action was subsequently endorsed by a number of members of the Organisation of Islamic Cooperation, its principal detractors have included the United States and some European states, oftentimes through their avoidance of recognition of the text entirely. The reasons for this state of affairs are no doubt complex and multilayered. Based on our experiences and involvement in many negotiations related to the Rabat Plan of Action, a number of suppositions may be made.

The first is related to the birth of the process of the Rabat Plan of Action, the origin of which lies in the 2009 Durban Review Conference held in Geneva and, further back, in the 2001 World Conference against Racism, Racial Discrimination, Xenophobia, and Related Intolerance, held in Durban. Both the United States and Israel had strongly objected to the decision to hold the Durban Review Conference, on the grounds of the perceived anti-Semitism that had dogged the original Durban conference. The Durban Review Conference was eventually boycotted by Australia, Canada, Germany, Israel, Italy, the Netherlands, New Zealand, Poland, and the United States. The Czech Republic discontinued its attendance on the first day, and twenty-three other European Union countries sent low-level delegations. Through its association with the Durban process, the Rabat Plan of Action was thus tainted from the beginning.

A second factor may be the intransigence of a dogmatic position within the U.S. State Department toward the First Amendment, which led the United States to reject the Rabat Plan of Action on the basis of its conflict with First Amendment precepts, even though the experts had sought to minimize the possibility of such conflict.[71]

A third reason concerns skepticism about the actual content of the Rabat Plan of Action itself. In many ways, the text appears to overlook the divergences and potential tensions across jurisdictions—particularly the American and European—and also between relevant international human rights law provisions on hate speech. Indeed, the provisions of the Rabat Plan of Action seems to indicate a clear preference, implicitly rejecting the standard indicated in Article 4 of the ICERD insofar as departs from Article 20 of the ICCPR,[72] while suggesting that these inconsistent international legal provisions are ultimately reconcilable.[73] The fact that the drafters of the Rabat Plan of Action were projecting a certain vision of international human rights law may well have been noted by some states' representatives in their subsequent decision not to rally behind it.

A fourth factor is that the specter of the debate on "defamation of religions" still remains strong, especially given the normative commitments to provisions prohibiting blasphemy and religious insult, which are regularly trumpeted within the council by powerful players such as Saudi Arabia, and by many other states. Moreover, though there have been historic advancements with the repeal of blasphemy laws in Europe over recent years—in states such as the Netherlands (2014), Iceland (2015), Norway (2015), Malta (2016), Denmark (2017), and

Ireland (2018)—at the regional level, the ECtHR has continued to legitimize blasphemy laws through its most recent case law on the issue.[74] In addition, the Istanbul Process, whose relationship with the UN human rights system was always unclear, has been deeply problematic over the years. While certain states, including the United States and members of the Organisation of Islamic Cooperation, have supported it over the years, it has lacked transparency and the possibilities for fuller civil society participation and has been viewed as a toothless "talking shop," serving the interests of the same states that most undermine religious tolerance and freedom of expression.[75]

CONCLUSION

This chapter has demonstrated how tensions between the underlying philosophical rationales for freedom of expression and those within international treaty law have served to frustrate global normative convergence on the issue of hate speech. Splits in the relative value placed upon the rationales for freedom of expression embraced by jurisdictions and the consequent legal approaches to hate speech have had siloing effects, with legal systems—whether at the international, regional, or national levels—further isolated from one another as a result. Courts have largely shied away from exploring or elaborating how censorship undermines human autonomy and dignity, concepts that have more usually been relied upon to justify restrictions on free speech. Important opportunities for a fuller understanding of how the positive exercise of freedom of expression (rather than its limitation) is essential to other rights, including and particularly equality, have thus been missed. More generally, international and regional jurisprudence on hate speech or incitement has disappointingly offered little elaboration or explanation of the complexity of ethical arguments justifying free speech.

We are persuaded that the differences between relevant provisions of international human rights treaties could have been, and still could be, mitigated by treaty bodies through a greater explicit awareness of those differences in their adjudicative and advisory functions, even though there has been little evidence of such efforts to date. Similarly, regional human rights courts and constitutional courts could promote greater convergence through the application of comparative approaches to hate speech, notwithstanding the idiosyncrasy of Article 17 of the ECHR in the European context. While the European Court of Human Rights has often turned to its doctrine of margin of appreciation to decide cases in the area, other regional courts have yet to consider hate speech issues. Prospects for the mitigation of differences in international treaty law lie in the embrace of soft law approaches by UN human rights bodies.

We therefore argue that the Rabat Plan of Action, in particular, should gain further traction as a credible basis for the emergence of a global norm on hate speech. Any stock-taking of its implementation, for instance, could present an ideal opportunity for states and other relevant stakeholders, including social media platforms, to expressly conceive the text as such. Enabling these soft norms to take root at the global level obviously would require the further and active support of the UN human rights bodies, including UN special procedures mechanisms, state representatives, and nongovernmental organizations working with such bodies. It also would require wider and deeper engagement, at the national and regional levels, by civil society organizations in their advocacy, by public prosecutors and judges in their decisions to prosecute and in their judgments, and by representatives of national human rights institutions. Beyond this, a greater public consciousness across regions and societies about the universality of freedom of expression and its interdependence with other rights has to be forged if a global norm on hate speech is ever to emerge.

NOTES

1. Report of the Special Rapporteur on Freedom of Opinion and Expression to the Human Rights Council, A/HRC/32/38, May 11, 2016 (on freedom of expression, states, and the private sector in the digital age).

2. Ishani Maitra and Mary Kate McGowan, eds., *Speech and Harm* (Oxford: Oxford University Press, 2013); Jeremy Waldron, *The Harm in Hate Speech* (Cambridge, MA: Harvard University Press, 2012); Michael Herz and Peter Molnar, eds., *The Content and Context of Hate Speech: Rethinking Regulation and Responses* (Cambridge: Cambridge University Press, 2012); Ivan Hare and James Weinstein, eds., *Extreme Speech and Democracy* (Oxford: Oxford University Press, 2010).

3. Frederick Schauer, "Freedom of Expression Adjudication in Europe and the United States: A Case Study in Comparative Constitutional Architecture," in *European and US Constitutionalism*, ed. Georg Nolte (Cambridge: Cambridge University Press, 2005), 49–69; Frederick Schauer, "The Exceptional First Amendment," in *American Exceptionalism and Human Rights*, ed. Michael Ignatieff (Princeton, NJ: Princeton University Press, 2005), 29–56.

4. Report of the Special Rapporteur on Freedom of Opinion and Expression to the Human Rights Council, A/HRC/38/35, April 6, 2018 (on regulation of user-generated online content); Report of the Special Rapporteur on Contemporary

Forms of Racism, Racial Discrimination, Xenophobia and Related Intolerance to the General Assembly, A/73/312, August 7, 2018 (on the contemporary use of digital technology in the spread of neo-Nazi and related intolerance).

5. United Nations, *United Nations Strategy and Plan of Action on Hate Speech*, May 2019, https://www.un.org/en/genocideprevention/documents/UN%20Strategy%20and%20Plan%20of%20Action%20on%20Hate%20Speech%2018%20June%20SYNOPSIS.pdf. The document states that "hate speech is understood as any kind of communication in speech, writing or behaviour, that attacks or uses pejorative or discriminatory language with reference to a person or a group on the basis of who they are, in other words, based on their religion, ethnicity, nationality, race, colour, descent, gender or other identity factor" (2).

6. United Nations General Assembly, Report of the Special Rapporteur on the Promotion and Protection of the Right to Freedom of Opinion and Expression, October 9, 2019, A/74/486.

7. Eric Barendt, *Freedom of Speech* (Oxford: Oxford University Press, 2005), 1–38; Andrew Nicol, Gavin Millar, and Andrew Sharland, *Media Law and Human Rights* (Oxford: Oxford University Press, 2009), 1–5; Geoffrey R. Stone, Louis Michael Seidman, Cass R. Sunstein, Mark V. Tushnet, and Pamela S. Karlan, *Constitutional Law*, 8th ed. (New York: Aspen, 2017), 1027–1037. See, generally, Frederick Schauer, *Free Speech: A Philosophical Inquiry* (Cambridge: Cambridge University Press, 1982).

8. Andras Sajó, *Freedom of Expression* (Warsaw: Institute of Public Affairs, 2004), 18.

9. Vienna Declaration and Programme of Action, adopted by the World Conference on Human Rights in Vienna on June 25, 1993, para. 5.

10. Each justification has its own individual critiques, not addressed here. See Barendt, *Freedom of Speech*, 7–23. Other justifications for freedom of expression also have been put forward. See Geoffrey R. Stone, Louis Michael Seidman, Cass R. Sunstein, Mark V. Tushnet, and Pamela S. Karlan, *The First Amendment*, 5th ed. (New York: Wolters Kluwer, 2016); Vincent Blasi, "The Checking Value in First Amendment Theory," *American Bar Foundation Research Journal* 2, no. 3 (1977): 521, 527–542; Lee C. Bollinger, *The Tolerant Society: Freedom of Speech and Extremist Speech in America* (Oxford: Oxford University Press, 1986), 9–10, 107; Vincent Blasi, "Free Speech and Good Character: From Milton to Brandeis to the Present," in *Eternal Vigilance: Free Speech in the Modern Era*, ed. Lee C. Bollinger and Geoffrey Stone (Chicago: University of Chicago Press, 2002), 61–62, 84–85.

11. John Stuart Mill, *On Liberty* (London: Longmans, Green, Reader and Dyer, 1869); John Milton, "Areopagitica: A Speech for the Liberty of Unlicensed Printing," in *Prose Writings* (London: Everyman, 1958).

12. Abrams v. United States, 250 U.S. 616, 630–631 (1919).

13. Alexander Meiklejohn, *Political Freedom: The Constitutional Powers of the People* (Oxford: Oxford University Press, 1965), 27.

14. In Procunier v. Martinez, 416 U.S. 396, 427 (1974), Justice Thurgood Marshall stated, "The human spirit . . . demands self-expression."

15. Ronald Dworkin, *Taking Rights Seriously* (London: Duckworth, 1977), 266–278, 364–368. See also Kent Greenawalt, "Free Speech Justifications," *Columbia Law Review* 89, no. 1 (1989): 119, 153.

16. Frederick Schauer, "Speaking of Dignity," in *The Constitution of Rights: Human Dignity and American Values*, ed. Michael A. Meyer and William A. Parent (Ithaca, NY: Cornell University Press, 1992), 178–179.

17. Guy E. Carmi, "Dignity—the Enemy from Within: A Theoretical and Comparative Analysis of Human Dignity as a Free Speech Justification," *University of Pennsylvania Journal of Constitutional Law* 9, no. 4 (2007): 957, 998.

18. European Court of Human Rights, Erbakan v. Turkey, application no. 59405/00, judgment of July 6, 2006, para. 56.

19. Carmi, "Dignity," 986–996.

20. Sajó, *Freedom of Expression*, 18; David Kretzmer and Eckhart Klein, foreword to *The Concept of Human Dignity in Human Rights Discourse*, ed. David Kretzmer and Eckhart Klein (Leiden: Brill, 2002), v–viii.

21. Article 19, *The Camden Principles on Freedom of Expression and Equality* (London: Article 19, 2009). https://www.article19.org/data/files/pdfs/standards/the-camden-principles-on-freedom-of-expression-and-equality.pdf.

22. General Assembly Resolution 59(1) calling for an international conference on freedom of information, December 14, 1946.

23. Adopted and proclaimed by General Assembly Resolution 217 A(3) of December 10, 1948.

24. See also Universal Declaration of Human Rights (UDHR), preambular para. 1 and 5, and Articles 22 and 23(3).

25. General Assembly Resolution 2200A(21) of December 16, 1966, entered into force March 23, 1976.

26. See UDHR, preambular para. 1 and 2.

27. UDHR, Articles 7, 10, 16, 21, 23, and 26; International Covenant on Civil and Political Rights (ICCPR), Articles 3, 14, 23–27; International Covenant on Economic, Social and Cultural Rights, Articles 2–3, 7, 10, 13.

28. Office of the High Commissioner for Human Rights, *United Nations Human Rights Management Plan 2018–2021* (Geneva: United Nations, 2018), 28–31.

29. General Assembly Resolution 260 A(3) of December 9, 1948, entered into force January 12, 1951.

30. United Nations General Assembly Resolution 2106(20), December 21, 1965, entered into force on January 4, 1969.

31. See "A Global Threshold," part 1 of this volume; Toonen v. Australia, CCPR/C/50/D/488/1992, views adopted March 31, 1994.

32. Nazila Ghanea, "Nature and Means of Effective Remedies," paper presented at Expert Workshops on the Prohibition of Incitement to National, Racial, or Religious Hatred, February 9–10, 2011, Vienna; Sandra Coliver, ed., *Striking a Balance: Hate Speech, Freedom of Expression, and Non-discrimination* (London: Article 19 and University of Essex: Human Rights Centre, 1992); Stephanie Farrior, "Molding the Matrix: The Historical and Theoretical Foundations of International Law Concerning Hate Speech," *Berkeley Journal of International Law* 14, no. 1 (1996): 8.

33. Malcolm Ross v. Canada, CCPR/C/70/D/736/1997, views adopted October 26, 2000.

34. Human Rights Committee, General Comment no. 34, para. 50.

35. UN General Assembly, Committee on the Elimination of Racial Discrimination, General Recommendation 15 on Article 4 of the convention, A/48/18, March 23, 1993, para. 2.

36. Human Rights Committee, General Comment 11 on Article 20 (Prohibition of propaganda for war and inciting national, racial or religious hatred), July 29, 1983, para. 2.

37. Human Rights Committee, General Recommendation 14, para. 3–4.

38. Paula Martins, "Freedom of Expression and Equality: The Prohibition of Incitement to Hatred in Latin America," paper presented at Expert Workshops on the Prohibition of Incitement to National, Racial, or Religious Hatred, October 12–13, 2011, Santiago.

39. Doudou Diene, "Study on the Prohibition of National, Racial, or Religious Hatred in Africa," paper presented at Expert Workshops on the Prohibition of Incitement to National, Racial, or Religious Hatred, April 6–7, 2011, Nairobi.

40. Louis-Léon Christian, "Background Study for the Workshop on Europe," paper presented at Expert Workshops on the Prohibition of Incitement to National, Racial, or Religious Hatred, February 9–10, 2011, Vienna. See, however, the definition of "hate speech" offered in Stern Taulats and Roura Capellera v. Spain, application no. 51168/15 and 51186/15, judgment of March 13, 2018, para. 41.

41. On the application of European Convention on Human Rights, Article 17, see Gündüz v. Turkey, application no. 35071/97, judgment of December 4, 2003, para. 41; and Perinçek v. Switzerland, application no. 27510/08, judgment of the Grand Chamber, October 15, 2005, para. 114–115.

42. See, for instance, Wingrove v. UK, application no. 13470/87, judgment of November 25, 1996.

43. Agnès Callamard, "Towards an Interpretation of Article 20 of the ICCPR: Thresholds for the Prohibition of Incitement to Hatred," paper presented at Expert Workshops on the Prohibition of Incitement to National, Racial, or Religious Hatred, February 9–10, 2011, Vienna. See also expert papers available at https://www.ohchr.org/EN/Issues/FreedomOpinion/Articles19-20/Pages/ExpertsPapers.aspx

44. Christian, "Background Study," 2.

45. Henry Maina, "The Prohibition of Incitement to Hatred in Africa: Comparative Review and Proposal for a Threshold," paper presented at Expert Workshops on the Prohibition of Incitement to National, Racial, or Religious Hatred, April 6–7, 2011, Nairobi.

46. Paula Martins, "Freedom of Expression and Equality: The Prohibition of Incitement to Hatred in Latin America," paper presented at Expert Workshops on the Prohibition of Incitement to National, Racial, or Religious Hatred, October12–13, 2011, Santiago.

47. Eduardo Bertoni, "A Study on the Prohibition of Incitement to Hatred in the Americas," paper presented at Expert Workshops on the Prohibition of Incitement to National, Racial, or Religious Hatred, October 12–13, 2011, Santiago.

48. Martins, "Freedom of Expression," 50.

49. Brandenburg v. Ohio, 395 US 444 (1969), 447.

50. R.A.V. v. City of St. Paul, 505 U.S. 377 (1992).

51. National Socialist Party of America v. Village of Skokie, 432 U.S. 43 (1977); Collin v. Smith, 578 F.2d 1197 (7th Cir. 1978); Smith v. Collin, 439 U.S. 916 (1978) (denying certiorari).

52. Jeremy Waldron, *The Harm in Hate Speech* (Cambridge, MA: Harvard University Press, 2012); Eric Heinze and Gavin Phillipson, *Debating Hate Speech* (Oxford: Hart Publishing, 2014).

53. There is scholarly consensus that the United States is an outlier when it comes to its position on hate speech. See, for instance, Schauer, "Exceptional First Amendment."

54. Sejal Parmar, "Uprooting 'Defamation of Religions' and the Emergence of a New Approach to Freedom of Expression at the United Nations," in *The United Nations and Freedom of Expression and Information: Critical Perspectives*, ed. Tarlach McGonagle and Yvonne Donders (Cambridge: Cambridge University Press, 2015), 373–427, at 375.

55. Office of the High Commissioner for Human Rights, "Rabat Plan of Action on the Prohibition of Advocacy of National, Racial or Religious Hatred that Constitutes Incitement to Discrimination, Hostility or Violence," Annual Report of the United Nations High Commissioner for Human Rights (appendix), A/HRC/22/17/Add.4, January 11, 2013.

56. For commentary, see Sejal Parmar, "The Rabat Plan of Action: A Critical Turning Point in International Law on Hate Speech," in *Free Speech and Censorship around the Globe*, ed. Peter Molnar (New York: Central European University Press, 2015), 211.

57. Rabat Plan of Action, para. 10.

58. Parmar, "Rabat Plan of Action: A Critical Turning Point," 213.

59. On the impact of the Rabat Plan of Action, see Sejal Parmar, "Taking Stock of the Impact of the Rabat Plan of Action, Towards Its Implementation and Reinvigoration," paper presented at the roundtable "The Rabat Plan of Action and Asia," organized by Asian Forum for Human Rights and Development (Forum Asia), Bytes for All, and Global Partners Digital, June 29, 2018, Geneva.

60. See, in particular, Office of the High Commissioner for Human Rights, "Beirut Declaration on 'Faith for Rights'," para. 7, https://www.ohchr.org/Documents /Press/21451/BeirutDeclarationonFaithforRights.pdf; UN Office on Genocide Prevention and the Responsibility to Protect, "Policy Options Preventing Incitement to Violence," para. 11 (and note 2) and 21, http://www.un.org/en/genocideprevention /advising-and-mobilizing.html; Fez Declaration, Morocco, April 24, 2015, preamble, p. 20; and UN Office on Genocide Prevention and the Responsibility to Protect, "Plan of Action for Religious Leaders and Actors to Prevent Incitement to Violence that Could Lead to Atrocity Crimes," July 14, 2017, http://www.un .org/en/genocideprevention/documents/Plan%20of%20Action%20Advanced%20 Copy.pdf.

61. Human Rights Council Resolution 37/32, A/HRC/RES/37/32, March 23, 2018, para. 18.

62. These have included the special rapporteurs on freedom of religion or belief, contemporary forms of racism, racial discrimination, xenophobia and related intolerance, freedom of opinion and expression, and minority issues.

63. Committee on the Elimination of Racial Discrimination, General Recommendation no. 35, CERD/C/GC/35, September 26, 2013, para. 15–16, 29, and 35. See also Committee on the Elimination of All Forms of Racial Discrimination, TBB Turkish Union v. Germany, CERD/C/82/D/48/2010, decision of February 26, 2013, individual opinion of committee member Mr. Carlos Manuel Vazquez (dissenting), April 4, 2013, notes 4, 7, and 11.

64. Opening statement of High Commissioner for Human Rights Zeid Ra'ad Al Hussein (as delivered by Ibrahim Salama) at the Rabat+5 Symposium on the Follow-Up to the Rabat Plan of Action, Rabat, December 6–7, 2017.

65. General Assembly, Report of the Special Rapporteur on the Promotion and Protection of the Right to Freedom of Opinion and Expression.

66. United Nations, *United Nations Guidance Note on Addressing and Countering COVID-19 Related Hate Speech*, May 11, 2020, https://www.un.org/en/genocidepreven

tion/documents/Guidance%20on%20COVID-19%20related%20Hate%20Speech
.pdf.

67. See Asian Forum for Human Rights and Development, "Jakarta Recommendations on Freedom of Expression in the Context of Religion," June 5, 2015, https://
www.forum-asia.org/?p=19179.

68. Human Rights Council, Resolution 16/18, A/HRC/RES/16/18, March 11, 2011.

69. General Comment no. 34, para. 48. See also Human Rights Council, *Report of the
Special Rapporteur on Freedom of Religion or Belief*, A/HRC/31/18, December 23,
2015, para. 59–61, 84; and A/HRC/28/66, December 29, 2014, para. 94.

70. For a notable exception, see Human Rights Law Centre, "Striking the Right
Balance—Freedom of Speech and Hate Speech: Submission to the Inquiry into
Racial Vilification Law in New South Wales," March 19, 2013.

71. Objections on First Amendment grounds were communicated to the authors on a
number of occasions by representatives of the U.S. government or civil society.

72. Sejal Parmar, "The Rabat Plan of Action: A Global Blueprint for Combating 'Hate
Speech,'" *European Human Rights Law Review*, no. 1 (2014): 21–31, at 27.

73. Rabat Plan of Action, para. 14 and 17.

74. ES v. Austria, application no. 38450/12, judgment of October 25, 2018. See Sejal Parmar, "Freedom of Expression Narratives after the Charlie Hebdo Attacks," *Human
Rights Law Review* 18, no. 2 (2018): 267, 281–282; and Agnès Callamard, "The Expression of Religious Beliefs: In the Name of Pluralism, Although Not Quite Religious,"
Religion and Human Rights 12 (2017): 153–163.

75. On criticism of the Istanbul Process meeting in Jeddah in June 2015, see Committee for Inquiry, Statement to the 28th Session of the Human Rights Council (General Debate on Item 4), March 17, 2015; and Amnesty International, "Saudi Arabia:
Every Lash of Raif Badawi Defies International Law," June 11, 2015, https://www
.amnesty.org/en/latest/news/2015/06/saudi-arabia-every-lash-of-raif-badawi
-defies-international-law/.

TWELVE

Social Media Platforms and Freedom of Expression Norms

CHINMAYI ARUN

In October 2017, Raya Sarkar wrote about what came to be known as a "list of sexual harassers in academia" on Facebook, instigating an acrimonious debate in India. Days later, her Facebook account was suspended and she was no longer able to post. At the time, Raya was halfway around the world, in the United States. She was unable to discuss her perspective in the important debate that she had triggered. Fortunately, she was able to reach out Facebook staff, and they speedily restored Raya's access to her account.[1] It was never made clear why the account was suspended in the first place, or what specifically had been seen as a potential violation of Facebook's terms and conditions.

It would have helped to understand why and how Raya's account ended up suspended, and whether it was restored because an exception was made or because the suspension was a mistaken application of Facebook's terms. I wondered about the normative standard and its application, as my Facebook news feed filled with heartbreaking #MeToo posts, with Indian women writing in intimate, spine-chilling detail about the violence they had experienced. If the #MeToo posts were reported, would they be taken down? How might one have them restored?

Social media platforms' self-regulatory norms affect freedom of expression and the audience's right to view an important public debate. Raya's Facebook post triggered a conversation that was very important for women's rights in India. The #MeToo movement did the same. It is important to ensure that speech like this remains a part of public discourse.

Social media platforms make difficult decisions about the speech that they permit and the speech they remove from their platforms. They permit heads of state to propagate ideas that are blocked when expressed by ordinary citizens.[2] They censor activists' demands for independent states, flagging them as hate speech terrorist content.[3] Since the social media platforms play a central role in public discourse, their self-regulatory norms matter.[4] Through the architecture of the platforms and powerful algorithms, social media companies control how users engage with one another and with the platform.[5] The architecture enables them to set the terms for engagement, from how users respond to arguments to how they share photographs or report abusive content. The algorithms enable fine distinctions of content moderation, with different content being seen in different jurisdictions, content that cannot be shared at all, and content that will be online but down-ranked so that it loses visibility.

This power that the social media companies wield over speech online, and therefore over public discourse more broadly, is being recognized as a new form of governance. It is uniquely powerful because the norms favored by social media companies can be enforced directly through the architecture of the social media platforms. There are no consultations, appeals, or avenues for challenge. There is little scope for users to reject a norm enforced in this manner. While a blatantly illegitimate norm may result in uproar, choices made by social media companies to favor existing local norms that violate international human rights norms are common enough.

This chapter is about the role of social media platforms. It discusses the role and influence of private companies, especially social media companies, in creating norms affecting freedom of expression. Toward this, it begins with an introduction to the role of the Internet in public discourse, followed by a discussion of how the architecture of the Internet enables social media companies to influence speech norms. The chapter then discusses the factors that influence the speech norms created by platforms and ends on a cautionary note about how the international human rights norm of freedom of expression may be threatened by the platforms' self-regulatory norm-setting for online speech.

A FREE MARKET FOR IDEAS

In its early years, the Internet was a medium humming with innovation and accessible information. Newspapers and magazines were rushing to digitize and to offer their content free, since the advertising model worked for them back then. Until recently, it was possible to find episodes of most popular television shows on major video sharing platforms. Oligopolies were yet to colonize our attention, and algorithms were not sophisticated enough for the fine-distinction filtering or personalized targeting of information at users in which they engage these days.

Previously, the major cause for concern was censorship in the form of the global blocking of content at the behest of one country. The *LICRA v. Yahoo!* series of cases is the classic illustration of the conflict of laws that might result in this. These cases came before the French and American courts because Yahoo! permitted a user to auction Nazi memorabilia on its platform, which was illegal in France but constitutionally protected the United States, leading to a French organization objecting because the content was visible in France.[6] Today, it is a simple thing for content to be blocked in one jurisdiction while it remains visible in others. This has led to rising demands from courts around the world to enforce national speech norms in particular countries.[7]

It was clear in the beginning that the Internet had the potential to come closer to Jürgen Habermas's ideal "public sphere" than any other medium.[8] Then and now, the Internet enables global public discourse on an unprecedented scale.[9] There is much scholarship that explains how dramatically the Internet changed the nature of the public sphere. Yochai Benkler, for example, identifies the major change from the "industrial information economy" to what he has christened the "networked information economy": the Internet radically lowered the costs of sharing information for individuals, such that content no longer had to be marketable, enabling a great diversity of content to be shared online.[10] The Internet was transformative not just because it was a networked information economy but also because it was global in nature. The global and offline influence of the Internet is now so apparent that Zepnep Tufekci refers to it as a "digitally networked public sphere" that covers the "complex interaction of publics, online and offline, all intertwined, multiple, connected and complex, but also transnational and global."[11]

This change is visible to those of us who can recall the sudden expansion of our worlds. Previously, we had access to news and reading material that fit our prevailing social norms and stayed within the bounds of our culture—this was the material made available in our libraries, via our newspapers and television channels. With the Internet, this was infinitely varied: a girl in India could become an avid reader of the *New Yorker* and a boy in London could read Pakistan's *Dawn* every day. Dalits in India could discuss racism and intersectionality with Americans of color, and young people could read about alternate sexuality and the many ways in which people live and love.

The ways in which we engaged with the media changed. Instead of passively consuming the curated offerings of the press or the television channels, we could have conversations on the Internet and could actively engage with the content that we were consuming.[12] Jonathan Zittrain has discussed the generative potential of the Internet in detail in his book.[13] These origins of the Internet remain visible in its original architecture, which still shines through the increasingly industrialized version of the Web that we now use. Although the social media companies control and commoditize the networked experience on their platforms,[14] they inherited the networked model from the early versions of the Internet. It is the networked model of social media that fundamentally changed the nature of the public sphere. The basic feature of social media, which distinguishes it from the mass media of the twentieth century, is that it is "participatory, many-to-many media."[15]

Without social media and its participatory design, Raya Sarkar would have had to persuade editors of the publication-worthiness of her controversial list of men who have been accused of sexual harassment, and she would only have been able to say her piece, as opposed to the continuous engagement with her supporters and her detractors that social media enabled. The many young women who posted their #MeToo stories received, in addition to a barrage of abuse, declarations of support that showed them that they were not alone. The many-to-many media meant that people reached out to them saying "I believe you," confirming their stories, responding with another, similar one, and offering concrete help in the form of legal support.

Many major political movements of our time lean on social media. #MeToo is a global phenomenon, with women across the world raising their voices together. Black Lives Matter inspired Dalit Lives Matter in India. From Tahrir Square to Occupy Wall Street to Tunisia's Jasmine Revolution, the Internet has enabled protests and solidarity. The deeply personal, sometimes anonymous, statements that are a part of the #MeToo movement may not have possible through any other media. The number of statements, and the number of women validating each statement, created a new norm. It is a norm that has been strongly resisted, even by feminists, but it will be difficult to change, now that it has taken hold. It is clear by now that the Internet transforms the public sphere, but the public sphere consists of more than the Internet.[16]

The generative structure and potential of the Internet has influenced the regulatory choices made by governments for social media companies. For many years, the reasoning was that minimal regulation would enable innovation on the Internet.[17] This did lead to a burgeoning of innovation. There was a time when consumers could actually choose between Blogger, Wordpress, and Live-Journal, between Orkut and Facebook, and between MSN Messenger and Google Talk. There was even a time when people routinely used search engines other than Google. However, this changed over time, such that a few companies controlled social media.

ARCHITECTURE AND SPEECH

The Internet's potential to be the Habermas ideal makes it necessary to scrutinize the limitations placed on speech by social media platforms. In the absence of regulation, and in response to some of the influences discussed later in this chapter, the platforms have developed and enforce their own content norms. These norms are a result of the difficult decisions that the social media companies regularly make about the speech that they permit and the speech they remove from their platforms. For example, most people would agree that child pornography should be censored. However, they might not consider the iconic Pulitzer Prize–winning photograph of "Napalm Girl," a nude nine-year-old screaming in pain as she runs on a public street, child pornography. Facebook initially took the stand that removing the iconic photograph should be acceptable in the interests of maintaining the consistent rule that no child nudity would be permitted on the platform—this is reasonable as a principle, since children are not old enough to consent. However, the platform eventually accepted that the Napalm Girl photograph was an exception, given its the history and significance—it was valuable political speech.[18] Here, the platform used a norm, but it was challenged until it was amended.

Through the architecture of the platforms, social media companies control how users engage with one another and with the platform. The architecture enables them to set the terms for all engagement, from how users respond to arguments to how they share photographs or report abusive content. Rebecca MacKinnon was among the early authors to build on Lawrence Lessig's theory that the architecture of the Internet, which Lessig refers to as "code," would regulate individual behavior. MacKinnon expanded on this by pointing out that code acts like law in that it shapes what people can do and what they can see.[19] Today, it has become clear that social media platforms wield a tremendous amount of power over speech through their architecture and their policies. Scholars are acknowledging this. Tarleton Gillispie has gone as far as to say that moderation is "*the* commodity that platforms offer." Kate Klonick has referred to them as the "new governors."[20] The child pornography/Napalm Girl conundrum illustrates that these content moderation choices can be complex, and platforms are not always able to get them right.[21]

However, the companies' choices affect what we can share and what we see. When Facebook removes *Kashmir Ink*'s cover with Burhan Wani's face on it, people around the world lose access to an important, although controversial story.[22] The Kashmiri press has the right to freedom of expression and plays an important role in shaping the public narrative on global politics. If only conservative views on Kashmir may be expressed on Facebook, the Kashmiri people lose the freedom to communicate their complex political situation to the world and to one another. As MacKinnon was astute enough to point out in 2012, Internet companies "provide and shape the digital spaces upon which citizens increasingly depend."[23]

Presently, it is evident and undisputed that platforms engage in heavy moderation. Their policies are complex and often controversial. Content moderation now accounts for local rules in different countries. This is a function of the sophisticated algorithms and the change in policies that have resulted in the platforms curating their online norms differently in different countries. This is not very surprising if one accepts that the moderation of speech by social media platforms is the key commodity that they offer. The platforms make decisions about speech.[24] These decisions seem to be shaped by various factors, including pressure from governments, the platforms' perception of what their "community" wants to see, as well as the increasing pressure on them to take action in the context of harmful speech.[25] In reaction, the platforms have created elaborate self-regulatory systems that resembles "legal or governance" systems.[26]

UN Special Rapporteur for Freedom of Expression David Kaye has referred to the companies as "enigmatic regulators, establishing a kind of 'platform law' in which clarity, consistency, accountability and remedy are elusive."[27] This suggests that, where they previously enabled the emergence, catalyzing, cross-pollination, and coexistence of norms, the platforms now are intervening and often are favoring one norm over the other, such as the idea that breast-feeding should not be seen in public, that a picture of Yasser Arafat with a gun might amount to terrorist propaganda, that critique of the Thai king is unacceptable in Thailand, and more.

INFLUENCING NORMS

If it is clear that platforms create norms and that these norms can reflect, modify, reshape, and even override existing speech norms, it is worth looking into the factors that influence the normative choices made by platforms. As discussed, the platforms initially were unable to moderate content, but over the years they have been able to do so in increasingly sophisticated ways. This has made it necessary to consider what shapes their decisions about speech, which appears to be law, public pressure, and market considerations, as may be the case for most for-profit companies.

The most influential factor, however, might be safe harbor laws. This began with section 230 of the Communication Decency Act, which granted information intermediaries immunity from liability for user content.[28] It is worth noting Julie Cohen's argument that the creation of platform immunity was a part of a constitutional strategy to use the First Amendment to protect from regulatory oversight all forms of commercial information processing and communication with consumers. Immunity was granted to platforms via section 230 on the assumption that this would ensure that the Internet was a vibrant marketplace of ideas.[29] Over time, analogous laws were passed in several other countries, offering the platforms immunity.[30]

This new norm of immunity for platforms for online speech diverged from the old norm of holding publishers liable for content they published. In some countries, the law had gone so far as to hold booksellers strictly liable for the contents of books that they sold, even if knowledge or intention of the illegal content could not be established.[31] The influence of the global Web-based platforms has been powerful enough to change this norm, and many countries around the world have adopted law that offers an unprecedented degree of immunity to online platforms with regard to content hosted by them. Germany's recent effort to deviate from this norm through its Netzwerkdurchsetzungsgesetz (Network Enforcement Law) has attracted criticism.

The reasoning, at the time of creation of legal immunity, was that it would be impossible for platforms to sift through and weed illegal content out of the enormous quantities of content that they hosted and linked to.[32] The expectation accompanying this immunity was that platforms would offer their users freedom of expression.[33] The narrative around immunity suggested that platforms were neutral and functioned as mere conduits through which people could transmit their speech.[34]

This did not, of course, account for the future in which algorithms were able to enable content moderation at scale. Over time, technology became more sophisticated, enabling the platforms to intervene and moderate content much more successfully. It became possible to create hashed databases of images that would automatically get removed from multiple platforms. Algorithms can be used to implement rules across the platforms,[35] and while the algorithms are not perfect, their use in content moderation has changed one of the foundational assumptions of the safe harbor immunity—that regulating content at scale would almost impossible. It is not only possible, it can be varied with subtlety—strategies available to social media companies include blocking content only in specific countries, down-ranking content so that it is technically published but not actually visible, and others.

If it was the immunity conferred by safe harbor laws that led to platform self-regulation, then the self-regulatory choices made by the platforms are influenced by a number of factors, including threats of legal intervention. Social media companies have been confronted by inconsistent national laws and government pressure to moderate content in particular ways, and the lack of harmonized laws across jurisdictions means that the platforms engage in extensive regulatory arbitrage.[36] They go to some trouble to avoid regulation and can be responsive to the threat of regulation or loss of market access.

For example, after YouTube was banned in Pakistan for three years, the company created a local version of YouTube, such that the Pakistani government could ask for content to be blocked for users in Pakistan.[37] This version may be consistent with the legal norms that the Pakistani government is attempting to create for freedom of expression, but YouTube is enabling the Pakistani government to privilege this national norm over the international human rights norm of freedom of expression. Such tensions between norms are common in the context of cross-border speech, and the choices made by social media companies can privilege in-country norms that are at odds with international human rights norms.

The platforms also sometimes change their policies in response to public criticism.[38] They have, for example, responded over time to the pressure to take action against accounts that are abusive toward women. However, this appears to depend on the platform's own attachment to particular policies. Facebook, for instance, has resisted public pressure to change its real-name policy, even though this impacts users' ability to speak anonymously. Julie Cohen has pointed out, in the context of the platform companies' role in helping create the apparatus for the surveillance society, that platform companies' commercial interests and business models also influence their conduct.[39] It is a reasonable argument, which suggests that if law can influence the architecture and policies of social media platforms, so can business.

In addition to the norms that control how users might publish or view content in the moment, platforms also engage in practices that impact user behavior in indirect ways. These practices affect the privacy of the user and involve the sharing of data and metadata with private companies and governments. In authoritarian countries, this can jeopardize dissident speakers and chill freedom of expression.[40]

CONCLUSION

The Internet offers a space for engagement and conversation, as opposed to the one-to-many role that the mass media used to play. The problem of sorting through the cacophony was inevitable, and some degree of curating was always necessary. However, this curating was never going to be simple. The Internet has always run into conflicting norms, owing to the number of countries, communities, social groups, and more that it spans.

The architecture through which speech is curated embeds norms and values and favors certain speech norms over others. As this architecture gets more sophisticated, it permeates all the content on social media. The nature of this content is complex and layered as a result of the many-to-many nature of the medium. The speech includes political and personal conversation merged so seamlessly that it is sometimes difficult to tell them apart. My former student's deeply personal story about their journey from being a lawyer to performing in drag was also valuable political speech about social norms, drag, and India. A video of a Palestinian woman performing at a poetry slam may help her audience to empathize with her people in a way in which complex essays and journalism cannot. Social media platforms are the means by which information and stories reach the world from regions where the media is not permitted to perform its function.

We have become accustomed to this unrestricted access to information because the Internet initially removed the points of control, or the gatekeeping function, that governments used to control the public sphere.[41] This changed the nature of the public sphere. The Internet's potential to uphold and enable values of freedom of expression and the freedom of the press in repressive countries has been discussed in powerful scholarly pieces such as Anupam Chander's "Googling Freedom." It is therefore of concern that, over time, governments have started to reassert control.

The online platforms' power over speech became clear when the Chinese government co-opted the data from companies like Yahoo!, Microsoft, and

Google to track and arrest dissidents and chill their speech.[42] Although the platforms did react and make commitments to human rights, they were permitted to continue to self-regulate, and it is not clear that their commitments have stayed as firm as was intended. Google has been in the news for the Dragonfly project, a proposal to create a search engine and a news feed aggregator that censors all content blacklisted by the Chinese government.[43] The full extent of how far the platforms can control freedom of expression, if they should be so inclined, is evident in China. For instance, WeChat censors even interpersonal conversations; images connected with Liu Xiaobo were filtered out of not just group conversations but also one-on-one conversations.[44]

It appears that platforms are under pressure to uphold repressive countries' norms for online content if they want access to markets around the world. The assumption that these private companies will always uphold the international norm of freedom of expression by defending users' human rights might have been unrealistic. If the norm of freedom of expression is to prevail, it is high time we asked ourselves what can be done to influence social media platforms such that they act and regulate in favor of the rights to freedom of expression and privacy, even when they are under pressure to act differently.

It would be a mistake to ignore the importance of the Internet in the context of the public sphere. My own eye-opening moment about the power of the Internet came when I first read *Baghdad Burning*, a blog by an anonymous young Iraqi woman, which went on to document ten years of armed conflict, from 2003 to 2013. The woman's story was moving and political. It remained uncensored, and she lived ten years to tell it, which is difficult to fathom today. In farewell, she signed off with "Lo khuliyet, qulibet . . . ," offering her translation: "If the world were empty of good people, it would end." If social media companies need regulation to make sure that they prioritize human rights norms over profits and pressure from authoritarian governments, perhaps that is a conversation that we should begin.

NOTES

1. See Aihik Sur, "Facebook Access Restored after Company's Staff in Palo Alto Was Contacted," *New Indian Express*, October 26, 2017, http://www.newindianexpress .com/nation/2017/oct/26/facebook-access-restored-after-companys-staff-in-palo -alto-was-contacted-raya-sarkar-1683449.html.
2. See, for example, Abby Ohlheiser, "The Three Loopholes that Keep Trump's Tweets on Twitter," *Washington Post*, July 23, 2018, https://www.washingtonpost.com

/news/the-intersect/wp/2018/01/03/the-3-loopholes-that-keep-donald-trumps-tweets-on-twitter/?utm_term=.31b81da7abd1.

3. Eli Rosenberg, "Facebook Censored a Post for 'Hate Speech.' It Was the Declaration of Independence," *Washington Post*, July 5, 2018, https://www.washingtonpost.com/news/the-intersect/wp/2018/07/05/facebook-censored-a-post-for-hate-speech-it-was-the-declaration-of-independence/?utm_term=.acaaf462f99e.

4. Kate Klonick, "The New Governors: The People, Rules, and Processes Governing Online Speech," *Harvard Law Review* 131, no. 6 (2018): 1615.

5. See Laura De Nardis, *The Global War for Internet Governance* (New Haven, CT: Yale University Press, 2014), 58; and Laura De Nardis and A. M. Hackl, "Internet Governance by Social Media Platforms," *Telecommunications Policy* 39 (2015): 762.

6. See Marc H. Greenberg, "A Return to Lilliput: The LICRA v. Yahoo! Case and the Regulation of Online Content in the World Market," *Berkeley Technology Law Journal* 18 (2003): 1191.

7. Agnès Callamard, "Are Courts Re-Inventing Internet Regulation?," *International Review of Law, Computers, and Technology* 31, no. 3 (2017): 323–339.

8. Anupam Chander, "Googling Freedom," *California Law Review* 99, no. 1 (2011): 1–45.

9. Human Rights Council, *Report of the Special Rapporteur on the Promotion and Protection of the Right to Freedom of Opinion and Expression*, A/HRC/38/35, April 6, 2018, para. 1. See also Chander, "Googling Freedom"; and Yochai Benkler, *Wealth of Networks: How Social Production Transforms Markets and Freedom* (New Haven, CT: Yale University Press, 2006).

10. Benkler, *Wealth of Networks*, 166–167.

11. Zeynep Tufekci, *Twitter and Tear Gas: The Power and Fragility of Networked Protest* (New Haven, CT: Yale University Press, 2017), 6.

12. See Benkler, *Wealth of Networks*, 180.

13. Jonathan L. Zittrain, *The Future of the Internet—and How to Stop It* (New Haven, CT: Yale University Press, 2008).

14. Julie E. Cohen, "Law for the Platform Economy," *UC Davis Law Review* 51, no. 133 (2017): 143–148.

15. Jack M. Balkin, "Fixing Social Media's Grand Bargain," Hoover Working Group on National Security, Technology, and Law, Aegis Series Paper 1814, October 16, 2018.

16. Tufekci, *Twitter and Tear Gas*, 6; Benkler, *Wealth of Networks*, 180.

17. See Cohen, "Law for the Platform Economy," 164–167.

18. Sam Levin, Julia Carrie Wong, and Luke Harding, "Facebook Backs Down from 'Napalm Girl' Censorship and Reinstates Photo," *Guardian*, September 9, 2016, https://www.theguardian.com/technology/2016/sep/09/facebook-reinstates-napalm-girl-photo. For a detailed discussion, see Tarleton Gillespie, *Custodians of*

the Internet: Platforms, Content Moderation, and the Hidden Decisions that Shape Social Media (New Haven, CT: Yale University Press, 2018), 1–5.

19. Lawrence Lessig, *Code 2.0* (New York: Basic Books, 2006), 81–82; Rebecca Mac Kinnon, *Consent of the Networked: The Worldwide Struggle for Internet Freedom* (New York: Basic Books, 2012), 115.

20. Gillespie, *Custodians of the Internet*, 13; Klonick, "New Governors."

21. Gillespie, *Custodians of the Internet*, 1–5.

22. Abhishek Saha, "Burhan Effect: Facebook Blocks Page of Kashmir Magazine, Deletes Cover of Issue," *Hindustan Times*, July 9, 2017, https://www.hindustantimes .com/india-news/burhan-effect-facebook-blocks-page-of-kashmir-magazine -deletes-cover-of-issue/story-FWxU7PnATmZc52jClkkloO.html.

23. MacKinnon, *Consent of the Networked*, 11.

24. Gillespie, *Custodians of the Internet*, 13.

25. See De Nardis and Hackl, "Internet Governance," 766–768.

26. Kate Klonick, "New Governors," 1602.

27. Human Rights Council, *Report of the Special Rapporteur*, para 1.

28. For a discussion of this, see De Nardis and Hackl, "Internet Governance," 766.

29. Cohen, "Law for the Platform Economy," 162, 164.

30. See Stanford Centre for Internet and Society, "World Intermediary Liability Map," https://wilmap.law.stanford.edu, accessed July 20, 2020; and Urs Gasser and Wolfgang Schulz, *Governance of Online Intermediaries: Observations from a Series of National Case Studies*, Berkman Klein Center for Internet & Society at Harvard University, Research Publication 2015-5 (February 18, 2015).

31. This was the case in India, for example, as discussed in detail in Chinmayi Arun, "Gatekeeper Liability and Article 19(1)(a) of the Constitution of India," *NUJS Law Review* 7 (2014): 73.

32. Mark Lemley, "Rationalizing Internet Safe Harbors," *Journal on Telecommunications and High Technology Law* 6 (2007): 100–112.

33. De Nardis and Hackl, "Internet Governance," 966.

34. Cohen, "Law for the Platform Economy," 164.

35. See Maayan Perel and Niva Elkin Koren, "Black Box Tinkering: Beyond Disclosure in Algorithmic Enforcement," *Florida Law Review* 69, no. 1: 183.

36. De Nardis and Hackl, "Internet Governance," 767; Cohen, "Law for the Platform Economy," 184.

37. Faras Ghani, "Censorship Fears Persist as YouTube Returns to Pakistan," *Al Jazeera*, January 19, 2016, https://www.aljazeera.com/news/2016/01/youtube-pakistan-16011907 1439119.html.

38. See discussion of public controversies, corporate values, and cultural norms in De Nardis and Hackl, "Internet Governance," 767.

39. Cohen, "Law for the Platform Economy," 196.

40. De Nardis and Hackl, "Internet Governance," 763–766, Chander, "Googling Freedom," 4–5; and Cohen, "Law for the Platform Economy," 193–196.

41. Benkler, *Wealth of Networks*, 180.

42. MacKinnon, *Consent of the Networked*, 133–139.

43. Alex Hern and agencies, "Google 'Working on Censored Search Engine' for China," *Guardian*, August 2, 2018, https://www.theguardian.com/world/2018/aug/02/google-working-on-censored-search-engine-for-china.

44. Masashi Crete-Nishihata, Jeffrey Knockel, Blake Miller, Jason Q. Ng, Lotus Ruan, Lokman Tsui, and Ruohan Xiong, "Remembering Liu Xiaobo: Analyzing Censorship of the Death of Liu Xiaobo on WeChat and Weibo," Citizen Lab, University of Toronto, https://citizenlab.ca/2017/07/analyzing-censorship-of-the-death-of-liu-xiaobo-on-wechat-and-weibo.

THIRTEEN

China, Information Technology, and
Global Freedom of Expression

*A Story of Sovereignty and
Global Capitalism*

SÉVERINE ARSÈNE

The development of information technology in China since the 1980s is a story of the ambivalent relationship between sovereignty and globalization. As soon as the Chinese Communist Party engaged in economic reforms in the early 1980s, and while Western countries and international organizations were racing to build "information superhighways," Chinese leaders decided that they could not miss this technological turn, and they invested massively in telecommunications. Jiang Zemin, who was minister of the electronics industry in the early 1980s, before he became president of the People's Republic, highlighted the importance of informatization in several important speeches.

Until now, telecommunications and the digital have consistently been mentioned in strategic and economic plans, such as the five-year plans, the Medium- and Long-Term Plan on the Development of Science & Technology 2006–2020, and the Made in China 2025 strategy, which cites "next-generation information technology" as the number one strategic priority for Chinese industry. Building a strong "indigenous" information technology industry and service sector is seen as one of the most important levers of economic development, one that would help China leapfrog to a leading position, regain economic strength and autonomy, and thus rebuild political legitimacy and recognition, both domestically and globally.[1]

This strategic choice implies important transformations of the political and industrial apparatus of the country, and it raised controversies among members of the Chinese party, administrations, and businesses. Among many issues, were the divergent interests and ideological views on whether to rely on foreign or domestically developed technology, whether to open Chinese markets to foreign capital, and to what extent, and under what conditions, access to information should be opened to the larger public. Many case studies show how diverse actors allied and lobbied to influence the restructuring of the telecommunication sector, the development of domestic technical standards, or the adoption of other specific policies.[2] This process also involved transnational coalitions of actors and revealed disparities among more or less internationalized actors in China, with geographic discrepancies between inland and coastal provinces, for instance.[3] Each of these apparently specific, technical, pragmatic decisions entailed complicated power dynamics enmeshed in the global political economy, which added nuance, if it did not undermine, the grand narratives of "techno-nationalism."[4]

As China joined the World Trade Organization in 2001, and as the profound implications of the Internet unfolded over the 2000s, the issues at stake—including the advent of social networks, e-commerce, and cybersecurity concerns—appeared to be overwhelmingly diverse and intertwined, ranging from industrial development to trade and state security. Of course, the development of information technologies and the Internet also completely reconfigured the media landscape and forced open a space for public speech, where the party could not ensure monopolistic control, though the state also gradually gained unprecedented surveillance capabilities.

Against this political and strategic background, in the mind of Chinese leaders and policy makers, public speech cannot be separated from, and must be subordinated to, other political, economic, and strategic priorities. In this chapter, I intend to highlight how this conflation of speech with other priorities in domestic policy translates into Chinese positions concerning free speech on the international stage, and how it resonates with a difficulty for the global community to find a common framework to discuss a hierarchy of norms in the digital sector. I also would like to shed light on how China's rise in the global information technology landscape is enmeshed in a global process of capitalist development and involves a diversity of public and private actors with competing agendas. This is bringing new, complicated challenges to freedom of expression, not only in China but also globally, as the influence and reach of Chinese actors extend beyond Chinese borders and beyond the mere question of censorship.

Precisely because free speech is intertwined with other aspects of information technology development, it is important to adopt a flexible definition that can grasp the various ways in which information technology can shape the agency and freedom of individuals. Therefore, for the purposes of this book on global norms of freedom of expression, I am including such aspects as access to information, the right to privacy, and control of one's personal data.

I first will focus on the implications of information technology development for free speech in China. This is essential to understanding the second topic, the logic behind the Chinese engagement in Internet governance and free speech norms globally. Finally, I will look at the more diverse, pragmatic ways in which Chinese norms, interests, and soft power are gaining ground, such as through localization regulations and increased engagement in crafting global technical norms.

RECONFIGURATIONS OF SPEECH THROUGH MEDIA REFORMS AND INFORMATIZATION

Public Speech in China: From State Monopoly to Conditional Privilege

From a legal point of view, although freedom of speech is protected by the 1982 Chinese constitution, the vagueness of legal definitions of terms such as "national interests" and "stability," and the weakness of the rule of law, practically render this protection ineffective. Chinese citizens are routinely arrested and convicted for expressing political opinions, charged with such crimes as "picking quarrels and provoking trouble" or "separatism."

Since the establishment of the People's Republic, public speech has essentially been the monopoly of the party. However, during the reform period, and particularly after 1992, when Deng Xiaoping formulated a renewed social contract based on the continuation of economic reforms in exchange for a political status quo, the party's monopoly over public speech had to be redefined toward a more open, if still politically controlled, ecosystem.

The media was open to private investment during the 1990s and 2000s, and all press outlets were encouraged to diversify their content in order to reach better profitability. This enabled the production of more relevant and appealing information formats, covering topics of interest in people's daily lives (such as consumption, education, and health) and testing the limits of censorship with discussion of more sensitive social issues, such as pollution or even corruption.

However, ownership and editorial choices always remained under the party's control, and the coverage of political topics was still strictly limited. Zhao Yuezhi noted that the Chinese media was torn "between the party line and the bottom line," while Daniela Stockmann underlined that their marketized look nevertheless enhanced their credibility in public opinion.[5] All in all, despite the apparent modernization of the media, public speech in China remains not "a right but a privilege. It is not an *entitlement* granted on the basis of equality before the law and pluralist philosophy, but a *power* granted on the basis of particularity and monism" (emphasis added).[6]

The Internet, an Instrument of Power and Development

The advent of the Internet transformed the media landscape even further. Now, with more than half of the Chinese population having Internet access, it has become an essential element of the social contract proposed by the Chinese Communist Party in the twenty-first century. It constitutes vivid evidence that China has entered the modern, globalized world and is a promise to the population that they can improve their quality of life through easier access to goods, entertainment, and even financial products. Chinese Internet users have largely embraced social networks and platforms that enable self-expression online—to share personal diaries, rate restaurants and films, join car-sharing groups, or write online novels. There is now more space than ever for individuals to express their identities and share concerns.

Despite many expectations, however, this has not marked a turn in the overall conception of freedom of speech on the part of the Chinese leadership. Whereas in Western democracies the rise of online speech triggered myths of discursive public spaces and deliberation (which failed to materialize in such idealized ways), the Chinese leadership allowed the development of online speech based on apparently opposite principles. The Internet was conceived of primarily as an instrument of power and development and access was granted to the population under strict conditions of political stability. It was also envisioned as a way to improve the state–society relationship by modernizing administration and providing more efficient public services, thereby enhancing centralized technocratic governance and accountability.[7]

Online Speech Subordinated to Political, Economic, and Security Concerns

The construction of Internet infrastructure and regulation over the past thirty years reflects these concerns. At a time when libertarian-oriented Western

Internet developers were proclaiming the "independence of cyberspace," China pioneered a combination of filtering techniques and industrial policies and regulations designed to make sure that the Internet would be the instrument of economic power and governance that it was intended to be, with limited political risks.[8]

Understandably, the increasing sophistication of censorship and surveillance of online exchanges drew most of the scholarly attention.[9] From the licensing system of Internet service providers to the real-name system that forced Internet users to provide identification before posting online, all measures were designed to reward political "responsibility" and to intimidate actors into self-censorship.

Beyond information control, these measures also played a role in the development of a strong indigenous Internet ecosystem, somewhat in tension with World Trade Organization engagements. With key American websites such as Google, Facebook, and Twitter being blocked in China, Chinese Internet champions Baidu, Alibaba, and Tencent had more room to acquire market share with distinct business models. Restrictions on foreign investments in key areas such as providing Internet service[10] or, more recently, content, such as through publishing outlets, also combine the purposes of controlling content and making room for "indigenous innovation."

Putting essential assets in the hands of Chinese actors and under the control of the Chinese government is also framed as a matter of national security, which has become a priority in a context where Chinese leaders are wary of cyber spying and criminality. That is probably the reason why the first actual law that brings together previously scattered measures and regulations of the Internet is a cybersecurity law. This focus on security made possible a number of actual protections for Internet users—for instance, limits on the collection of personal data—but it also came together with a consolidation of the real-name system, forcing platforms to collect the identity of their users. As underlined by Shanthi Kalathil, the use of the term "information security" in the law signals a broader view that conflates speech issues with other dimensions, "framing domestic and international speech, assembly, surveillance and privacy issues as issues of cybersecurity."[11]

A Normative Framework under Constant Negotiation

It must be emphasized, however, that this framing of public speech is the result of constant negotiation within the party itself, and it is diversely perceived in Chinese society. Internet policy is notoriously the object of a turf battle between different ministries and agencies. Efforts by the central government to central-ize policy making through the establishment of the Cyberspace Administration of China have only partially solved this problem, and only to enhance the role of control and propaganda in conjunction with cybersecurity.[12]

In addition, the question of free speech generates heated debates between more conservative or liberal factions inside the Communist party. Some believe that opening some space for expression is essential for the modernization of the country and to maintain popular support for the regime, while others believe that it constitutes a major threat to the one-party regime and stability. More-over, as mentioned, the interests of different administrations or local govern-ments can differ depending on their scope of action or their links with local or transnational businesses. In this context, we can assume that the regulation of the media and the Internet is the result of constantly renegotiated compromises, with additional uncertainty in implementation due to local variations in politi-cal perceptions and interests.

The role and limits of public speech are also a matter of debate and negotia-tion in Chinese society. On the one side, official discourses emphasize morality and "social orderliness" and encourage moral panics that, to a certain extent, resonate with the people's own concerns and sociocultural frames.[13] In a series of interviews I conducted in Beijing in 2006 and 2007, I observed that political constraints are combined with other social norms and values, like politeness, "modernity," and "civilization," into a loosely defined normative frame condu-cive to self-censorship.[14] The effectiveness of these norms often relies on a sense of distinction among middle-class, urban Internet users.

On the other side, daily practices and incidents show that there is a lot of space for interpretation, renegotiation, and contestation, thereby carving out more space for free speech. First, the boundary between personal, intimate expression and public speech is very blurry in an online ecosystem with very diverse publication platforms. Secondly, the very terms of the social contract are subject to redefinition on a daily basis, particularly when it comes to dis-cussing the "modern" quality of life that is promised by the regime. Over the years, people have expressed grievances concerning private property, health, environmental issues, and in many other areas where they hold the authorities accountable for their own promises. Finally, many citizens and activists are unhappy about the proposed framework for speech and keep pushing the boundaries, inventing new vocabulary and symbols, devising tactics to spread messages, and, more generally, contesting the limits of censorship.[15]

Nevertheless, in recent years, censorship and information control have increasingly been conducted in an open and assertive way, accompanied and justified by propaganda efforts. This trend developed just as the Chinese Internet was becoming one of the most prolific, innovative, and profitable online environments in the world. Perhaps this should not be seen as a contradiction, as the successes and attractiveness of the Chinese Internet sector allow for more assertiveness in implementing a specific Chinese norm for the management of public speech.

Indeed, in an important milestone, the 2010 white paper on the Internet in China clarified that the Internet, as a new space for self-expression, is considered essential to the Chinese regime but conditional upon political stability.[16] The white paper also underlined that this fragile balance relies upon the guaranteed sovereignty of the Chinese state over online activities. In other terms, maintaining control over public speech within the borders of China is necessarily articulated with a global Internet governance regime that limits foreign interference in China.

CHINA AS THE LEADING ADVOCATE FOR CYBER SOVEREIGNTY

A Key Moment to Influence Global Internet Governance in the Making

This concern is expressed in a context in which global Internet governance is undergoing growing pains. In the Chinese academic literature, as well as in the official discourse, global cyberspace is often described as an "unregulated" or "anarchic" space, where transnational circulation of information and data generates exposure to risk, foreign influence, and crime.[17] This is a debatable argument, as individuals and corporations are in fact liable for their online behavior and assets in multiple jurisdictions, according to their country of residence, their activity, or the location of data servers, for instance. However, this multiplicity of legal frameworks and norms does enhance risk, uncertainty, and costs, particularly when it comes to finding and punishing authors of cyber crime, such as fraud or identity theft, but also in the case of protecting free speech or preventing abuse.

Finding a common regime to regulate online behavior at the global level is a daunting task, given the diverse facets and layers of the Internet, and because norms and values are highly diverse across continents, cultures, and political regimes—for example, criticism of religion or politics, or negationist speech are diversely tolerated across the world. Multiple attempts to initiate a global dialogue, including the UN-sponsored World Summit on the Information Society, in 2003 and 2005, the subsequent Internet Governance Forum, and other government-initiated forums, such as the NETmundial Initiative (Brazil, 2015), have borne little in the way of concrete results, apart from broad statements of principle.

Faced with these difficulties, governments, service providers, and other actors, such as copyright owners, are turning to technical measures and infrastructure to regain control of the circulation of online content, with major implications for freedom of speech.[18] These developments have put the more technical institutions of Internet governance, such as the Internet Corporation for Assigned Names and Numbers (ICANN) or the Internet Engineering Task Force, under the spotlight, with increased criticism and contention. Some questions revolve around the cost of participation; the respective weight of different categories of stakeholders, such as the industry, governments, or civil society participants; the potential influence of lobbies; the processes of decision and accountability; and the weight of the United States, which plays (depending on the case) an institutional role (ICANN, until its reform) or a de facto dominant role through corporations, civil society, and individual participants.

Meanwhile, specific issues like cybersecurity or copyright are dealt with unilaterally, bilaterally, or through regional treaties like the Budapest Convention on Cybercrime or trade agreements that contain controversial measures on intellectual property. In this ecology, the sources of the norms that shape freedom of expression have multiplied. In addition to national and international law, trade agreements and contracts also play a crucial role, as do technological standards, for instance.

Here, again, freedom of expression is entangled with multiple competing concerns. With the advent of the "information society," the global circulation of information has become a matter of trade and copyright,[19] and after Edward Snowden's revelations of massive U.S. surveillance of global networks, the stakes in terms of national security and global stability have taken an even more important place in the debate. In this context, it has proved difficult to effectively consolidate a hierarchy of norms at the global level that would put freedom of speech or human rights at the top, or even to agree on the appropriate framework of governance to achieve that kind of dialogue with regard to the cyber domain.

Chinese Advocacy for an International Regime Under the UN

Most Chinese experts agree that this constitutes a key moment for the Chinese government to take a more active part in the development of new governance frameworks and to obtain a regime that may be more favorable to China. The

Chinese leadership consistently puts forward the notion of cyber sovereignty, claiming that a Westphalian framework offers more efficient protection and is better adapted to local variations in terms of applicable norms for freedom of speech.

The 2010 white paper is very clear about the Chinese leadership's preference for a United Nations framework. It states that "the Internet of various countries belongs to different sovereignties, which makes it necessary to strengthen international exchanges and cooperation in this field. . . . China supports the establishment of an authoritative and just international Internet administration organization under the UN system through democratic procedures on a worldwide scale." A white paper on diplomacy, published in 2013, stressed that China "opposes the use of the Internet to interfere with other countries' domestic politics."[20] Article 1 of the cybersecurity law, which came in force on June 1, 2017, again highlights the relationship between domestic development goals, national security, and cyber sovereignty, naming as goals "to ensure cybersecurity, safeguard cyberspace sovereignty and national security, and social and public interests, to protect the lawful rights and interests of citizens, legal persons, and other organizations, and to promote the healthy development of the informatization of the economy and society."[21]

During the past two decades, Chinese representatives have consistently pressed the international community to bring Internet governance under an intergovernmental framework. In 2011 and 2015, China, Russia, Tajikistan, and Uzbekistan proposed to the General Assembly of the United Nations (without success) a code of conduct for information security. This document pleaded for "multilateral, transparent and democratic international Internet governance."[22] It insists that states should be free to balance national security and public order with free speech as they see fit. In 2017, these principles were reiterated in the International Strategy of Cooperation on Cyberspace. The strategy defines sovereignty as the "respect [of] each other's right to choose their own path of cyber development" and asks for equal participation of countries in a multitiered governance platform where the UN would play a leading role, and "countries should promote cooperation at the bilateral, regional and international levels."[23]

By establishing a yearly World Internet Conference in the city of Wuzhen, China clearly expressed an intention to position itself as the leading advocate for cyber sovereignty. This meeting, however, has been met with mixed reactions so far, as some Western companies were represented but most developed countries sent only lower-ranking representatives.

The idea that states are better equipped to defend the interests of citizens in the cyber realm is very seductive to many governments. Presumably, an intergovernmental framework would give more weight to developing countries, which are chronically underrepresented in all Internet governance instances as a consequence of the digital divide, and which are sensitive to threats of Western hegemony and technical domination.[24] In a "post-Snowden" context, privacy and cybersecurity concerns also have become important drivers of increased governmental involvement. Countries such as Brazil, France, and Germany, as well as the European Union as a whole, have expressed more balanced views on the relative role of states vis-à-vis other actors. Nevertheless, they remain strong supporters of an open, multistakeholder model. The use of the word "multilateral" in conjunction with the term "multistakeholder" in the final report of the ten-year review of the World Summit on the Information Society, published in December 2015, was seen as a small victory for China.[25]

These debates culminated in a showdown at the International Telecommunication Union's World Conference on International Telecommunications in Dubai in 2012, between the signatories of an agreement on new international telecommunication regulations (mostly developing countries, China, and Russia) and countries that refused to sign, including the United States and European countries.

Complex Domestic and Transnational Coalitions of Interests

Despite these apparently Manichean oppositions, each country's position in these negotiations is the result of complex dynamics. In the Chinese case, Peixi Xu suggests that the very phrase "multilateral, democratic, and transparent" was initially inserted by "a lower bureaucrat," to align with the language of the 2005 World Summit on the Information Society declaration in Tunis, and that it continued to shape the Chinese reluctance on multistakeholderism for a decade, until Xi Jinping's 2014 speech in Brazil.[26] It took until the beginning of the 2010s, with a more dominant position in terms of Internet penetration and in the business landscape, and with a change of leadership, for Chinese representatives to publicly underline the fact that they do not oppose multistakeholderism in principle. Li Yan, an expert at the influential China Institutes of Contemporary International Relations think tank, proposes to redress "misconceptions" by clarifying that China advocates the "flexible, pragmatic, multiple application of the multistakeholder model."[27] These statements leave the door open for various definitions of the concept, including one where multistakeholder participation would simply become a form of consultation of civil society organizations, experts, and businesses in a government-led decision-making process.

This gradual evolution of the Chinese position and strategy with regard to global Internet governance can be seen, in Hong Shen's words, "as the result of multifaceted power interactions among a group of power-holders, including different state agencies and business units."[28] According to Xu Peixi, "The multistakeholder model is supported by transnational information technology companies, many grassroots entities and a considerable number of governments. The traditional model preferring a larger degree of isolation, fragmentation, and confrontation is favored by those who either cling to traditional/conservative thinking, or can profit from the new Cold War mentality in the cyberspace, or . . . worry about becoming victims of the cyber attacks."[29] While it is difficult to know anything specific about these internal debates, the increased openness of Chinese representatives to the principle of multistakeholder participation can be seen not simply as the adoption of an internationally recognized norm but also as a negotiated, pragmatic, and ad hoc embrace of the current status quo, which some Chinese experts, such as Shen Yi, describe as the only rational strategy for China.[30]

Chinese experts' and policy makers' strong emphasis on pragmatism should also draw our attention to the fact that the Chinese influence on global norms of expression is not limited to the traditional channels of international negotiations and institutions of Internet governance. In addition to these, freedom of expression in China and beyond is affected by concrete, day-to-day bureaucratic, commercial, and technical measures.

TECHNICAL NORMS AND MARKET DOMINATION AS SOURCES OF SOFT POWER

Many Chinese experts of cyber policy appear to be readers of Lawrence Lessig's *Code and Other Laws of Cyberspace*, published in 1999, which, very early on, described how the architecture of networks and technical choices contribute to shaping users' agency and therefore have a considerable impact on our liberties. This work is often cited in China to underline how American domination of technology, services, and businesses implies that Chinese actors do not have a say in the design of the cyber environment and must rely on choices that may not align with their needs and values.

More generally, the field of science and technology studies has provided a wealth of case studies showing the political importance of technical decisions. Technical standards for online communication do not simply ensure transmission of data from one place to another. They also entail choices and priorities in terms of, for instance, data safety, network stability, and privacy. Design and ergonomics also determine the users' "affordances," the options for action that are open to them, and they indicate the norms of good behavior on any given platform. The political economy of technology also plays an essential role, as the owners of "pipes" and websites, typically private companies, play an essential role as gatekeepers, while there is little awareness or consent on the side of users.[31]

Weighing In on the Global Standards War

In light of the digitization strategy of the Chinese government, regaining control of technical designs is clearly a central concern and a core motivation to move up the value chain and accelerate the development of Chinese digital champions. It also entails a strategy to weigh in on the adoption of technical standards in the telecommunications and digital sectors.

Although China was frustrated with the multistakeholder system and the country's overall lack of representation in standards-setting organizations, Chinese engineers never stopped participating in the working groups and meetings they thought were key. For example, researchers from the Chinese Academy of Sciences, along with Taiwanese, Korean, and Japanese counterparts, were jointly developing standards to enable domain names in Chinese characters, even as government representatives did not attend ICANN meetings in the early 2000s. These researchers' proposal was adopted as a global standard and was recognized by ICANN.[32] This certainly underlines the difference between the agenda of engineers, who pursue a goal of scientific and technological advancement, and that of diplomats, who pay more attention to geopolitical issues. It also may indicate a willingness of Chinese officials to tolerate and perhaps even encourage such grassroots, low-profile international collaboration, in order to collect the benefits without compromising China's bargaining power on the international stage.

There were attempts to develop Chinese standards separately and to impose them on the Chinese market, but these were met with critical reactions from Chinese as well as international actors. One of the most well-studied cases is that of a standard for wireless mobile communication called WAPI, which was promoted for some time as a competitor of the Wi-Fi standard. It was even briefly made compulsory for devices for the Chinese market. However, coalitions of domestic and international companies lobbied the authorities to lift this obligation, notably by putting together competing narratives about China's national interests in the technology world.[33] In this case, domestic techno-nationalists were mostly industrial and bureaucratic actors, such as the state defense and national security apparatus, which had the most to lose in the globalization process, and actors located inland, rather than actors in the information technology industry, which is mostly located in coastal regions and is much more integrated into global industrial networks.[34] In other words, domestic factors largely account for China's strategy vis-à-vis the international governance and technical system, while reciprocally, transnational capitalist interests (including some state actors) also represent "significant structural forces undermining the techno-nationalist agenda."[35]

These failed attempts to impose domestic information technology standards probably led the Chinese central authorities to recognize that science and technology battles must be fought at a global level. Some even argued that the interest of China was aligned with the "global public interest," in the development of open source systems,[36] although this is not a mainstream point of view. In recent years, China has been well represented in all major Internet governance venues. The Internet Engineering Task Force held a meeting in China in 2010 for the first time. In 2013, ICANN's forty-sixth meeting was held in Beijing, and it subsequently opened an "engagement center" there. Lu Wei, then the head of the Cyberspace Administration of China, was listed as a member of the NETmundial council, along with Jack Ma, founder of Alibaba. Over the years, China has become the second most frequent contributor to the task force at the IETF (behind the United States), with 326 proposals for new standards. This effort comes from the private sector as well. In 2017, Huawei was the second most frequently contributing company, with fifty-nine cumulated proposals. This certainly can be counted as a success for Chinese "techno-globalists," who contribute to Chinese soft power through active participation in the definition of global standards.

The effectiveness of this strategy is in part determined by the fact that China has reached a critical size in terms of online population (with 751 million Internet users in 2017, according to the China Internet Network Information Center) and constitutes the largest e-commerce market. Now Chinese private companies like Alibaba, Baidu, Tencent, or Huawei have enough human resources, cash, and technological knowledge to attend major international conferences and to represent their interests alongside government representatives. The increased global presence of Chinese companies undoubtedly enhances the effectiveness of Chinese soft power, even if their relationship with the state is very complicated and ambiguous. On the one hand, they prolong and project the influence of the Chinese jurisdiction beyond the country's territory, sometimes even with the help of more liberal regulatory frameworks, as in the *Zhang v. Baidu* case, where a New York district judge protected the right of the Chinese giant to censor content, on the ground that Baidu's decisions are protected in the United States by the First Amendment. On the other hand, Chinese companies have an agenda that is distinct from that of the government, and companies like Alibaba, Tencent, or Huawei have occasionally made public their doubts about Chinese policies such as the cybersecurity law. The specifics of the Chinese political economy, with formal and informal mechanisms connecting the management of large companies with the party-state, particularly in such a sensitive area as the digital, also contribute to blurring the lines when it comes to distinguishing the roles of Chinese public and private actors on the global stage.

Bringing Foreign Actors Under Chinese Jurisdiction

The size of the Chinese Internet market also exercises a strong force of attraction for foreign organizations and businesses. There are many practical and technical reasons for businesses in the Internet sector to set up infrastructure as close as possible to their target customers, which therefore means falling under Chinese jurisdiction. With the threat of having a foreign website blocked or slowed down, the Great Firewall enhances the pressure to run services from Chinese territory, while new regulations are regularly reinforcing Chinese authorities' grasp on the domestic Internet sector—with, for instance, a prohibition of foreign ownership in online publishing, local registration of domain names, and local storage of users' personal data for "critical network infrastructures."

Despite this increasingly constraining regulation, many companies are ready to make great concessions, particularly in terms of censorship, in order to access the Chinese market. Some famous cases include LinkedIn and Apple—the latter removed virtual private networks from its App Store in China. Google, in a remarkable saga, finally withdrew its flagship search engine from China in 2010. The dilemma is now extending to the field of academic publishing, as Cambridge University Press was pressured (but finally refused) to censor hundreds of articles from two of its academic journals, *China Quarterly* and *Journal of Asian Studies*, on its Chinese website. Springer Nature, on the contrary, unapologetically yielded to the pressure and removed content from its catalog.

Some of these localization measures are motivated by a will to control online content. Other measures, like security assessments of information technology products and localization of essential data and infrastructure, raise suspicion of industrial espionage, although they are officially justified by cybersecurity concerns, in a context where we can assume that Chinese leaders are genuinely worried about the potential occurrence of a cyber war. Foreign countries are also expressing doubts about whether constraining measures would disproportionately affect foreign companies, thus amounting to barriers to competition.[37] A report to the American Chamber of Commerce warns against worrying trends of "deglobalization" in this area.[38]

Moreover, localization might seem contradictory with the "Going Out" policy, whereby the Chinese government encourages companies and state-run media to expand in overseas markets. Private companies like Baidu and Huawei also have international ambitions, which can at times conflict with the authorities' information control agenda.[39] Ironically, many Chinese agencies run social media platforms abroad for public relations, using services such as Twitter or Facebook that are blocked in China.

Despite these contradictions, localization measures and the export of Chinese devices and services may be two sides of the same coin. The acquisition of new users overseas contributes to the Chinese influence and reach beyond the Chinese territory. These companies may contribute to the global extension of Chinese governance, as practical measures, bureaucracy, and technical and business choices will define the norms of what is clickable or publishable online, a norm-setting role that was previously overwhelmingly held by American companies.

CONCLUSION

By putting informatization at the heart of its nation-building and economic development strategy, the Chinese government certainly set itself on a path of greater convergence with the global community. This is despite the fact that this choice initially fulfilled "techno-nationalistic" goals, with the motive of restoring national power and accelerating economic development. In particular, the development of the Internet is an element of the renewed social contract between the Communist party and the populace, a guarantee of prosperity and a modern lifestyle, granted under conditions of political stability. In line with these principles, the Chinese government has consistently defended a preference for "cyber sovereignty" and has supported a stronger role for the UN in Internet governance.

Nevertheless, Chinese representatives gradually incorporated some of the concepts elaborated in global Internet governance forums into their own discourses and practices, albeit with room for reinterpretation. Notions of privacy and protection of personal data have been more clearly established in the 2016 cybersecurity law, with language on consent and proportionality inspired by Organisation for Economic Co-operation and Development norms. The "multistakeholder" model is no longer dismissed altogether but rather has been reformulated as a form of consultation that includes a variety of interested parties in the decision-making process, as long as the state remains in a leading position. Overall, Chinese leaders seem to have adopted a pragmatic position and have increased participation in existing Internet governance institutions and meetings.

One might wonder whether this indicates that China has been "socialized" into the global Internet governance system. However, the Chinese literature on the matter suggests a more "realist" position, with Chinese experts arguing that the current status quo cannot be changed and thus that participation in the status quo is the best choice in the short term.[40] Another point of view could be that China, with the largest online market and huge potential in terms of e-commerce and big data, has now reached a critical mass and can expect to weigh more in global decision-making, whatever the institutional setup. This certainly has enhanced China's bargaining power, as most organizations now consider China to be an essential discussion partner that cannot be left out.

In any event, the rise of awareness and criticism concerning the pitfalls of the current global Internet governance framework, and the difficulties of finding a proper alternative, constitute a key opportunity for Chinese leaders to take a more assertive position on the global stage, as in other fields of global governance. Controversies over such issues as privacy, the "right to be forgotten," or copyright protection measures have all underlined the difficulty of establishing a hierarchy of norms that would make freedom of expression the highest priority when set against other concerns, such as security or trade, in the current balance of power among states, corporations, civil society organizations, and other stakeholders. In this context, Chinese cyber sovereignty positions have found some support in a number of developing countries concerned with Western domination and the digital divide. They sometimes converge with European concerns about the legitimate role of the state in protecting the interests of citizens and communities. Nonetheless, Chinese efforts to build up support for cyber sovereignty, notably by establishing a yearly World Internet Conference, have not yet tipped the balance toward the adoption of a different governance and normative framework.

However, one has to pay attention to different, more pragmatic and trivial forms of norm-setting to really grasp the impact of China's digital rise on global freedom of expression. The rise of China as the largest Internet market means it is now a leading producer of usage data, e-commerce opportunities, and innovative services, all of which present an enormous incentive for global companies to localize some assets in the Chinese jurisdiction—and therefore to comply with censorship and surveillance requirements, and sometimes with invasive security assessments.

China has already given birth to national giants in the Internet sector, from hardware to software and content production, some of which are now expanding overseas, thus extending the reach of Chinese norms beyond the Chinese borders. It also means that the Chinese private sector now actively participates in defining technical norms and standards for the global Internet, with the possibility to defend technical choices more advantageous to them, and that may impact users' privacy and agency. While the fact that private companies have exclusive control over essential elements of freedom of speech globally already raises democratic concerns, the rise of Chinese companies on the global stage is now a prominent factor in this equation.

As shown by many cases of domestic and international negotiations over technical standards and policies, this state of affairs is not only a matter of China establishing boundaries and controls to regain sovereignty over transnational flows of information. Fierce debates between Chinese "techno-globalists" and "techno-nationalists" partly reveal how the turn to digitization in China contributed in a redistribution of the cards between Chinese inland and coastal regions, and between specific stakeholders in the party-state, through the mobilization of transnational coalitions and business interests. These competing views and interests have revealed and enhanced the existence of some pluralism within China, but the political choice on the part of the central government to align with global standards and participate more in global Internet governance institutions has not necessarily entailed more democratic or inclusive decision-making. This might just as easily be viewed, as Qiu has argued, as centralized, elite, capitalist power establishing dominance over the underprivileged classes and inner provinces, which often are more likely to be unsettled by globalization.

The outcomes of such power plays, in terms of freedom of expression, are not completely straightforward. For instance, while Chinese Internet giants have a very close and complicated relation to the party-state, they also have a vested interest in building a more open Internet where vivid communities can thrive, and in benefiting from an environment where individuals and businesses can trust that their sensitive data is secure. One central issue for the global community to re, together with Chinese actors, is how to disentangle free speech issues and prioritize them against other policy concerns, such as free trade and copyright, and even more importantly, against cybersecurity, particularly at a time when terrorism and cyber espionage tend to take the lion's share of global attention.

AFTERWORD

Since the drafting of this chapter in 2017, information control has become tighter within China and has been enhanced outside China. Overseas, China has stepped up media capabilities and various forms of propaganda and social media influence to control its image and critiques abroad. The country also has been at the forefront of innovation in terms of using data and algorithms to power commerce and governance, with grave implications in terms of privacy, surveillance, and human rights. The rise of the Chinese model has become a significant factor in the global race for the deployment of big data and artificial intelligence tools, also empowering corporate interests around the world. Overseas, China has stepped up media capabilities and various forms of propaganda and social media influence.

In addition, the wider geopolitical context is marked by an acceleration of "deglobalization" in response to trade wars, cybersecurity concerns, and human rights issues. However, global supply chains and economies are so deeply intertwined that such a disentangling might not be a straightforward process.

In the face of such developments, it has never been more important for the global community to find effective ways of protecting free speech and privacy. Despite fierce technological competition, it is important to make the time and space for democratic debate about the kind of digital societies we want.

NOTES

1. Christopher R. Hughes and Gudrun Wacker, *China and the Internet: Politics of the Digital Leap Forward* (London: Routledge, 2003).
2. Eric Harwit, *China's Telecommunications Revolution* (Oxford: Oxford University Press, 2008); He Zhou, "A History of Telecommunications in China: Development and Policy Implications," in *Telecommunications and Development in China*, ed. Paul S. N. Lee (Cresskill, NJ: Hampton Press, 1997), 55–87.

3. Jack Linchuan Qiu, "Chinese Techno-nationalism and Global WiFi Policy," in *Reorienting Global Communication: Indian and Chinese Media beyond Borders*, ed. Michael Curtin and Hemant Shah (Chicago: University of Illinois Press, 2010), 284–303.

4. Yuezhi Zhao, "China's Pursuits of Indigenous Innovations in Information Technology Developments: Hopes, Follies and Uncertainties," *Chinese Journal of Communication* 3, no. 3 (2010): 266–289.

5. Yuezhi Zhao, *Media, Market, and Democracy in China: Between the Party Line and the Bottom Line* (Urbana: University of Illinois Press, 1998); Daniela Stockmann, *Media Commercialization and Authoritarian Rule in China* (Cambridge: Cambridge University Press, 2013).

6. Rogier Creemers, "The Privilege of Speech and New Media: Conceptualizing China's Communications Law in the Internet Era," in *The Internet, Social Media, and a Changing China*, ed. Jacques deLisle, Avery Goldstein, and Guobin Yang (Philadelphia: University of Pennsylvania Press, 2014).

7. Jesper Schlaeger, *E-Government in China: Technology, Power and Local Government Reform* (London: Routledge, 2013).

8. Li Yonggang, 我们的防火墙 [Our Great Firewall] (Guilin: Guangxi Normal University Press, 2009). In Chinese.

9. For a good overview, see Margaret E. Roberts, *Censored: Distraction and Diversion Inside China's Great Firewall* (Princeton, NJ: Princeton University Press, 2018).

10. Irene S. Wu, *From Iron Fist to Invisible Hand: The Uneven Path of Telecommunications Reform in China* (Stanford, CA: Stanford University Press, 2009).

11. Shanthi Kalathil, *Beyond the Great Firewall: How China Became a Global Information Power*, Center for International Media Assistance, National Endowment for Democracy (March 2017), 20. http://docs.uyghuramerican.org/pdf/CIMA-Beyond -the-Great-Firewall_150ppi-for-web.pdf.

12. Rogier Creemers, "The Pivot in Chinese Cybergovernance: Integrating Internet Control in Xi Jinping's China," *China Perspectives* 4 (2015): 5–13.

13. Di Cui and Fang Wu, "Moral Goodness and Social Orderliness: An Analysis of the Official Media Discourse about Internet Governance in China," in "Convergence and Liberalization in China's ICT Sector: New Market and New Ecosystem," special issue, *Telecommunications Policy* 40, no. 2–3 (2016): 265–276; Marcella Szablewicz, "The Ill Effects of 'Opium for the Spirit': A Critical Cultural Analysis of China's Internet Addiction Moral Panic," *Chinese Journal of Communication* 3, no. 4 (2010): 453–470.

14. Séverine Arsène, "From Self-Censorship to Social Protest," *Revue Française de Science Politique (English)* 61, no. 5 (2012): 53–74.

15. Yongnian Zheng, *Technological Empowerment: The Internet, State, and Society in China* (Stanford, CA: Stanford University Press, 2008); Johan Lagerkvist, *After the*

Internet, Before Democracy: Competing Norms in Chinese Media and Society (Berlin: Peter Lang, 2010).

16. Information Office of the State Council, *The Internet in China*, white paper, June 8, 2010, http://china.org.cn/government/whitepaper/node_7093508.htm.

17. Séverine Arsène, "Global Internet Governance in Chinese Academic Literature: Rebalancing a Hegemonic World Order?," *China Perspectives* 2 (2016): 25–36.

18. Francesca Musiani, Derrick L. Cogburn, Laura DeNardis, and Nanette S. Levinson, eds., *The Turn to Infrastructure in Internet Governance* (New York: Palgrave Macmillan, 2016).

19. Tim Wu, "The World Trade Law of Censorship and Internet Filtering," *Chicago Journal of International Law* 7, no. 1 (2006): 263–287.

20. 2013 中国外交白皮书: 中国维护领土主权决心坚定 [2013 China White Paper on Diplomacy: China Is Firmly Determined to Safeguard Territorial Sovereignty], *Tianya*, July 17, 2013, http://bbs.tianya.cn/post-worldlook-827386-1.shtml (in Chinese).

21. "Cybersecurity Law of the People's Republic of China," ed. Rogier Creemers, trans. Paul Triolo, *China Copyright and Media*, November 7, 2016, https://chinacopyrightandmedia.wordpress.com/2016/11/07/cybersecurity-law-of-the-peoples-republic-of-china.

22. UN General Assembly, *Letter Dated 9 January 2015 from the Permanent Representatives of China, Kazakhstan, Kyrgyzstan, the Russian Federation, Tajikistan and Uzbekistan to the United Nations Addressed to the Secretary-General*, A/69/723, January 13, 2015, https://digitallibrary.un.org/record/786846?ln=en.

23. "Full Text: International Strategy of Cooperation on Cyberspace," *Xinhuanet*, March 1, 2017, http://news.xinhuanet.com/english/china/2017-03/01/c_136094371.htm.

24. Abu Bhuiyan, *Internet Governance and the Global South: Demand for a New Framework* (Basingstoke: Palgrave Macmillan, 2014).

25. See Monika Ermert, "WSIS+10: Roles, Responsibilities Remain Hot; Cybersecurity Treaty Demanded By Many States," *Intellectual Property Watch*, December 16, 2015, http://www.ip-watch.org/2015/12/16/wsis10-roles-responsibilities-remain-hot-cybersecurity-treaty-demanded-by-many-states/.

26. Peixi (Patrick) Xu, "From ICANN57 Hyderabad to the 3rd WIC Wuzhen Summit: A Moment of Consensus on Internet Governance," *CircleID*, December 6, 2016, http://www.circleid.com/posts/20161206_from_icann57_hyderabad_to_the_3rd_wic_wuzhen_summit.

27. Li Yan, "Reforming Internet Governance and the Role of China," *Focus Asia: Perspective and Analysis* 12 (Stockholm: Institute for Security and Development Policy, February 2015). http://isdp.eu/content/uploads/images/stories/isdp-main-pdf/2015-LiYan-Reforming-Internet-Governance-and-the-role-of-China.pdf.

28. Hong Shen, "China and Global Internet Governance: Toward an Alternative Analytical Framework," *Chinese Journal of Communication* 9, no. 3 (2016): 304–324.

29. Xu, "From ICANN57 Hyderabad."

30. Shen Yi, "全球网络空间治理原则执政与中国的战略选择" [The Controversy over Global Internet Governance Principles and China's Strategic Choices], *Waijiao pinglun* 2 (2015): 1–15. In Chinese.

31. Rebecca MacKinnon, *Consent of the Networked: The Worldwide Struggle for Internet Freedom* (New York: Basic Books, 2012).

32. Séverine Arsène, "Internet Domain Names in China: Articulating Local Control with Global Connectivity," *China Perspectives* 4 (2015): 25–34.

33. Scott Kennedy, "The Political Economy of Standards Coalitions: Explaining China's Involvement in High-Tech Standards Wars," *Asia Policy* 2, no. 1 (2011): 41–62.

34. Qiu, "Chinese Techno-nationalism."

35. Zhao, "China's Pursuits," 274.

36. Wang Shaochuan, Linux expert, cited in Zhao, "China's Pursuits," 285.

37. Cynthia Liu, "Internet Censorship as a Trade Barrier: A Look at the WTO Consistency of the Great Firewall in the Wake of the China–Google Dispute," *Georgetown Journal of International Law* 42 (2010): 1199.

38. Rhodium Group and Covington, *Preventing Deglobalization: An Economic and Security Argument for Free Trade and Investment in ICT* (Washington, DC: United States Chamber of Commerce, 2016), https://www.uschamber.com/sites/default/files/documents/files/preventing_deglobalization_1.pdf.

39. Adam Segal, "The Great Cannon and the Globalization of Chinese Internet Companies," blog post, Council on Foreign Relations, April 14, 2015, https://www.cfr.org/blog/great-cannon-and-globalization-chinese-internet-companies.

40. Yi, "全球网络空间."

The Rise of Global Counternorms   **FOURTEEN**

ALEXANDER COOLEY

Since the great financial meltdown of 2008, it has become commonplace to think of the West as being in normative retreat. The financial crisis undercut the perception that Western economic systems are superior, touched off an ongoing crisis in the Eurozone, and saw the sitting prime minister of an EU country (Hungary's Viktor Orbán) openly doubt whether liberal democracies can remain globally competitive. In parallel, revelations about National Security Agency surveillance and the release of the U.S. Senate report on CIA torture have reinforced perceptions that the United States acts hypocritically and applies double standards when it comes to so-called values issues. Under the Trump administration, Secretary of State Rex Tillerson's decision to remove the promotion of democracy as a core mission of the agency reinforced President Trump's populist campaign message that the United States would refrain from championing liberal values in other countries.

Beyond the West's own current confrontation with populist and illiberal movements, a larger international backlash against liberal democracy has grown and gathered momentum. Over the past decade, authoritarians have experimented with and refined a number of new tools, practices, and institutions that are meant to shield their regimes from external criticism and to erode the norms that inform and underlie the liberal international political order. The important debate about whether there has been a democratic recession over the past decade—about how to understand these trends and how to classify stagnating polities and decaying institutions—also requires us to examine the broader global political changes and systemic shifts that have produced new counternorms and counterpractices.[1]

Policy makers and academics have been hesitant to acknowledge some of these recent cross-regional trends. Many deeply held and still highly influential assumptions about the nature of the liberal political order, the normative fabric of global governance, and the diffusion of democratic norms are products of the years just after the Cold War. Back then, in the 1990s, when the Soviet Union had just collapsed and former Communist countries had begun economic and political transitions, liberal democratic values appeared triumphant and free of significant ideological competition. At the same time, U.S. power was unrivaled, U.S. control of global institutions was strong, and there was a broad perception that a U.S.-led liberal world order would continue to set the rules, standards, and norms for international interactions. In light of the "pushback" in which authoritarian regimes are now engaged, upbeat assumptions about liberal democracy's effortless dominance require careful scrutiny.

The truth is that norms privileging state security, civilizational diversity, and traditional values over liberal democracy now have significant backing, and they are reshaping the international environment—including the West itself. The effects are most visible in the narrower political space that nongovernmental organizations (NGOs) are now facing, the shifting purposes that regional organizations are embracing, and the rising influence of non-Western powers as international patrons. Together, these dynamics reveal an international political climate that has made the work of spreading of democratic norms far more difficult than it was two decades ago.

Perhaps most disturbingly, authoritarians have pursued these tactics and counterpractices because they are proving effective: The activities of NGOs can be successfully restricted, regional organizations can be repurposed to support the political agendas of authoritarian member states, and international investment and assistance can be procured from new donors without accompanying political conditions. Success breeds imitation, and more authoritarian regimes (plus some backsliding democracies) across Eurasia, Latin America, the Middle East, and Africa are beginning to emulate these practices.

COUNTERNORMS VERSUS LIBERAL DEMOCRACY

Just as the backlash against liberal democracy spans different regions and countries, it also contains various alternative narratives and norms. The most commonly voiced critiques stress the primacy of state sovereignty and security, while charging that liberal democratic governments and international organizations are too prone to meddle in the domestic affairs of other countries. Liberal democracy's universalism—its claim to be the sole legitimate form of human governance—comes under challenge, with liberal democratic discourse said to be serving as cover for U.S. and Western geopolitical interests. Counternorms are thus also grounded in changing power balances, as the post–Cold War era of U.S. hegemony gives way to a more multipolar world—a shift often summed up (not without irony) as the "democratization of international relations."

Counterterrorism and Security

The most powerful single source of counternorms has been the post-9/11 turn toward counterterrorism and security. Since the 2001 terror attacks, there has been a collective acceptance, stretching well beyond the confines of the United States, that the tradeoff between security and individual liberty should be rebalanced in favor of security. As Kim Lane Scheppele has observed, this "international state of emergency" has empowered governments to expand executive authority, increase areas of secrecy and state privilege, set up exceptional legal procedures, expand domestic surveillance, bypass national asylum procedures, and establish forms of cooperation among security services that escape transnational oversight.[2] While the 1990s saw the steady expansion of global civil society and transnational networks, the 2000s witnessed the globalization of anticonstitutionalist measures for purposes of fighting terrorism and strengthening state security.

Among the most powerful counterterrorist norms to arise thus far has been the widespread acceptance of organized blacklisting of suspected terrorists and their supporters. The legal basis for this practice dates from almost two years before 9/11, when UN Security Council Resolution 1267 of October 1999 created a sanctions committee charged with listing all Al Qaeda affiliates. Resolution 1373, adopted on September 28, 2001, required states to criminalize terrorist financing and authorized governments to establish their own domestic blacklists. According to scholars and legal advocates, international blacklisting has had ill effects on political rights worldwide.[3] With no clear criteria for listing and no procedure for delisting, the "terrorist" designation has become a weapon that authoritarians can wield against political foes. It has also spawned the rise of "parallel" systems of administrative interventions that supplant the criminal justice system and weaken the rule of law. Moreover, blacklisting appears to have generated a type of intergovernmental "logrolling," in which states do each other favors by readily accepting each other's decisions to list this group or that as "terrorist."[4]

A related concern, heightened by blacklisting, has been the growing abuse of the red-notice system that the International Criminal Police Organization (INTERPOL) uses to ask states to find, apprehend, and extradite individuals wanted for prosecution or the serving of a criminal sentence elsewhere. According to the legal watchdog Fair Trials, the governments of Belarus, Indonesia, Iran, Russia, Sri Lanka, Turkey, and Venezuela have played a large role in driving up the number of red notices issued, from 1,277 in 2002 to 8,132 a decade later.[5]

Public conversations over security and sovereignty have also been used by governments to justify their increased monitoring, censorship, and control of cyberspace. Russia and China have been at the forefront of advocating for a "digital sovereignty" model of Internet regulation, empowering states to actively regulate Internet activity within their national jurisdictions, as opposed to empowering an international organization with the function.[6]

Civilizational Diversity

Appeals to "civilizational diversity" and the principle of noninterference in the domestic affairs of sovereign states form another class of emerging counternorms. The People's Republic of China is the leading supporter of this manner of critiquing liberal democracy's universalism as well the political conditionality that international institutions adopt to further universal democratic norms.

The "respect for civilizational diversity" counternorm is the operating principle of the Shanghai Cooperation Organization (SCO), a regional group founded in 2001 by China, Russia, and four Central Asian states (Kazakhstan, Kyrgyzstan, Tajikistan, and Uzbekistan). Chinese official statements and commentary repeatedly refer to the group's embodiment of the foundational "Shanghai spirit," a norm that enshrines respect for state sovereignty and noninterference, promotes the "democratization of international relations," and rejects the imposition of political and economic conditionalities by global governance institutions.[7] As David Lewis has observed, in Central Asia the SCO's norms have displaced the liberal democratic principles that the Organisation for Security and Co-operation in Europe (OSCE) has traditionally promoted across the former Soviet space, and have even prompted the OSCE to water down its regional projects that deal with "democratic values."[8]

The New Traditional Values Agenda

A third distinct group of counternorms concerns the defense of "traditional values." Here, Russia is the main backer. Proponents of the "values" school of thought, which is rooted in strands of neo-Eurasianist thinking and fueled by Russia's stand against what the Kremlin sees as Western encroachment, maintain that Western individualism has gone over the edge into a state of crisis and moral decay. This accounts for the challenge now being posed to Western decadence worldwide by a turn toward sources of national culture, heritage, and religion.

The Kremlin is pushing the traditional values agenda as normative cement for the new economic and security architecture that it is seeking to build across Eurasia.[9] As part of these efforts, LGBTQ communities and civil society representatives have found themselves targeted by stigmatization campaigns and legislative restrictions. Eurasian countries are introducing bans on "homosexual propaganda" similar to the one that Russia passed in 2011. Kyrgyzstan's parliament, widely thought to be one of the region's more pluralistic, in October 2014 overwhelmingly approved a bill criminalizing "propaganda for non-traditional sexual relations" and banned information alleged to promote "homosexual lifestyles." The senate of neighboring Kazakhstan passed a similar draft bill in February 2015. When Almaty was a candidate city for the 2022 Winter Olympics, activists and athletes intensively lobbied the International Olympic Committee to pressure the government of Kazakhstan to reject the legislation.

Outside the region, Russia has acquired partners willing to introduce the traditional values agenda in international forums. On September 27, 2012, a resolution of the UN Human Rights Council, sponsored by Russia and the Arab League, called for "a better understanding and appreciation of traditional values" to be applied in human rights work. The vote was 25 for and 15 against, with seven countries abstaining.[10] In a sharp criticism of the text, the EU affirmed that human rights are "universal and inalienable," while warning that traditional values are "inherently subjective and specific to a certain time and place." The EU's statement went on to worry that introducing "the concept of 'traditional values' into this discourse can result in a misleading interpretation of existing human rights norms, and undermine their universality."[11] Although emphasizing different goals, the counterterror, civilizational diversity, and traditional values agendas all question the feasibility or desirability of liberal democracy's universal aspirations. Basic changes in the international order over the past two decades have powered the rise of each of these sources of counternorms.

Russia's support for "traditional values" also informs much of its support for illiberal parties and movements throughout the West. From Moscow's support of France's Front National to its increased activities opposing actors aligned with the Euro-Atlantic community in the Balkans and its alleged interference in the 2016 U.S. presidential elections, Russia supports political outsiders and antisystemic actors who are critical of migrants, multiculturalism, liberal values, and democratic norms. The weaponization and spread of "fake news" has been matched by Russia's active networking with U.S.-based right-wing groups advocating gun rights, Christian fundamentalism, family values organizations, and the individual state sovereignty campaigns advocating secession from the United States.[12]

TRANSMISSION FAILURE: FROM NGOS TO GONGOS AND ZOMBIES

Nowhere is the contrast between the relatively democratization-friendly world of twenty years ago and today's harsher international environment more apparent than in the realm of nongovernmental organizations. In the 1990s, academics and policy makers heralded the rise of NGOs. These independent actors in international politics, it was said, were achieving a new prominence and fueling a shift away from traditional state power. The most influential scholarly study of the topic claimed that NGOs regularly "boomerang" around recalcitrant governments to effect positive change, exerting pressure via transnational networks that include other NGOs, international organizations, and like-minded states.[13]

In hindsight, this celebratory account appears clearly premature. Such optimistic studies assumed that NGO campaigns and activities would enjoy a clear field indefinitely, while the severity and effectiveness of future state responses went unanticipated. The turning point came after the so-called color revolutions that flared in the former Soviet Union during the first half of the 2000s. In Georgia (2003), Ukraine (2004), and Kyrgyzstan (2005), street protests following flawed elections swept regimes from power. Experts still debate whether Western-funded NGOs played a decisive role.

Whatever the case may be, a broad perception arose that Western democracy promoters were using NGOs as political weapons. "Color revolution" became a synonym for "foreign-sponsored regime change," and governments began to treat democracy monitors as potential security threats. Within eighteen months of Kyrgyzstan's 2005 "Tulip Revolution," all five former Soviet Central Asian republics enacted restrictive NGO registration laws. In 2011, the Arab Spring drew more attention to the role that foreign-funded civil society groups (and social media) might play in political unrest. Three years after that, the Euromaidan protests in Ukraine brought down a Russian-backed president and again heightened the anxiety felt in certain quarters about the political weight of foreign-backed civil society groups.

In response, governments across the world have developed a "counterrevolutionary playbook" that targets NGOs and democracy monitors and prioritizes state information security. The common charge is that NGOs act on behalf of outside interests eager to influence domestic political outcomes. New legal restrictions limit NGOs' access to foreign funds and even stigmatize the groups as Trojan horses that covertly serve the West. In addition to the best-known cases in Eurasia and the Middle East, countries such as Ecuador, Ethiopia, Hungary, India, Mexico, Pakistan, Sudan, Venezuela, Vietnam, and even Canada have moved, over the past ten years, to put a squeeze on the activities of foreign-funded NGOs within their borders. Measures range from outright bans on foreign funding (in Eritrea and Saudi Arabia), to restrictions on foreign funding of political work, to burdensome mandates that force NGOs to secure government approval of any outside funding and to meet stringent reporting requirements.[14]

Darin Christensen and Jeremy Weinstein's 2013 study of ninety-eight countries found that twelve governments had prohibited the foreign funding of the civil society, while thirty-eight had imposed restrictions on outside funding (twenty of them since 2002).[15] Another recent academic survey identified forty-five countries that have imposed laws restricting foreign funding of domestic NGOs since 1993, noting that thirty-eight of them have adopted these restrictions since 2003.[16] Demonstration effects also seem to be important: studies suggest that countries carefully pay attention to and emulate the normative practices of their neighbors.[17] Far from being a temporary measure, the clampdown on NGOs is a growing global trend.

Evidence from the latest crackdowns strongly suggests that these new restrictions are accomplishing their political objectives. In Russia, ground zero of the NGO backlash, a 2012 law required NGOs receiving outside funds to register as "foreign agents" on pain of fines. Few chose to register at first, so the law was amended to allow the Russian justice ministry to decree whether a group qualifies as independent or not. The ministry has since formally warned twenty groups that they must register, while at least six groups—including election watchdogs, legal societies, and LGBTQ organizations—chose to close rather than accept the stigmatizing label of "foreign agent."[18] In Ethiopia, a pioneering study exploring the effects of a restrictive 2009 NGO law found that 90 percent of domestic NGOs concerned with political or human rights issues either folded or shifted to work in less contentious areas such as economic development or social services.[19] Governments have learned that they will face few international consequences for cracking down on NGOs and that such "sovereignty-preserving" efforts have the encouragement of China, Russia, and other non-Western powers.

Even as they ramp up their repression of independent NGOs, governments have been promoting pseudo NGOs and fake democracy monitors that emulate the form but not the substance of true civil society groups. The proliferation of government-organized nongovernmental organizations (GONGOs) has been especially striking. Unhappy with a civil society that independently monitors and challenges them, authorities have been busy building their own tame simulacrum of it that collaborates with power rather than criticizing it. In like manner, governments have begun funding youth movements, such as the Russian group Nashi, that stress themes of national pride and sovereignty.

The rise of what I call "zombie" election monitors offers another dramatic case in point. Traditionally, election monitoring has been the mission of a few skilled NGOs and international organizations such as the OSCE, acting through its Office for Democratic Institutions and Human Rights (ODIHR). These groups bring to their work extensive experience, technical expertise, and a code that lays out the best practices to be followed in observing and evaluating elections, including measures such as long-term monitoring. Over the past decade, many authoritarian governments and ruling parties have continued to avow their acceptance of external election observation as a norm but have undercut it in practice by using zombie monitors. Zombie monitors try to look like democratic observers but serve autocratic purposes by pretending that clearly flawed elections deserve clean bills of health.

Authoritarians have increasingly hired or deployed zombies on election days without regard to their expertise, competence, or credibility. Azerbaijan's October 9, 2013, presidential election appears to have marked a watershed in the practice—many of the forty-two invited organizations that were there to observe the elections had never been heard of before. The process ended with incumbent president Ilham Aliyev claiming a third term (he has been free to run indefinitely since engineering a 2009 constitutional change that erased term limits) on the basis of almost 85 percent of the vote. The process began with the national election commission accidentally releasing a "result"—before voting had even started—that showed Aliyev as the winner, with nearly 73 percent. Among the reports that observer groups issued on the electoral process, only the ODIHR's was critical.[20]

It may be tempting to dismiss zombie monitors as laughably phony and hence powerless to undermine international standards with their bogus assessments, or to reverse general international impressions of an election's poor quality. Yet, critically, zombies are not meant to function as perfect substitutes for Western democratic watchdogs. Instead, their role is less ambitious, and thus easier to play: regimes use zombies with the intention to confuse and distract, to sow uncertainty by promoting progovernment "narratives," and to boost the plausibility of government complaints that critical foreign observers are biased.[21] What is more, zombies allow authoritarians to gradually redefine of the very purpose and role of outside election observation as a political norm. Instead of being a neutral activity that evaluates the quality of electoral processes objectively and openly, even if this might "undermine" sovereignty, election observation becomes, in authoritarian eyes, a "sovereignty-enhancing" partnership between invited observers and the governments that summon them.

THE NEW AUTHORITARIAN REGIONALISM

Another international development that has fostered the rise of counternorms involves various regional organizations and the new legal frameworks and activities that they have been championing. As had been the case with NGOs, scholars who studied regional organizations in the wake of the Cold War believed that on the whole they would assist democratic consolidation.[22] The expansion of the EU and its adoption of the strict Copenhagen criteria for membership spread an impression that deeper regional integration would reinforce democratic consolidation and institutional transformation. The EU standards, for instance, gave democrats in such aspirant countries (at the time) as Slovakia and Romania a basis for criticizing the democratic shortcomings of their own governments. There was scholarly criticism of this view, but it stopped short of questioning the basic idea that regional organizations would by and large promote the diffusion of democratic norms.[23]

Such optimism now seems less warranted. Across Eurasia, the Middle East, Africa, and Latin America, new regional organizations are flourishing. Yet their

political agendas seem to be drifting away from reaffirming democratic principles and even veering toward new practices that serve to shield their authoritarian members from outside criticism of what they do at home. As Latin America
expert Christopher Sabatini has observed with regard to the Bolivarian Alliance for the Peoples of Our Americas (ALBA, founded 2004) and the Union of
South American Nations (UNASUR, founded 2008), these new organizations
rely on "anti-imperialist" sentiment plus what he calls "the vague basis of norms
of regional solidarity."[24]

Of particular concern are the agreements and treaties that some regional
organizations have been forging, often in the name of new norms of regional
security, stability, or counterterrorism. These compacts are creating legal
frameworks that could serve to institutionalize authoritarian and anticonsti-
tutional practices. For instance, the SCO's 2009 antiterrorism treaty and the
2012 joint security agreement of the Gulf Cooperation Council give executive
authorities and security services a number of extraterritorial powers that
bypass traditional domestic legal checks and international norms. Each compact provides for a common blacklist of suspected terrorists and "extremists,"
and each allows any member state to extradite suspects to any other member
state on the basis of a mere accusation, with no clear standards of evidence. The
security services of member states, meanwhile, may conduct investigations on
one another's territory, with information about suspects and targeted individuals to be shared upon request.[25]

Not surprisingly, human rights watchdogs have criticized both of these
treaties for undermining political rights in member countries.[26] Kuwait's legislature delayed ratification of the Gulf Cooperation Council pact amid worries—
voiced by lawmakers and civil society groups—that the compact would undermine the country's constitutional principles. After its ratification, these concerns
appeared justified, as three prominent Kuwait activists were reportedly detained
at the request of Saudi authorities in 2015.[27]

When not dreaming up agreements that embed authoritarian practices,
regional organizations have been busy diluting democratic standards and incu-
bating fresh zombie monitors. In Eurasia, the Commonwealth of Independent
States Election Monitoring Observers (founded 2005) like to associate themselves with international standards and Western organizations such as the
OSCE, but in fact have offered an assessment opposite to the ODIHR's in every
regional election that the two groups have observed, save one (Ukraine's 2010
elections). In Latin America, UNASUR wants its monitors to "accompany" host
governments throughout the electoral process and to reach accommodation
with the results. It does not expect monitors to assess either the political

environment that precedes the voting or the conduct of the election itself.[28] And even the African Union, which in other ways has embodied democratic principles—it has a policy against according recognition to coups, for instance—has proven too accommodating in its assessments. Thus, its observation team was quick to declare the Democratic Republic of Congo's November 2011 presidential election a success, even as EU and U.S. observers were reporting chaotic conditions and irregularities that had damaged the quality of the vote.[29]

Why do regional organizations so often fail to show firmness when upholding democratic standards? A major and perhaps surprising role in the failure is played by leading regional powers. States such as Brazil and South Africa are preoccupied with leveraging their newfound prominence in regional organizations to cement coveted status as regional bellwethers and "emerging" global powers. They seem to fear that criticizing neighboring governments will arouse unwanted resentment, while embattled authoritarians are practiced in the art of using appeals to regional solidarity to deflect international opprobrium. The 2015 assumption of the African Union's rotating presidency by Zimbabwe, for example, gave that country's nonagenarian strongman, Robert Mugabe, a welcome new platform from which to repeat his denunciations of "imperialists and colonialists."[30]

None of this means that regional organizations are playing a solely negative role, of course. On the contrary, groups such as the African Union and the Association of Southeast Asian Nations openly reflect on democratic issues and conduct regular outreach to civil society. And yet the broader analytical point remains: regional groups themselves have become institutional arenas where democratic norms are contested and counternorms are introduced. Indeed, even the OSCE, long the embodiment of the 1975 Helsinki Accords' normative "human values" agenda, has come under siege as a group of Eurasian states led by Russia has proposed to reduce the ODIHR's budget and autonomy.

NEW PATRONS AND MEDIA PROVIDERS

A third international trend that has reinforced the rise of counternorms is the advent of alternative providers of international public goods. Since the 2008 financial crisis, it has become commonplace to speak of the West's economic retrenchment and the rise of emerging powers as major players in the world economy. Although obituaries of the Western-led liberal economic order seem premature—overall world trade recovered by 2010 and, in 2013 dollars, constituted more than 60 percent of global reserve holdings, and dollar transactions accounted for more than 80 percent of global trade finance—the one area where Western economic hegemony has markedly waned is in providing development aid, including project finance, stabilization assistance, and concessionary loans.

Emerging donors, especially China and the Gulf states, have transformed the dynamics of international development lending. China now has the world's second-largest economy, smaller only than that of the United States (though, by some reckonings, China's may even have recently nosed into first place). Beijing's stock in trade is to offer packages that defy traditional distinctions between aid and investment, often accepting as security for its loans access to host country energy resources, commodities, or other assets.

Whatever China's intentions, its influence as a political model is unavoidably linked to its growing economic engagement and international patronage. The availability of alternative donors, who demand fewer democratic conditions and good governance guarantees, makes it easier for state recipients throughout the developing world to reject Western funding if the prodemocratic "strings" attached to it are considered too constricting. The prestige of these economically successful authoritarians gives other leaders who are bent on deviating from liberal democratic norms a plausible alterative to having to submit to liberal values and Western criticism. Thus, Turkish president Recep Tayyip Erdoğan has repeatedly brought up the idea of dropping talks with the EU in order to seek membership in the SCO. That organization, he says, "is better and more powerful [than the EU], and we have common values with them."[31]

The rise of alternative patrons is transforming the development landscape. Over the past decade, China has lent more money in Latin America than have the World Bank and the Inter-American Development Bank combined. In Africa, China has doubled its development financing, going from $10 billion lent from 2009 through 2012 to twice that amount for the period from January 2013 to February 2015.[32] Beijing has also become the leading lender to Central Asia, and it is playing a major role in the Caribbean as well as in the island states of the Pacific. Together with this, a shift from grants to loans secured by concessions has raised further concerns about repayment terms, political conditions, and the demands that Beijing might make on its debtors in the future.

In other cases, emerging donors have stepped in to aid countries not serviced by the Western-led aid community. Since the instability of the Arab Spring, the oil-rich Gulf states have sent tens of billions of dollars abroad and now provide the lion's share of development aid to Bangladesh, Egypt, the Maldives, and Yemen. Other cases suggest that in postconflict settings, governments that have been shunned or sanctioned by the West can now readily find new patrons as alternatives to the liberal peace-building complex. After the Sinhalese-dominated Sri Lankan government launched its ruthless and successful 2009 military offensive against Tamil insurgents, it bypassed Western donors and their human rights concerns by turning to China and India for postconflict assistance.[33] Angola, Sudan, and Tajikistan can also be seen as part of this growing new "illiberal" peace-building complex.

In 2014, Beijing strongly backed, and indeed capitalized, two new lending organizations in order to challenge the West's monopoly control over official international financial institutions. The New Development Bank (originally called the BRICS Development Bank) and the Asian Infrastructure Investment Bank are supposed to perform tasks resembling those of the World Bank and Asian Development Bank, with an emphasis on financing large-scale infrastructure projects in developing countries. Interestingly, while U.S. officials were cautiously supportive of the New Development Bank, they publicly campaigned against the Asian Infrastructure Investment Bank, to the point of lobbying allies such as Australia to forgo membership.[34]

Yet U.S. geopolitical influence now appears weak, as fifty-three states have joined the bank, including Western states such as the United Kingdom, Germany, and France, and even, after a change of mind, Australia. Whether these banks can truly devise workable lending practices without imposing Western-style oversight and conditions remains to be seen. Yet their political significance as alternative sources of international financing should not be underestimated. As China develops its Belt and Road infrastructure projects across Eurasia, the Middle East, South Asia, and Europe, it seems likely that recipient countries will become more reluctant to criticize China's political practices and counternorms.

Another former Western monopoly of the liberal order that has been broken is the field of global media. As the United States and other Western countries have continued to whittle down their presence in international news gathering (few U.S. newspapers maintain permanent foreign bureaus or correspondents anymore), Russia and China have been pouring state funds into news and broadcasting operations. As of 2013, according to one report, China Central Television had set up seventy international bureaus, including twenty in Africa and a dozen in Latin America, with a plan to broadcast (in local languages) to regions and countries where China has made big investments.[35]

Russia has upped its international media presence by expanding the reach of its television channel Russia Today (now rebranded simply as RT), and by launching (in November 2014) a state-run multimedia outlet called Sputnik in thirty-four countries across five continents. Sputnik's stated goal is to counter "Western propaganda" worldwide.[36] In practice, RT and Sputnik have proven particularly effective not in promoting Russia's own political model or foreign policy but in amplifying stories that highlight Western hypocrisy and double standards, especially on social and political issues. Going forward alongside these efforts are the activities of global outlets such as Iran Press TV, the Venezuelan-run Telesur consortium, and several Gulf broadcasters. Together, they pose a serious, amply funded challenge across large swaths of the world in covering news, setting journalistic standards, and editorializing about political events.

In the 1990s, the West still had a nearly exclusive role as *the* provider of international funding and information the world over. Emerging donors and alternative patrons have changed that. In development assistance, in project finance, and in global media, emerging powers are displacing the West. The upshot of these trends is more contention over the normative foundations of the international order (with nonliberal voices having a bigger say than before), more authority for counternorms such as noninterference in countries' internal affairs, and more influence for various authoritarian alternatives to liberal democracy.

HANDLING THE INFLUENCE OF THE NEW

As we have seen, rising new counternorms are threatening to straitjacket liberal democracy's power, even as they chip away at its status as the most influential source of norms for global governance. The appearance of these counternorms is not adventitious but has a basis in fundamental changes that have been altering the post–Cold War international order. Changes in the legal status and role of NGOs, the conversion of regional organizations into arenas of contestation, and the rise of alternative patrons have turned a world that was once relatively favorable to the spread of democratic norms into one where authoritarians can push back—and have learned to do so in innovative ways. Whatever the exact extent of worldwide democratic regression, it is clear that counternorms to liberal democracy have taken root and are helping authoritarians to retain power.

What can democracy advocates and prodemocratic policy makers do about all this? A key challenge is to disentangle, as much as possible, the issue of perceived Western political decline from the fate of liberal democracy.

The first need is to combat the rise of counterdemocratic practices embodied in new regional frameworks or the proliferation of zombies. Here, policy makers should concentrate on benchmarking these new phenomena against existing international standards or introducing new standards against which the credibility of such practices and frameworks must be tested. For example, a code of standards governing election observation does exist, and long-standing UN principles undergird it. Similarly, new regional treaties and agreements should not be passively accepted but should instead be actively scrutinized in light of international human rights laws and countries' commitments to such standards. Identifying best practices in election observation, news coverage, legal development, blacklisting, and data sharing are critical for stopping the "anything goes" thinking that is too often assumed to be a natural concomitant of multipolarity.

Moreover, diplomats and foreign policy officials should reconsider how emerging powers can gain status by adopting, rather than rejecting, standards that respect good governance and democracy. Recent scholarship has shown that political practices such as gender quotas for legislatures tend to spread not on principled grounds but rather because countries get the impression that adopting them is the "high-status" thing to do.[37] In view of this, liberal democracies should do all they can to reinscribe principles such as good governance, transparency, and respect for the due autonomy of civil society in the honor roll of "things that enhance a country's standing in the world." Appeals to national pride and prestige are likely to have more effect on emerging powers than will lectures about democratic shortcomings.

Finally, Western representatives charged with public diplomacy and regional engagement must resist the urge to decouple normative from geopolitical issues. If the West were to reduce its support for liberal norms and a rule-based international order for the sake of political expediency, it would only hasten the erosion of its own normative standing and emphasize that we are now in a world of competitive patronage dynamics where the highest bidder wins. Instead, the onset of multipolarity, when it truly emerges, should be embraced with a clear sense of liberal democracy's purpose and unique standing in the universe of competing norms and counternorms. Without confidence in its own values, the West not only will continue to lose its global appeal but also will lose itself.

NOTES

A version of this essay was previously published as Alexander Cooley, "Authoritarianism Goes Global: Countering Democratic Norms," *Journal of Democracy* 26, no. 3 (July 2015): 49–64.

1. Larry Diamond, "Facing Up to the Democratic Recession," *Journal of Democracy* 26, no. 1 (2015): 141–155; Steven Levitsky and Lucan Ahmad Way, "The Myth of the Democratic Recession," *Journal of Democracy* 26, no. 1 (2015): 45–58.

2. See Kim Lane Scheppele, "Law in a Time of Emergency: States of Exception and the Temptations of 9/11," *University of Pennsylvania Journal of Constitutional Law* 6 (2004): 1001–1008; and Scheppele, "The Migration of Anti-Constitutional Ideas: The Post-9/11 Globalization of Public Law and the International State of Emergency," in *The Migration of Constitutional Ideas*, ed. Sujit Choudhry (New York: Cambridge University Press, 2006).

3. Gavin Sullivan and Ben Hayes, *Blacklisted: Targeted Sanctions, Preemptive Security and Fundamental Rights*, European Center for Constitutional and Human Rights, December 2010, https://www.ecchr.eu/fileadmin/Publikationen/Blacklisted .pdf.

4. Alexander Cooley, *Great Games, Local Rules: The New Great Power Contest in Central Asia* (New York: Oxford University Press, 2012), chap. 6.

5. Fair Trials International, *Strengthening Respect for Human Rights, Strengthening INTERPOL*, November 2013, https://www.fairtrials.org/wp-content/uploads /Strengthening-respect-for-human-rights-strengthening-INTERPOL4.pdf.

6. Andrei Soldatov and Irina Borogan, *The Red Web: The Struggle Between Russia's Digital Dictators and the New Online Revolutionaries* (New York: Public Affairs, 2015).

7. Thomas Ambrosio, "Catching the 'Shanghai Spirit': How the Shanghai Cooperation Organization Promotes Authoritarian Norms in Central Asia," *Europe–Asia Studies* 60 (2008): 1321–1344.

8. David Lewis, "Who's Socialising Whom? Regional Organisations and Contested Norms in Central Asia," *Europe–Asia Studies* 64 (2012): 1219–1237.

9. Alexander Lukin, "Eurasian Integration and the Clash of Values," *Survival* 56 (2014): 43–60.

10. See United Nations, "Resolution 21/3: Promoting Human Rights and Fundamental Freedoms through a Better Understanding of Traditional Values of Humankind: Best Practices," in *Report of the Human Rights Council*, A/67/53/Add.1 (September 10–28 and November 5, 2012), 18–19. https://www.ohchr.org/Documents /HRBodies/HRCouncil/A-67-53-Add-1_en.pdf.

11. See European Union, Permanent Delegation to the United Nations and Other International Organizations in Geneva, "Contribution of the European Union: Traditional Values," February 15, 2013, www.ohchr.org/Documents/Issues/HRValues /EU.pdf.

12. Casey Michel, "How Russia Became the Leader of the Global Christian Right," *Politico*, February 9, 2017.

13. Margaret E. Keck and Kathryn Sikkink, *Activists beyond Borders: Advocacy Networks in International Politics* (Ithaca, NY: Cornell University Press, 1998).

14. Thomas Carothers and Saskia Brechenmacher, *Closing Space: Democracy and Human Rights Support Under Fire* (Washington, DC: Carnegie Endowment, 2014).

15. Darin Christensen and Jeremy M. Weinstein, "Defunding Dissent: Restrictions on Aid to NGOs," *Journal of Democracy* 24 (2013): 77–91.

16. Kendra Dupuy, James Ron, and Aseem Prakash, "Stop Meddling in My Country!: Governments' Restrictions on Foreign Aid to Non-governmental Organizations," November 23, 2014, https://ssrn.com/abstract=2529620.

17. Beth A. Simmons, *Mobilizing for Human Rights: International Law in Domestic Politics* (Cambridge: Cambridge University Press, 2009).

18. Human Rights Watch, "Russia: Government vs. Rights Groups," June 18, 2018, https://www.hrw.org/russia-government-against-rights-groups-battle-chronicle.

19. Kendra Dupuy, James Ron, and Aseem Prakash, "Who Survived? Ethiopia's Regulatory Crackdown on Foreign-Funded NGOs," *Review of International Political Economy* 22 (2015): 419–456.

20. Christopher Walker and Alexander Cooley, "Vote of the Living Dead," *Foreign Policy*, October 31, 2013.

21. Judith Kelley, "The More the Merrier? The Effects of Having Multiple International Election Monitoring Organizations," *Perspectives on Politics* 7 (2009): 59–64.

22. Jon Pevehouse, *Democracy from Above: Regional Organizations and Democratization* (Cambridge: Cambridge University Press, 2005).

23. See Amitav Acharya, "How Ideas Spread: Whose Norms Matter? Norm Localization and Institutional Change in Asian Regionalism," *International Organization* 58 (2004): 239–275; and Acharya, "Norm Subsidiarity and Regional Orders: Sovereignty, Regionalism, and Rule-Making in the Third World," *International Studies Quarterly* 55 (2011): 95–123.

24. Chris Sabatini, "Meaningless Multilateralism," *Foreign Affairs*, August 8, 2014.

25. Alexander Cooley, "The League of Authoritarian Gentlemen," *Foreign Policy*, January 30, 2013, https://foreignpolicy.com/2013/01/30/the-league-of-authoritarian -gentlemen.

26. Human Rights in China, "Counter-Terrorism and Human Rights: The Impact of the Shanghai Cooperation Organization," March 2011; and Human Rights Watch, "GCC: Treaty Imperils Rights," April 27, 2014, www.hrw.org/news/2014/04/26/gcc -joint-security-agreement-imperils-rights.

27. Madawi Al-Rasheed, "Kuwaiti Activists Targeted Under GCC Security Pact," *Al-Monitor*, March 20, 2015, http://www.al-monitor.com/pulse/originals/2015/03 /saudi-gcc-security-dissident-activism-detention-opposition.html#.

28. Sabatini, "Meaningless Multilateralism."

29. Judith Kelley, "Watching the Watchmen: The Role of Election Observers in Africa," *Think Africa Press*, May 21, 2013.

30. Sam Jones, "Robert Mugabe Assumes African Union Helm with Familiar Battle Cry," *Guardian*, January 30, 2015.

31. Emrulla Usru, "Turkey Debates the SCO as an Alternative to the EU," *European Dialogue*, February 8, 2013.

32. See Margaret Myers, "Chinese Lending to LAC in 2014: Key Findings," blog post, *China and Latin America*, February 27, 2015, http://chinaandlatinamerica.com /2015/02/27/chinese-lending-to-lac-in-2014-key-findings; Yun Sun, "China's Aid to Africa: Monster or Messiah?," Brookings Institution, February 2014; and Charles Wolf Jr., Xiao Wang, and Eric Warner, *China's Foreign Aid and Government-Sponsored Investment Activities: Scale, Content, Destinations, and Implications* (Santa Monica, CA: RAND, 2013).

33. David Lewis, "The Failure of a Liberal Peace: Sri Lanka's Counter-insurgency in Global Perspective," *Conflict, Security and Development* 10 (2010): 647–671.

34. Human Rights Watch, "Russia."

35. Anne Nelson, *CCTV's International Expansion: China's Grand Strategy for Media?* (Washington, DC: Center for International Media Assistance, 2013).

36. Peter Pomerantsev and Michael Weiss, *The Menace of Unreality: How the Kremlin Weaponizes Information, Culture, and Money* (New York: Institute of Modern Russia, 2014).

37. Ann E. Towns, *Women and States: Norms and Hierarchies in International Society* (New York: Cambridge University Press, 2010).

Interactive Global Jurisprudence | **PART IV**

New York Times Co. v. Sullivan   **FIFTEEN**

HAWLEY JOHNSON

The U.S. Supreme Court case of *New York Times Co. v. Sullivan* was more than a landmark case. It set a new constitutional privilege for the protection of freedom of expression and had a significant influence on free speech standards in national and regional courts globally. Legal scholar David Partlett describes *Sullivan* as a normative beacon for American ideals and values, "turn[ing] on the assumption that free speech, unshackled from other norms like privacy and community precepts, would further democratic values, drive us to truth or make us better citizens."[1] *Sullivan*'s radical prioritizing of the right to freedom of the press, over the right to reputation, privacy, and dignity, is as controversial as it is influential. The jurisprudential recognition that a free press is "critical" to enable public oversight of elected officials and is at the heart of a functioning democracy, self-development, and the foundation of a great society would challenge other jurisdictions to plot their standards on the legal continuum, with *Sullivan*'s "actual malice" doctrine marking the most liberal extreme.

This chapter surveys seventy-seven court decisions from around the world that cite *Sullivan*, to demonstrate how its key principles and the actual malice doctrine have been interpreted by other jurisdictions, and where it has acted as a liberalizing force to expand protections of political speech by the press. This is by no means an exhaustive list but a comprehensive selection of some of the most important and representative rulings from civil (twenty-nine) and common law (forty-eight) jurisdictions. However, the impact of *Sullivan* is far greater than can be proved by direct citations. The language of *Sullivan*—specific terms and turns of phrase like "actual malice," "reckless disregard for the truth," and "breathing space," to name a few—are now deeply embedded in the lexicon of international law, invoking the spirit of the ruling, even when the case is not directly mentioned.

BACKGROUND

In 1960, L. B. Sullivan, a police commissioner in Montgomery, Alabama, brought the case in response to a paid advertisement in the *New York Times*, which claimed that public officials throughout the southern states were colluding to derail the civil rights movement and had wrongly arrested Dr. Martin Luther King Jr. and his supporters on various occasions. The ad was paid for by the Committee to Defend Martin Luther King and the Struggle for Freedom in the South and included signatures of one hundred prominent Americans in support of Dr. King. Fewer than four hundred copies of the paper were sold in Alabama.

Although Mr. Sullivan was not mentioned by name or identifying characteristics, he claimed that the comments about the Montgomery police implicated him and that there were factual inaccuracies that harmed his reputation. The Alabama Supreme Court affirmed a lower court verdict that awarded Sullivan $500,000 in damages, which the *New York Times* appealed to the United States Supreme Court.

The Supreme Court recognized that this was no ordinary libel suit and that the established common law defense of fair comment would not have protected the *New York Times* from the errors in the advertisement. In an unprecedented move, the court extended constitutional protections to alleged libel by invoking the First and Fourteenth Amendments to prohibit elected officials from recovering damages for false statements made regarding their official conduct, unless it could be proven with clear and convincing evidence that the statements were made with "actual malice," defined as "knowledge of its falsity or with reckless disregard of whether it was true or false."[2]

Moreover, this created a fault standard, different from the common law understanding of malice as ill will or spite. The justices made that leap beyond common law libel because they viewed the substance of the case as addressing government suppression of speech on matters of significant public interest, or, in this case, attempts by public officials to silence criticism of their policies and practices related to the civil rights movement.[3]

For the purposes of this global analysis, the legacy of *Sullivan* is broken down into two widely supported principles and the more narrowly endorsed actual malice doctrine.

PRINCIPLES

1. *Constitutional democracy requires tolerance of criticism of public officials.* Justice William J. Brennan Jr. famously wrote, "We consider this case against the background of a profound national commitment to the principle that debate on public issues should be uninhibited, robust and wide open, and that it may well include vehement, caustic, and sometimes unpleasantly sharp attacks on government and public officials."[4] This effectively broadened the scope of the common law defense of fair comment to protect speech about the official conduct of public officials. Nani Jansen Reventlow and Jonathan McCully, in chapter 3 of this volume, state that this principle, the right to hold and disseminate political *opinions*, as distinct from *fact*, has been largely adopted on the international level and is now slowly being adopted on the national level, as evidenced by the cases in this chapter.

2. *Erroneous statements made in the public interest must be protected to prevent chilling effect.* The court ruled that erroneous statements are inevitable in free debate and that it must be protected if the freedoms of expression are to have the "breathing space" that they "need ... to survive."[5] In the words of Frederick Schauer, possible falsity is protected because "it is the only way to protect truth from self-censorship."[6] This is potentially the most contentious protection to emerge from *Sullivan*, with many jurisdictions finding the allowance of false statements of fact to be a slippery slope toward disinformation. The court also recognized this concern and clarified that the spreading of known falsities has no social value and therefore no constitutional protections.

DOCTRINE: ACTUAL MALICE DOCTRINE

This federal rule set a very high bar for public officials to bring libel suits against the press and "implicitly, it subjected all action for defamation to constitutional scrutiny."[7] The court further established that the burden of proof should fall on the plaintiff, because otherwise it could create a chilling effect where "would-be critics of official conduct may be deterred from voicing their criticism, even though it is believed to be true and even though it is in fact true, because of doubt whether it can be proved in court or fear of the expense of having to do so."[8] No longer were allegedly defamatory statements presumed to be false unless the defendant could prove otherwise.

Due to the uniquely broad protections granted by the ruling, *Sullivan* has rarely been adopted wholesale by other jurisdictions and has often inspired intense scrutiny by other courts considering its merits. One of the oft-cited perilous social costs is that the actual malice doctrine protects the dissemination of falsehoods, either as fact or as personal opinion, which can distort public opinion and weaken confidence in public institutions. In 1991, well before our era of "fake news," First Amendment scholar Lee C. Bollinger presciently wrote that the media can "distort knowledge of public issues not just by omission but also through active misrepresentation and lies."[9] This level of freedom could also lead to a loss of credibility of the press if it is not held accountable for its accuracy and truth.[10] Bollinger warns that "in many cases [the U.S. Supreme Court] seems to have gone out of its way—to the brink of misrepresentation—to ignore the risk that the press can become a threat to democracy rather than its servant."[11]

ENDORSEMENT OF THE ACTUAL MALICE DOCTRINE

The actual malice doctrine has been endorsed by some courts in Latin American, Europe, and Asia. Though there is evidence that it is slowly being integrated into national case law in some jurisdictions, it has not become truly settled law in any of the countries surveyed.

India has been one of the foremost supporters, with the Supreme Court of India employing the actual malice standard in a seminal 1994 ruling, *Rajagopal v. State of Tamil Nadu*. The Madras High Court began its July 20, 2009 opinion in *A. Raja v. P. Srinivasan* with a lengthy quote from Sullivan, to "set the tone for a decision in this case," finding that "the Government, local authority and other organs and institutions exercising governmental power . . . cannot maintain a suit for damages for defaming them." The court further maintained that according to an independent rule relating to public figures, the remedy of action for damages is simply not available with respect to their acts and conduct relevant to the discharge of their official duties. This is so even where the publication is based upon facts and statements which are not true, unless the official establishes that the publication was made (by the defendant) with reckless disregard for truth. In such a case, it would be enough for the defendant (member of the press or media) to prove that he acted after a reasonable verification of the facts; it is not necessary for him to prove that what he has written is true.[12]

The Bombay High Court, in *National Stock Exchange of India v. Moneywise Media Pvt. Ltd. and 2 Ors* (2015) also found that the plaintiffs did not meet the actual malice standard, having demonstrated neither "intentional falsehood" nor "a failure to attempt a verification." The Supreme Court again cited *Sullivan* in *Shreya Singhal v. Union of India* (2015), in reference to the potential chilling effect of overly broad restrictions on freedom of speech.

Argentina was an early adopter of the actual malice doctrine and has expanded on its principles, while localizing the ruling to account for the country's unique circumstances and need to balance freedom of expression in the public interest with the right to honor and dignity.[13] Beginning in 1987, the Argentina Supreme Court cited *Sullivan* in *Costa, Hector R. v. Municipalidad de La Capital y Otros* (1987) to distinguish between private individuals and public figures and to establish the principle of responsible journalism.[14] In a series of important cases—the Vargo case (1991), the case of Morales Sola (1996), and the case of Pandolfi (1997)—the court slowly adopted the actual malice doctrine. In 2008, in *Jose Angel Patito v. Diario La Nacion*, the court rejected the presumption of falsehood and ruled that the plaintiff must prove actual malice on the part of the news organization, with clear and convincing evidence. Since it could not be proven in that case, the court found that "intolerance of error would lead to self-censorship, depriving the citizenry of the crucial information necessary for making decisions about their representatives."[15]

This standard was again upheld in *Di Salvo, Miguel Ángel v. Diario La Mañana on daños y perjuicios* (2010)[16] and in *Dahlgren v. Editorial El Chaco* (2010), where the court protected "breathing room" for "erroneous statements," concluding, "This Court ratifies the doctrine that arises from applying the jurisprudential standards of the United States Supreme Court in the case *New York Times v. Sullivan* (376 U.S. 254) and that results from the constitutional parameters that govern the scrutiny of demonstrations on matters of public interest."[17] Legal scholar Kyu Ho Youm points out that Argentina applies the doctrine equally in civil and criminal contexts and has in practice expanded on the doctrine by requiring libel plaintiffs to prove both malintent and knowledge of falsity. Argentinian courts have further upheld a broad understanding of who is a public figure, and it established the "Campillay doctrine," which incorporated the American neutral reporting privilege to provide even greater protection for the news media than was provided by the actual malice doctrine.[18]

Courts in Mexico, Panama, and Uruguay have also upheld the *Sullivan* doctrine in various rulings. The Mexican Supreme Court of Justice cited the potential chilling effect of the presumption of falsity in Direct *Amparo* Appeal 2044-2008, June 17, 2009,[19] and in *Former Governor of the State of Aguascalientes v. General Director of the Newspaper "Tribuna Libre la Voz del Pueblo"* (2014). Similarly, the 17th Criminal Circuit Court of the First Circuit in Panama acquitted three journalists of defamation for offending the honor of an official of the Panama national police force, finding that the journalists "did not act with actual malice, as there is no indication of a reckless disregard for the truth."[20] In June 2010, the Criminal Appeals Court of Uruguay overturned a conviction of the managing director of the weekly *Tres Puntos* in relation to two articles about police corruption, finding that the plaintiff failed to provide sufficient evidence to prove any actual malice or intent to violate privacy on behalf of the defendant.[21]

Youm has written extensively about Sullivan's influence in Asia, including how Taiwan first applied the *Sullivan* doctrine in criminal defamation, and later expanded it to civil cases (Supreme Court 93 Shang Tzi 851 Civil Judgment, April 29, 2004). In the seminal 1997 case *Liu Tai-ying v. Wang Shu-yuan*, he explains, the High Court of Taiwan upheld a District Court of Taipei ruling, which found that American and Taiwan journalists who had produced an investigative report of significant public interest, on U.S. influence peddling in Taiwan, had not acted with malice but had adequately verified the facts before publication.[22] In a significant move, in 2009, to expand press freedom in Korea, and diverting from previous case law, the Seoul Central District Court held that government agencies cannot bring libel claims against individuals without proof of actual malice and that the state has the burden of proof—but it is not yet clear if this will be adopted by higher courts.[23]

In Europe, the Federation of Bosnia-Herzegovina applied the actual malice standard to both public and private figures in its defamation statute, and used nearly the Brennan Court's wording to hold liable those who disseminated falsehoods while knowing that an "expression was false or acted in reckless disregard for its veracity."[24]

On the regional level, the Inter-American Commission and the Special Rapporteur for Freedom of Expression of the Inter-American Commission on Human Rights have argued for inclusion of the actual malice standard under Article 13 of the American Convention on Human Rights.[25] The special rapporteur recommended that Organization of American States member states adopt an actual malice standard in their defamation laws, in 1997, and issued a declaration of principles in 2000, which stated that public figures, or private persons who become voluntarily involved in public matters, should never be allowed to bring criminal defamation actions, and that when bringing a civil suit, the plaintiff must prove the speaker was aware of the falsity, acted with negligence and disregard for truth or falsity, and/or acted with an intent to inflict harm.[26] In a 2017 report, Special Rapporteur Edison Lanza advocated for the application of the actual malice standard in national civil defamation proceedings involving statements about public officials, which were made in the public interest in accordance with inter-American principles of proportionality and reasonableness.[27]

REJECTION OF THE ACTUAL MALICE DOCTRINE

Many jurisdictions have rejected the actual malice doctrine, for various reasons, ranging from culture (such as *Jeyaretnam Joshua Benjamin v. Lee Kuan Yew* in Singapore and *Hill v. Church of Scientology* in Canada), to the type of legal system they have, to the balancing of constitutional protections for freedom of speech with reputation and human dignity (*Khumalo and Others v. Holomisa* in South Africa).[28]

Jurisdictions such as Taiwan and Singapore find that "persons holding public office or politicians . . . are equally entitled to have their reputations protected as those of any other persons."[29] Yet, even as they reject it, courts in these countries still engage with the actual malice doctrine as a reference point when developing their own approach, such as in Spain's neutral reporting doctrine (*Antena 3 v. Extraconfidencial, S.L.*, STS 2957/2015), which protects accurate and disinterested reporting. Commonwealth courts have tended to expand the common law defenses of fair comment or qualified privilege, such as the UK ten-point Reynolds duty-interest test, to balance the rights based on the context on a case-by-case basis; the Australian "reasonableness" standard (*Lange v. Australian Broadcasting Corporation* (1997) 189 CLR 520), which extends a very narrowed privilege for speech about "what is necessary for the effective operation of that system of representation and responsible government provided for by the constitution"; and the New Zealand privilege for political speech about parliamentarians, provided there is no evidence of malice.[30] The Supreme Court of Canada issued a landmark rejection of *Sullivan* in *Hill v. Church of Scientology* (1995), arguing that the burden of proof should remain on those who make the statements. The court noted that *Sullivan* prevents effective remedies to damaged reputations and that only true statements of fact contribute to meaningful public debate.[31]

EVOLVING SUPPORT

Courts in a range of jurisdictions have either partially endorsed the actual malice doctrine or have referenced it positively to justify a rebalancing of the right to freedom of the press over the right to reputation, which may signify a slow integration of the standard into national and regional case law—but time will tell. Hungary is one example of a European civil law jurisdiction making strides in adopting a modified version of the *Sullivan* doctrine in both civil and criminal law, protecting opinions and statements of fact, insofar as no actual malice can be proved by the defendant, rather than by the plaintiff.[32]

The actual malice doctrine has been upheld by the Supreme Court of the Philippines in civil and criminal defamation proceedings (including *Babst v. National Intelligence Board, Borjal v. Court of Appeals*, and *Ciriaco "Boy" Guingguing v. the Honorable Court of Appeals*), recognizing the role of a free press in monitoring public officials and the inevitability of errors in public debate, but it has yet to be fully adopted.[33] In criminal complaints, for instance, the burden of proof still falls on the defendant to prove their honest intent rather than on the plaintiff to prove malice under the "presumed malice rule." In 2014, two Supreme Court of the Philippines justices, Antonio Carpio and Arturo Brion, wrote separate opinions on the Cybercrime Prevention Act, citing *Sullivan* to argue shifting the burden in cases involving public officials. Carpio found the "presumed malice rule" to be a "gross constitutional anomaly" and that public officials should be legally required to provide evidence that the statement was false and made with "reckless disregard" for its truth or falsity.[34]

In an unprecedented decision in 2015, the High Court of Zambia applied the actual malice standard in *Sondashi v. Daily Nation*[35] to dismiss a defamation claim, finding criticism of public officials to be part of robust political debate so long as that criticism isn't made with actual malice. It was a significant turnaround from *Mmembe and Another v. People* (1996), where the court found *Sullivan* protections could lead to the wholesale character assassinations of public figures.

Two important rulings from the Supreme Court of Canada, *Grant v. Torstar* (2009) and *Crooks v. Newton* (2011), recognized the need for "incremental adjustments" in defamation law to rebalance Canadian common law in favor of freedom of expression, in light of technological developments. In *Grant v. Torstar* (2009), the court established the "responsible communication" defense to the tort of defamation to reduce the risk of "chilling" expression. This went beyond *Sullivan*, ruling that this defense could be applied to all communications, not just communications by journalists, and it expanded the definition of public interest: "Public interest is not confined to publications on government and political matters, as it is in Australia and New Zealand. Nor is it necessary that the plaintiff be a "public figure," as in the American jurisprudence since *Sullivan*."[36]

In 2013, the United Kingdom passed the Defamation Act, which abolished the common law Reynolds defense and, as legal scholar Mark Tushnet notes, "replaced it with a 'public interest' defense, insulating publishers from liability for all statements, including false ones, if the statement was on a matter of public interest" and the publisher "reasonably believed that publishing the statement . . . was in the public interest." Tushnet observes that, on the one hand, this is a weaker standard than *Sullivan*, as it puts the burden on the publisher to prove the defense, but on the other hand, it provides broader protections to publishers for making false statements of facts on matters of public interest, even in situations where the publisher may have known the facts to be false. By establishing a higher threshold of "serious harm," it aimed to prevent unnecessary claims. Tushnet puts the irony this way: "The United Kingdom thus appears to have moved from a judicially developed law that rejected *New York Times v. Sullivan* because it was too generous to publishers to a legislatively enacted statute that rejects *New York Times v. Sullivan* because it is not generous enough to publishers."[37]

REGIONAL COURTS

The Inter-American Court of Human Rights, the European Court of Human Rights, and the Economic Community of West African States (ECOWAS) Community Court of Justice have each engaged with Sullivan to different extents. The Inter-American Court of Human Rights effectively applied the actual malice standard but failed to use the term in *Tristan Donoso v. Panama* (2009), finding that a journalist had not acted with knowledge of falsity in making claims about a public figure who must tolerate a high degree of scrutiny. Legal scholar Edward Carter believes this could be a positive sign that the court is beginning to integrate the standard into its own case law.[38]

On February 13, 2018, the ECOWAS court handed down the landmark decision *Federation of African Journalists v. the Republic of The Gambia*, which quoted *Sullivan* to affirm that an "erroneous statement is inevitable in free debate, and that it must be protected if the freedoms of expression are to have the 'breathing space' that they need . . . to survive," and that placing the burden of proving the truth of a reported statement on the journalist has a chilling effect, deterring criticisms of official conduct.[39] Thus, while recognizing key principles from the ruling, the court did not clearly adopt the doctrine.

The European Court of Human Rights has recognized *Sullivan*'s influence on the development of the principle of responsible journalism (as in *Pentikäinen v. Finland*, 2015), but it has repeatedly rejected the actual malice doctrine (as in *Kasabova v. Bulgaria*, 2011, and *McVicar v. the UK*, 2002), finding "it is not, in principle, incompatible with Article 10 to place on the defendant in libel proceedings the burden of proving to the civil standard the truth of defamatory statements."[40]

CONCLUSION

A variety of headwinds have shaped how *Sullivan* has traveled, including historical, cultural, and political differences. Just as *Sullivan* is very much a representation of the values, history, and political system of the United States, each court will weigh the *Sullivan* standards and principles against its prevailing social or legal norms. Jurisdictions may not accept *Sullivan* in it entirety, but its key principles have navigated their way into the case law. Above all, *Sullivan* created an international reference point for other jurisdictions to use to define their national values as they relate to the role of the press in a democratic society, the right to reputation, the scope of political speech and the boundaries to set for its protection, and how they should properly balance political speech with reputational rights.

NOTES

1. David Partlett, "*New York Times v. Sullivan* at 50 Years: Defamation in Separate Orbits," in *Comparative Defamation and Privacy Law*, ed. Andrew Kenyon (Cambridge: Cambridge University Press, 2016), 60.
2. New York Times Co. v. Sullivan, 376 U.S. 254 (1964), 265–292. See also Partlett, 59.
3. Elena Kagan, "A Libel Story: *Sullivan* Then and Now (reviewing Anthony Lewis, *Make No Law: The Sullivan Case and the First Amendment* (1991))," *Law and Inquiry* 18, no. 1 (1993): 197–217, at 204.
4. *Sullivan*, 271. This principle was later extended in subsequent case law to cover public figures, such as celebrities and others who are well known in the public sphere. Gertz v. Robert Welch, Inc. 418 U.S. 323, 347 (1974).
5. *Sullivan*, 272.

6. Frederick Schauer, "Social Foundations of the Law of Defamation: A Comparative Analysis," *Journal of Media Law and Practice* 1, no. 1 (1980): 11.

7. Robert D. Sack, *Sack on Defamation: Libel, Slander, and Related Problems*, 4th ed. (New York: Practising Law Institute, May 1, 2010), 1–7.

8. Sack, *Sack on Defamation,* 279–280.

9. Lee C. Bollinger, *Images of a Free Press* (Chicago: University of Chicago Press, 1991), 26.

10. András Koltay, "Around the World with *Sullivan*: The *New York Times v. Sullivan* Rule and Its Universal Applicability," *Iustum Aequum Salutare* 2, no. 3–4 (2006): 6.

11. Bollinger, *Images of a Free Press,* 34.

12. A. Raja v. P. Srinivasan, application no. 2919 of 2009, July 20, 2009, para. 1. https://indiankanoon.org/doc/114007/.

13. Susana N. Vittadini Andres, "US Actual Malice Doctrine in Argentine Constitutional Law," *Tamkang Journal of International Affairs* (1991).

14. Kyu Ho Youm, "The "Actual Malice of *New York Times Co. v. Sullivan*: A Free Speech Touchstone in a Global Century," in "New York Times v. Sullivan at 50," special issue, *Communication Law and Policy* 19, no. 2 (2014): 185–210. See also Vittadini Andres, "US Actual Malice Doctrine."

15. Inter-American Commission on Human Rights (IACHR), *National Jurisprudence on Freedom of Expression and Access to Information*, Office of the Special Rapporteur for Freedom of Expression, OEA/Ser.L/V/II.147 CIDH/RELE/INF.10/13, March 5, 2013, para. 108.

16. IACHR, *National Jurisprudence*, para. 108.

17. Dahlgren v. Editorial Chaco, November 9, 2010, Fallos 333.2079, p. 32.

18. Youm, "Actual Malice," 5.

19. IACHR, *National Jurisprudence*, para. 109.

20. IACHR, *National Jurisprudence*, para. 112; Republic of Panama, 17th Criminal Circuit Court of the First Circuit, Judgment of Acquittal no. 13 of July 17, 2012. Panama has not adopted actual malice as a rule, but its penal code does provide for a defense that goes beyond protecting mere political speech. Article 198 of the Criminal Code states, "The discussions, critiques, and opinions about official acts or omissions of public servants, related to the exercise of their functions and also about literary, artistic, historic, scientific, or professional critique will not be a 'crime against honor.'" Committee to Protect Journalists, "Criminal Defamation Laws in Central America," https://cpj.org/reports/2016/03/central-america.php.

21. IACHR, *National Jurisprudence*, para. 111.

22. Youm, "Actual Malice," 7.

23. Youm, "Actual Malice," 8.

24. Youm, "Actual Malice," 8.

25. Edward Carter, "Actual Malice in the Inter-American Court of Human Rights," *Communication Law and Policy* 18, no. 4 (2013): 395, 420.

26. Carter, "Actual Malice," 405; IACHR, *National Jurisprudence*, 41–44.

27. Edison Lanza, *Annual Report of the Inter-American Commission on Human Rights 2017*, OEA/Ser.L/V/II. Doc. 210/17, December 31, 2017, 416.

28. High Court of Singapore, Jeyaretnam Joshua Benjamin v. Lee Kuan Yew, [1992] 2 SLR 310; Supreme Court of Canada, Hill v. Church of Scientology, [1995] 2 S.C.R. 1130; Constitutional Court of South Africa, Khumalo and Others v. Holomisa, 2002 (5) SA 401 (CC).

29. Benjamin v. Lee Kuan Yew, para. 62.

30. Koltay, "Around the World with *Sullivan*," 110–111.

31. Hill v. Church of Scientology, paras. 135–137.

32. Constitutional Court of Hungary, Decision 36/1994, on Defamation of Public Officials and Politicians, June 24, 1994. See Youm, "Actual Malice," 5.

33. Supreme Court of the Philippines, Babst et al. v. National Intelligence Board et al., 132 SCRA 316,330 (1984); Borjal v. Court of Appeals, 301 SCRA (1999); Ciriaco "Boy" Guingguing v. the Honorable Court of Appeals, G.R. no. 128959 (2005). See also Youm, "Actual Malice," 4.

34. Buena Bernal, "Shift Burden in Libel Cases to Public Officials, Say 2 Justices," *Rappler*, February 22, 2014, https://www.rappler.com/nation/51269-sc-carpio-brion-libel-cybercrime-law.

35. Research contributed by Marietta Cauchi.

36. Columbia University, Global Freedom of Expression, "Grant v. Torstar," https://globalfreedomofexpression.columbia.edu/cases/grant-v-torstar/.

37. Mark Tushnet, "*New York Times v. Sullivan* Around the World," *Alabama Law Review* 66, no. 2 (2014): 355–356.

38. Carter, "Actual Malice," 422.

39. Economic Community of West African States (ECOWAS) Community Court of Justice, *Federation of African Journalists v. the Republic of The Gambia*, ECW/CCJ/JUD/04/18 (2018), 43–44.

40. European Court of Human Rights, Kasabova v. Bulgaria, application no. 22385/03 (2011), para 58. http://hudoc.echr.coe.int/eng?i=001-104539.

Handyside v. the United Kingdom | SIXTEEN

AMALIE BANG

The judgment in *Handyside v. the United Kingdom* (1976) set an important standard for the protection of freedom of expression. The case concerned the publication of the *Little Red Schoolbook*, a book originally written by two Danish authors, which contained passages providing sexual education. Though the book had already been published and distributed in a number of countries, the British courts decided to seize it in the United Kingdom and prohibit its distribution. The argument for the seizure was the protection of morals. The European Court of Human Rights found that the seizure had not amounted to a violation of Article 10 of the European Convention on Human Rights. However, the case resulted in a landmark ruling, as the court firmly underlined the importance of freedom of expression in a democratic society.

The court elaborated on the concept of a margin of appreciation, "given both to the domestic legislator ('prescribed by law') and to the bodies, judicial amongst others, that are called upon to interpret and apply the laws in force." It noted that it is for the national authorities to make the initial assessment of the reality of the pressing social need implied by the notion of "necessity" in this context. The court also underlined that the domestic margin of appreciation goes hand in hand with European supervision. Though the court did not find a violation, it strongly emphasized that freedom of expression

> constitutes one of the essential foundations of [a democratic] society, one of the basic conditions for its progress and for the development of every person. Subject to paragraph 2 of Article 10, it is applicable not only to "information" or "ideas" that are favorably received or regarded as inoffensive or as a matter of indifference, but also to those that offend, shock or disturb the State or any sector of the population. Such are the demands of that pluralism, tolerance and broadmindedness without which there is no "democratic society." This means, amongst other things, that every "formality," "condition," "restriction," or "penalty" imposed in this sphere must be proportionate to the legitimate aim pursued.[1]

The *Handyside* ruling has been cited in a large number of cases all over the world because of the court's recognition of the importance of freedom of expression in a democratic society. The European Court itself, too, has frequently recalled *Handyside* in later rulings.[2]

The Inter-American Court of Human Rights has cited *Handyside* in a number of cases.[3] In *Herrera-Ulloa v. Costa Rica*, for instance, the court referred to *Handyside* when stating,

> Freedom of expression constitutes one of the essential pillars of democratic society and a fundamental condition for its progress and the personal development of each individual. This freedom should not only be guaranteed with regard to the dissemination of information and ideas that are received favorably or considered inoffensive or indifferent, but also with regard to those that offend, are unwelcome or shock the State or any sector of the population. Such are the requirements of pluralism, tolerance and the spirit of openness, without which no "democratic society" can exist. . . . This means that . . . any formality, condition, restriction or sanction imposed in that respect, should be proportionate to the legitimate end sought.[4]

The UN Human Rights Committee referred to *Handyside* in *Sergei Govsha, Viktor Syritsa and Viktor Mezyak v. Belarus*. It noted that the ban on the organization of peaceful assembly at stake in the case was not necessary in a democratic society, the cornerstone of which is free dissemination of information and ideas not necessarily favorably received by the government or the majority of the population.[5] The committee made a similar reference to *Handyside* in its views concerning the communication in *Irina Fedotova v. Russian Federation*.[6]

A large number of national courts all over the world have referred to *Handyside*.[7] In a March 30, 1989, ruling, the Supreme Court of India cited *Handyside* in *S. Rangarajan v. Janjivan*. The court quoted the European Court's dictum that "freedom of expression constitutes one of the essential foundations of [a democratic] society, one of the basic conditions for its progress and for the development of every person" in striking down a ban on a movie concerning caste and education rights in India. Also in 1989, the Supreme Court of Canada referred to *Handyside* in a case in which the court reasoned that there was a pressing and substantial government objective to protect children from manipulation by advertising. Therefore, a ban on children's advertising resulted in minimal impairment of freedom of expression.[8] The Supreme Court of Canada again referred to *Handyside*, in 1990, in a case concerning a high school teacher who was prosecuted for communicating in his classroom hateful sentiments against the Jewish community. The court found it justifiable that his freedom of expression had been limited, as it found the limitation reasonable in a democratic society, in order to protect target groups from hateful propaganda.[9] The court noted that "the European Court of Human Rights also upheld prosecution of a bookseller in Northern Ireland for distributing *The Little Red Schoolbook* . . . on the grounds that the prosecution was "for the protection of health or morals."

The Supreme Court of Hong Kong referred to *Handyside*, in 1994, when noting that "freedom of expression is also applicable to 'information' or 'ideas' that offend, shock or disturb."[10] The Australian High Court quoted *Handyside* in its ruling in *Leask v. Commonwealth* (November 5, 1996) when finding that, in the view of the European Court of Human Rights, proportionality has been interpreted as meaning that a restriction must be "proportionate to the legitimate aim pursued." In 2000, the Supreme Court of Sri Lanka referred to *Handyside* when stating that freedom of expression constitutes one of the essential foundations of a democratic society.[11]

The Supreme Court of Zimbabwe made a similar reference to *Handyside* in a May 2000 judgment. The court quoted the European Court's adage that freedom of expression is applicable "not only to 'information' or 'ideas' that are favorably received or regarded as inoffensive or as a matter of indifference, but also to those that offend, shock or disturb."[12] South Africa's Supreme Court of Appeal referenced *Handyside* in the case *National Media Ltd. and Others v. Bogoshi*, quoting the passage that "freedom of expression constitutes one of the essential foundations of a democratic society."[13] The High Court of South Africa, in a different case from 2003, referred to *Handyside* when noting that the European Court of Human Rights allows member states a margin of appreciation.[14]

In 2006, the Constitutional Court of Guatemala referred to *Handyside* when finding that articles criminalizing threats, defamation, and insult of public officials were unconstitutional and violated freedom of expression guarantees.[15] The Supreme Court of Brazil referred to *Handyside* in a ruling from 2009 when finding the Brazilian Press Act, issued in 1967, during the military dictatorship, to be incompatible with the Brazilian constitution of 1988.[16] In 2014, the Constitutional Court of Hungary referred to *Handyside* when acquitting a local politician of the criminal charges of defamation.[17] And the Constitutional Court of Turkey referred to *Handyside* in 2015 when finding that a columnist should not be convicted for insulting public officials.[18]

As these examples demonstrate, international and national courts have referred to and continue to refer to *Handyside*. Different citations have been used in different contexts. However, it remains clear that *Handyside* has had significant influence on the development of freedom of expression jurisprudence all over the world.

NOTES

1. European Court of Human Rights, Handyside v. the United Kingdom, application no. 549372, December 7, 1976, para. 48, 49.
2. See, for example, Von Hannover v. Germany (no. 2); Gough v. the United Kingdom; Animal Defenders International v. the United Kingdom; Dink v. Turkey; Lillo-Stenberg v. Norway; Pavel Ivanov v. Russia; Vural v. Turkey; Feret v. Belgium; Murphy v. Ireland; Haldimann v. Switzerland; The Sunday Times v. the United Kingdom; The Sunday Times v. the United Kingdom (no. 2); I.A. v. Turkey; Otto-Preminger-Institut v. Austria; Müller v. Switzerland; Gündüz v. Turkey; Karttunen v. Finland; Vejdeland and Others v. Sweden; Couderc v. France; Tusalp v. Turkey; M'Bala M'Bala v. France; Görmüş v. Turkey; Pinto Coelho v. Portugal (no. 2); Bédat v. Switzerland; Sousa Goucha v. Portugal; Cojocaru v. Romania; Lingens v. Austria; Mikkelsen and Christensen v. Denmark; Castells v. Spain; Dupuis v. France; Romanenko v. Russia; Stoll v. Switzerland; and Fressoz and Roire v. France.
3. See, for example, Velásquez Rodríguez v. Honduras, July 29, 1988; Godínez Cruz v. Honduras, January 20, 1989; Herrera-Ulloa v. Costa Rica, July 2, 2004; Suárez Peralta v. Ecuador, May 21, 2013; and Ivcher Bronstein v. Peru, February 6, 2001.
4. Inter-American Court of Human Rights, Herrera-Ulloa v. Costa Rica, July 2, 2004. A similar reference was made by the court in Ivcher Bronstein v. Peru, February 6, 2001; and Ricardo Canese v. Paraguay, August 31, 2004.

5. UN Human Rights Committee, Sergei Govsha, Viktor Syritsa, and Viktor Mezyak v. Belarus, Communication, no. 1790/2008, UN Doc. CCPR/C/105/D/1790/2008 (2012).

6. Irina Fedotova v. Russian Federation, Communication no. 1932/2010, UN Doc. CCPR/C/106/D/1932/2010 (2012).

7. The following cases are not an exhaustive compilation but only key examples of rulings referring to *Handyside*.

8. Supreme Court of Canada, Irwin Toy Ltd. v. Quebec, April 27, 1989. Columbia University, Global Freedom of Expression, "Irwin Toy Ltd. v. Quebec," https://globalfreedomofexpression.columbia.edu/cases/irwin-toy-ltd-v-quebec.

9. Supreme Court of Canada, R. v. Keegstra, December 13, 1990. Columbia University, Global Freedom of Expression, "R. v. Keegstra," https://globalfreedomofexpression.columbia.edu/cases/r-v-keegstra.

10. Supreme Court of Hong Kong, Re Luoi Wai Po, January 20, 1994, para. 71.

11. Supreme Court of Sri Lanka, Sunila Abeysekera v. Ariya Rubasinghe, Competent Authority and Others, May 15, 2000.

12. Supreme Court of Zimbabwe, Chavunduka v. Minister of Home Affairs, May 22, 2000.

13. Supreme Court of Appeal of South Africa, National Media Ltd. and Others v. Bogoshi (579/96), September 29, 1998.

14. High Court of South Africa, Cape of Good Hope Provincial Division, Victoria & Alfred Waterfront (PTY) Ltd. v. Police, December 23, 2003.

15. Constitutional Court of Guatemala, Action Challenging the Constitutionality of the Offense of Criminal Defamation in Guatemala, February 1, 2006. Columbia University, Global Freedom of Expression, "Action Challenging the Constitutionality of the Offense of Criminal Defamation in Guatemala," https://globalfreedomofexpression.columbia.edu/cases/action-challenging-constitutionality-offense-defamation-guatemala.

16. Supreme Court of Brazil, PDT v. President of Republic and National Congress, April 30, 2009. Columbia University, Global Freedom of Expression, "PDT v. President of Republic and National Congress," https://globalfreedomofexpression.columbia.edu/cases/pdt-v-president-of-republic-and-national-congress.

17. Constitutional Court of Hungary, Public Prosecutor v. Ottó Szalai, April 18, 2014. Columbia University, Global Freedom of Expression, "Public Prosecutor v. Ottó Szalai," https://globalfreedomofexpression.columbia.edu/cases/public-prosecutor-v-otto-szalai.

18. Constitutional Court of Turkey, Case of Bekir Coşkun, July 1, 2015. Columbia University, Global Freedom of Expression, "The Case of Bekir Coşkun," https://globalfreedomofexpression.columbia.edu/cases/the-case-of-bekir-coskun.

Claude Reyes et al. v. Chile   **SEVENTEEN**

A Global Trailblazer

SOFÍA JARAMILLO-OTOYA

In 2006, the Inter-American Court of Human Rights (IACtHR) decided the case *Claude Reyes et al. v. Chile*. This landmark case was prompted by Chile's refusal to provide members of an environmental organization with all the information they had requested from the Chilean Foreign Investment Committee regarding the potential environmental impact of a forestry exploitation project. The state authorities did not provide any reasons for withholding information from the public.

The IACtHR ruled that the "right to freedom of thought and expression includes the protection of the right to access state-held information" (para. 77). According to the court, the right to access information is an essential requisite for democracy, necessary for the formation of public opinion, participation in public administration, and control of the performance of public functions.

The decision identified key principles with regard to an access to information regime. These include the principle of maximum disclosure, according to which restrictions must be exceptional and meet the three-part test (para. 91), and the principle of universality, according to which individuals should be granted access to state-held information, without having to prove a personal or direct interest, and should be able to circulate the information.

The decision had an "extraordinary impact," by influencing the adoption of access to information (ATI) legislation throughout Latin America. It also became the key reference in subsequent national jurisprudence dealing with ATI, some of which is highlighted here. Civil society organizations played a key role in disseminating the decision regionally and internationally and in ensuring that it influenced legislative processes in Latin America and beyond.[1]

This chapter provides a short analysis of the journey toward the globalization of the *Claude Reyes* decision and the global judicial integration it has unleashed. This decision will be shown to constitute a pivotal step by the IACtHR toward the creation of a global norm on access to government-held information as a human right.[2] Lastly, the application of this decision by courts and legislative bodies around the world will be described, which should confirm some degree of global convergence.

RECOGNITION OF THE RIGHT OF ACCESS TO INFORMATION AS A HUMAN RIGHT

The recognition of access to information as a human right has progressively evolved within the framework of international human rights law. The inter-American human rights system played a fundamental role in this endeavor with the *Claude Reyes* decision.[3] Indeed, the decision is a pioneering ruling that marks the first time an international court recognized the right to access public information as a human right.

The court stated that "by expressly stipulating the right to 'seek' and 'receive' 'information,' Article 13 of the [American] Convention protects the right of all individuals to request access to State-held information, with the exceptions permitted by the restrictions established in the Convention. . . . In this way, the right to freedom of thought and expression includes the protection of the right to access State-held information, which also clearly includes the two dimensions, individual and social, of the right to freedom of thought and expression that must be guaranteed simultaneously by the State" (para. 77).

The IACtHR's recognition of ATI as a human right has provided courts in Latin America with legal tools to give content to guarantee and protect the right to access information in those jurisdictions that do not or did not have a specific ATI law at the time of ruling.

In Costa Rica, the Constitutional Chamber of the Supreme Court of Justice has developed a rich and varied jurisprudence to strengthen some constitutional provision on ATI, given that there is no specific law on ATI. In 2014, the chamber referenced *Claude Reyes* to emphasize that the right to information is a conventional and constitutional right that can only be exceptionally restricted and that it is not necessary to accredit a direct interest or involvement to request information.[4]

While the Colombian constitution has recognized ATI as a fundamental right since 1991, the institutional practice privileged opacity.[5] The Colombian Constitutional Court has had a long tradition of incorporating international standards. In at least five judgments before the enactment of the 2014 ATI law, the *Claude Reyes* decision was referenced to highlight the existence of a conventional and constitutional right to access information.[6]

In Argentina, before the enactment of the 2016 ATI law, the *Claude Reyes* decision influenced a 2012 ruling by the Argentine Supreme Court recognizing the right to information as an autonomous, constitutional right.[7] In Paraguay, the IACtHR decision allowed courts to give content to the right. For instance, in 2007, the Court of Liquidation and Judgment referred to *Claude Reyes* to strengthen the legal basis to recognize, for the first time, access to information as a human right.[8]

In some jurisdictions that already had specific laws on ATI, the IACtHR decision contributed to invigorate the discussions and protections of the right to information. The relationship between the *Claude Reyes* decision and the right to access information in Mexico has been a "reciprocal" one. As Catalina Botero-Marino explains in chapter 8 of the present volume, Mexican civil society and Mexican Judge García Ramírez—president of the IACtHR—were key to the *Claude Reyes* decision. In turn, the IACtHR decision has been important to advance the strengthening of the protection of the right to information in Mexico.[9]

In the Dominican Republic, the *Claude Reyes* decision was key to the implementation of the law on ATI that had been enacted in 2005 but left dormant. Specifically, it was used to reinvigorate the debate and recognize the right to information as a human right.[10] Jurisprudentially, the Constitutional Court granted access, in 2012, to information concerning the names and income of congressional advisors working for the House of Representatives. The court referenced *Reyes* to stress that ATI is a human right and that states have the obligation to guarantee it, and to highlight the importance of this right to the exercise of democratic control of the public administration.[11]

Outside Latin America, experts have repeatedly suggested that *Claude Reyes*, along with other factors, inspired the European Court to recognize access to information as a human right. The wording of Article 10 of the European Convention on Human Rights (ECHR) does not explicitly reference the right to "seek" information. Therefore, the European Court on Human Rights (ECtHR) was left to consider whether the right to information could be viewed as falling within the ECHR provision. In 2009, in *Társaság a Szabadságjogokért (TASZ) v. Hungary*, the ECHR made a "cautious" confirmation of the right to information as linked to the right to freedom of expression.[12]

In 2016, the ECtHR confirmed the 2009 ruling, in *Magyar Helsinki Bizott-ság v. Hungary*. While the ECtHR was "clearer and firmer" than ever before in the recognition of ATI as part of the right to freedom of expression, it did not acknowledge the right to information as a "fully fledged right" under Article 10.[13] According to the court, Article 10 does not include a *self-standing* right to information or a positive obligation on a state to disclose information. However, the state obligation may arise when an enforceable judicial order has imposed the disclosure of information, and in circumstances where ATI is "instrumental" for the individual's exercise of their right to freedom of expression, "and where its denial constitutes an interference with that right."[14] The ECtHR highlighted the *Claude Reyes* decision as the most "noteworthy" precedent concerning the recognition of a right to ATI.

MAXIMUM DISCLOSURE AND THE THREE-PART TEST

The recognition of ATI as a human right also implies that any restriction is subject to a limited system of exceptions. In the *Claude Reyes* decision, the court specified that state authorities must be governed by the principle of maximum disclosure. According to this principle, restrictions must be exceptional and meet the three-part test: they must be provided by law; they must pursue an objective permissible under the American Convention (to ensure respect for the rights of others, and to protect national security, public order, or public health or morals); and they must conform to the strict tests of necessity and proportionality.

Around the world, the Inter-American decision has been referenced to evaluate the legitimacy of restrictions that have been imposed on the right to information. For instance, with regard to the legality of restrictions, the Constitutional Chamber of the Supreme Court of Justice of El Salvador declared a section from the Regulation of the Law on Access to Public Information unconstitutional. This regulation, established via decree by the president, included grounds to categorize information as classified. The court cited the *Claude Reyes* decision to emphasize that all restrictions on ATI should only be established by a duly enacted law. The court reiterated that a *law* demands to be adopted by the legislature and promulgated by the executive.[15]

When deciding the constitutionality of the Anti-hawking Law of the State of Chiapas, the Supreme Court of Mexico referenced *Claude Reyes* to emphasize the importance of the maximum disclosure principle. The court considered that restrictions to ATI established by the Anti-hawking Law did not satisfy the requirements of the three-part test.[16] These principles were also echoed in the case *Director of Magazine Proceso v. Congress of Mexico*.[17]

In October 2013, the Supreme Court of Paraguay issued a decision in which it "internalized" the jurisprudence of *Claude Reyes*.[18] The Office of the Ombudsman brought an action before the Supreme Court due to the refusal of the city of San Lorenzo to disclose salary information on a number of public officials. While acknowledging that the right to access state-held information admits limitations, the court stated that the refusal of information in this case did not meet the conditions set forth by the IACtHR on the *Claude Reyes* decision. The court privileged the right to information over the right to privacy.[19] According to civil society, the court's 2013 decision generated the social and political conditions for the approval of the ATI law in 2014. Since then, *Claude Reyes* has inspired all the cases that have been decided so far.[20]

Argentina and Colombia also have referenced *Reyes* to analyze whether restrictions to freedom of information were legitimate.[21] In at least four cases, the IACtHR has analyzed the legitimacy of restrictions, citing the *Claude Reyes* precedent, including *Kimel v. Argentina*, *Usón Ramírez v. Venezuela*, *Omar Humberto Maldonado Vargas v. Chile*, and *Álvarez Ramos v. Venezuela*.[22]

For its part, the African Commission on Human and People's Rights, in *Egyptian Initiative for Personal Rights and Interights v. Egypt* (2011), referenced the *Claude Reyes* decision to emphasize that "the freedom of expression and to receive information is broadly conceived to include information of all types of knowledge including in political terms . . . and the Respondent State has an obligation to ensure that this information is accessible without impediment."[23]

UNIVERSAL CHARACTER OF THE RIGHT TO INFORMATION: NO NEED TO DEMONSTRATE A PARTICULAR INTEREST

The right to access information is a universal human right. Consequently, as established in the *Claude Reyes* decision, all individuals have the right to request access to information. The court further specified that individuals should be granted ATI without having to prove a personal or direct interest and that they should be able to disseminate acquired information.

In *Center for the Implementation of Public Policies Promoting Equity and Growth v. Ministry of Social Development*, the Argentine Supreme Court referenced *Claude Reyes* to recognize a broad legal standing for those wanting to exercise their right to access information, stating that information belongs to the public and not the state. In *Rubén H. Giustiniani v. Y.P.F.S.A.* (2015), the Argentine Supreme Court ruled that the person requesting information does not need to provide a motive or direct personal interest in their request, a position reiterated in *Fundación Poder Ciudadano v. National Chamber of Deputies*.[24] In 2014, the court of Appeals of Uruguay cited the IACtHR decision to emphasize that ATI is a human right, that it has a double dimension, that petitioners do not need to have a direct interest, and that any denial of information must be substantiated.[25]

When deciding on the constitutionality of the access to information law, the Constitutional Court of Guatemala referenced various IACtHR decisions. The court highlighted that the movement to guarantee the right to access publicly held information is not unique to Guatemala but rather a result of an international concern about the issue. The court reiterated all principles that were identified in *Claude Reyes*.[26]

The ECtHR has not recognized the principle of universal access as established by the *Claude Reyes* decision. In fact, in the ruling on *Magyar Helsinki Bizottság v. Hungary*, the ECtHR referred to the IACtHR *Claude Reyes* decision but rejected its approach and set out four different principles, focused on the persons requesting the information, to determine whether a denial of ATI interferes with the right to freedom of expression. The four principles are that the requested information must be *necessary* to exercise the right to freedom of expression; the requested information must meet a "public-interest test"; those seeking to access information must do so with "a view to informing the public in the capacity of a public 'watchdog,'" which includes not only nongovernmental organizations (NGOs) and the press but also "bloggers and popular users of social media"; and the requested information must be "ready and available."

POSITIVE STATE OBLIGATIONS

The IACtHR decision also had a transformative effect on Latin American legal systems and a broader impact on the effectiveness of the right to access to information. Indeed, the court identified necessary elements and guarantees to design a regime that allows access to information to be effective. Specifically, the court ordered Chile to "adopt the necessary measures to guarantee the protection of the right of access to state-held information, and these should include a guarantee of the effectiveness of an appropriate administrative procedure for processing and deciding requests for information, which establishes time limits for taking a decision and providing information, and which is administered by duly trained officials" (para. 163).

In Chile, the *Claude Reyes* decision had "immediate effects" and became a catalyst for the recognition of the right to information and the creation of the Council for Transparency, a body designed to protect and promote this right.[27] In 2007, the Constitutional Court—although not mentioning the *Claude Reyes* decision—stated that the right to access public information was constitutionally recognized in Chile.[28] A year later, the Chilean Congress enacted the ATI law after taking into account the IACtHR decision.[29]

Shortly after the *Claude Reyes* decision, a group of states enacted laws on ATI. Two months after the IACtHR decision, Honduras enacted its ATI law.[30] According to NGOs, the IACtHR decision has been essential in implementing this law, to claiming the right to information as a fundamental right, to accountability initiatives, and to the fight against corruption.[31] In 2008, Nicaragua, Guatemala, and Uruguay[32] enacted their own ATI laws. Nicaraguan civil society organizations promoting the approval of the ATI law relied extensively on *Claude Reyes*. In the Nicaraguan parliament, the decision created debates on the importance and responsibility of the state in guaranteeing the approval of laws that are aimed at improving the living conditions of citizens.[33] In Uruguay, the *Claude Reyes* decision also was central to the campaign to promote the adoption of the ATI law and its regulation.[34]

In 2010, the Organization of American States General Assembly approved the Model Inter-American Law on Access to Public Information and the Guide for its Implementation. The general assembly *reaffirmed* "the [IACtHR] decision in *Claude Reyes v. Chile*, which formally recognized the right of ATI as part of the fundamental right to freedom of expression." The Model Law is also expressly governed by the principles of maximum disclosure and universal access. Furthermore, the Commentary and Guide to the Model Law states, "Regardless of its moral justification, states parties to the American Convention on Human Rights are legally obliged to comply with the holding of the *Claude Reyes v. Chile* case, where the [IACtHR] mandates to amend existing legislation contrary to the principles of the right of access to information."[35] Five months later, in *Gomes Lund et al. v. Brazil*, the IACtHR echoed the arguments of *Claude Reyes* when it found that the state had failed to provide timely information to the relatives of the victims of military operations of the Brazilian army during the years 1973 and 1974.[36]

Subsequently, in 2011, El Salvador[37] and Brazil[38] enacted their ATI laws. According to civil society in El Salvador, the *Claude Reyes* decision had a great influence on the public and legislative debate on access to public information, which resulted in the approval of its law.[39] In Brazil, the NGO Article 19 relied on key ATI principles included in the *Claude Reyes* decision to carry out several campaigns that aimed to encourage participation in the legislative debate of the 2011 ATI law.[40]

In 2014, Colombia and Paraguay[41] approved their ATI laws. In Colombia, the *Claude Reyes* decision contributed to invigorating the debate on ATI, and according to Transparency Colombia and the Foundation for Free Press, the decision helped to highlight ATI as a human right and to describe the specific positive actions that it imposes on the state.[42] In Argentina, the *Claude Reyes* decision also largely influenced the adoption of the 2016 ATI law.[43]

In Venezuela, *Claude Reyes* has been an important reference in academic debates, forums, and activities carried out by citizens and organizations. In addition, the IACtHR decision served as the basis for the Access to Information Bill, approved in first discussions by the Venezuelan parliament (2016).[44] However, the Supreme Tribunal of Justice of Venezuela has repeatedly denied the exercise of this right.[45]

In conclusion, the IACtHR's *Claude Reyes* decision has significantly influenced jurisprudence and legislative developments around the world. The decision has been picked up by at least ten different courts in thirty different cases, and by the three regional courts for the protection of human rights—six by the Inter-American Court, two by the European Court, and one by the African Court. This decision has also greatly influenced public debates, resulting in the adoption of legislation on access to information. *Claude Reyes* has allowed a global judicial integration to the extent that it has been a key reference to advance the protection and guarantee of the right to access information.

NOTES

The title of this chapter comes from Toby Mendel, who called *Claude Reyes* a global trailblazer. See Mendel, "ELLA Expert Review: Transparency and Access to Information," ELLA Network, November 6, 2012, http://ella.practicalaction.org/knowledge-review/ella-expert-review-transparency-and-access-to-information.

1. See Catalina Botero-Marino, "The Role of the Inter-American Human Rights System in the Emergence and Development of Global Norms on Freedom of Expression," chapter 8 of the present volume. See also Moisés Sánchez, "Una década de

acceso a la información en las Américas," in *A 10 años del fallo Claude Reyes: Impacto y Desafíos* (Santiago: Consejo para la Transparencia, 2016), 68; and Karina Banfi and Daniela Urribarri, *Fuerza colectiva: Aprendizajes de la Alianza Regional para la Incidencia* (Alianza Regional, 2013).

2. See Sandra Coliver, "The Right to Access Information Held by Public Authorities: Emergence as a Global Norm," chapter 2 of this volume.

3. Inter-American Commission on Human Rights, Special Rapporteur for Freedom of Expression, *Special Study on the Right of Access to Information*, 2007. In Spanish.

4. Supreme Court of Justice, Fernández v. Costa Rican Social Security Fund, Expediente: 13-012328-0007-CO, March 21, 2014.

5. Marcela Restrepo Hung, Ana María Avella, and Pedro Vaca, "Acceso a la información pública en Colombia," in *Saber Más VIII: Una década de Acceso a la Información en Las Américas* (Alianza Regional, 2016), 5.

6. Colombian Constitutional Court, judgments T-580/12, T-691/10, T-167/13, T-451/11, and T-511/10.

7. Argentine Supreme Court, Asociación por los Derechos Civiles v. EN-PAMI, December 4, 2012, judgment A.917.46. See also Torcuato Sozio and Diego de Francesco, "Acceso a la Información Pública en Argentina," in *Saber Más VIII* (Alianza Regional, 2016), 22–24.

8. Court of Liquidation and Judgment, S.D. no. 40, July 31, 2007; Supreme Court of Justice, "El acceso a la información pública en el Paraguay: Aportes desde la Justicia a un derecho fundamental para la democracia" (2015).

9. Haydeé Pérez Garrido, Justine Dupuy, and Sarahi Salvatierra, "Acceso a la información pública en México," in *Saber Más VIII* (Alianza Regional, 2016), 102–105.

10. Carlos Pimentel, "A la información pública en República Dominicana," in *Saber Más VIII* (Alianza Regional, 2016), 125–126.

11. Dominican Republic Constitutional Court, TC/0042/12, September 21, 2012.

12. Helen Darbishire, "Primeros pasos en el camino hacia el derecho a la información: el caso Claude Reyes visto desde Europa," in *Saber Más VIII* (Alianza Regional, 2016), 7–11.

13. Nani Jansen Reventlow and Jonathan McCully, "The European Court of Human Rights and Access to Information: Clarifying the Status, with Room for Improvement," *Cyberlaw Clinic*, Berkman Klein Center for Internet & Society, Harvard Law School, November 22, 2016, https://clinic.cyber.harvard.edu/2016/11/22/the-european-court-of-human-rights-and-access-to-information-clarifying-the-status-with-room-for-improvement/.

14. European Court of Human Rights, Magyar Helsinki Bizottság v. Hungary, application no. 18030/11, November 8, 2016.

15. El Salvador, Supreme Court of Justice, Sentencia 13-2012, December 5, 2012.

16. Mexico, Supreme Court of Justice, Amparo en Revisión AR-492/2014, May 20, 2015.

17. Mexico, Supreme Court of Justice, Amparo en Revisión AR-173/2012, February 6, 2013.

18. Ezequiel Santagada, "Acceso a la información pública en Paraguay," in *Saber Más VIII* (Alianza Regional, 2016), 119–120.

19. Supreme Court of Paraguay, Decision 1306, October 15, 2013.

20. Santagada, "Acceso a la información pública en Paraguay," 119.

21. Supreme Court of Argentina, Center for the Implementation of Public Policies Promoting Equity and Growth v. Ministry of Social Development, judgment C.830.46, March 26, 2014; Colombian Constitutional Court, Sentencia C-540/12.

22. Inter-American Court of Human Rights (IACtHR), Kimel v. Argentina, Merits, Reparations and Costs, judgment of May 2, 2008, Series C 177, para. 52, 83, and 87; IACtHR, Usón Ramírez v. Venezuela, Preliminary Objections, Merits, Reparations and Costs, judgment of November 20, 2009, Series C 207, para. 55, 83, and 129; IACtHR, Omar Humberto Maldonado Vargas et al. v. Chile, Merits, Reparations and Costs, judgment of September 2, 2015, Series C, No. 300; IACtHR, Álvarez Ramos v. Venezuela, Merits, Reparations and Costs, judgment of August 300, 2019, Series C, No. 380, para. 108.

23. African Commission on Human and People's Rights, Communication 323/06: Egyptian Initiative for Personal Rights and Interights v. Egypt, December 2011.

24. Supreme Court of Argentina, Giustiniani, Rubén Héctor v. Y.P.F. S.A., judgment CAF 037747/2013/CS001, November 10, 2015; Chamber 2 of the Federal Court in Administrative Matters, Fundación Poder Ciudadano v. National Chamber of Deputies, judgment 2445/2015, September 29, 2015.

25. Court of Appeals of Uruguay, Decision 0002-050654/2014, December 5, 2014.

26. Guatemala, Constitutional Court, Decisions 1373-2009, 1412-2009, and 1413-2009, November 30, 2010.

27. Edison Lanza, "Prólogo," in *A 10 años del fallo Claude Reyes: Impacto y Desafíos* (Santiago: Consejo para la Transparencia, 2016), 11.

28. Chile, Constitutional Court, STC no. 634, August 9, 2007.

29. Library of the National Congress of Chile, "Historia de la Ley no. 20.285 Sobre acceso a la información pública," 166, 175, 275, 343–344, 350–353, and 384.

30. Honduras, Decreto no. 170-2006, *La Gaceta*, December 30, 2006.

31. José León Aguilar et al. "Acceso a la Información Pública en Honduras," in *Saber Más VIII* (Alianza Regional, 2016), 91–93.

32. Nicaragua, Law no. 621 of May 16, 2007, *La Gaceta* 118, June 22, 2007; Guatemala, Decree no. 57-2008 of October 23, 2008, *Diario de Centro América* 285, no. 45; and Uruguay, Law no. 18.381 of October 17, 2008, *Diario Oficial*, November 7, 2008.

33. Cristiana Chamorro Barrios and Guillermo José Medrano, "Acceso a la información pública en Nicaragua," in *Saber Más VIII* (Alianza Regional, 2016), 113–114.

34. Martín Prats, "Acceso a la información pública en Uruguay," in *Saber Más VIII* (Alianza Regional, 2016), 129–130.

35. Organization of American States, AG/RES. 2607 (XL-O/10), June 8, 2010.

36. IACtHR, Gomes Lund et al. ("Guerrilha do Araguaia") v. Brazil, para. 106–112, 230–231.

37. See recital 1 of the law. Decree no. 534, *Diario Oficial* 391, no. 70, December 2, 2010. Adopted in 2011.

38. Law No. 12.527, *Diário Oficial da União*, November 18, 2011.

39. Javier Castro de León et al., "Acceso a la información pública en El Salvador," in *Saber Más VIII* (Alianza Regional, 2016), 74–76.

40. Paula Martins, Joara Marchezini, and Bárbara Paes, "Acceso a la información pública en Brasil," in *Saber Más VIII* (Alianza Regional, 2016), 31–32.

41. Colombia, Law no. 1.712, *Diario Oficial* no. 49.084, March 6, 2014; Paraguay, Law no. 5.282 of September 18, 2015, *Registro Oficial* no. 180, September 19, 2014.

42. Restrepo Hung, Avella, and Vaca, "Acceso a la información pública en Colombia," 5.

43. Argentina, Law no. 27.275, *Boletín Oficial* no. 33.472, September 14, 2016. See also Sozio and de Francesco, "Acceso a la Información," 22–24.

44. Mercedes de Freitas and Carlos Correa, "Acceso a la información pública en Venezuela," in *Saber Más VIII* (Alianza Regional, 2016), 137–141; Transparencia Venezuela, *Proyecto de Ley de Transparencia, Divulgación y Acceso a la Información Pública*.

45. Venezuela, Supreme Tribunal of Justice, judgment 745, July 15, 2010; Supreme Tribunal of Justice, judgment 01177, August 5, 2014.

Lohé Issa Konaté v. Burkina Faso   **EIGHTEEN**

A Tipping Point for Decriminalization
of Defamation in Africa

HAWLEY JOHNSON

On December 5, 2014, the African Court on Human and Peoples' Rights handed down a landmark ruling in *Lohé Issa Konaté v. The Republic of Burkina Faso*, unanimously finding custodial sentences, suspension of news outlets, and excessive damages for criminal defamation to be disproportionate interferences with the right to freedom of expression where civil remedies were sufficient. This was the court's first case pertaining to freedom of expression, and its second merits judgment, presenting the court with an important opportunity to reinforce the principles and protections laid out in the African Charter of Human and Peoples' Rights, uphold international standards, and set precedent in the region. While the court stopped short of finding criminal defamation unconstitutional, the strength of the decision is its careful reasoning on the issues of necessity and proportionality, and the judgment has inspired a range of other courts to decriminalize defamation in their jurisdictions.

The African Court, through the *Konaté* ruling, gave binding force to protections long established in soft law in the region dating as far back as 1991, and effectively created a tipping point for the decriminalization of defamation on the continent.

The court relied heavily on international and regional jurisprudence to over-turn the criminal conviction of a journalist, Lohé Issa Konaté, for defaming a state prosecutor. The judgment cites some thirteen international conventions and treaties, fifteen judgments from the European Court of Human Rights, three judgments from the Inter-American Court of Human Rights, and two decisions from the UN Commission on Human Rights, as well as seven from the African Court. By late 2018, *Konaté's* influence could be seen on rulings in Kenya, Leso-tho, and Africa's two subregional courts, the Economic Community of West African States (ECOWAS) Community Court of Justice and the East African Court of Justice (EACJ), with additional cases pending in Nigeria, in Uganda, and before the EACJ. Petitioners, third-party interveners, and courts have cited *Konaté* to affirm that in democratic societies, public officials must endure public and media scrutiny of their professional duties and that journalists should never be subject to unwarranted imprisonment for holding the powerful to account.

BACKGROUND

The case concerned Lohé Issa Konaté, an editor and owner of a weekly newspa-per, *L'Ouragan* (*The Hurricane*), in Burkina Faso, who was found guilty of crim-inal defamation and sentenced to a twelve-month prison term and damages of $12,500 (equivalent) for a series of articles investigating allegations that the state prosecutor, Placide Nikiema, had been involved in counterfeiting and traffick-ing fake bank notes. The court ordered the suspension of the weekly *L'Ouragan* for six months. The decision was subsequently upheld by the Ouagadougou Court of Appeal.

In June 2013, an application was filed on behalf of Konaté before the African Commission on Human and Peoples' Rights, claiming that the excessive penal-ties violated his rights to freedom of expression.[1]

Konaté also challenged Articles 109, 110, and 111 of Burkina Faso's Informa-tion Code, which protect the honor and image of public officials from defama-tion by means of direct publication or reproduction of an allegation through "disparaging, contemptuous or insulting language."[2] In its defense, Burkina Faso claimed the restrictions were provided by law, citing the colonial French law of July 29, 1881,[3] on press freedom as well as jurisprudence from the Euro-pean Court of Human Rights to assert that the law would be considered "acces-sible and predictable under Article 10 (2) of the ECHR."[4]

In recognition of the potential significance of the case, a group comprising the most influential legal and media advocacy organizations in the region submitted an amicus brief to the court.[5] The brief recommended that the court strike down Burkina Faso's defamation and insult laws as incompatible with the right to freedom of expression as guaranteed by Article 9 of the African Charter.

The African Court was in a strong position to make a courageous ruling. In 1990, the African Commission on Human and Peoples' Rights passed Resolution 169, On Repealing Criminal Defamation Laws in Africa. Beginning in the 1990s numerous countries in Africa, such as Benin, Central African Republic, Ghana, Mauritania, Niger, Togo, and most recently, Zimbabwe, rewrote their constitutions or related laws to protect internationally recognized human rights such as freedom of expression and freedom of the press. Since 2000, there has been a succession of declarations promoting independent and pluralistic media, such as the 2007 Declaration of Table Mountain and the Pan-African Parliament's 2013 Midrand Declaration, calling for greater press freedom as a prerequisite for good governance and development. Six months prior to the *Konaté* decision, in a landmark ruling, the Constitutional Court of Zimbabwe, in *Madanhire v. Attorney General*, declared the offense of criminal defamation unconstitutional and inconsistent with the protection of freedom of expression under the country's former constitution.[6]

THE RULING

During the admissibility phase, the court rejected Burkina Faso's claim that Konaté did not qualify as a journalist due to his failure to follow administrative requirements established by the state,[7] and affirmed that Article 9 of the charter and Article 19 of the covenant both guarantee the right to freedom of expression to all people, without exception.[8] Since the African Charter does not contain a general limitation clause to freedom of expression,[9] the court applied the three-part test of Article 19 of the International Covenant on Civil and Political Rights.

The court found that the restriction was within the law and served the legitimate aim of protecting the reputation of public figures. In evaluating whether the restrictions were necessary for the stated purpose, the court found that the custodial sentence, as well as the heavy damages, were "disproportionate to the aim pursued." On this issue, the court relied heavily on international standards and ruled that sections 109 and 110 of the Burkinabe Information Code, as well as section 178 of the penal code, were contrary to the state's obligations under Article 9 of the African Charter and Article 19 of the covenant. Furthermore, the court found that custodial sentences constitute disproportionate interferences under the revised ECOWAS treaty.[10]

The court further ruled that Burkina Faso had not demonstrated that the suspension of the newspaper for six months was necessary to protect the rights and reputation of the prosecutor.[11] To support that finding, the court drew from the amici and cited the African Commission in *Constitutional Rights Project, Civil Liberties Organization and Media Rights Agenda v. Nigeria*, which found that the banning of publications was disproportionate and in violation of Article 9(2) of the charter.[12]

In assessing proportionality, the court relied on the 2009 African Commission decision in *Zimbabwe Lawyers for Human Rights & Associated Newspapers of Zimbabwe v. Zimbabwe*, the UN Human Rights Committee General Comment no. 34, and case law from the European Court (*Tolstoy Miloslavsky v. the United Kingdom*) and the Inter-American Court (*Tristan Donoso v. Panama*).[13]

One of the most significant findings by the court was that that criminal defamation laws should only be used as a last resort and within the context of what is necessary in a democratic society. The court agreed that only under circumstances of incitement or threats against persons or groups due to race, religion, color, or nationality could custodial sentences be justified.[14]

In a minority separate opinion, four of the ten judges found that the Burkinabe laws and the incarceration of Konaté were in clear violation of Article 9 of the charter, and moreover that a state's responsibility to protect national security and morality can never justify the criminalization of expression. The judges also stated that the possible exception for incitement or hate speech was too broadly defined, and that if such a crime occurred, it would fall under legislation for sedition or high treason, rendering criminal defamation laws useless.

INFLUENCE ON NATIONAL COURTS

Konaté demonstrates how a ruling from a newly established regional court can set precedent and thereby facilitate the codification of international norms and standards nationally, regionally, and even beyond the continent. The African Court's influence is, in principle, rather limited in that its decisions are only binding on parties to the case,[15] but as Pansy Tlakula, chairperson and former Africa Special Rapporteur on Freedom of Expression and Access to Information, has reminded states parties to the African Charter that they are obligated to align their laws with their regional obligations to protect the right to freedom of expression.[16] In practice, *Konaté's* influence has spread through a range of instruments and actors referencing it to defend journalists' freedom of expression and role in democratic societies.

India: *Subramanian Swamy v. Union of India*

Konaté made its way to India in the May 2016 ruling *Subramanian Swamy v. Union of India*, where it was cited by the petitioners in their pleadings, but not ultimately by the Supreme Court of India in its judgment. Unlike the African Court, India's Supreme Court found criminal defamation in this case to be proportionate, relying on a standard that evaluated the reasonableness and proportionality of the law's interest to the general public, rather than the proportionality of the punishment of the defendants.[17]

Kenya: *Okuta v. Attorney General*

A big win came on February 7, 2017, in *Okuta v. Attorney General*, when the High Court of Kenya declared the offense of criminal defamation under section 194 of the Kenyan penal code to be unconstitutional—a ruling in line with the bolder minority dissent from *Konaté*.[18]

A third-party intervention submitted by Article 19—Eastern Africa, in December 2016, argued that any law criminalizing defamation constitutes a violation of freedom of expression and is outdated, unduly harsh, unnecessary, and disproportionate to protecting individuals' reputations.[19] The brief included a lengthy eight-paragraph discussion of *Konaté*.

Significantly, the court's ruling cited the *Konaté* judgment twice and ruled according to *Konaté* in its finding that civil remedies are sufficient for penalizing defamation and therefore criminal remedies are inappropriate. In the spirit of the *Konaté* decision, the court recognized the peril of the chilling effect of criminal defamation, stating, "The overhanging effect of the offense of criminal defamation is to stifle and silence the free flow of information in the public domain. This, in turn, may result in the citizenry remaining uniformed about matters of public significance and the unquestioned and unchecked continuation of unconscionable malpractices."[20]

Lesotho: *Peta v. Minister of Law, Constitutional Affairs and Human Rights*

Lesotho followed suit, and on May 18, 2018, the Constitutional Court of Lesotho declared that the law on criminal defamation was unconstitutional and should be struck down. In *Peta v. Minister of Law, Constitutional Affairs and Human Rights*, the court held that much of the terminology related to defamation in the penal code was overbroad and vague and could lead to unjustified restrictions on freedom of expression. The Constitutional Court relied heavily on international jurisprudence and soft law and noted, in particular, the unanimous *Konaté v. Burkina Faso* decision.[21] The court concluded that the criminal defamation laws have a chilling effect on freedom of expression and hence that criminal defamation was "not reasonable and demonstrably justifiable in a free and democratic society," and thus it declared the articles in the penal code to be unconstitutional.[22]

INFLUENCE ON REGIONAL COURTS

Both subregional courts in Africa, the ECOWAS Community Court of Justice and the EACJ, rendered judgments in 2018 that upheld Article 9 of the African Charter and standards set in *Konaté* protecting the right to freedom of expression and press from arbitrary bans and disproportionate restrictions.[23] Collectively these rulings are binding for twenty countries on the continent, and codify international and regional standards on the subregional level.

ECOWAS Community Court of Justice: *Federation of African Journalists and Others v. the Republic of the Gambia*

In a landmark freedom of expression ruling, *Federation of African Journalists and Others v. the Republic of The Gambia*, the ECOWAS Community Court of Justice ruled, on March 13, 2018, that The Gambia's sedition, libel, and false news laws, as well as the detention and torture of two journalists, were a gross violation of international standards and the right to freedom of expression of the four applicant journalists.

A brief of amici curiae, submitted by sixteen international and regional organizations on behalf of the Federation of African Journalists, cited and relied heavily on *Konaté*, including on the key questions of proportionality and necessity, and highlighted the potentially chilling effect of criminal sanctions on the free exercise of expression, especially around matters of public interest.[24] The ruling referenced a compendium of international standards and comparative jurisprudence, including the *Konaté* ruling, to uphold the standard that restrictions must be "assessed within the context of a democratic society," and that it is a "proportionate measure to achieve the set objective," and that public figures must tolerate a higher degree of criticism over matters of public import.[25]

The court found that sedition laws function as a form of censorship and that "the existence of criminal defamation and insult laws are indeed inacceptable instances of gross violation of free speech and freedom of expression." The court referenced the Human Rights Committee's General Comment no. 34 as well as the U.S. Supreme Court decision in *New York Times Co. v. Sullivan*, 376 U.S. 254 (1964) to affirm the potential chilling effect of defamation laws, even when speaking the truth, and the need for "breathing space" for erroneous statements.[26] The court ordered The Gambia to decriminalize its legislation on sedition, criminal libel, defamation, and false news publication to bring its laws in line with its international obligations.[27] In its closing, the court additionally thanked the amicus curiae for "the insightful submission," which assisted the court "in taking an informed Decision."[28]

The East African Court of Justice: *Managing Editor of Mseto v. Attorney General of Tanzania*

On June 21, 2018, the East African Court of Justice ruled in *Managing Editor of Mseto v. Attorney General of Tanzania* that the banning of a weekly newspaper for three years was "unlawful, disproportionate and did not serve any legitimate or lawful purpose."[29] The weekly newspaper *Mseto* had been banned from print and online publishing for three years for its reporting on alleged corruption during elections and for what the minister of information claimed was irresponsible journalism. Referencing *Konaté*, the defendants (the editor and publisher of *Mseto*) had argued that the president and the deputy minister, as public officials, are legitimate subjects of press scrutiny, that the banning order could have a potential chilling effect on the publication of information in the public interest, and that the order, "contributed to a systemic practice that stifles the independent press and free speech in Tanzania."[30] While the final court judgment did not reference *Konaté*, it did uphold its established standards, affirming that criticism of the president of a partner state in newspaper articles "is the price of democracy and public watchdogs like the press must be allowed to operate freely within lawful boundaries."[31]

THE JOURNEY FORWARD

While the seeds for decriminalization in Africa were planted in 1990, the African Court's *Konaté* decision in 2014 energized the process and gave the decriminalization a seal of greater legitimacy. Various jurisdictions have pending cases relying on *Konaté* which could provide opportunities for further strengthening of the standards.

An important EACJ case to watch, in light of the *Mseto* ruling in Tanzania, is *Ronald Ssembuusi v. the Attorney General of the Republic of Uganda*, which could reinforce the decriminalization pattern of defamation in East Africa. The court granted permission to Special Rapporteurs on Freedom of Expression Pansy Tlakula of the African Union and David Kaye of the United Nations, as well as coalition of twenty African and international nongovernmental organizations, to submit interventions.[32]

In Nigeria, a challenge to the constitutionality of sections 24 and/or 38 of the Cybercrime Act 2015 (*Solomon Okedara v. Attorney General of the Federation*) relies on *Konaté* to argue that a conviction under the act would ultimately result in excessive fines and/or imprisonment, which has been found to be a disproportionate restriction under regional and international law. The case is on appeal before the Federal High Court Lagos Judicial Division. It references *Konaté* to argue that criminal defamation has a chilling effect and that the penalties under "Section 24(1) of the Cybercrime Act [are] clearly excessive and patently disproportionate as held in *Lohé Issa Konaté v. the Republic of Burkina Faso*."[33]

Konaté has been referenced multiple times in the context of a lawsuit brought against Angolan investigative journalist Rafael Marques de Morais, who has been charged numerous times for defamation due to his reporting on corruption. For instance, fifty concerned personalities published a letter addressed to the president of the Republic of Angola claiming the criminal defamation case "stands in opposition to the December 2014 judgment of the African Court on Human and Peoples' Rights, which ruled in the case of *Lohé Issa Konaté v. Burkina Faso* that except in very serious and exceptional circumstances, 'violations of laws on freedom speech and the press cannot be sanctioned by custodial sentences.'"[34] The American Bar Association trial observation report, which documented numerous irregularities throughout the court proceedings, also referenced *Konaté* as an example that a prison sentence is rarely, if ever, a proportional punishment for expressions of opinion.[35] The Marques de Morais case is likely to be brought before the African Commission.[36]

While *Konaté* has been most influential in Africa, it is more generally relevant to all jurisdictions where criminal defamation lingers due to colonial legacies or authoritarian regimes. Legal scholar and Middle East expert, the late Matt Duffy, and his coauthor Mariam Alkazemi believed that the *Konaté* ruling helped establish best practices in international defamation law and that it could potentially strengthen protections for journalists in the Middle East and North Africa, specifically Algeria, Egypt, Libya, and Tunisia.[37] Further, Duffy and Alkazemi credit the African Court's ruling in *Konaté* for creating a consensus among the regional courts—the European Court of Human Rights, the Inter-American Court of Human Rights, and the African Court—and hence for contributing to the establishment of a global norm that libel and slander should be addressed as civil rather than criminal offenses.[38] In four short years, the African Court on Human and Peoples' Rights ruling in *Konaté* has had great impact on the continent regionally, subregionally, and nationally, but its journey has just begun.

NOTES

1. African Commission on Human and Peoples' Rights, "169 Resolution on Repealing Criminal Defamation Laws in Africa," ACHPR/Res.169(48)10 (2010). http://www. achpr.org/sessions/48th/resolutions/169/.

2. African Court on Human and People's Rights, Lohé Issa Konaté v. the Republic of Burkina Faso, application no. 004/2013, para. 32.

3. The French Law of July 29, 1881, acknowledged the need for restrictions on press freedom in order to balance the right of freedom of speech with the protection of individual rights and public order.

4. *Konaté*, para. 33.

5. The amicus brief was submitted by the Center for Human Rights, Committee to Protect Journalists, Media Institute of Southern Africa, Pan African Human Rights Defenders Network, Pan African Lawyers Union, Pen International and Malawi Pen, Pen Algeria, Pen Nigeria Center, Pen Sierra Leone, South Africa Pen Center, Southern Africa Litigation Center, and the World Association of News papers and News Publishers. https://globalfreedomofexpression.columbia.edu/wp-content/uploads/2015/02/Amici-Brief-in-Issa-Konate-Case-28Submitted-Version29.pdf.

6. On June 12, 2014, the Constitutional Court of Zimbabwe ruled that the offense of criminal defamation was unconstitutional and inconsistent with the protection of freedom of expression under the country's former constitution, in a case related to an investigative journalism article into the practices of a medical aid company. Columbia University, Global Freedom of Expression, "Madanhire v. Attorney General," https://globalfreedomofexpression.columbia.edu/cases/madanhire-v-attorney-general. On February 6, 2016, the court declared the offense of criminal defamation to be unconstitutional under the new constitution, except in cases where it could be proved that there had been "malicious injury to a person's reputation or dignity." Columbia University, Global Freedom of Expression, "MISA-Zimbabwe et al. v. Minister of Justice et al.," https://globalfreedomofexpression.columbia.edu/cases/misa-zimbabwe-et-al-v-minister-justice-et-al.

7. Konaté did not possess a press card, nor had he registered his newspaper with the tax authorities, as required by the state. See *Konaté*, para. 54.

8. *Konaté*, para. 58.

9. See Catherine Anite, "The African System: A New Actor of Normative Integration?," chapter 9 of the present volume.

10. *Konaté*, para. 164.

11. *Konaté*, para. 169.

12. *Konaté*, para. 150.

13. *Konaté*, para. 152–154. Specifically, see notes 25–26, which discuss the key issues raised and legal reasoning applied in the cases.

14. *Konaté*, para. 161

15. Oliver Windridge, "Konaté to the Rescue? How Konaté Can Help Others Facing Criminal Defamation Charges," *ACtHPR Monitor*, March 26, 2015, http://www .acthprmonitor.org/konate-to-the-rescue-how-the-konate-case-can-help-others -facing-criminal-defamation-charges/.

16. Lianna Merner, Sarah Clarke, and Romana Cacchio, eds., "Stifling Dissent, Impeding Accountability: Criminal Defamation Laws in Africa," PEN International, November 22, 2017, 6. http://pensouthafrica.co.za/wp-content/uploads/2017/11 /Stifling-Dissent-Impeding-Accountability-Criminal-Defamation-Laws-in-Africa .pdf.

17. Anna Liz Thomas, "Subramanian Swamy v. UoI: Unanswered Arguments," *CCG Blog*, Centre for Communication Governance, National Law University Delhi, May 27, 2016, https://ccgnludelhi.wordpress.com/tag/lohe-issa-konate/.

18. Nani Jansen Reventlow and Catherine Anite, "Kenyan Court Knocks Down Criminal Defamation, Safeguards Freedom of Expression," *Cyberlaw Clinic*, Berkman Klein Center for Internet & Society, Harvard Law School, February 8, 2017, https:// clinic.cyber.harvard.edu/2017/02/08/kenyan-court-knocks-down-criminal -defamation-safeguards-freedom-of-expression/.

19. Article 19, Interested Party Submission in Constitutional Court of Kenya, Okuta v. Attorney General & 2 others [2017] eKLR p. 9, para. 51 and 70.

20. *Okuta*, 11.

21. Lesotho, Peta v. Minister of Law, Constitutional Affairs and Human Rights, CC 11/2016, p. 32.

22. *Peta*, 34.

23. The Economic Community of West African States (ECOWAS) Community Court of Justice, based in Abuja, Nigeria, issues binding decisions for the member states of Benin, Burkina Faso, Cape Verde, The Gambia, Ghana, Guinea, Guinea Bissau, Ivory Coast, Liberia, Mali, Niger, Nigeria, Sierra Leone, Senegal, and Togo. The East African Court of Justice, based in Arusha, Tanzania, issues judgments for partner states Burundi, Kenya, Rwanda, Tanzania, and Uganda. "The African Regional Human Rights Courts," Leigh Day, https://www.leighday.co.uk/getattachment

/Asserting-your-rights/Human-rights/Human-Rights-resources/Regional-Human
-Rights-Courts-in-Africa/Regional-human-rights-courts-in-Africa-factsheet.pdf
.aspx.

24. Consolidated brief of amici curiae in ECOWAS, Federation of African Journalists
v.TheGambia,ECW/CCJ/APP/36/15(2018),para.12http://globalfreedomofexpression
.columbia.edu/wp-content/uploads/2016/04/201610-Consolidated-Amicus-Brief
-FAJ.docx; *Konaté*, para. 143.

25. ECOWAS Community Court of Justice, Federation of African Journalists and
Others v. the Republic of The Gambia, ECW/CCJ/JUD/04/18 (2018), p. 5.

26. *Federation of African Journalists*, 41.

27. *Federation of African Journalists*, 48. The court further ordered The Gambia to pay
the fourth and fifth applicants 2 million Gambian dalasi each (approximately
$42,000 in March 2018) for the violation of their human right to freedom of expres-
sion and the right to freedom from torture. Subsequently, The Gambia failed to fully
implement the ECOWAS judgment. On May 9, 2018, the Gambian Supreme Court,
in *Gambia Press Union v. the Attorney General*, declared the criminal defamation
and false news laws unconstitutional but upheld the sedition law as it pertains to
expression about the president. The Media Legal Defense Initiative supported both
the ECOWAS case as well as the Gambian Supreme Court cases. "Gambia: A Mixed
Result as the Supreme Court Delivers Judgment in Important Constitutional Challenges to Free Speech Law," Media Legal Defence Initiative, May 16, 2018, https://
www.mediadefence.org/news/gambia-mixed-result-supreme-court-delivers
-judgment-important-constitutional-challenges-free.

28. *Federation of African Journalists*, 62.

29. East African Court of Justice at Arusha, First Division, Managing Editor Mseto
and Hali Halshi Publishers Ltd. v. the Attorney General of the United Republic of
Tanzania, reference no. 7 of 2016 (June 21, 2018), para. 69.

30. *Mseto*, para. 69.

31. *Mseto*, para. 72.

32. Nani Jansen Reventlow and Catherine Anite, "Kenyan Court Knocks Down Criminal Defamation, Safeguards Freedom of Expression," *Cyberlaw Clinic*, Berkman
Klein Center for Internet & Society, Harvard Law School, February 8, 2017, https://
clinic.cyber.harvard.edu/2017/02/08/kenyan-court-knocks-down-criminal
-defamation-safeguards-freedom-of-expression.

33. Nigeria, *Solomon Okedara v. Attorney General of the Federation*, FHC/L/CS/937/
2017, p. 30.

34. Human Rights Watch, "Joint Letter Re: Prosecution of Rafael Marques de Morais,"
May 27, 2015, https://www.hrw.org/news/2015/05/27/joint-letter-re-prosecution-rafael
-marques-de-morais#.

35. American Bar Association Center for Human Rights, "Trial Observation Report: The Case of Rafael Marques Demorais," June 2015, https://www.americanbar.org /content/dam/aba/administrative/human_rights/trialobservationreport_rafael marques.authcheckdam.pdf.

36. Although Angola is a signatory to the African Charter, it has not signed the Court Protocol. This means that De Morais could bring his case to the African Commission, claiming violation of his rights under the African Charter, but not to the African Court. See Windridge, "Konaté to the Rescue?"

37. Matt J. Duffy and Mariam Alkazemi, "Arab Defamation Laws: A Comparative Analysis of Libel and Slander in the Middle East," *Communication Law and Policy* 22, no. 2 (2017): 189–211.

38. Duffy and Alkazemi (footnote 9) cite the following three landmark cases for setting the norm: Inter-American Court of Human Rights, Herrera-Ulloa v. Costa Rica, section C, no. 107 (2004); Konaté v. Burkina Faso; and European Court of Human Rights, Lingens v. Austria, no. 9815/82 (1986).

Fast, Far, and Deep

NINETEEN

The Journey of the Right to Be Forgotten

BACH AVEZDJANOV

The concept of the right to be forgotten (RTBF) was born in Europe in the 1970s[1] and remained largely dormant until 2014, when the Court of Justice of the European Union (CJEU) digitized the concept in the *Google Spain SL v. Agencia Española de Protección de Datos* decision. The CJEU, emphasizing the fundamental rights to privacy and the protection of personal data, found that individuals had the right to request search engines to "forget" them by deindexing search results that contained outdated or private information.[2] Within just a few years, tribunals and legislators around the world adopted, or at least considered adopting, the right to deindex, often referring back to the *Google Spain* judgment. On its global journey, the CJEU's RTBF decision was often reinterpreted and modified, including in Europe. The fast, far, and deep journey of the right to be forgotten (figure 19.1) is an example of "judicial convergence across borders, and of an emerging and interactive globalized jurisprudence as far as de-listing is concerned."[3]

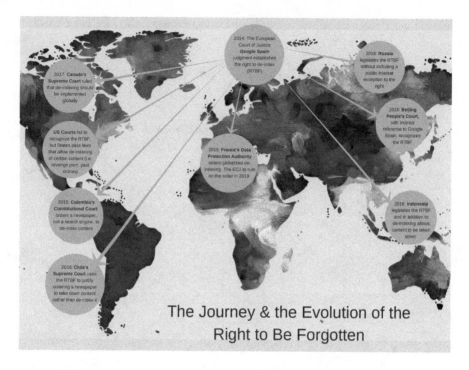

The Journey & the Evolution of the
Right to Be Forgotten

Figure 19.1 The journey and evolution of the right to be forgotten.

RIGHT TO BE FORGOTTEN JOURNEYS FAST AND FAR

Shortly after the CJEU rendered the *Google Spain* decision, the right to be for-gotten began its global journey. Tribunals and legislators introduced or consid-ered introducing the RTBF in Asia, Africa, Central and Latin America, and Europe. In the vast majority of cases, the judicial and legislative bodies referred to *Google Spain*. No region reacted more swiftly to the *Google Spain* decision than Central and Latin America, possibly because of a legal history on matters related to the right to be forgotten, and preceding the CJEU decision. Courts in Argentina,[4] Brazil,[5] Colombia,[6] Chile,[7] Mexico,[8] and Peru[9] adjudicated cases concerning the right to be forgotten just months after the CJEU judgment. Additionally, lawmakers in Brazil and Panama introduced bills on the RTBF.[10] Eventually, even national courts that had first rejected the right to be forgotten succumbed to the trend, as was the case in Brazil.

Since 2015, high courts in Brazil had repeatedly ruled against imposing on search engine operators the responsibility to deindex links, due to worries about turning them into digital censors.[11] However, in May 2018, the nation's Superior Court of Justice ordered search engines to deindex search results in a case concerning a judge who allegedly helped commit fraud.[12] In 2006, a newspaper published articles claiming that the judge had helped his family gain an unfair advantage during a judicial exam. The judge demanded that all search results tying his name to the allegations be deindexed, but lower courts rejected the request. Eventually, the Superior Court of Justice of Brazil endorsed the judge's right to be forgotten. The high court held that the RTBF allowed an individual to enjoy reasonable anonymity, without an automated recollection of dated disreputable information by search engines.

In China, in a case concerning deindexing from Baidu search results, the Beijing court refused to rely on the *Google Spain* decision because foreign law could not be used in the adjudication of cases in China.[13] Nonetheless, the court extracted the RTBF from the Chinese tort law's definition of the right to personality, which "protects the subject's personal interests, and encompasses both those personal interests that have already been categorized as legally defined rights, as well as those legitimate legal interests that have not been so categorized but which should receive the protection of law."[14] Similarly, the Supreme Court of Japan did not reference the CJEU's RTBF decision but applied analogous reasoning, holding that an individual may demand a search engine operator to deindex URLs and other items from the search results if "the legal interest of such [information] not being published is greater than the legal interest of publishing [it]."[15]

In other parts of Asia, lawmakers introduced the right to be forgotten by revising existing laws or adapting new ones. In 2016, Indonesia amended its 2008 Electronic Information and Transactions Law to introduce the right to be forgotten.[16] The same year, South Korea's Communication Commission released nonbinding Guidelines on the Right to Request Access Restrictions on Personal Internet Postings, in response to the *Google Spain* decision, which recommended that website administrators and search engines satisfy Internet users' requests to deindex and delete information containing personal details.[17] In 2017, the Indian Committee of Experts, appointed by the government, recommended to codify the RTBF into any future data protection legislation and stated that "the recognition of the right to privacy envisages within its contours the right to protect personal information on the Internet. Consequently, from this right, it follows that any individual may have the derivative right to remove the 'shackles of unadvisable past things' on the Internet and correct past actions."[18] In its reasoning, the committee explicitly referred to the *Google Spain* judgment.

In Russia, several months after the CJEU decision, the head of Roskomnad-zor, the country's information watchdog, publicly voiced approval for the right to be forgotten.[19] Less than a year later, in July 2015, the Russian Parliament added an RTBF provision to the nation's information law.[20] However, the Russian law had a major drawback—it did not include "limitations on the 'right to be forgotten' when the personal information at issue [was] in the public interest and/or concerns public figures."[21] In Kazakhstan, some members of parliament reacted to the *Google Spain* decision and twice proposed but failed to introduce the RTBF, in part as a response measure to misinformation and the increasing popularity of fake social media accounts.[22]

Courts in the United States have yet to accept the right to be forgotten. In the first reference to the *Google Spain* judgment, in 2014, the United States Court of Appeals for the Ninth Circuit highlighted the RTBF as one potential solution to remedy reputational harm. However, it noted that the right had not been domestically recognized.[23] Despite the American judiciary's lack of support for the RTBF, it has still managed to find a place in the country's digital life. In 2015, Google announced that it would permit victims of revenge porn to request deindexing of search results that lead to sexually explicit images shared without their consent.[24] In late 2017, New York State passed amendments to its Criminal Procedure Law that allowed former convicts to seal information about their past criminal history.[25] Information about one's past crimes is just a Google search away, and to fulfill the amendments' directives, individuals could in theory request that their criminal records be deindexed.

These examples illustrate that the CJEU's *Google Spain* judgment swiftly reverberated across judicial and legislative halls around the world. Although attempts to introduce the RTBF have not always been successful, one cannot deny that the *Google Spain* decision made millions of Internet users, including judges, parliamentarians, and politicians, rethink the balance between freedom of expression and privacy rights online.

THE SLIPPERY SLOPE

At the time of its adoption, the CJEU decision was heavily criticized by freedom of expression activists on the grounds that it ignored free expression values that are vital to online journalism and represented a "radical break from the carefully constructed legal philosophies underscoring privacy, which is already a newer and much more volatile right than the free expression values with which it often collides."[26] Another criticism of the right to be forgotten, voiced by freedom of expression defenders, was that it "could override the public interest in the information remaining available."[27] Some four years later, while many legal risks appear to have been avoided and search engines have fully operationalized deindexing, there remain some worrying instances that deserve attention.

Blame the Publisher

As the right to be forgotten spread around the world, it was reinterpreted in some jurisdictions to impose on publishers, rather than on search engines, the obligation to deindex content. This interpretation of the RTBF has origins in Central and Latin America. In 2015, Colombia's Constitutional Court rejected an individual's request to order Google to deindex links to an article about her alleged criminal past.[28] Instead, the court ordered the publisher, the *El Tiempo* newspaper, to take steps to render the article invisible to Google. A year later, Chile's Supreme Court ordered the newspaper *El Mercurio* to delete digital versions of news articles referring to decade-old criminal proceedings against a certain individual. In justifying its decision, the Chilean court stated that it could not see a benefit to freedom of expression in ensuring that an old article remained detectable by a search engine.[29] Some courts in Europe followed suit and expanded to the original publishers of information the obligation to implement the RTBF. In 2015, the Higher Regional Court of Hamburg, Germany, ordered a newspaper to deindex certain articles from its archive so that they would not appear in online search results.[30] "The Court stated that, if such claims to delink certain content could be brought against search engines, as decided by the European Court of Justice in the Google Case, all the more reason to decide they could be brought against the original provider of such content," clearly misinterpreting the CJEU decision.[31]

In another 2015 decision, Italy's Supreme Court of Cassation penalized the newspaper *PrimaDaNoi* for failing to deindex information in a timely manner and concluded that despite the importance of the right to report, private information should not be publicly available indefinitely. This opened a pathway for online users to request publishers to delete certain information about them after a set period of time, which the Italian Court fixed, in a rather arbitrary manner, at two and a half years.[32] In 2016, the Belgian Court of Cassation used the RTBF to order a newspaper to anonymize the name of a person in its online archive, thus making the name disappear in search engines worldwide.[33] The same year, Turkey's Constitutional Court similarly imposed on a newspaper the responsibility of deindexing articles it had published, to satisfy the right to be forgotten.[34]

Imposing on publishers the obligation to implement the RTBF has several drawbacks, some of which the CJEU addressed in the *Google Spain* judgment, when Google attempted to shift the responsibility for implementing the RTBF onto publishers. The CJEU rejected the search engine's argument.[35] The court explained that information on the Internet could easily be replicated or archived, and thus to better protect personal data, it was more effective to require a search engine to deindex certain hyperlinks. Additionally, the CJEU noted that, unlike search engines, some websites publish personal information purely for journalistic purposes and thus enjoy a higher degree of protection.

Another issue, not addressed by the CJEU, is that of cost. Many publishers do not have the financial or human resources to respond to lawsuits. In fact, media around the world is struggling to survive financially in the digital age.[36] Regrettably, persistent right to be forgotten lawsuits forced the newspaper *PrimaDaNoi* to suspend its publication on the anniversary of its thirteenth year in operation, on September 26, 2018.

These decisions in Belgium, Chile, Colombia, Germany, and Italy have not been replicated elsewhere thus far. Search engines continue to bear the vast majority of the responsibility for implementing the RTBF, as the CJEU recommended.

Don't Just Forget the Content. Delete It!

In some parts of the world, the CJEU's interpretation of the right to be forgotten was expanded to include deletion of content online. For instance, as mentioned earlier, in 2016 South Korea's Communication Commission unveiled its nonbinding guidelines concerning Internet posts. These guidelines "allow consumers to request that search engines and website operators restrict access and ultimately remove online information."[37] In Indonesia, under the 2016 amendments that introduced the right to be forgotten, individuals may request an electronic systems owner, defined as anyone who processes, stores, displays, transmits, or disseminates data, to delete their personal data, both online and offline, upon obtaining a court order.[38]

Some courts likewise interpreted the right to be forgotten to include deletion of information, in addition to deindexing. As discussed, in 2016, the Supreme Court of Chile ordered the newspaper *El Mercurio* to delete all news articles about a decade-old criminal case concerning a certain individual. The court felt that its judgment did not restrict freedom of expression because, even after the articles were deleted online, they still could be found offline by anyone who might be interested in them.[39]

Extraterritorial Reach for an Extraterritorial Right?

The right to be forgotten continues to evolve. In 2015, Agnés Callamard, one of the editors of the present volume, pointed out that the issue dominating legal and policy debates concerning the right to be forgotten was "no longer so much about delisting requests (whether the request was well-founded or not) but instead over the extraterritorial reach of delisting decisions."[40] In Canada and France, courts have already demanded worldwide deindexing of search results. The French data protection authority, CNIL, ordered Google to deindex twenty-one links from its search results worldwide, rather than simply on Google.fr.[41] Google appealed to the French Conseil d'Etat, which in turn sought advice from the CJEU. The CJEU ultimately held that since the European data protection laws were silent on the scope of deindexing, Google was not obliged to apply deindexing orders globally in every case. The court explained that national courts need to determine the necessary scope of the deindexing based on the context of each case.[42]

Canada's Supreme Court ruled in *Google v. Equustek* that Google can be forced to delist search results worldwide to enforce the decisions of Canadian courts.[43] However, Google successfully requested an injunction against the Canadian judgment in front of the District Court for the Northern District of California. This latter court held that the Canadian order disregarded section 230 of the Communications Decency Act of 1996 and undermined free speech on the global Internet, which section 230 protects.[44]

Technical alternatives to deindexing could result in extraterritorial effects, as when the Belgian court ordered a newspaper to anonymize a name in its online archive and thus remove it from search engines worldwide. Overall, ordering publishers to deindex or anonymize may lead to global deindexing. Publishers can hide information from search engines by relying on two technical tools (tags, such as "no-index" or "meta," or robot.txt files), which must be tailored to deliver geolocalized effects. It may be that publishers have an incentive to deindex content globally in order to avoid additional lawsuits stemming from the availability of nationally deindexed information through virtual private networks or search engines in other regions.

CONCLUSION

In 2014, the Court of Justice of the European Union rendered the *Google Spain* judgment and introduced to the Internet the concept of the right to be forgotten. Within a very short period, the judgment and the concept traveled the globe. However, as the mushrooming digital right moved from one jurisdiction to another, tribunals and legislators molded it. Rather than making search engines responsible for the "forgetting," as the CJEU had done, courts in Belgium, Chile, Colombia, and Germany imposed responsibility for its implementation on publishers of content. The evolution of the RTBF continues, as questions over extraterritorial deindexing are raised and are pending at the time of publication. Despite differences in interpretation of the right to be forgotten, its international journey across courtrooms and legislative halls offers strong evidence that these bodies listen to and communicate with each other across national and jurisdictional borders.

NOTES

1. Paul Bernard, "A Right to Delete?," *European Journal of Law and Technology* 2, no. 2 (2011): 2.

2. Court of Justice of the European Union, Google Spain SL, Google Inc. v. Agencia Española de Protección de Datos (AEPD), Mario Costeja González, C-131/12, ECLI:EU:C:2014:317 (May 13, 2014); "Google Spain SL v. Agencia Española de Protección de Datos," Columbia University, Global Freedom of Expression, https://globalfreedomofexpression.columbia.edu/cases/google-spain-sl-v-agencia-espanola-de-proteccion-de-datos-aepd/.

3. Agnès Callamard, "Comity for Internet? Recent Court Decisions on the Right to be De-indexed," *National Law Review*, August 12, 2015, p. 2, https://www.natlawreview.com/article/comity-internet-recent-court-decisions-right-to-be-de-indexed.

4. Edward L. Carter, "Argentina's Right to be Forgotten," *Emory International Law Review* 27 (2013): 25–31.

5. "RTBF in the Brazilian Courts," InternetLab blog, February 2, 2017, http://www.internetlab.org.br/en/opinion/4special-week-rtbf-in-the-brazilian-courts.

6. Katitza Rodriguez and Sarah Myers West, "Google to France: We Won't Forget It For You Wholesale," Electronic Frontier Foundation, August 3, 2015, https://www.eff.org/deeplinks/2015/08/google-france-we-wont-forget-it-you-wholesale.

7. Pedro Angutta Ramirez, "The Right to Be Forgotten in Chile: Doctrine and Jurisprudence," *Blogdroiteuropéen*, June 8, 2017, https://blogdroiteuropeen.files.wordpress.com/2017/06/article-pedro-chile-final-version.pdf.

8. Mexico, Google México, S. de R.L. de C.V., Instituto Federal de Acceso a la Información y Protección de Datos, PPD.0094/14 (July 26, 2015); "Anonymous Applicant v. Google Mexico," Columbia University, Global Freedom of Expression,

https://globalfreedomofexpression.columbia.edu/cases/fiaipd-anonymous
-applicant-v-google-mexico/.

9. Martin Borgioli, "Google es sancionado por primera vez en Perú por desconocer el
   derecho al olvido" [For the First Time, Google Is Sanctioned in Peru on the Basis
   of the Right to Be Forgotten], *Hiperderecho*, June 21, 2016, http://hiperderecho.org
   /2016/06/google-sancionado-datos-personales-peru-derecho-olvido/.

10. *Latin America in a Glimpse*, Human Rights and the Internet, Internet Gover-
    nance Forum, Mexico 2016, Derechos Digitales, November 10, 2016, 4–6,
    https://derechosdigitales.org/wp-content/uploads/Latin-America-in-a-Glimpse
    -eng.pdf.

11. "RTBF in the Brazilian Courts."

12. Brazil, Superior Court of Justice, Recurso Especial no. 1.660.168–RJ (2014/0291777-
    1), June 8, 2018, https://www.conjur.com.br/dl/direito-esquecimento-indexacao
    .pdf; "DPN vs. Google Brasil Internet Ltda.," Columbia University, Global Free-
    dom of Expression, https://globalfreedomofexpression.columbia.edu/cases/dpn-vs
    -google-brasil-internet-ltda.

13. China, Beijing First Intermediate People's Court, Ren Jiayu v. Beijing Baidu Netcom
    Technology Co., Ltd., December 25, 2015, http://wenshu.court.gov.cn/content/content
    ?DocID=789e76ed-c084–41bb-8e75-a092cba58912.; "Ren Jiayu v. Baidu," Columbia
    University, Global Freedom of Expression, https://globalfreedomofexpression
    .columbia.edu/cases/ren-jiayu-v-baidu/.

14. "An Overview of China's First 'Right to be Forgotten' Lawsuit," *Fei Chang Dao*
    (blog), May 16, 2016, http://blog.feichangdao.com/2016/05/an-overview-of-china
    -first-right-to-be.html.

15. Japan, Tokyo High Court, Plaintiff v. Google, 71 Minshu 1, 2016 (Kyo) 45, January 31,
    2017, http://www.courts.go.jp/app/hanrei_en/detail?id=1511; "Plaintiff X v. Google,"
    Columbia University, Global Freedom of Expression, https://globalfreedomofexpression
    .columbia.edu/cases/plaintiff-x-v-google/.

16. Nadine Freischlad, "Controversial 'Right to Be Forgotten' Finds Its Way into Indo-
    nesian Law," *Tech in Asia*, December 1, 2016, https://www.techinasia.com/indonesia
    -recognizes-right-to-be-forgotten.

17. James Lin, "South Korea Releases Right to Be Forgotten Guidance," Bloomberg
    BNA, May 9, 2016.

18. India, Ministry of Electronics and Information Technology, Committee of Experts,
    Data Protection Framework for India, December 18, 2018, p. 138, http://meity.gov.in
    /writereaddata/files/white_paper_on_data_protection_in_india_18122017_final
    _v2.1.pdf.

19. "Roskomnadzor Predlagaet Obsudit' 'Pravo na Zabvenie' Priminitelno k Polzo-
    vatelyam Runeta" [Roskomnadzor Suggests to Discuss the Applicability of "the

Right to be Forgotten" to Russia's Internet], TASS, November 5, 2014, https://tass.ru/obschestvo/1552936.

20. O Vnesenii Izmeneniy v. Federalnyi Zakon "Ob Informatsii, Informatsionnyh Tekhnologiyah, i o Zashite Informatsii" [Amendments to the Federal Law "On Information, Information Technology, and Protection of Information"], 2015, no. 264, https://rg.ru/2015/07/16/informacia-dok.html.

21. "Legal Analysis: Russia's Right to Be Forgotten," Article 19, September 16, 2015, https://www.article19.org/resources/legal-analysis-russias-right-to-be-forgotten.

22. "Deputat Potreboval Obespechit Kazakhstantsev 'Pravom na Zabvenie' v. Internete" [Parliamentarian Wants Kazakhs to Enjoy the "Right to Be Forgotten"], NUR, https://www.nur.kz/883972-deputat-potreboval-obespechit-kazakh.html.

23. US 9th Circuit, Cindy Lee Garcia v. Google Inc., 786 F.3d 733 (2015).

24. Amit Singhal, "'Revenge Porn' and Search," *Google Public Policy Blog*, June 19, 2015, https://publicpolicy.googleblog.com/2015/06/revenge-porn-and-search.html.

25. New York Assembly Bill A3009C, January 23, 2017, https://legislation.nysenate.gov/pdf/bills/2017/A3009C; Mahir Nisar, "New York Law Permits 'Sealing' of Criminal Records from Potential Employers," Nisar Law Group, November 22, 2017, http://www.nisarlaw.com/blog/2017/november/new-york-law-permits-sealing-of-criminal-records.

26. Geoffrey King, "Two Continents, Two Courts, Two Approaches to Privacy," Committee to Protect Journalists, April 27, 2015, https://cpj.org/2015/04/attacks-on-the-press-two-continents-two-courts-two-approaches-to-privacy.php.

27. "Viviane Reding Responds to Reporters Without Borders' Criticism of 'Right to be Forgotten,'" Reporters Without Borders, January 20, 2016, https://rsf.org/en/news/viviane-reding-responds-reporters-without-borders-criticism-right-be-forgotten.

28. Rodriguez and West, "Google to France."

29. Supreme Court of Chile, Aldo Graziani Le Fort v. Empresa El Mercurio S.A.P. [Aldo Graziani Le Fort v. El Mercurio Newspaper], case no. 22.243-2015, January 21, 2016, 10–11; "Graziani v. El Mercurio," Columbia University, Global Freedom of Expression, https://globalfreedomofexpression.columbia.edu/cases/graziani-v-el-mercurio.

30. Germany, Higher Regional Court of Hamburg, openJur 2015, 12831, July 7, 2015; "Plaintiff X v. Newspaper X," Columbia University, Global Freedom of Expression, https://globalfreedomofexpression.columbia.edu/cases/plaintiff-x-v-newspaper-x/.

31. Tobias Raab, "Germany: Court Orders Newspaper to Delink Online Articles so They Do Not Appear in Searches and Uphold the Right to be Forgotten," European Centre for Press and Media Freedom, October 16, 2015, https://www.ecpmf.eu/archive/news/legal/archive/germany-court-orders-newspaper-to-delink-online

-articles-so-they-do-not-appear-in-searches-and-uphold-the-right-to-be-forgotten
.html.

32. Italy Supreme Court of Cassation, Prima sezione civile, n.13161/16, November 11, 2015;
"Plaintiff X v. PrimaDaNoi," Columbia University, Global Freedom of Expression,
https://globalfreedomofexpression.columbia.edu/cases/plaintiff-x-v-primadanoi.

33. Belgian Court of Cassation, no. C.15.0052.F, April 29, 2016; "P.H. v. O.G.," Columbia University, Global Freedom of Expression, https://globalfreedomofexpression
.columbia.edu/cases/p-h-v-o-g/.

34. Constitutional Court of Turkey, N.B.B. Başvurusu [N.B.B. Case], Başvurusu
no. 2013/5653 [2016], http://www.resmigazete.gov.tr/eskiler/2016/08/20160824-14.pdf
?lipi=urn%3Ali%3Apage%3Ad_flagship3_pulse_read%3B5OJo8gj%2FTTSN9gVHz
%2BnVJg%3D%3D; "The Case of N.B.B.," Columbia University, Global Freedom of
Expression, https://globalfreedomofexpression.columbia.edu/cases/case-n-b-b/.

35. *Google Spain SL*, para. 83–88.

36. Nic Newman, with Richard Fletcher, Antonis Kalogeropoulos, David A. L. Levy,
and Rasmus Kleis Nielsen, *Reuters Institute Digital News Report 2018*, Reuters
Institute for the Study of Journalism, 10, https://agency.reuters.com/content/dam
/openweb/documents/pdf/news-agency/report/dnr-18.pdf.

37. Lin, "South Korea Releases Right to Be Forgotten Guidance."

38. "Legal Updates: Amendment to Law No. 11 of 2008 on Electronic Information and
Transactions," *Global Business Guide, Indonesia*, November 8, 2016, http://www
.gbgindonesia.com/en/main/legal_updates/amendment_to_law_no_11_of_2008
_on_electronic_information_and_transactions.php/; Mark Innis, "Indonesia:
New Regulation on Personal Data Protection," *Global Compliance News*, Baker
McKenzie, January 25, 2017, https://globalcompliancenews.com/argentina-regulation
-personal-data-protection-20170125/.

39. *Graziani*, 10–11.

40. Callamard, "Comity for Internet?," 1.

41. Nani Jansen Reventlow, Vivek Krishnamurthy, and Christopher T. Bavitz, "A
French Court Case against Google Could Threaten Global Speech Rights," *Washington Post*, December 22, 2016, https://www.washingtonpost.com/news/global
-opinions/wp/2016/12/22/a-french-court-case-against-google-could-threaten
-global-speech-rights/?utm_term=.b6982a2c7776.

42. "Google LLC v. National Commission on Informatics and Liberty (CNIL)," Columbia University, Global Freedom of Expression, https://globalfreedomofexpression
.columbia.edu/cases/google-llc-v-national-commission-on-informatics-and
-liberty-cnil/.

43. Supreme Court of Canada, Google Inc. v. Equustek Solutions Inc., [2016] 2017 S.C.R.
34, 2017 SCC 34; "Google Inc. v. Equustek Solutions Inc.," Columbia University,

Global Freedom of Expression, https://globalfreedomofexpression.columbia.edu/cases/equustek-solutions-inc-v-jack-2/; Agnès Callamard, "Are Courts Re-Inventing Internet Regulation?," *International Review of Law, Computers, and Technology* 31, no. 3 (2017): 330, https://doi.org/10.1080/13600869.2017.1304603.

44. United States District Court for the Northern District of California, San Jose Division, Google LLC, Plaintiff, v. Equustek Solutions Inc. et al., Defendants., 2017 U.S. Dist. LEXIS 182194, 2017 Comm. Reg. (P & F) 55, 2017 WL 5000834, November 2, 2017, https://advance.lexis.com/api/document?collection=cases&id=urn:contentItem:5PW0-MRR1-F04C-T450-00000-00&context=1516831.

Contributors

Catherine Anite is a lawyer from Uganda and the founding director of the Freedom of Expression Hub, an organization that promotes and defends freedom of expression in Africa. In 2019, she was appointed to the High Level Panel of Legal Experts on Media Freedom by Lord David Neuberger and Amal Clooney. She also serves on the advisory council of the International Center for Not-for Profit Law (ICNL) and is an expert with the Global Freedom of Expression project at Columbia University. She holds a Bachelor of Laws degree from Makerere University and an LLM in international human rights law from Notre Dame University.

Séverine Arsène, a political scientist and China scholar, is adjunct assistant professor at the Chinese University of Hong Kong and an associated researcher at the médialab at Sciences Po, Paris. Arsène has published extensively on Chinese cyber policy, notably as a researcher at the Centre for Research on Contemporary China (CEFC) in Hong Kong and as a former editor in chief of *China Perspectives*. She previously held teaching and research positions at the University of Lille, the CNRS Communication and Politics Laboratory, and Orange Labs in Paris and Beijing, and she was a Yahoo! Fellow at the Institute for the

Study of Diplomacy, Georgetown University. She holds a PhD in political science from Sciences Po, Paris.

Chinmayi Arun is an assistant professor of law at National Law University Delhi. She is also the founding director of the Centre for Communication Governance at the same university. She has been a resident fellow of the Berkman Klein Center of Internet and Society at Harvard University, and she is currently a resident fellow of the Information Society Project at Yale Law School. She is an alternative board member of the Global Network Initiative and an expert affiliated with Columbia University's Global Freedom of Expression project.

Bakhtiyor "Bach" Avezdjanov is a program officer at Columbia University's Global Freedom of Expression project and a legal adviser to the UN Special Rapporteur on extrajudicial, summary, or arbitrary executions. His current interests lie in digital rights and the prevention of threats against speakers. Previously, he supported human rights programs for vulnerable groups with the UN High Commissioner for Refugees (UNHCR) in Sudan and the UN Office of the High Commissioner for Human Rights (OHCHR) in Kyrgyzstan. He also researched model torture preventative mechanisms at the American University of Central Asia. Avezdjanov holds a law degree from Boston University and is fluent in Russian.

Amalie Bang holds an LLM from Copenhagen University and a master's degree from the European Inter-University Centre for Human Rights and Democratization. She has worked with human rights and freedom of expression issues throughout her career, including at the Danish Institute for Human Rights, the Council of Europe, and the European Union Delegation to the United Nations, as well as for the Danish government. She has conducted extensive research in the field of freedom of expression and media law for the Global Freedom of Expression project at Columbia University. From September 2017, she has worked as deputy judge in Copenhagen, Denmark.

Lee C. Bollinger became Columbia University's nineteenth president in 2002 and is the longest-serving Ivy League president. He is Columbia's first Seth Low Professor of the University, a member of the Columbia Law School faculty, and one of the country's foremost First Amendment scholars. Each fall semester, he teaches the "Freedom of Speech and Press" course to Columbia undergraduate students. His latest book, *The Free Speech Century*, co-edited with Geoffrey R. Stone, was published in the fall of 2018 by Oxford University Press.

Bollinger is a director of Graham Holdings Company (formerly the Washington Post Company) and serves as a member of the Pulitzer Prize Board. From 2007 to 2012, he was a director of the Federal Reserve Bank of New York, where he also served as chair from 2010 to 2012. From 1996 to 2002, Bollinger was the president of the University of Michigan at Ann Arbor. He led the university's historic litigation in *Grutter v. Bollinger* and *Gratz v. Bollinger*, Supreme Court decisions that upheld and clarified the importance of diversity as a compelling justification for affirmative action in higher education. He speaks and writes frequently about the value of racial, cultural, and socioeconomic diversity through columns, interviews, and appearances around the country and across the world.

Catalina Botero Marino is a lawyer, the dean of the law school at the University of Los Andes, the co-chair of the Facebook and Instagram's Oversight Board, and a member of the International Bar Association's Human Rights Institute Council. She is also the director of UNESCO Chair on Freedom of Expression, an associate professor at American University, and the co-chair of the Colombian ICON-S chapter. She has been a guest lecturer at universities in more than twenty countries and published numerous articles on human rights and freedom of expression, which have been translated into several languages. She is an expert on constitutional and international human rights law and is a member of Columbia University's Global Freedom of Expression project.

Agnès Callamard, PhD, was appointed the UN Special Rapporteur on extrajudicial, summary, or arbitrary executions on August 1, 2016. She is currently the director of Columbia University's Global Freedom of Expression project, an initiative seeking to advance understanding of the international norms and institutions that protect freedom of expression. Previously, she spent nine years as the executive director of Article 19, and she was chef de cabinet for the Secretary General of Amnesty International (AI) and AI's research policy coordinator, leading AI's policy work and research on women's human rights. She has advised senior officials at high levels of multilateral organizations and governments around the world and led human rights investigations in more than thirty countries.

Sandra Coliver is the senior managing legal officer for freedom of information, expression, assembly, and association with the Open Society Justice Initiative. Previously, she directed the Center for Justice and Accountability and worked in Bosnia after the genocide for the United Nations, the Organization for Security and Co-operation in Europe (OSCE), and the International Crisis Group. As Article 19's first law program director, she developed groundbreaking resources on hate speech, national security, freedom of expression, and access to information. She also clerked for the Ninth Circuit Court of Appeals and taught at the American University and UC Berkeley law schools.

Alexander Cooley is the Claire Tow Professor of Political Science at Barnard College and director of Columbia University's Harriman Institute for the Study of Russia, Eurasia, and Eastern Europe. He is the author and/or editor of seven academic books on the international relations, sovereignty, and governance of post-Soviet states, including *Dictators Without Borders: Power and Money in Central Asia* (2017, with John Heathershaw) and *Exit from Hegemony: The Unravelling of the American Global Order* (2020, with Daniel Nexon). In addition to his academic research, Cooley serves on international advisory boards engaged with the post-Soviet states and has testified for the U.S. Congress. His opinion pieces have appeared in *New York Times, Foreign Policy*, and *Foreign Affairs*. Cooley earned both his MA and PhD from Columbia University.

Richard Danbury is an academic lawyer, a journalist, and a former practicing barrister. He directs the MA in Investigative Journalism program at City University of London, coordinates Channel 4's investigative journalism training scheme, is the BBC's advanced legal trainer, and is a member of the Scott Trust Review Panel, the organization that deals with editorial complaints in relation to the *Guardian*'s content. He is an associate research fellow at the Institute for Advanced Legal Studies at the University of London, an associate at the Centre for Intellectual Property and Information Law at the University of Cambridge, and an expert at Columbia University's Global Freedom of Expression project. His undergraduate degree in philosophy is from Cambridge University, and his doctorate in media law is from Oxford University.

Nani Jansen Reventlow is the founding director of the Digital Freedom Fund, which supports partners in Europe to advance digital rights through strategic litigation. She is a recognized international lawyer and expert in human rights litigation responsible for standard-setting freedom of expression cases across several national and international jurisdictions. Jansen Reventlow is a lecturer in law at Columbia Law School, an adjunct professor at Oxford University's Blavatnik School of Government, and an associate tenant at Doughty Street Chambers. She is also a senior fellow at Columbia Law School's Human Rights

Institute and an affiliate at the Berkman Klein Center for Internet and Society at Harvard University. She has been an advisor to Harvard's Cyberlaw Clinic since 2016.

Sofia Jaramillo-Otoya is the Digital Rights Fellow and co-supervisor of the International Justice Clinic at the University of California, Irvine. Previously, she was the legal officer at Columbia University Global Freedom of Expression. Jaramillo-Otoya has devoted much of her career to international human rights mechanisms: she served as legal advisor to the UN Special Rapporteur on freedom of opinion and expression and the UN Special Rapporteur on extrajudicial, summary, or arbitrary executions, and as a human rights specialist for Special Rapporteurs for freedom of expression of the Inter-American Commission on Human Rights. She has consulted and worked for regional organizations such as Dejusticia, Civitas, the Foundation for Free Press, and the Inter-American Press Association.

Hawley Johnson is associate director of Columbia University's Global Freedom of Expression project. Since 2014, she has managed the Case Law Database, which hosts analyses of seminal freedom of expression court rulings from more than 130 countries. From 2013–2014, she worked with the award-winning Organized Crime and Corruption Reporting Project to launch the Investigative Dashboard (ID), a joint effort with Google Ideas that offers specialized databases and research tools for journalists. From 2000–2007, she was associate director of the Media and Conflict Resolution Program at New York University. She has a PhD in communications from Columbia University's Graduate School of Journalism.

Jonathan McCully is legal adviser to the Digital Freedom Fund, an organization that supports strategic litigation to advance digital rights in Europe. Prior to this role, he held a senior legal position at the Media Legal Defence Initiative, an NGO that provides legal assistance to journalists. He has worked on several significant free speech cases, including cases before the European Court of Human Rights, the East African Court of Justice, and the United Nations Working Group on Arbitrary Detention (UNWGAD). He sits on the Legal Affairs Committee of the European Centre for Press and Media Freedom and the advisory board of Investigate Europe. He has published widely on freedom of expression, privacy, and intellectual property. He holds an LLB from Trinity College Dublin and an LLM from the London School of Economics.

Tarlach McGonagle, PhD, is professor of media law and information society at Leiden Law School, Leiden University, and a senior researcher/lecturer at the Institute for Information Law (IViR) at Amsterdam Law School, University of Amsterdam. He is the founder and co-chair of the Working Group on Human Rights in the Digital Age in the Netherlands Network for Human Rights Research and a member of the Euromedia Research Group. He regularly advises and writes expert studies for the Council of Europe, the OSCE, and other intergovernmental organizations. He is a member of the Council of Europe's committee of experts on hate speech.

Toby Mendel is the founder and executive director of the Centre for Law and Democracy, a Canadian-based international human rights NGO that provides legal and capacity-building expertise regarding foundational rights for democracy, including the right to information, freedom of expression, the right to participate, and the rights to assembly and association. Prior to that, he was senior director for law at Article 19, a human-rights NGO that focuses on freedom of expression and the right to information. He has collaborated extensively on law reform efforts with intergovernmental actors as well as governments and NGOs in countries all over the world. He has also published extensively on a range of freedom of expression, right to information, communication rights, and refugee issues.

Peter Noorlander is a lawyer with twenty-five years' experience of working in the human rights movement, focusing on the promotion of freedom of expression and the empowerment of civil society. His expertise is internationally recognized. In 2015, Columbia University awarded its inaugural Award for Excellence in Legal Services to the Media Legal Defence Initiative, which Peter co-founded and led. He has been at the heart of numerous cases and campaigns on issues ranging from promoting the right to information to ending the imprisonment of journalists for defamation.

Jan Oster, LLM, is an assistant professor for EU law and institutions at Leiden University. His research interests broadly lie in the areas of information and communication law, EU law, and the regulation of electronic communication networks and services. His publications include *Media Freedom as a Fundamental Right* (2015) and *European and International Media Law* (2017). Oster studied law at the Johannes Gutenberg University of Mainz, Germany, and the University of California, Berkeley. Between 2009 and 2013, he worked as Lecturer in Law at the King's College London School of Law. He has given speeches and presentations in Australia, Belgium, Finland, France, Germany, Luxembourg, the Netherlands, Turkey, the United Kingdom, and the United States.

Sejal Parmar is a lecturer at the School of Law at the University of Sheffield. She was previously an assistant professor in the Department of Legal Studies at the Central European University; a senior adviser to the OSCE Representative on Freedom of the Media (on secondment from the UK Foreign and Common-wealth Office); and a senior legal officer at Article 19. Her main field of research, teaching, and policy engagement is international and European human rights law, with a particular focus on issues of freedom of expression, media freedom, and digital rights. She regularly serves as an expert consultant for intergovern-mental organizations and NGOs.

Frederick Schauer is the David and Mary Harrison Distinguished Professor of Law at the University of Virginia, and was previously, for nineteen years, the Frank Stanton Professor of the First Amendment at Harvard University. A fel-low of the British Academy and the American Academy of Arts and Sciences, he has also been a Guggenheim Fellow and the Eastman Visiting Professor at Oxford University. He is the author of *Free Speech: A Philosophical Enquiry* (1982); *Playing By the Rules: A Philosophical Examination of Rule-Based Decision-Making in Law and in Life* (1991); *Profiles, Probabilities, and Stereotypes* (2003); *Thinking Like a Lawyer: A New Introduction to Legal Reasoning* (2009); and *The Force of Law* (2015).

Joel Simon has been executive director of the Committee to Protect Journalists since 2006. He writes and speaks widely on press freedom issues and is the author of three books, mostly recently *We Want to Negotiate: The Secret World of Kidnapping, Hostages, and Ransom* (2018). Prior to joining CPJ in 1997 as Americas program coordinator, Simon worked for a decade as a journalist in Latin America.

Emmanuel Vargas Penagos works as a legal and grants officer at the Media Legal Defence Initiative. He previously worked in Colombia at the Foundation for Press Freedom (FLIP) in different roles, dealing with project coordination, advocacy, and litigation regarding freedom of expression and access to public information. He has also worked as consultant on freedom of expression and access to public information for several entities, including the Inter-American Commission on Human Rights. Vargas Penagos studied law and journalism at the University of Los Andes in Colombia, and he has an LLM in information law from Amsterdam University.

Elisabeth Witchel has worked for over twenty years in human rights and journalism. In 2007, she launched the Committee to Protect Journalists's ongoing Global Campaign Against Impunity. Witchel has written numerous reports on the impunity and safety of journalists published by CPJ, including ten editions of its global impunity index. In 2019, she curated *The Last Column*, a collection of last works by journalists who have been killed. Witchel has also worked on publications on safety of journalists for the Denmark-based group International Media Support and UNESCO, among other organizations.

Index

Note: Page numbers in italics refer to figures. Those followed by n refer to notes, with note number.